The Diachrony of Written Language Contact

Brill's Studies in Historical Linguistics

Series Editor

Jóhanna Barðdal
(Ghent University)

Consulting Editor

Spike Gildea
(University of Oregon)

Editorial Board

Joan Bybee (*University of New Mexico*) – Lyle Campbell (*University of Hawai'i Manoa*) – Nicholas Evans (*The Australian National University*) Bjarke Frellesvig (*University of Oxford*) – Mirjam Fried (*Czech Academy of Sciences*) – Russel Gray (*University of Auckland*) – Tom Guldemann (*Humboldt-Universität zu Berlin*) – Alice Harris (*University of Massachusetts*) Brian D. Joseph (*The Ohio State University*) – Ritsuko Kikusawa (*National Museum of Ethnology*) – Silvia Luraghi (*Università di Pavia*) Joseph Salmons (*University of Wisconsin*) – Søren Wichmann (*MPI/EVA*)

VOLUME 15

The titles published in this series are listed at *brill.com/bshl*

The Diachrony of Written Language Contact

A Contrastive Approach

By

Nikolaos Lavidas

BRILL

LEIDEN | BOSTON

The Library of Congress Cataloging-in-Publication Data is available online at https://catalog.loc.gov
LC record available at https://lccn.loc.gov/2021052530

Typeface for the Latin, Greek, and Cyrillic scripts: "Brill". See and download: brill.com/brill-typeface.

ISSN 2211-4904
ISBN 978-90-04-46375-2 (hardback)
ISBN 978-90-04-50356-4 (e-book)

Copyright 2022 by Koninklijke Brill NV, Leiden, The Netherlands.
Koninklijke Brill NV incorporates the imprints Brill, Brill Nijhoff, Brill Hotei, Brill Schöningh, Brill Fink, Brill mentis, Vandenhoeck & Ruprecht, Böhlau Verlag and V&R Unipress.
All rights reserved. No part of this publication may be reproduced, translated, stored in a retrieval system, or transmitted in any form or by any means, electronic, mechanical, photocopying, recording or otherwise, without prior written permission from the publisher. Requests for re-use and/or translations must be addressed to Koninklijke Brill NV via brill.com or copyright.com.

This book is printed on acid-free paper and produced in a sustainable manner.

Contents

Acknowledgements   IX
List of Figures and Tables   XI

PART 1
Written Language Contact and Grammatical Change in English and Greek

1 **Written Language Contact and Translations**   3
  1.1 Introduction   3
  1.2 Terminology of Language Contact   9
  1.3 Written Language Contact   11
      1.3.1 *Translations and Diachronic Linguistics. Translations as a Source of Change and as Evidence of Change*   14
      1.3.2 *Translations as a Typical Example of Written Language Contact*   15

2 **Early History of Translations and Grammatical Change: Landmarks in the Development of Early Translations**   29
  2.1 Introduction   29
  2.2 Early History of Translations and Grammatical Change in English   34
      2.2.1 *Biblical vs. Non-biblical Translations in the History of English*   39
            2.2.1.1 Biblical Translations and Grammatical Change in English: An Overview of the Major Landmarks   39
            2.2.1.2 Non-biblical Translations and Grammatical Change in English   45
      2.2.2 *Written Contact and Grammatical Change vs. Translation Effects in the History of English*   46
      2.2.3 *The Role of Retranslations in Diachronic Linguistic Studies*   50
  2.3 Greek in Written Contact: History of Early Translations   53
      2.3.1 *Introduction. Translations in the History of Greek*   54
      2.3.2 *History of Translation and Language History: Later Developments in the Diachrony of Greek*   55
      2.3.3 *Greek Intralingual Translations and Their Characteristics*   56

VI   CONTENTS

    2.3.4   *The Case of Biblical Greek* 60
          2.3.4.1 Introduction 60
          2.3.4.2 Semitisms in Biblical Greek 60
    2.3.5   *Biblical Translations into Later Greek* 63
          2.3.5.1 Greek Biblical Translations: Brief Overview 63
          2.3.5.2 Major Landmarks of Biblical Translations into Greek:
                    Their Position in the History of the Language 65

3 Biblical Translations 75

    3.1   The Corpus of Biblical Translations: Source of Evidence of
        Grammatical Change 75
        3.1.1   *Biblical Translations as a Corpus* 75
        3.1.2   *Biblical Translations: The Parameter of Intralingual*
              Translations 81
    3.2   Biblical Translations as Factor of Grammatical Change 83
    3.3   English Biblical Translations: Examples of Corpus-Based Surveys 85

4 Intralingual Translations: Two Directions—to the Past or to the Present 90

    4.1   Introduction 90
    4.2   Intralingual Translations as Evidence of Grammatical Change 91
    4.3   Types of Greek Intralingual Translations 92
    4.4   Retranslations and Their Relation to Intralingual Translations 98

5 Examples of Studies on Grammatical Change in English through Translations 103

    5.1   Introduction 103
    5.2   Translations and Multilingualism in the History of English 103
    5.3   Grammatical Characteristics and the Effect of Other Languages in the
        Diachrony of English 106

6 From *Syntactic Diglossia* and *Universal Bilingualism* to What Diachronic Translations Can Tell Us about *Grammatical Multiglossia* 110

    6.1   A Theoretical Proposal: *Grammatical Multiglossia* 110
    6.2   Historical Grammatical Multiglossia, L2 and Bilingualism 115
    6.3   Historical Grammatical Multiglossia and Ferguson's Diglossia 118
    6.4   Historical Grammatical Multiglossia as Related to (Semi-)natural
        Change 122

CONTENTS VII

PART 2
Data: English and Greek Translations and Grammatical Change

7 **English Data** 129
  7.1 Introduction 129
  7.2 Voice, Argument Structure and Transitivity in English Biblical Diachronic Retranslations 130
     7.2.1 *English Diachronic (Re)translations of the New Testament* 136
  7.3 Voice and Transitivity in English Diachronic Biblical vs. Non-biblical Translations 173
     7.3.1 *Corpus Survey* 178
  7.4 English Biblical vs. Non-biblical Diachronic Retranslations: Borrowing of Word-Formation Morphology 189
     7.4.1 *Corpus Survey* 194
        7.4.1.1 Case study I: Old English suffix *-ness* vs. the innovative Romance suffix *-itie* (/*-ity*) 194
     7.4.2 *Concluding Remarks* 208

8 **Greek Data** 210
  8.1 Greek Diachronic Retranslations of the New Testament: Voice and Argument Structure 210
     8.1.1 *Data* 216
  8.2 Greek Diachronic Retranslations: Phrase Matching Approach 267
     8.2.1 *Qualitative and data-driven analysis. Phrase matching approach* 267
     8.2.2 *Data* 272
        8.2.2.1 Case Study I: Translation/ paraphrasis of Anna Komnene's *Alexiad* (books XI–XII) 273
        8.2.2.2 Case study II: An early 13th-century translation of Nikephoros Blemmydes' *Basilikos Andrias* 284
        8.2.2.3 Case study III: Two versions of "Life of Aesop"; Accursiana vs. Version W 292
        8.2.2.4 Case study IV: Two versions of "Life of Aesop"; Version W vs. Version G 303
        8.2.2.5 Case study V: Two versions of "Digenis Akritis"; Grottaferrata vs. Escorial 313
  8.3 Greek vs. English Data: An Approach to the Diachrony of Written Language Contact 316

9 Conclusion 319

Appendix 1: Further Information on the Texts of the Corpus 325
Appendix 2: (i) The Corpus of Translations of Biblical Texts; (ii) The
Corpus of Translations of Boethius' De Consolatione
Philosophiae 329
References 332
Index 372

Acknowledgements

This book is an original research monograph. It belongs to the broad area of my research work, which includes my PhD thesis on argument structure in diachrony, my postdoctoral research on the diachrony of word order from a language change—language acquisition perspective, and a series of articles and organized workshops on contrastive Greek-English diachronic analyses and Indo-European linguistics, from the perspective of language change and bilingualism.

Nobody can deny that an account of grammatical change that takes written contact into consideration is a significant challenge for any theoretical perspective. The main contribution of the present book is to add a diachronic dimension to the study of written contact by examining aspects of the history of translation as they relate to grammatical changes in English and Greek in a contrastive way. In this respect, emphasis is placed on the analysis of diachronic retranslations. I examine translations from earlier periods of English and Greek in relation to various grammatical characteristics of these languages in different periods and in comparison to non-translated texts. Moreover, I add a second parameter of examination: translations can be seen as a source of evidence of grammatical change; a new grammar demands a new translation. The book has two clear-cut sections: (i) a theoretical one that discusses the history of translations in relation to grammatical changes in Greek and English, as well as the theoretical framework of the study of the relation between translations and diachrony; and (ii) a more research-based section that presents the results of corpus-based studies in the history of translations in English and Greek. Most of the data in the second part are related to characteristics of voice and argument structure.

First, I would like to thank Jóhanna Barðdal for her enormous help, support, essential guidance, and endless discussions of several parts of the book. I would also like to thank Elisa Perotti for her great help, patience, trust in me, and excellent collaboration. Brill was on my side from the first moment until all preparations for the book were completed. In addition, I wholeheartedly thank the two anonymous reviewers for successful suggestions and fruitful criticism. Needless to say, all errors remain mine.

I owe a sincere thank you to all the people who have supported me since the start of this project. The idea of the project started when I was member of the Department of Theoretical and Applied Linguistics, Faculty of English, School of Philosophy, Aristotle University of Thessaloniki. Most of its parts were completed when I was member of the Department of Language and Linguistics,

Faculty of English, School of Philosophy, National and Kapodistrian University of Athens. I learned much about the way one should work with diachronic and developmental data and about modern methodologies of linguistic research, and I owe much to all linguists of the Schools of Philosophy of the Aristotle University of Thessaloniki and of the National and Kapodistrian University of Athens.

In 2015 Elly van Gelderen (Arizona State University) and Alexander Bergs (University of Osnabrück) invited me to create the first version of the Naxos Summer School of Old and Middle English, which later became the Naxos Summer School on Diachronic Linguistics. Ioanna Sitaridou (University of Cambridge) joined our common efforts, and we managed to broaden the scope of the summer school. I owe Elly, Alex, and Ioanna much of my enthusiasm and energy. They felt my anxieties, they discussed with me several ideas for research projects, and they were always present, to strengthen academic initiatives and to start new "risky" ones.

Leonid Kulikov (University of Ghent), Donka Minkova (UCLA), Olga Fischer (University of Amsterdam), Dag Haug (University of Oslo), Þórhallur Eyþórsson (University of Iceland), Igor Yanovich (University of Tübingen, University of Vienna), Antonio Revuelta Puigdollers (Universidad Autónoma de Madrid), and Artemij Keidan (Sapienza Università di Roma) were always great friends, "teachers," and collaborators, supporting me during the long period of preparing this book. I do not have words to thank them; the project owes them much, too. My gratitude also goes to a wonderful team of researchers, PhD candidates under my supervision, Theodora Panagiotidou (she completed her PhD Dissertation in March 2021), Thomi Gamagari and Vassilis Symeonidis.

My last thank you goes to all Teachers I have met and to all my Students who will believe in themselves.

Figures and Tables

Figures

2.1 Source texts and variation in faithfulness of a translation 33

2.2 Lexical correspondences in Boethius' translations by Alfred, Chaucer and Elizabeth (Romaine 1985: 460) 52

7.1 Active vs. non-active/ marked voice forms in the corpus of English translations of the New Testament (See the list of selected verbal meanings: Table 7.2) 138

7.2 Distribution of voice forms in anticausative constructions in the corpus of English translations of the New Testament (See the list of selected verbal meanings: Table 7.2) 140

7.3 Active voice forms in transitive and anticausative constructions in the corpus of English translations of the New Testament (See the list of selected verbal meanings: Table 7.2) 141

7.4 Animate subjects of active verbs vs. animate subjects of non-active/ marked verbs—Inanimate subjects of active verbs vs. inanimate subjects of non-active/ marked verbs in the corpus of English translations of the New Testament (See the list of selected verbal meanings: Table 7.2) 146

7.5 Animate vs. inanimate subjects in the corpus of English translations of the New Testament (See the list of selected verbal meanings: Table 7.2) 147

7.6 Distribution of active vs. non-active/ marked voice forms in the diachrony of English non-translated texts (See the list of selected verbal meanings: Table 7.2); Penn Parsed Corpora of Historical English 151

7.7 Distribution of voice forms in anticausative constructions in the diachrony of English non-translated texts (See the list of selected verbal meanings: Table 7.2); Penn Parsed Corpora of Historical English 152

7.8 Transitive and anticausative constructions with active voice forms in the diachrony of English non-translated texts (See the list of selected verbal meanings: Table 7.2); Penn Parsed Corpora of Historical English 153

7.9 Voice, transitivity and subject animacy: The verb "grow" in the corpus of English translations of the New Testament 155

7.10 Animate vs. inanimate subjects: The verb "grow" in the corpus of English translations of the New Testament 156

7.11 Voice, transitivity and subject animacy: The verb "dry" in the corpus of English translations of the New Testament 158

7.12 Animate vs. inanimate subjects: The verb "dry" in the corpus of English translations of the New Testament 159

7.13 Voice, transitivity and subject animacy: The verb "heal" in the corpus of English translations of the New Testament 160

7.14 Animate vs. inanimate subjects: The verb "heal" in the corpus of English translations of the New Testament 161

7.15 Voice, transitivity and subject animacy: The verb "tear" in the corpus of English translations of the New Testament 165

7.16 Animate vs. inanimate subjects: The verb "tear" in the corpus of English translations of the New Testament 166

7.17 Voice, transitivity and subject animacy: The verb "clean" in the corpus of English translations of the New Testament 167

7.18 Animate vs. inanimate subjects: The verb "clean" in the corpus of English translations of the New Testament 168

7.19 Voice, transitivity and subject animacy: The verb "close" in the corpus of English translations of the New Testament 170

7.20 Animate vs. inanimate subjects: The verb "close" in the corpus of English translations of the New Testament 171

7.21 Transitive vs. intransitive constructions in finite, matrix clauses in the corpus of English biblical translations (See the list of selected verbal meanings: Table 7.6). See also Appendix 2 (i) for details on the sample included in the corpus 180

7.22 Transitive vs. intransitive constructions in finite, matrix clauses in the corpus of English translations of Boethius' De Consolatione Philosophiae (See the list of selected verbal meanings: Table 7.6). See Appendix 2 (ii) for details on the sample included in the corpus 181

7.23 Transitive vs. intransitive constructions in finite, matrix clauses in the diachrony of English non-translated texts. (See the list of selected verbal meanings: Table 7.6); Penn Parsed Corpora of Historical English 182

7.24 Object pronouns vs. object nouns in the corpus of English biblical translations. (See the list of selected verbal meanings: Table 7.6). See Appendix 2 (i) for details on the sample included in the corpus 184

7.25 Object pronouns vs. object nouns in the corpus of English translations of Boethius' De Consolatione Philosophiae. (See the list of selected verbal meanings: Table 7.6). See Appendix 2 (ii) for details on the sample included in the corpus 185

7.26 Object pronouns vs. object nouns in the diachrony of English non-translated texts (See the list of selected verbal meanings: Table 7.6); Penn Parsed Corpora of Historical English 186

7.27 Active vs. marked voice forms in the corpus of English biblical translations. (See the list of selected verbal meanings: Table 7.6). See Appendix 2 (i) for details on the sample included in the corpus 187

FIGURES AND TABLES

7.28 Active vs. marked voice forms in the corpus of English translations of Boethius' De Consolatione Philosophiae (See the list of selected verbal meanings: Table 7.6). See Appendix 2 (ii) for details on the sample included in the corpus   188

7.29 Voice in the diachrony of English non-translated texts (See the list of selected verbal meanings: Table 7.6); Penn Parsed Corpora of Historical English   190

8.1 Distribution of voice morphology in the corpus of later Greek translations of the New Testament (See the list of selected verbal meanings: Table 8.1).   217

8.2 Distribution of voice morphology of verbs in anticausative constructions in the corpus of later Greek translations of the New Testament (See the list of selected verbal meanings: Table 8.1).   218

8.3 Distribution of active morphology of verbs in anticausative vs. transitive constructions in the corpus of later Greek translations of the New Testament (See the list of selected verbal meanings: Table 8.1)   219

8.4 Distribution of voice morphology of verbs with animate and inanimate subjects in the corpus of later Greek translations of the New Testament (See the list of selected verbal meanings: Table 8.1)   224

8.5 Distribution of animate vs. inanimate subjects in the corpus of later Greek translations of the New Testament (See the list of selected verbal meanings: Table 8.1)   226

8.6 Distribution of (active vs. non-active) voice morphology in the corpus of non-translated texts. All verbs as one verbal class. Word list: καθαρίζω katharízō katharizo 'clean', κλείνω kleínō klino 'close', στεγνώνω stegnónō stegnono 'dry', βράζω vrázō vrazo 'boil', σαπίζω sapízō sapizo 'rot', λιώνω liónō liono 'melt'. Part of the data is based on data from Lavidas et al. (2012)   230

8.7 Distribution of (active vs. non-active) voice morphology in the corpus of non-translated texts. Word list: καθαρίζω katharízō katharizo 'clean', κλείνω kleínō klino 'close', στεγνώνω stegnónō stegnono 'dry', βράζω vrázō vrazo 'boil', σαπίζω sapízō sapizo 'rot', λιώνω liónō liono 'melt'. Part of the data is based on data from Lavidas et al. (2012)   231

8.8 Distribution of voice morphology of verbs in anticausative constructions in the corpus of non-translated texts. All verbs as one verbal class. Word list: καθαρίζω katharízō katharizo 'clean', κλείνω kleínō klino 'close', στεγνώνω stegnónō stegnono 'dry', βράζω vrázō vrazo 'boil', σαπίζω sapízō sapizo 'rot', λιώνω liónō liono 'melt'. Part of the data is based on data from Lavidas et al. (2012)   232

8.9 Distribution of voice morphology of verbs in anticausative constructions in the corpus of non-translated texts. Word list: καθαρίζω katharízō katharizo 'clean', κλείνω kleínō klino 'close', στεγνώνω stegnónō stegnono 'dry', βράζω vrázō vrazo 'boil', σαπίζω sapízō sapizo 'rot', λιώνω liónō liono 'melt'. Part of the data is based on data from Lavidas et al. (2012)   233

XIV FIGURES AND TABLES

8.10 Active voice forms in anticausative and transitive constructions in the corpus of non-translated texts. All verbs as one verbal class. Word list: καθαρίζω katharízō katharizo 'clean', κλείνω kleínō klino 'close', στεγνώνω stegnónō stegnono 'dry', βράζω vrázō vrazo 'boil', σαπίζω sapízō sapizo 'rot', λιώνω liónō liono 'melt'. Part of the data is based on data from Lavidas et al. (2012)   235

8.11 Active voice forms in anticausative and transitive constructions in the corpus of non-translated texts. Word list: καθαρίζω katharízō katharizo 'clean', κλείνω kleínō klino 'close', στεγνώνω stegnónō stegnono 'dry', βράζω vrázō vrazo 'boil', σαπίζω sapízō sapizo 'rot', λιώνω liónō liono 'melt'. Part of the data is based on data from Lavidas et al. (2012)   236

8.12 Distribution of active and non-active voice morphology with animate subjects in the corpus of non-translated texts. See the list of selected verbal meanings: καθαρίζω katharízō katharizo 'clean', κλείνω kleínō klino 'close', στεγνώνω stegnónō stegnono 'dry', βράζω vrázō vrazo 'boil', σαπίζω sapízō sapizo 'rot', λιώνω liónō liono 'melt'. Part of the data is based on data from Lavidas et al. (2012)   241

8.13 Distribution of voice morphology in the corpus of non-translated texts. Word list: καθαρίζω katharízō katharizo 'clean', κλείνω kleínō klino 'close'. Part of the data is based on data from Lavidas et al. (2012)   243

8.14 Distribution of voice morphology in the corpus of non-translated texts. Word list: στεγνώνω stegnónō stegnono 'dry', βράζω vrázō vrazo 'boil', σαπίζω sapízō sapizo 'rot', λιώνω liónō liono 'melt'. Part of the data is based on data from Lavidas et al. (2012)   245

8.15 Distribution of voice morphology of verbs in anticausative vs. transitive constructions and subject animacy in the Koine Greek New Testament and the corpus of later Greek biblical translations (and in the LXX): The verb afxano 'grow'   249

8.16 Subject animacy in the Koine Greek New Testament and the corpus of later Greek biblical translations (and in the LXX): The verb afxano 'grow'   250

8.17 Distribution of voice morphology of verbs in anticausative vs. transitive constructions and subject animacy in the Koine Greek New Testament and the corpus of later Greek biblical translations (and in the LXX): The verb anigo-anignimi 'open'   253

8.18 Subject animacy in the Koine Greek New Testament and the corpus of later Greek biblical translations (and in the LXX): The verb anigo-anignimi 'open'   254

8.19 Distribution of voice morphology of verbs in anticausative vs. transitive constructions and subject animacy in the Koine Greek New Testament and the corpus of later Greek biblical translations (and in the LXX): The verb therapevo 'heal'   256

FIGURES AND TABLES

8.20 Subject animacy in the Koine Greek New Testament and the corpus of later Greek biblical translations (and in the LXX): The verb therapevo 'heal' 258

8.21 Distribution of voice morphology of verbs in anticausative vs. transitive constructions and subject animacy in the Koine Greek New Testament and the corpus of later Greek biblical translations (and in the LXX): The verb katharizo 'clean' 260

8.22 Subject animacy in the Koine Greek New Testament and the corpus of later Greek biblical translations (and in the LXX): The verb katharizo 'clean' 261

8.23 Distribution of voice morphology of verbs in anticausative vs. transitive constructions and subject animacy in the Koine Greek New Testament and the corpus of later Greek biblical translations (and in the LXX): The verb kli(n)o 'close' 263

8.24 Subject animacy in the Koine Greek New Testament and the corpus of later Greek biblical translations (and in the LXX): The verb kli(n)o 'close' 265

Tables

1.1 Parameters involved in contact of English with Latin, Scandinavian, Celtic and French (Fischer 2013: 24) 13

1.2 Factors and outcome of language contact through translation (Kranich et al. 2011: 18) 22

1.3 Infinitival endings in MS C [MS Cotton Tiberius D. vii] and Caxton's version of the Polychronicon (Iyeiri 2010: 115) 26

1.4 The forms ne, ne … not, not in MS C [MS Cotton Tiberius D. vii] and Caxton's version of the Polychronicon (Iyeiri 2010: 120) 27

1.5 Single and multiple negation in MS C [MS Cotton Tiberius D. vii] and Caxton's version of the Polychronicon (Iyeiri 2010: 122) 27

2.1 The frequency and weight of head-initial PPs with and without a PP in the source text, comparing non-translations with biblical and non-biblical translations (Taylor 2008: 354; Table 14) 48

2.2 Formal translation correspondences between Biblical Greek and Hebrew and Aramaic (Thompson 1985: 53) 62

3.1 Comparison between the Greek definite article and its correspondent words in the Authorized Version (Dahl 2007: 178) 79

3.2 Comparison between the Greek definite article and its correspondent words in the French Louis Segond translation (Dahl 2007: 179) 79

3.3 Greek future tense and T-scores in English biblical translations (Dahl 2007: 180) 80

3.4 Types of change in intralingual translations (Screnock 2018: 527) 82

FIGURES AND TABLES

7.1 Anticausatives acquiring the same form as the causatives in various periods of English (based on data from Krahe & Meid 1969) 133

7.2 Word list for the corpus surveys on voice and argument structure 135

7.3 Chronologies/ Divisions of the time periods and abbreviations used in the corpus surveys (according to the Penn Parsed Corpora of Historical English) 136

7.4 Overview of changes in case form and function in the history of English (Fischer et al. 2017: 4) 174

7.5 Overview of changes in voice-system in the history of English (Fischer et al. 2017: 4) 175

7.6 Word list for the corpus surveys on voice and argument structure (it repeats Table 7.2) 179

7.7 Chronologies/ Divisions of the time periods and abbreviations used in the corpus surveys, following the Penn Parsed Corpora of Historical English: M3-E3 179

7.8 The corpus: English translations of the Latin text of Boethius' De Consolatione Philosophiae and English translations of the New Testament 191

7.9 -ness and -ity formations in Alfred's, Chaucer's and Elizabeth's translations of Boethius' De Consolatione Philosophiae: data from Romaine 1985 192

7.10 Synonymous Germanic and Romance suffixes in Middle English (van Gelderen 2014: 133) 193

7.11 Chronologies/ Divisions of the time periods and abbreviations used in the document classification study, following the Penn Parsed Corpora of Historical English: M3-E3 (it repeats Table 7.7) 194

7.12 Accuracy data (machine learning approach and document classification) 195

7.13 -ity vs. -ness with nouns that are good discriminators in Chaucer's (14th-century) vs. Elizabeth's (16th-century) translation of Boethius' De Consolatione Philosophiae 196

7.14 -ity vs. -ness with nouns that are good discriminators of the 14th-century (Chaucer's) vs. the 16th-century (Colville's) translation of Boethius' De Consolatione Philosophiae 198

7.15 -ity vs. -ness with nouns that are good discriminators of the 14th-century (Chaucer's) translation of Boethius' De Consolatione Philosophiae [sample] and of the 14th-century non-translated text [Purvey's General Prologue to the Bible; date: a1450 (a1397); genre: religious treatise] 198

7.16 -ity vs. -ness with nouns that are good discriminators between the 14th-century (Wycliffe's) and the 16th-century (Tyndale's) translation of the New Testament 199

7.17 Synonymous Germanic and Romance suffixes in Middle English (van Gelderen 2014: 133). It repeats Table 7.10 200

FIGURES AND TABLES

7.18 List of good discriminators of the 14th-century (Chaucer's) translation if compared to the 16th-century (Colville's) translation 200

7.19 Romance vs. Germanic derivational suffixes [of Table 7.17] in the list of good discriminators of the 14th-century (Chaucer's) translation if compared to the 16th-century (Colville's) translation 201

7.20 Romance vs. Germanic derivational suffixes [of Table 7.17] in the list of good discriminators of the 1695 (Preston's) translation if compared to the 1785 (Ridpath's) translation 202

7.21 Derivational suffixes [of Table 7.17] in the list of good discriminators of the 14th-century translated text (Chaucer's translation [sample]) if compared to the 14th-century non-translated text (Purvey's text; General Prologue) 203

7.22 Romance vs. Germanic derivational suffixes [of Table 7.17] in the list of good discriminators of the 1611 translation of the New Testament (Authorized Version) if compared to the 1764 (Purver's) translation of the New Testament 204

7.23 Accuracy numbers (document classification): (i) Middle English vs. Early Modern English translations of the corpus; (ii) Middle English vs. 18th-century translations of the corpus 206

7.24 Non-biblical translations: Romance vs. Germanic derivational suffixes [of Table 7.17] in the list of good discriminators of the 14th-century (Middle English) translation if compared to the 18th-century translations of Boethius' De Consolatione Philosophiae 206

7.25 New Testament translations: Romance vs. Germanic derivational suffixes [of Table 7.17] in the list of good discriminators of the 14th-century (Middle English) New Testament translation if compared to the 18th-century New Testament translations of the corpus 208

8.1 Word list for the corpus surveys on voice and argument structure (it repeats Table 7.2) 212

8.2 Voice morphology in Ancient Greek (following Lavidas et al. 2012: 392) 215

PART 1

Written Language Contact and Grammatical Change in English and Greek

∵

CHAPTER 1

Written Language Contact and Translations

1.1 Introduction

Without question, an account of grammatical change that takes into consideration written contact is a significant challenge for any theoretical perspective. The challenge becomes even greater if one takes a historical-structural theoretical perspective that attempts to link the main characteristics of grammar to language acquisition. However, according to many recent studies, it is evident that (oral) language contact has a central role in grammatical change, either as a factor that changes the input of language acquisition, or as an important trigger of grammatical borrowing. Language contact has also been considered by some as being the sole cause of systematic grammatical change, and especially in those approaches in which language change is seen as related to language acquisition: that is, language contact introduces new grammatical characteristics in the input or changes the distribution and frequency of grammatical characteristics (on the central role of contact in grammatical change, cf., among many others, Heine & Kuteva 2005, Koptevskaja-Tamm 2006, Matras 2009, Robbeets & Cuyckens 2013).

The aim of the present book is to describe in detail another type of language contact: written contact. *Written contact* of earlier periods or written contact from a diachronic perspective refers to contact through translation.[1] The main contribution of this book is that it adds a diachronic perspective to the study of written contact, in that it examines aspects of the history of translation in relation to grammatical change in English and Greek, in a contrastive way. In this respect, emphasis is placed on an analysis of diachronic retranslations—that is, translations of the same source text by various translators in different periods of the history of the target language (see Chapters 2–4, and empirical data in Chapters 7 and 8): I examine translations in earlier periods of English and Greek focusing the attention on different grammatical characteristics of these languages across different periods. Moreover, I add a second parameter of examination: translations can be viewed as another *source of evidence of grammatical change*, given that, for instance, a new grammar demands a new translation

---

1 On the contrary, types of written contact of contemporary times—that does not relate to translation—may also refer to contact of non-native speakers/ writers of a language on internet, for example, in the case of social media.

© KONINKLIJKE BRILL NV, LEIDEN, 2022 | DOI:10.1163/9789004503564_002

(new translations can, of course, be triggered by several other factors, but my focus here is on the different grammatical characteristics of different retranslations). In this respect, one of the basic research questions of my study concerns the ways diachronic retranslations are related to the development of grammar.

Accordingly, the book begins with a brief history of translations in the context of English and Greek, as a method of testing the ways through which translations—and, mainly, retranslations in earlier periods of English and Greek—are related to grammatical change. The primary goal is to present a theoretical background that can account for the relation between grammatical characteristics of diachronic retranslations and the development of the grammatical systems of the languages. After considering all the relevant data, I hypothesize that the relation is not direct, that is, retranslations do not reflect grammatical change in a direct way. The relation should be considered more complex and should be explained in the context of a grammatical multiglossia that can refer to the multiple grammatical systems that coexist in a "peaceful" way within one synchronic period. Grammatical multiglossia has its starting point in Kroch's (1989, 2001) "syntactic diglossia"/ "parallel grammars" (*Competing Grammars Hypothesis*) but emphasizes the coexistence and the *contact* between the parallel grammars that results in transfer from the one—for example, grammar of translated texts—to the other system—for example, grammar of non-translated texts.

The data presented in this book concern two languages, English and Greek, which have been in written contact for many centuries, and in particular through biblical translations. We should not, however, ignore the fact that the situation regarding the involved languages is complex, again: for instance, the earliest English translations of the New Testament were prepared through a Latin translation (the Vulgate) of the Koine Greek source text. I examine biblical translations and their role in grammatical change, following relevant previous studies, adding the parameter of intralingual translation in the case of biblical translations to the equation. The Greek data are rich in terms of intralingual retranslations of biblical texts from the 16th century onwards, but also include the early translations of the Old Testament from Biblical Hebrew. A discussion of the relation between the history of translations and grammatical change can be fully enriched if we take into consideration data related to intralingual translations. For this reason, the data of intralingual retranslations in the history of Greek provide a comparative basis for an analysis of similarities/ differences between interlingual and intralingual retranslations— and their role in the history of the languages. This contrastive perspective is a current that runs throughout the entire study. For instance, a comparison between English and Greek data reveals a continuity of characteristics of voice-argument structure in English vs. change in voice-argument structure in Greek.

The book includes two clear-cut sections: (i) a theoretical one, that discusses the history of translations (not in general—but in relation to grammatical change in Greek and English), as well as the theoretical framework of the study of the relation between translations and diachrony; (ii) a more research-based section that presents the results of corpus-based studies in the history of translations in English and Greek. Most of the data of the second part speak to the characteristics of voice and argument structure. Both parts are directly connected to the main research questions of the book. Part 1 analyzes the main aspects of the history of translations in English and Greek in relation to grammatical change. In addition, Part 1 shows how the above examination is linked to a broad theoretical framework of written contact. Part 2 investigates examples of grammatical characteristics and their development as reflected in diachronic retranslations. The development of the examined grammatical characteristics in retranslations is compared to the development of the same grammatical characteristics in non-translated texts. Part 2 also includes corpus-based surveys of different types, all which have their starting point in previous relevant studies and which contribute to a well-established theoretical discussion of central grammatical phenomena.

Both the English and Greek data derived from diachronic (inter- and intralingual) retranslations and the theoretical discussion of the development of grammatical characteristics in retranslations and in the history of English and Greek non-translated texts confirm the hypothesis that translations represent parallel systems of grammar as evidenced both in the example of continuity of grammatical characteristics (English) and in the example of change (Greek).[2] The overall picture becomes clearer if we distinguish between translation effects (transfer from the source text) and grammatical characteristics of translations reflecting a parallel grammar to the grammar represented in non-translated texts. The example of biblical translations is even more complicated, because in Greek, for instance, a possible influence from Biblical Hebrew through the translation of the Septuagint can be witnessed in later translations of the New Testament, as well. In a similar way, English biblical translations are not a simple case either. Besides the Koine Greek or the Biblical Hebrew

---

2 In other words, translations may demonstrate characteristics of syntactic diglossia (Kroch 1989), according to which coexistence of more than one grammar is possible in transitional periods. See Chapter 6.

original text, we must always consider interference from Latin. In addition, the results of the corpus surveys confirm the hypothesis that diachronic retranslations do not reflect directly the changes that the grammar underwent between the period of an early and the period of a later retranslation. Retranslations do not reflect directly contact-induced changes either. They demonstrate a parallel grammatical system that has its own development and is in contact with the grammatical system of non-translated texts. The contact between the grammar of non-translated texts and the grammar of translated texts triggers bidirectional influence, and grammatical borrowing is evident both in translations and non-translations.

In the first sections of Part 1, I discuss the terminology related to language contact, and in particular, to written language contact, as well as the basic types of contact and contact-induced changes. I then introduce the main characteristics of the relation between the study of translations and diachronic linguistics and the twofold status of translations in this context as a source of grammatical change and as an evidence of change (Chapter 1). One of the main aims of the first section is to present a history of early translations, with an emphasis on their relation to grammatical change, in a contrastive manner, first in English and then in Greek (Chapter 2). Previous studies have revealed the differences between biblical and non-biblical translations and the fact that, in the case of biblical translations, both direct and indirect translation effects are available—that is, not only transfer of a characteristic in passages where it appears in the source text but a broader influence on the target text, also in other passages where the relevant characteristic does not appear in the source text—in contrast to non-biblical translations (Chapter 3). In this respect, I distinguish between examples of translation effects and results of written contact and grammatical change in the history of English.

Biblical translations have a more central position in the history of Greek. Thus, I describe the main characteristics of Biblical Greek, and present a history of early translations into Greek, with a special emphasis on its relation to grammatical change. Biblical translations, of course, involve intralingual translations of the Koine Greek New Testament into later Greek. I analyze intralingual translations—which refer to target texts written in later periods of the source language—as a type of retranslation (on the characteristics of intralingual translations, see Chapter 4). Biblical translations also form a valuable corpus that can be used in any examination of change, even though, according to my main hypothesis, retranslations should not be seen as directly reflecting grammatical change but as a parallel grammatical system in contact with the grammar represented in non-translated texts. A detailed discussion of (intralingual) biblical translations into later Greek again reveals a significant distinction between written contact—and written contact-induced grammatical change—and translation effects.

Chapter 4 provides a detailed presentation of the characteristics of intralingual translations in the history of Greek and English. I analyze the basic types of intralingual translations and the way they are related to characteristics of retranslations and to approaches to retranslations. In Chapter 5, I discuss previous studies on possible grammatical change attributed to translations in the history of English. I mainly present grammatical characteristics and constructions of English that have been considered as influenced by translations. It appears that there are no similar case studies that reveal grammatical characteristics or constructions influenced by another language through translation in the case of Greek.

The last chapter of Part 1 (Chapter 6) presents the theoretical background of my analysis of translations, the *Hypothesis of Grammatical Multiglossia*. The idea starts with Kroch's (1989, 2001) "syntactic diglossia" and Roeper's (1999, 2016) "universal bilingualism", and show how historical grammatical multiglossia, as reflected in the parallel development of grammatical characteristics of non-translated and translated texts, is related to L2 and bilingualism. Historical grammatical multiglossia is also connected to traditional diglossia contexts, starting with Ferguson's (1959) analysis. I consider the existence of grammatical multiglossia as directly related to the two types of grammatical change: natural and semi-natural change. Written learned language and its effects—how it influences the development of grammar—can trigger semi-natural grammatical change (Weiß 1998, 2001, 2005a), which has different characteristics than grammatical change connected to L1/ L2 (and/ or adult L2) acquisition.

Part 2 discusses the results of several corpus surveys that examine the development of voice and argument structure in English and Greek. All corpus surveys concern a word list, a limited number of verbs with similar meanings (change-of-state verbs). Each sub-section of Part 2 begins with a presentation of the most important aspects of the development of the relevant grammatical characteristics, according to previous studies. A corpus survey of non-translated texts adds significant information on the frequencies of the characteristics under investigation in non-translated texts from different periods.

The first corpus survey of English concerns the development of voice and argument structure (Section 7.2). The data derive from a corpus of English retranslations of the New Testament from the 14th, 16th, 17th, 19th and 21st century. A comparison is carried out between frequencies of characteristics of the whole group of verbs under examination in the translations and frequencies of these characteristics of the same group of verbs in non-translated texts of the same periods. I also examine the development of separate verbs of the group of verbs under examination in different case studies. Further, I analyze parameters related to voice morphology and transitivity.

The second subpart of the English corpus survey examines the contrast between English biblical vs. non-biblical retranslations (Section 7.3). The grammatical characteristics investigated again concern voice and transitivity. The non-biblical data derive from retranslations of Boethius' text *De Consolatione Philosophiae* "Consolation of Philosophy". I then analyze the following parameters: transitives vs. intransitives in English biblical vs. non-biblical translations; object nouns vs. pronouns; morphology of voice. The second corpus survey of English translations has the form of a corpus-driven study, involving an investigation of the borrowing of features of word formation morphology (derivational suffixes) in retranslations of Boethius' text *De Consolatione Philosophiae* (Section 7.4). The starting point of this corpus survey is Romaine's (1985) study on derivational suffixes in retranslations of Boethius' text.

The second section of Part 2 includes a discussion of results derived from a Greek corpus of biblical and non-biblical translations (Chapter 8). The research methodology is the same as the one applied in the English corpus surveys (Chapter 7). This involves an examination of a limited number of verbs that form a verbal class (change-of-state verbs—word list methodology). The first corpus survey (Section 8.1) analyzes the development of characteristics of voice and argument structure as reflected in Greek diachronic retranslations of the New Testament (17th, 19th, 20th century). All results from the translated corpus are evaluated against tendencies observed in a corpus of non-translated texts from the same periods. The parameter of lexical conceptual structure is also included in case studies that present results of the same corpus surveys but now related to some of the verbs separately and not to the whole verbal class. The second part of the Greek corpus survey is a corpus-driven research that includes a qualitative analysis (Section 8.2). This involves a phrase matching approach, including a study of paraphrases in later periods of Greek. According to the methodology of this corpus survey, I analyze only passages where the paraphrased/ target text follows the source text—that is, where the target text uses the same words and main structure as the source text—focusing in particular on the small modifications in grammatical characteristics of the target text. The data derive from translations/ paraphrases that render the source texts closer to the vernacular language (Karla & Lavidas 2004):

(i) an early 14th-century (according to the Thesaurus Linguae Graecae: "post A.D.12") translation of Anna Komnene's *Alexiad*, books XI–XII; (ii) a translation of the early 13th-century *Basilikos Andrias* of Nikephoros Blemmydes by Georgios Galesiotes and Georgios Oinaiotes; (iii) a paraphrasis of *Life of Aesop* into the vernacular language of the period (Vita W (vita Aesopi Westermanniana) vs. Vita Pl vel Accursiana (sub auctore Maximo Planude) vs. Vita G (e cod. 397 Bibliothecae Pierponti Morgan)); (iv) Digenis Akritis' Grottaferrata version vs. Escorial version (the source text was prepared approximately in the 12th century).

Part 2 of this book concludes with an overall discussion of how the proposed theoretical model of analysis of written language contact, presented in detail in Part 1, may be applied on the data in the English and Greek corpus surveys presented in Section 8.3. Then a summary follows of the major conclusions regarding the central questions and hypothesis of the present study.

1.2   Terminology of Language Contact

There is no agreement between scholars on the terminology related to contact-induced grammatical change. In the present section, I discuss concepts that have been used to describe types of grammatical change through language contact with an emphasis on studies on written language contact. I follow Hickey's (2010a) analysis of the concepts related to language contact. In the following, I present Hickey's typology:[3]

(i)   *Borrowing* describes the process of "copying" from one language to the other without language shift. This form of contact-induced change is a characteristic of "cultural" contact, for instance between Latin and early English or between contemporary English and other European languages (Kastovsky & Mettinger, eds, 2000; Poplack & Levey 2010; Miller 2011; Operstein 2015). Other scholars prefer the term *copying* (Johanson 2008, 2011) instead of the term *borrowing* (see also Hickey 2010a who considers copying as a more accurate concept than borrowing). The focus of the present study, that is, *written contact and its effects, belongs to the first type of change through contact* ("*borrowing or copying*") as described by Hickey.

(ii)   The term *transfer* is related to the transfer of linguistic features in the case of language switching, that is, when (bilingual) speakers "switch" to another language. Transfer can be supportive or innovative depending on whether the transferred linguistic features already existed in the target language, even with differences in some of their properties.

---

3   Classical descriptions and accounts of language contact include the studies of Weinreich 1979 [1953], Thomason & Kaufman 1988, Winford 2003, Heine & Kuteva 2005, Thomason 2006, 2008, Matras 2009, Drinka 2013, 2017. On historical language contact, see, among others, Janse 2002 (on Greek) and the special issue of *Linguistics Vanguard* (2020a) edited by Lavidas & Bergs (on English). Cf. also Lavidas & Bergs (2020b).

(iii) *Imposition* describes borrowing from a variety of a minority with high-status into a variety of a majority with low-status, providing that the variety of the minority is a shift variety. *Shift varieties* are the result of a community giving up their L1 in favor of a foreign language: see, for example, the shift variety of Singapore English or Irish English. I should note that, for van Coetsem (1995, 2003) and Winford (2003), imposition is similar to transfer (they do not distinguish between them).

(iv) *Metatypy* refers to common structures between languages that become increasingly more similar after a long period of contact (Ross 2003, 2013). These common structures lead to the emergence of a Sprachbund (see, among others, Lavidas 2019b).

(v) *Convergence* describes the coexistence of influence through contact and through internal development in the case of a single feature. The same concept has also been used in the literature instead of the concept *metatypy* for cases where two languages become more and more similar structurally (Hickey 2010a; Muysken 2010).

In a similar manner, relevant studies recognize two broad types of *change* that are related to language contact:

(a) contact-induced changes which are connected to full bilingualism and prevalent code-switching, that is, the "alternating use of different languages within a given situation" (Sankoff & Poplack 1981) (see Section 6.2);

(b) shift-induced interferences which are connected to imperfect learning (Thomason 2003: 709).

Moreover, there is consensus in the literature that shift-induced interference (or imposition) demonstrates source-language agentivity. Source-language agentivity is related to imperfect learning in cases where the source language is dominant (van Coetsem 1995, 2000, 2003). Recipient-language agentivity results in borrowing when the recipient language is the dominant language. Dominance is a key issue in studies of language contact, and, as seen, the recipient language can be dominant—and, in this case, mainly lexicon is involved. Alternatively, the source language can be dominant—and, if so, mainly phonology or syntax is involved. Studies have also shown that, in the case of recipient-language agentivity, a mechanism of imitation plays a significant role; whereas a mechanism of adaptation (through imperfect learning) plays a significant role in the case of source language agentivity (Fischer 2013; Fischer et al. 2017—Miller 2012).

In addition, several studies have analyzed the role of social forces in language contact (cf., among many others, Sitaridou 2014, 2016, 2022). For instance, social forces can easily be recognized in certain situations, e.g., contact due to immigration or conquest, or the mere geographical proximity (Sankoff 2008).

Important social factors that intervene in cases of language contact in earlier periods include immigration, imperfect learning and substratum[4] as well as conquest and the geographical proximity of communities. In cases of immigration, one should take into consideration the number of newcomers in comparison to the number of native population. Moreover, several studies have revealed the role of the social and prestige status of the languages in contact. In the case of substratum, standard language and bilingualism form significant factors that influence the results and characteristics of language contact.

Contact in the case of imperfect language learning—in particular, short-term contact that involves adult population—results in *simplification* of the variety of the broader community language (Trudgill 2001, 2004, 2009, 2012). On the contrary, *complexification* emerges with bilingualism, in particular, with long-term contact that involves children. Transfer of grammatical categories and Sprachbund formation is more plausible in the latter case. Accordingly, Trudgill connects the type of contact situation to the type of grammatical change: simplification is the result of a contact situation of brief interaction; complexification is the result of extended contact.

The investigation of the grammatical systems of target and source languages, as well as the quantitative comparative analysis of the constructions in the target language before and after a period of contact, form the starting points of any type of study of language contact. Syntactic transfer strongly depends on the availability of analogous constructions in the target language (cf., for instance, Fischer 2013). The typological characteristics of the languages that are in contact also determine the direction of change: for instance, if the languages are mutually intelligible, this can lead to the emergence of a *Koine*. Mixing of languages in these cases, together with reduction, as a type of attrition, may result in simplification and levelling (Kerswill 2003), whereas, with Koines, assimilation emerges only after mixing (Britain & Trudgill 1999; on the role of mixing, see also Section 6.4.).

1.3 Written Language Contact

Written language contact is usually seen in connection to ancient languages in religious contexts (Thomason & Kaufman 1988: 78–79), where *cultural* borrowing has been recognized as a type of contact-induced change (Häcker 2011),

---

4 Substratum refers to traces of the original language that forms the basis for or influences another language that later replaces the original language.

as evidenced in cases of borrowing from Latin and Greek into later European languages, or from English into modern languages (see also Adams et al., eds, 2002). Fischer (2013: 21) clearly recognizes the possibility of written language contact:

> It is also possible that contact takes place via written or indirect oral sources (books, the internet, radio/TV etc.) without any speakers directly communicating, in which case the effect of the contact is usually less strong [...].

A major question regarding *cultural* borrowing concerns the *spread* of borrowings from the individual to the community. In Fischer's (2013: 24; Table 2.1) classic table of contact-induced change in the history of English,[5] Latin and French appear to be true opposites mainly in parameter (x): fewer loanwords have their origin in Latin (see Table 1.1). Fischer's explanation includes, among other factors, the written type of contact with Latin (2013: 23), which is related to the fact that communication in terms of Latin was far more indirect, mostly via translators of texts.

Contact with Latin was never intensive or long, but always concerned native speakers of English with competence of Latin. In terms of my approach (see Chapter 6), this would mean that this type of contact always concerns speakers with at least "double competence" of Latin grammar in addition to another grammar (on double competence, see Weiß 2005a). Adams (2003, 2007) provides several examples of historical bilingualism of similar type (see 6.2 below). Studies of language contact through written discourse also include Musacchio (2005) and Taylor (2005).

To mention only an example here of language contact through translation in the case of English (see further Chapters 2 and 5 below), *three English biblical translations* play a significant role in relation to several main aspects of the *development of English*, according to Božović (2014): the Wycliffite Bible (1382; 1388), William Tyndale's translation (1526) and the King James/ Authorized Version (1611). Wycliffe's method was mainly based on glossing the Latin source text in order to preserve the style of the source.

William Tyndale prepared the first printed English translation of the New Testament from Greek. Tyndale translated the New Testament from the original Greek source text and the Old Testament from the original Hebrew text. It is

---

5   On contact in the history of English, cf., among many others: Hadley & Richards (2000), Kastovsky & Mettinger (eds) (2000), Filppula et al. (2008), Hickey (2010a, b), Schendl & Wright (2011), Miller (2012), Schreier & Hundt (eds) (2013).

WRITTEN LANGUAGE CONTACT AND TRANSLATIONS

TABLE 1.1   Parameters involved in contact of English with Latin, Scandinavian, Celtic and French

Parameters (social and linguistic)		Latin Contact— Old English (OE)/ Middle English (ME) period and Renaissance	Scandinavian contact—OE (/ME) period	Celtic contact— OE/ ME period and beyond (in Celtic varieties of English)	French contact— mainly ME period
(*i*)	*Type of language agentivity (primary mechanism)*	Recipient agentivity (imitation)	Source agentivity (adaptation)	Source agentivity (adaptation)	Recipient agentivity (imitation)
(*ii*)	*Type of communication*	Indirect	Direct	Direct	(In)direct
(*iii*)	*Length and intensity of communication*	Low	High	Average (?)	Average
(*iv*)	*Percentage of population speaking the contact language*	Small	Relatively large	Relatively large	Small
(*v*)	*Socio-economic status*	High	Equal	Low	High
(*vi*)	*Language prestige*	High	Equal	Low	High
(*vii*)	*Bilingual speakers (among the English speakers)*	Yes (but less direct)	No	No	Some
(*viii*)	*Schooling (providing access to target language)*	Yes	No	No (only in later periods)	Some
(*ix*)	*Existence of standard in source/ target language*	Yes/ Yes	No/ No	No/ No (only in later periods)	Yes/ No
(*x*)	*Influence on the lexicon of the target language (types of loanword)*	Small (formal)	Large in the Danelaw area (informal)	Small (except in Celtic varieties of English) (informal)	Very large (mostly formal)
(*xi*)	*Influence on the phonology of the target language*	No	Yes	Yes? (clearly in Celtic varieties of English)	Some
(*xii*)	*Linguistic similarity with target language*	No	Yes	No	No

FISCHER 2013: 24

worth mentioning that Tyndale hypothesized an affinity between English and Hebrew syntax, and, therefore, he followed a word-for-word strategy in several cases. Accordingly, a Hebrew influence can be evident, for example, due to his tendency to follow the Hebrew source language with regard to word order, in the *NP-of-NP construction*, with superlative forms and with cognate noun constructions; for instance, *the holy of holies* instead of *the holiest*. Tyndale's role in the development of English has been recognized in his contribution to the emergence of an "English plain style", even in terms of remarks such as the following from Bobrick (2001: 105), "without Tyndale, no Shakespeare".

The Authorized Version of the Bible retained the archaic elements of earlier biblical translations. One should note that the instructions to the Authorized

Version translation team were to be careful *not* to depart from the Bishop's Bible (1568), which actually constituted a revision of the Great Bible (1539) which in turn revised Matthew's Bible (1537) which also revised Tyndale's text (1525). English biblical translations appear to include archaic characteristics always, and this fact comes in contrast to the character of ordinary (non-archaized) Greek/ Koine Greek, which could be translated into ordinary (non-archaized) English.

In the present section, I have introduced the concept of written language contact, providing some indicative examples from the history of English. In the following section, I further discuss some main characteristics of translations that can be seen as connected to written language contact.

1.3.1 *Translations and Diachronic Linguistics. Translations as a Source of Change and as Evidence of Change*

Discussions on written language contact may be found in studies on the general characteristics of language contact especially as related to ancient languages used for religious purposes (see Chapter 3), such as in the case of Koine Greek, Latin, Sanskrit, or Classical Arabic (Thomason & Kaufman 1988: 78–79; Cf. also Panagiotidou 2021, Gamagari & Lavidas 2022, Gamagari [to-appear]). For instance, there is a consensus in the studies on the diachrony of English that the introduction of Latin loanwords into English was accomplished through the written language because any type of oral use of Latin was restricted even within the clergy (see also Lakoff 1972; van Hoecke & Goyens 1990; Delisle & Woodsworth 2012).

Translations typically crop up in the historical linguistic context in different types of studies (Blake 1992), in works examining the history of education or ideas, in studies of vocabulary, but also in studies of historical syntax. However, as Blake (1992: 4) states, translations receive only incidental mention in histories of language and their influence on the language remains out of the scope of historical linguistic research.

McLaughlin (2011) also describes the relation between translations and historical linguistic studies in terms of tools of analysis of language change and in terms of research methodology as well as in cases where translations trigger change (cf. Haug & Jøhndal 2008). Even though many studies accept the role of translations in several cases of grammatical change, the earlier scholarship has not demonstrated how exactly translation operates as a factor of change. Translations from earlier periods differ substantially from translations of today. There is no consensus with regard to the period when the significant change in the translation methodology occurred, but most studies concur that it was quite recent, during the 19th century. In modern times, the focus is on the translation of the *content* of a text from one language to another—and not on the faithfulness of the translation, as in the case of early translations of religious texts. In early times, the aim and character of translations were different; this fact is also probably related to the status of the translators, which is evident if we consider the names of early translators: King Alfred, Chaucer, Elizabeth I, Pope and Dryden—many of whom are well known as original authors as well.

Translations served as exemplars of the ideal state of the language in the sense that they could express the content of religious, classical, well-received, influential source texts, and functioned as a model for other writers. Accordingly, the main point in the present study is that *there is not only antagonism between parallel grammars in the diachrony of languages but also coexistence and contact between early and late grammars—as well as between grammars reflected in translations and native grammars* (see Chapter 6). The examination of early translations reveals aspects of how translation affected the manner according to which the language developed: the early translations led to a situation of contact between features of the translations and native features of the language.

Translations also play a significant role in the development of the prestige of a language. This fact is directly related to the translation of ancient works into European languages of the late medieval and Renaissance period, which is considered as an important factor in the emergence of vernacular written languages. Standardized languages and earlier forms of the language are prestigious and can function as source languages that favor change through translations. More specifically, the contact between a standardized or an ancient language and a non-standardized language is the most favorable condition for translation-induced changes (McLaughlin 2011). This conclusion is directly related to the role of Latin in the development of standard languages in Europe—see Section 6.3. Written contact with Latin (and/ or another language) as a source language becomes weaker when earlier written (prestigious) varieties of the same language are available. As a result, a new type of written language contact emerges that concerns the contemporary language and an earlier written form of the same language. For instance, as described above, the contact of English with Latin or Greek is strong until later periods of English and until the emergence of a new contact situation/ a type of diglossia of the contemporary language with an earlier form of English.

1.3.2 *Translations as a Typical Example of Written Language Contact*
Translations are considered a typical example of written language contact, and several studies have investigated possible examples of change through translation. Two major types of translations can be recognized—and are relevant to the present study: translations that are oriented towards functional

equivalence—or covert translations, according to House (1997)—and translations that are oriented towards formal equivalence—or overt translations, in terms of House (1997) (see also Nida 1964; House 1997; Koller 1998).

In addition, two translation "laws" appear to be significant in any discussion on the role of early translations in contact-induced change: the *law of interference*, according to which the characteristics of the source language can be transferred into the target text, and the *law of growing standardization*, according to which the target text rather follows the preferences of the target language (Toury 2012: 267–278; Wollin 2002, 2005; Cf. also Becher et al. 2009, among others). In cases of high prestige of the source language, the law of interference prevails. Translations also apply a cultural filtering to adapt the translated text to preferences and norms of the target language (House 2008; Kranich et al. 2011).

Previous studies demonstrate the existence of the following inherent features of translated texts, namely, of universals of translation.[6] The universals of translation can be described as follows (Baker 1996; cf. also Laviosa 1998; Lanstyák & Heltai 2012):

- Explication: translated texts show a preference to spell out all elements of the meaning, rather than leave them implicit;
- Simplification: translated texts show a tendency to simplify the constructions used in the target text;
- Normalization: translated texts tend to exaggerate characteristics of the target language;
- Levelling out: translated texts prefer stylistically unmarked ways of expression. (On an opposite view, see House 2008 and Becher 2010).

Recently, further studies have highlighted the similarities between translation studies and contact linguistics (among others, House & Rehbein (eds) 2004; Steiner 2005, 2008; House 2008; Baumgarten & Özçetin 2008; Becher et al. 2009). For instance, Lanstyák & Heltai (2012) propose that translation studies are a subdivision of contact linguistics because (i) both translation and bilingual communication involve two languages and (ii) translators are a subgroup of bilinguals. Moreover, according to Lanstyák & Heltai's approach, translation universals are in reality language contact universals. In this respect, for

---

6 Note that we leave issues related to translation strategies and the role of translators open for future research. Instead, the aim is *a linguistic analysis of the interrelation between translations and linguistic diachrony; in broad terms: a linguistic study of the history of translations as related to grammatical change.* On possible relations between the history of translations and the history of language, see also Olohan (2014: 15). Cf. also Delisle & Woodsworth (2012); Lavidas (2021).

Lanstyák & Heltai, both translations and bilingual communication may lead to special (written or spoken) *contact varieties*. However, bilingual communication means independent language use—whereas translation is identified with text production dependent on a source text.

As discussed above, there is a consensus on the existence of universals of translation: most scholars agree on the universals of simplification, normalization, explicitation, as well as (according to several studies) discourse transfer/ interference and distinctive distribution of lexical items (Laviosa 2010; Lanstyák & Heltai 2012). There is less of an agreement on the universals of language contact. In most cases, scholars refer to *contact-induced changes* (Thomason & Kaufman 1988; Siemund 2008) and stress the fact that various social factors may affect language change in the context of language contact. The results of contact-induced changes can be described as areal diffusion or the transfer of linguistic characteristics/ elements from one language, a model language, to another, a replica language (Weinreich 1979 [1953]: 7–8, 32). Note, however, that universals are not a central issue for contact linguistic studies—even though Lanstyák (2003) recognizes a number of universals of language contact which share common characteristics with universals of translation.

Some of the proposed similarities between *universals of language contact* and *universals of translation* are the following, according to Lanstyák & Heltai (2012), in particular: (i) Contact effects (in language contact) and discourse transfer (in translations). Toury (2012) proposes the translation universal of discourse transfer/ law of interference—see also above, Section 1.2: translated texts are different than non-translated texts because of direct transference or due to a different distribution of lexical items and syntactic constructions. The above generalization has its parallel in contact effects or contact interference in the case of bilingual speech. Contact effects are present in all contact situations at the level of linguistic system and at the level of discourse. Moreover, contact effects appear in both languages of the bilinguals: both in their L1 and their L2; both in their dominant and their non-dominant language. Transfer in translation can be analyzed as a similar phenomenon to distributional differences in case of contact effects. The distributional contact effects derive from textual and linguistic differences that concern cases where the translated text follows the source text without ignoring, without disrespecting, the grammatical norms of the target language. The situational contact effects, however, refer to phenomena that are not dependent on the characteristics of the source language. These phenomena probably present parallels to what is expected to be translation universals, that is, to characteristics of the target text that are related to the process of translation and not to specific features of the source text.

(ii) Both translation and bilingual speech lead to the emergence of contact varieties. In the case of bilinguals, contact effects can derive a new variety if they incorporate into the linguistic system of the L1 (Lanstyák & Heltai 2012). Contact varieties demonstrate universals probably connected to the language contact situation. Accordingly, translations give rise to a new bilingual contact variety, to the variety of the translated language. The latter variety is different than contact varieties in that it also shows universal features non-dependent on the source language. Moreover, translators are a very specialized and numerically restricted population group, which may cast more general doubts on the possibility of translations affecting the development of the grammatical system of a given language: see the discussions in Sections 2.1, 3.3 and 5. However, as mentioned above, bilinguals may also use a contact variety of their L1. Thus, according to Lanstyák & Heltai (2012), contact and translation varieties may play a role in change in the target language in terms of register and general language.

Other studies have also stressed the relation between translations, language contact and grammatical change. Steiner (2008), for instance, argues that one language can affect another in a contact situation through its instantiations in discourses and texts only if there is a contrast between these languages. According to Steiner, translations are "a prime example of contact varieties" (2008: 322) (cf. also Appel & Muysken 2005). Moreover, Steiner (2008: 9) has examined translations as a significant "venue of influence" in language contact, a different one than traditional venues of contact.

In addition, Koller (1998) argues that translations from other languages have played a significant role, for example, in the diachrony of German both in the *development of the grammar* and the *preferences in style*. According to Koller, the total of German written texts consists of both translations and original texts in all periods and there is no clear differentiation of the one group of texts from the other. The influence of translations is related to language standardization, mainly, and the process of addition of prestige to the target language, which is shown to have the means to express the content of classical and wellreceived/ influential texts of the source language. Therefore, the influence of translations led to an incorporation of grammatical and stylistic characteristics of the source languages into German (Koller 1998).

Koller's conclusion is that cross-linguistic communication challenges the target language to find equivalent means for the expression of similar meanings. The equivalent means can be the result of introduction of characteristics of the source language or of re-definition and re-function of existent linguistic features (on reorganization of the grammar, with examples from the history of Greek, see Lavidas [2018b]). For Koller (1998), the introduction of new characteristics can be triggered either through "innovations on the level of the language system" (*Systeminnovationen*) or through "innovations on the level of norms of usage or stylistic innovation" (*Norm-/Stilinnovationen*). Stylistic/norm innovations can be further distinguished into quantitative and qualitative norm innovations.

In general, it is obvious that stylistic preferences and usage norms are *more susceptible* to innovations than the grammatical system. The quantitative norm innovations refer to cases where the frequent translation of structures of the source language through less productive—even though fully acceptable—structures of the target language leads to new prevailing norms of usage in translation. The new preferences become more productive and central for the target language through their establishment as *prescriptive* stylistic principles.

There is also agreement that translations transfer culture-specific concepts —probably modified by the translations—into different cultures (Häcker 2011; Luraghi 2013). For instance, Luraghi & Cuzzolin (2007) have shown how translations transfer culture-specific concepts into different languages with the examples of translations of Luke's Gospel into Latin, Gothic and Old Church Slavonic. It is evident that one expects a significant difference between the transfer of culture-specific linguistic elements coming from religious texts and the transfer of linguistic elements from other translated texts. The translation of religious text is also connected to a whole system of thoughts and values (see Chapter 3 on biblical translations).

Biblical Greek—both Old Testament Greek and New Testament Greek—is also affected by Semitic characteristics. In addition, Biblical Greek developed indirect contact with several other languages through two major translations, mainly the Latin Vulgate and the Old Church Slavonic translation. The Latin Vulgate has played a significant role in the process of transfer of constructions and meanings. Luraghi & Cuzzolin (2007), for example, examine the translation of the preposition ἐπί *epí* 'on' in Luke's Gospel into Latin, Gothic and Old Church Slavonic. Luraghi & Cuzzolin demonstrate for the Vulgate that Jerome's translation introduced new usages of lexical items and new constructions. This fact can be illustrated with examples of translations of the preposition *epí* in the New Testament. The Koine Greek preposition *epí* had no translational equivalent in Latin. Therefore, Jerome decided to limit its translation to two prepositions: *in* and *super*; earlier translations, prepared in different periods and locations, had shown, however, a variety of translations of the preposition *epí*, which was not found in the Vulgate (Luraghi & Cuzzolin 2007; Luraghi 2013). It thus appears that one may recognize established translation equivalents that could be used in various contexts in the target text (Kerr 2011; Porter

2013c, 2016a). It is evident that translation equivalents are also related to translation universals (see above) and features of biblical translations (cf. Chapter 3).

Observe that equivalence refers to structural similarities between languages but also to cases of manifestation of contact through translation, or, in terms of Heine & Kuteva (2005: 4), to the way speakers conceptualize the correspondences between languages in contact, as it is shown, for instance, in translational conventions and practices. Heine & Kuteva argue that translation constitutes a significant factor in cases of intense language contact—but a constrained one in a number of ways. Equivalence relations can be regarded as *translational equivalence*, which is defined in terms of speakers' linguistic behavior related to what speakers treat as equivalent features or patterns in contexts of contact. *The study of translations can be a significant way to reconstruct this linguistic behavior.* Heine & Kuteva (2005: 222) state that the study of translational works is the most obvious procedure to reconstruct what speakers in situations of contact conceive of and treat as equivalent use patterns or categories. The process of establishing translational equivalence is complex.

For instance, in the case of contact between German and Estonian (note that German has definite and indefinite articles, whereas Estonian has no grammaticalized articles), Lehiste (1979, 1999) concludes that the translators use the Estonian demonstrative pronoun *see* as a correspondent word for the German definite article, and the Estonian numeral *üks* 'one' for the German indefinite article. *Their strategy follows the universal principles* that determine the grammaticalization of articles in the diachrony of several languages (Heine & Kuteva 2003). German provides the model for replication—the indefinite article in German derived from the German numeral—and, based on this fact, Heine & Kuteva account for the above development in Estonian as a case of replica grammaticalization or polysemy copying.

Accordingly, translational equivalence concerns equating a category of the model language with a grammaticalization process in the replica language: that is, in the previous example, the definite article in German with the grammaticalization of the demonstrative into an article in Estonian. However, the numeral 'one' is a common source of grammaticalization of the indefinite article cross-linguistically, which means that one cannot exclude a parallel development.

Nau (1995) also presents several examples of the way that *written registers have enhanced or triggered contact-induced grammaticalization.* For instance, the grammaticalization of the locative (path) prepositions into more abstract (non-locative) prepositions in German and other European language has been considered as being replicated in Finnish and Latvian through the influence of biblical translations as well as of other translations from German (or Swedish). Therefore, for instance, the Latvian preposition *caur* with a new non-locative meaning is restricted to the written language (Nau 1995: 145).

Moreover, biblical translations have been described as a factor that has assisted in the development of grammaticalized futures with the modal verbs *pitää* 'should, must' and *tahtoa* 'want, intend' in Finnish. This type of grammaticalization does not affect spoken Finnish (Nau 1995: 99–104; Heine & Kuteva 2005: 104).

The spread of the replacement of the infinitive by finite subordinate clauses in the Balkans has also been considered as a result of Church influence, through Byzantine and Medieval Greek (Banfi 1990)—among many other possible hypotheses. Note, however, that oral forms of discourse are the first to be affected by contact-induced change in cases that do not involve written contact; after a period of time, the new features and constructions appear in written discourse as well. In contrast, if language contact is mainly related to written registers, written discourse can be affected first.

The question that arises is whether it is possible to recognize a specialized type of language contact through translation and even a different type of grammatical change due to contact through translation. Several studies have supported the idea of specialized *Language Contact Through Translation* (LCTT) that describes *innovations limited to translated texts or integrated into the target language*—as parts of specific registers or not (Kranich et al. 2011—Lehiste 1999; Božović 2014). As described above, translated texts show universal/ common features: for instance, according to Baker (1996), the language of (non-biblical) translations has a more simplified, normalized—with exaggeration of features of the target grammar, explicit and stylistically unmarked character. For Kranich et al., several linguistic as well as socio-political and cultural factors determine language contact through translation:
- intensity and length of contact,
- prestige of the source language and dominance relations,
- attitude towards the source language and the orientation of the translator,
- standardization of the target language and establishment of the particular genre in the target language,
- typological closeness between the target and the source language,
- functional equivalence between particular linguistic elements.

Translations can demonstrate a particular type of contact even though the changes due to translations can remain *restricted only to translated texts*.

However, this type of change can gradually be incorporated to the recipient language in a particular genre or in general (Blake 1992; Gottlieb 1999,

22   CHAPTER 1

TABLE 1.2   Factors and outcome of language contact through translation

Factors in language contact through translation

i.   Orientation of the translator towards free or literary translations
ii.   Intensity of contact
iii.   Length of contact
iv.   Sociopolitical dominance relations
v.   Prestige of source language
vi.   Attitude towards the source language
vii.   Degree of standardization of the target language
viii.   Degree of establishment of the genre in target language
ix.   Typological proximity
x.   Potential for establishing functional equivalence between particular
        linguistic items

Outcome of language contact through translation

I.   Lexical
II.   Morphological
III.   Syntactic
IV.   Pragmatic/ stylistic
V.   Different degree of explicitness of encoding in translated texts as com-
        pared to comparable non-translated text

KRANICH ET AL. 2011: 18

2005), because of the high prestige that the translation of classical or influential and well-received source texts can offer to the target language; the target
language is shown to have the means to express the content of the source texts,
which can be important for the development of the prestige of a language (see
Chapter 6). Translations may affect only specific genres (Koch & Oesterreicher
1994; Lehiste 1999, Böttger & Bührig 2003, Baumgarten et al. 2004; Ross 2011;
Baumgarten 2008) or even only specific syntactic features and constructions
(Cichocki & Lepetit 1986; McDonough 2002). Koch (2011) argues that translation effects are also limited if the target and source languages are typologically
distinct to a significant degree (Becher et al. 2009; Teich 2003).

    Kranich et al. (2011) propose a model for the classification of cases of lan-
guage contact through translation. Their model is based on two variables of
factors: one is related to typological features of the languages involved and the
other is related to the socio-political background of contact. This model is summarized in Table 1.2.

Following the parameters presented in Table 2.1 above, Kranich et al. provide two examples of types of contact situations: one example of early contact between Latin and Old Swedish and another example of modern contact between contemporary English and German. Late Medieval Sweden was a triglossic linguistic area, with the following varieties: Old Swedish, which constituted the vernacular; Medieval Latin, which constituted a *lingua franca* and a written language for religious, literary or administrative functions; Middle Low German which functioned as an additional *lingua franca*. In the Late Medieval period, Old Swedish can be described as being in the first stage of becoming a literary language. Translations from Latin into Old Swedish showed a significant increase. Latin was a language of prestige in the domains of liturgy and Scripture and was considered a more "logical" language than the Swedish vernacular. The early produced translations were of the functional equivalence type. However, late Old Swedish translations (circa 1400–1526) aimed at formal equivalence—and the new tendency resulted in a higher formal correspondence between translated and source texts. According to Kranich et al., the contact situation between Old Swedish and Latin after 1400 can be described as follows: (i) there was a preference for an overt translation strategy; (ii) the source language, Latin, was a language of high prestige; (iii) the contact was intense but restricted to a small community; (iv) the degree of standardization and the establishment of the relevant genres in Swedish was low; (v) Latin and Swedish were typologically similar but not closely related.

Observe that the above characteristics apply to the cases of *translations from Latin and Greek into English*, as well as to the *intralingual biblical translations* or *retranslations*: see Part 2. Based on the above description of the situation of language contact, Kranich et al. predict a significant effect of Latin on Swedish through translations. Even though contact was restricted to a small community, it seems that translations of religious, classical and well-received/ influential texts may trigger a significant spread of new linguistic characteristics, in the form of semi-natural grammatical change (cf. Chapter 6). According to their view, the written variety of Old Swedish includes many examples of code-switching and lexical transfer (Wollin 2007, among others). In addition, Kranich et al, argue that several grammatical changes can be attributed to the influence of Latin translations; for instance, changes in clause linking strategies, relativization, participial constructions, word order patterns in subordinate clauses, particle verbs, and gerundive forms.

Translations may affect all types of linguistic characteristics—but, of course, not in a similar way. Regarding the morphological characteristics, for example, there is no direct influence on borrowing of affixes from a source language. The first stages of borrowing of affixes mainly include loan affixes only as parts of words that are borrowed. A prime example are the affixes of French origin used in loanwords from French in the late 14th-century work of Chaucer (see Part 2: Section 7.4): *mesurable, servysable, chivalrye, briberye, argument, avisement.* However, French affixes appear very rarely with a native stem. In Chaucer, for instance, they are attested only in the examples of: *unknowable, housbondrye, robberie,* and *eggement* (Fischer 2007: 26). The above contrast in this development constitutes evidence of the long period required for the adaptation of foreign affixes in the native system of English.

With regard to syntactic constructions, in the case of glosses, which are extremely close / word-by-word translations, borrowed constructions are likely to be literal and directly affected by the source text. Therefore, glosses do not provide significant evidence of change in this case. However, they can be an important source of information if the glossator followed a phrase-by-phrase translation strategy or if the glossator translated the text in an idiomatic manner. In any case, such data should be used in comparison to the relevant constructions in original texts.

A challenge appears with translated constructions that also occur in non-translated texts in later periods of the language (on Greek and relevant examples in the case of the Septuagint, see Lavidas 2014, 2019a). It is debatable, then, whether such syntactic constructions are a development of native constructions that existed in earlier periods—or whether they were borrowed and became possible because they were part of the grammar of the source texts. A criterion to distinguish between borrowed constructions and native developments is whether the texts that include such constructions are extremely different from non-translated texts, and/ or whether the texts contain a huge amount of loanwords (Fischer 2007; 2013). Fischer (2007: 28) also refers to useful conclusions that may derive from a comparison of different translations of the same text (see Section 7.3): according to her, factors that may help to decide which grammatical properties are borrowed or not include the questions of presence—absence of heavy lexical borrowing, of how clumsily or not a translated text reads in comparison to native/ non-translated texts, and of the types of alternations inserted into the structure of the foreign text that can probably make the structure closer to a native one. Fischer (2007) states that it is interesting to compare translations of the same text (retranslations) in cases such as the above.

Moreover, even though there is an agreement in the scholarship that the borrowing of lexical foreign elements is more frequent in translations than the borrowing of other features, there is no agreement on the status of syntactic borrowing. Several researchers support the view that imperfect learners of a foreign language and substratum are required for syntactic borrowing to be possible—that is, there is a need for *intense and prolonged oral contact*. If the contact is not intense or prolonged (e.g., in the case of contact with a prestige, ancient source language), syntactic borrowing is possible *only when* the borrowed construction fits to the grammar of the target language (Thomason & Kaufman 1988; van der Wurff 1990; Fischer 1992; Harris & Campbell 1995; Bisang 1998; Aitchison 2001). Thomason's (2001: 70–71) 'borrowing scale' indicates that *syntactic constructions can be borrowed* if several factors favor their transfer from the one language to the other, such as length and intensity of contact, existence of bilingual speakers, social circumstances that support the borrowing (see also the 'hierarchy of borrowability' in Lass 1997: 189). However, for Harris & Campbell (1995: 120–150), syntactic borrowing should be seen as much more frequent and not bound to such restrictions as the ones mentioned above.

A clear example of translations as a factor of grammatical change and of the position of translations in the history of languages concerns the diachrony of infinitives in English. The development of infinitivals in English provides significant examples of the role of contact in the development of English (see also Chapter 5). For instance, Miller (2002) shows that Exceptional Case Marking (that is, case marking of the embedded subject by the matrix verb) with infinitives in constructions with wh-movement (e.g., *Whom I believe to be a liar*) was marginally grammatical only after verbs of mental perception ('know', 'believe', 'consider') in Old English (cf. also Stein & Trips 2012). Miller bases his conclusions about the diachrony of infinitivals exclusively on evidence from texts dependent on Latin: the translations of Bede's *Historia Ecclesiastica Gentis Anglorum* ['Ecclesiastical History of the English people'], the Benedictine Rule, and the glosses in Ælfric's Latin grammar.

Another example from English is reported by Iyeiri (2010) who investigates two versions of Trevisa's translation of Higden's Polychronicon (MS Cotton Tiberius D. VII, MS C, and Caxton's 1482 edition). Iyeiri's aim is to trace which features change in the process of textual transmission and which features can be used to estimate the date of a text. Trevisa's Middle English translation used as its source text the Latin Polychronicon which was written by Ranulph Higden who died in 1363/1364 (Lawler 1983). The text survived in more than 120 manuscripts, from the 14th century and later, as well as in copies in 14 full manuscripts and three early printed editions.

I should underline that, according to McIntosh (1963: 9), later Middle English manuscripts that are copies and include non-original texts show characteristics of translations (see Section 8.2 on Greek later versions of the same text). The relevant Middle English manuscript is MS C which dates from circa 1400 or few years earlier—whereas Caxton's edition was published in 1482 (Waldron 1991,

26 CHAPTER 1

TABLE 1.3   Infinitival endings in MS C [MS Cotton Tiberius D. VII] and Caxton's version of the Polychronicon

	-e retained	zero ending (loss of -en complete)
MS C	97.54 %	2.46 %
Caxton's version	87.31 %	12.69 %

IYEIRI 2010: 115

2001; Waldron (ed.) 2004). The stemma of manuscripts shows no direct relation between these texts.

Iyeiri (2010) examines the cases of (i) the adverbial suffixes -liche and -ly; (ii) infinitival forms; and (iii) negated constructions. The examples in (1a–b) (from Iyeiri 2010: 111) demonstrate the adverbial suffixes -liche and -ly. The Oxford English Dictionary relates the -ly forms to the Old English -lic(e), which was attested as -lik in northern dialects and as -liche in southern dialects. According to the data in the Oxford English Dictionary, both -liche and -ly can be found in the 15th century; the latter was used in all contexts by the end of the 15th century.

(1)   a. MS Cotton Tiberius D. VII of John Trevisa's translation based upon Ranulph Higden's Polychronicon (MS C), 223r
        [...] was *strongliche* despysed [...]
     b. Caxton's edition (1482) of John Trevisa's translation based upon Ranulph Higden's Polychronicon, 286v
        *But the kynge pursued hym soo **strongly** [...]*

The data in Book VI of the text under examination shows that MS C (which dates to around 1400) offers 154 relevant examples and all of them have the form -liche. Caxton's edition which dates to 1482 offers 158 relevant examples and all of them have the form -ly.

The second case study in Iyeiri's article concerns the infinitival forms. The loss of the infinitival ending -en was not complete in the two versions of the Polychronicon. Table 1.3 from Iyeiri (2010) presents the frequencies of the presence/ absence of the infinitival ending -e in the two texts; verbs with a stem ending with a vowel are excluded from the frequencies. The infinitival ending has left a trace before its complete loss, with the morpheme -e in various instances: MS C maintained -e almost in all passages, whereas Caxton's edition did not retain -e to such a degree and showed a zero ending more frequently than found in MS C.

TABLE 1.4 The forms *ne, ne ... not, not* in MS C [MS Cotton Tiberius D. VII] and Caxton's version of the Polychronicon

	ne	*ne ... not*	*not*
MS C	5.33%	0.67%	94.00%
Caxton's edition	4.70%	-	95.30%

IYEIRI 2010: 120

TABLE 1.5 Single and multiple negation in MS C [MS Cotton Tiberius D. VII] and Caxton's version of the Polychronicon

	Single negation	**Multiple negation**
MS C	87.79%	12.21%
Caxton's edition	88.30%	11.70%

IYEIRI 2010: 122

The distribution of the form *ne* and the forms *ne ... not* and *not* also illustrates the variation of negated constructions in the two texts.[7] The construction with *ne* was already found in Old English and was the earliest one. Table 1.4 (from Iyeiri 2010: 120) presents the frequencies of the three constructions in the versions of MS C and Caxton's edition. The decline of the multiple negation was attested in late Middle English, and the data show that multiple negation was not productive in the two versions of the Polychronicon (Table 1.5 from Iyeiri 2010: 122).

Caxton's aim was to modify the text to make it *absolutely readable for his contemporary target audience*. It seems, though, that Caxton did not modify negated constructions. The differences between Caxton's version and the MS C version are not significant with respect to negated constructions, even though the chronological order of the two versions is reflected, to a limited degree only, in the frequencies of the negated constructions (Iyeiri 2010).

---

7 Iyeiri (2010) also examines negated constructions and the editorial practices in various versions of Chaucer's *Boece*.

The above observations also favor the hypothesis that retranslations do not reflect the diachrony of the language (as attested in non-translated texts): later retranslations do not include innovative characteristics only. Retranslations "create" a parallel diachrony as they represent a parallel grammar that may reflect earlier periods of the language too. However, retranslations may demonstrate the same order of changes as the diachrony of non-translated texts, in that frequencies of later innovative characteristics become higher in later retranslations. The fact that retranslations follow the order of changes, as seen in the corpus study presented above, can be accounted for in terms of a development of retranslations that follows broad characteristics of grammatical change but do not directly follow the changes in the oral language which are represented in the non-translated texts.

CHAPTER 2

Early History of Translations and Grammatical Change: Landmarks in the Development of Early Translations

2.1 Introduction

The aim of the present chapter is not to include a detailed discussion of the history of translation (see Lavidas 2021 for a presentation of the history of translation in the West; cf. also Chapter 3). Rather, the aim is to present a brief introduction to *the main landmarks in the history of early translations*, focusing in particular on the development of early translations in English and Greek. After presenting an overview of early translations, I analyze the relation between the history of translations and grammatical change in English (Section 2.2) and the history of Greek translations and grammatical change in Greek (Section 2.3).

The first evidence of translations can be traced to 3000 BC in Pharaonic Egypt (area of Elephantine): bilingual inscriptions of this area refer to supervisors of interpreters (Kurz 1985—cf. also Kelly 1979; Bassnett 1991; Berchin 1998; Rigolio 2016). Kumārajīva's, a Buddhist monk's, work who translated Sanskrit Buddhist texts into Chinese in the late fourth century also marks a significant early stage of the history of translations. This early stage of translations includes the Arabic translations of Ancient Greek scientific and philosophical works.

The translation of the Hebrew Old Testament into Greek (the Greek Septuagint/ LXX) in the third century BC is the first major translation in the western world (see Lavidas 2021).[1] The name of the translation, *Septuagint*, refers to a myth according to which 72 translators prepared the translation of the Hebrew Bible in Alexandria, Egypt. The Greek translation also constituted a source text of later translations into Latin, Coptic, Armenian, and other languages. The translation of the Septuagint is a typical example of the translations into Greek from speakers of languages of the near East that were prepared from the third century BC, i.e., from a period when Greek is established as a lingua franca.

The well-known narration in Aristeas' epistle states that, in around 200 BC, a committee of 72 rabbis undertook the task to translate the first five books of

---

1 Note that the Greek Septuagint contains Greek original texts as well—see Section 2.3.5.2 where the Septuagint is discussed in detail.

© KONINKLIJKE BRILL NV, LEIDEN, 2022 | DOI:10.1163/9789004503564_003

the Old Testament into Greek (Naudé 2009). Greek-speaking Jews, who were located outside Palestine and had started to forget Hebrew and Aramaic, were the target of the translation. According to Philo of Alexandria (circa 25 BC–AD 40), the 72 translators produced the same translation, even though they worked in isolation from one another: this story provided the necessary authentication to this early biblical translation (see Chapter 3).

Aristeas' epistle aimed at presenting the translation of sacral texts as a work inspired of God. The collective responsibility protects translators from any accusation of personal style and from experiencing ultimate danger, as in the case of William Tyndale because of his English translation work of the Bible (see Section 2.2.1). The Septuagint also reflects a case of *language attrition*, i.e., of loss of an L1 or L2 once acquired or learned, because the Jews of this period and region could not understand Hebrew and therefore needed a Greek translation.

Another important early period in the history of translation is the second century BC when Greek comedies were translated into Latin. The debate between word-for-word and sense-for-sense translation also begins in that period (Polkas 2006). Cicero, for instance, developed the following view on the debate: "I did not think I ought to count them [the words] out to the reader like coins, but to pay them by weight, as it were" (*De Oratore*, 55 BC; Kumaniecki 1969). The 4th century AD demonstrates the emergence of a need for freer translations. In that period, Jerome of Stridon (circa 347–419/ 420) prepared one of the most important translations of the Bible, which succeeded the earlier Latin translations of *Vetus Latina* or *Itala* and was named in later times, after the 16th century, *Vulgata*. Jerome had based his translation of the New Testament on the Koine Greek text and the translation of the Old Testament on the Hebrew original text, rather than on the Septuagint. Boethius (470/ 475–524) also had his own translation program: his aim was to translate Aristotle's and Plato's works into Latin (Burnley 1992; Polkas 2006; Varmazis 2006).

The early history of translations into English starts with Alfred the Great who was responsible for important translations from Latin into the Old English of the 9th century, such as Bede's *Ecclesiastical History* and Boethius' *Consolation of Philosophy* (Wittig 1982; see also Chapter 3). Another important aspect of early European translations concerns the works of the *Toledo School of Translators* in the 12th and 13th century, which were translations of religious, medical and philosophical Arabic, Greek and Hebrew texts into Latin and Spanish. Roger Bacon (1220–1292), an English Franciscan monk, also played a significant role in the translation theory and practice of the 13th century. In his *Opus Maius* (1268), his main claim was that it is not possible for a translation to include all points of the source text due to the differences between the source and the target language. Bacon is considered the first to distinguish between two types of translations: the "vertical" type, where an earlier strong language is translated—for instance, Latin—into a contemporary, spoken language, and the "horizontal" type, where both the source and the target language have the same prestige (Polkas 2006).

Chaucer's English translations of Boethius' works from Latin and of the work "Roman de la Rose" from French as well Wycliffe's biblical translations (14th century) constitute examples of significant Middle English translations. The late 15th century was also an important period of the history of English translations: Malory, for instance, prepared the work "Le Morte d'Arthur" (an adaptation/free translation of romances about King Arthur). In several cases, the translator added original material.

The Renaissance, with renewed interest in the classical antiquity and the introduction of printing press to several European countries, provided translation with an important role in the process of bringing the European vernacular languages into contact with the classical works (Boutcher 2000; Lianeri & Zajko (eds) 2008). In the first ten years of the 16th century, translations of classical works and biblical translations were four times more frequent than in the previous 50 years. Regarding ancient Greek authors, translations of the following authors were prepared during this period either directly from Greek or through other languages: Demosthenes, Isocrates, Plutarch and Homer (Polkas 2006). One of the major translators of Homer is George Chapman: his complete English translation of the *Iliad* was published in 1611, followed by the *Odyssey* in 1616.

Many translators discussed the question of prestige of classical languages in their prefaces or in other works. Some translators regarded translations of this period as an action to support their native language, whereas, in other cases, translations were considered to be disruptive to the commonly recognized characteristics of the target language (Polkas 2006). In the 16th century, Martin Luther translated the Bible into German (New Testament: 1522; Old and New Testaments with Apocrypha: 1534) and was the first European translator to state that a satisfactory translation can be achieved *only toward the first language of the translator.*

In the list of early modern translations, one can find several important biblical translations, such as the Polish *Jakub Wujek Bible* (*Biblia Jakuba Wujka*) (1535) and the English *King James/ Authorized Version* (1604–1611) (on biblical translations, see Chapter 3). Other early, non-religious, English translations include John Dryden's translation of Virgil (Polkas 2006). In the end of the 17th century, John Dryden (1631–1700) and Alexander Pope (1688–1744) were the leading figures in the area of translations. According to Dryden, there are three basic types of translations: *translation*, which is actually word-by-word translation, *paraphrasis*, which means the transfer of interpretation of a text into another language, and *imitation*, which leads to the abandonment of the source text.

In the 18th century, Alexander Pope, in cooperation with Elijah Fenton and William Broome, translated the *Iliad* (1715–1720) and the *Odyssey* (1725–1726). Thomas Bentley (1735) and Cowper (1791) criticized the above translations because these approached the source text through other English—as well as French and Latin—translations (Polkas 2006). Furthermore, Alexander Fraser Tytler published his *Essay on the Principles of Translation* in 1791; according to Tytler, the main aim of a translator is to produce an equivalent work that can overcome linguistic and cultural differences between the source and target language.

From the Renaissance until the 18th century, the main aim of translations was the naturalization of the source language based on the target language. By contrast, in the 19th century, translations appear to have similar characteristics to the characteristics of the source text. Translations of Homer were very frequent in the 19th century England: Mathew Arnold (1822–1888), a translator of passages of the Homeric epics, for instance, introduced four criteria to evaluate the Homeric style and its translation: speed, simplicity, honesty and politeness (Steiner 2004). It was considered a duty of the translator to be as faithful as possible to the original text (Brock 1979; Polkas 2006).

As already seen, the history of translation clearly demonstrates that people mainly translate what a culture finds interesting in another culture (Bolgar 1954; Iartseva 1981). For instance, in early modern Europe, several translations of the following works were published: the Bible, *Imitatio Christi* 'Imitation of Christ' (by Thomas à Kempis; circa 1418), Greek and Latin classics, Erasmus' Latin texts, Luther's Latin and German texts, Calvin's Latin and French texts (Burke 2007b; see also Lavidas 2021, among others). The source and target languages in early translations mainly included Greek and Latin as source languages, and Latin (in translations from Greek) and European vernaculars as target languages. The opposite direction, from European vernaculars into Latin, reveals many aspects of the linguistic ideology of various periods of time, as well as significant characteristics of the development of languages (see Chapter 4).

Burke (2007b) mentions approximately 1200 translations from European vernaculars into Latin, completed between 1500 and 1800. Most of these translations are translations of scientific and religious books (Calvin, Luis de Granada, Galileo, Newton)—but there are also translations of poems, plays, histories and travel books. A list of plays translated into Latin includes the fol-

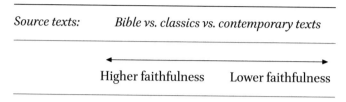

FIGURE 2.1 Source texts and variation in faithfulness of a translation

lowing: Ariosto's *Suppositi* and *Negromante, Celestina* of Fernando de Rojas, Tasso's *Aminta*, Giambattista Della Porta's *Astrologo*; Epics: *Orlando Furioso, Gerusalemme Liberata, Os Lusíadas, Paradise Lost*; Long poems: Dante's *Divina Commedia*, Brant's *Narrenschiff*, Spenser's *Shepherd's Calendar*, Dryden's *Absalom and Achitophel* (Grant 1954; Burke 2007b).

Moreover, it is obvious that a comparison of the early modern translations with, for instance, the translations before 1500 or after 1800 reveals changes in the practice of translation. In the Middle Ages, the methodology supported a word for word translation; in the Early Modern period, translations favor a much freer domestication strategy, whereas *the period after 1800* was the period of rise of a *foreignizing tendency*. Koskinen (2012: 13) provides the following definition of domestication vs. foreignization:

> Domestication and foreignization are often seen as two opposing poles of an axis where one set of translation strategies replaces all unfamiliar elements with domestic variants to help the reader approach the text with ease and familiarity, while the other one follows the original text very closely, ruthlessly ignoring all potential difficulties of comprehension or barriers of reception.

In addition, Figure 2.1 represents the variation in faithfulness of a translation depending on the type of the source text.

In terms of change in the practice of translation, translations of classical texts, for instance, have followed a foreignizing method, as evidenced in Newman (1853). This foreignizing method appeared with the form of archaisms in Newman's translation of Horace, for example (cf. Burke 2007a; Venuti 2008). However, in his translation of Homer, it had the form of an effort to achieve an historical analogy between early English and Greek. Newman (1856: vi) argues that the translation of Homer's texts should be as much "Saxo-Norman" as possible, without many elements of classical learning.

In this respect, Homer's style requires a particular English style in the translation, according to Newman who also did not attempt to write in an English "style" (as he called it) that existed at an earlier period. Newman's his main aim was to solve the "artistic problem"; that is, to attain an aspect of moderate antiquity while being intelligible (Newman 1856: x). The result of the application of his methodology was an artificially constructed archaism without attention to historical consistency.

The tendency for foreignizing translations can be seen in intralingual translations as well. For instance, Ezra Pound identified foreignization with archaism: His translation of *The Seafarer* (1912) was kept close to the Anglo-Saxon text, with regard to compounds and alliteration (Venuti 2008). He also included archaisms from later periods of English, as is shown in the list in (2) (from Venuti 2008).

(2) *bitre breostceare*   translated as → *bitter breast-cares*
     merewerges   → *mere-weary*
     corna caldast   → *corn of the coldest*
     floodwegas   → *flood-ways*
     hægl scurum fleag   → *hail-scur flew*
     mæw singende fore medodrince   → *the mews' singing all my mead-drink*
                                                                (Venuti 2008)

Several of Pound's archaisms became poetical words of later English: *brine, laud, ado*. In this respect, it appears that a foreignizing translation can be achieved with domestic elements that are anachronistic, in Venuti's (2008) words, i.e., specific to later periods.

2.2 Early History of Translations and Grammatical Change in English

In this section, I discuss in detail some aspects of a possible relation between the diachrony of English translations and grammatical change in English. I begin the section with a brief presentation of translations which constitute milestones within early translations into English. The aim of this section is to identify the particular properties that characterize early translations into English, as well as identify the interaction of translations and the development of the language, in general. The issue will also be further explored in Chapter 7 where specific corpus studies are presented.

In the Old English period, King Alfred's work played a significant role in the first phase of English translations. Alfred is considered the "father of Old English prose". Alfred promoted English as *a written language*, as before him, literacy was only related to Latin (Donoghue 2008; Ellis & Oakley-Brown 2009).

He commissioned or produced several translated works: Boethius' *Consolation of Philosophy*, Pope Gregory's *Pastoral Care*, St. Augustine's *Soliloquies*, Bede's Latin Ecclesiastical History, and most likely Pope Gregory's *Dialogues*, as well as the Spanish priest Orosius' *Historia adversus Paganos* (Swanton 1993; Timofeeva 2018).

Alfred formed a circle of translators, exactly like in the case of committees of translators in several biblical translations (see Sections 2.1.1 and 3, and also Irvine & Godden 2012). Probably, Alfred himself translated St. Augustine's *Soliloquies*, Boethius' *Consolation of Philosophy*, Pope Gregory's *Pastoral Care*, the first fifty Psalms and Orosius' book (Donoghue 2008). No other names of Alfred's collaborators are still known today except for the name of the translator of the *Dialogues*, Werferth. Several studies have attempted to uncover possible transfer from the source language to Alfred's translated texts (Fischer 1992): Nehls (1974), for example, has shown a possible influence of Latin on progressive forms; in the translation of the Old English Orosius, the rate of progressive forms is 518 /100,000 words, in contrast to the rate of progressive forms in the Middle English *Polychronicon* (another chronicle translated from Latin), which is 6 /100,000 words.

Ælfric (*c.* 950–*c.* 1010), Abbot of Eynsham, was the leading person of the other significant translation project in the Old English period, which resulted in several translations and adaptations of the Old Testament and other religious texts. Ælfric's work had a different orientation than King Alfred's: he aimed at faithful translations that could safeguard Latin learning. Ælfric prepared a late West Saxon translation of the Old Testament of the 4th century Latin Vulgate, *Ælfric's Heptateuch* (Ellis & Oakley-Brown 2009). However, there is uncertainty with respect to his share in the Old Testament translation. West Saxon Gospels, prepared at the beginnings of the 11th century, are related to a religious reform, the Benedictine Reform; the surviving manuscripts retained a text written in idiomatic prose and very faithful to the source text. It is worth noticing that Ælfric offered a Latin preface, for instance, to the first book of Gospel homilies, but an English preface to Genesis (Skeat 1878).

Some Old English translations are literal—for instance, Bede's *Ecclesiastical History*—other translations are freer—for instance, Boethius' *De Consolatione Philosophiae*. In addition, 10th-century collections of saints' lives and homilies by Ælfric and Wulfstan contain translated passages; all of the texts, translated and non-translated, were inspired by Latin works. Interlinear glosses have been analyzed as a source that includes dubious evidence but also as a source that can provide interesting data if treated with special consideration (Fischer et al. 2017). For instance, there are constructions with sequence of verbs that appear only in interlinear glosses in Old English (Koopman 1990). This means that these constructions are a word-by-word translation of Latin and were probably ungrammatical in Old English. Glosses, however, provide an interesting evidence for dialectical features as pointed out in a study by Kroch & Taylor (1997), who examined the 10th century Northumbrian glosses of the Latin Vulgate Bible. For instance, northern glosses used subject pronouns in a different position from what is attested in southern texts, in passages where the Latin source text omitted the subject pronoun (see Section 5.3).

For most part of the Middle English period, two vernaculars are available, English and Anglo-Norman. Most Middle English translations are anonymous until the mid-14th century, except for cases like Richard Rolle's translation (1290?–1349), whose Psalter came to be used for hundred years and more (Ellis & Oakley-Brown 2009). Observe that the Auchinleck MS (circa 1330), which contains anonymous translations of Anglo-Norman romances, has been given much importance and has been regarded as a case where "a general editor" supervised the work of his translators (Pearsall 1977a: 145–146).

Late 12th-century translations of French texts also include, for instance, Layamon's Brut. Layamon's Brut is a translation of Wace's French version of Geoffrey of Monmouth's *Historia regum Britanniae* (Brook & Leslie 1963, 1978; Blake 1992). The French direct source of Layamon's Brut survives in two late 13th-century manuscripts (Brook & Leslie 1963, 1978; Turville-Petre 2008; Timofeeva & Ingham 2018). Other translations of the 13th century include Kentish sermons in the MS Laud Misc. 471 from French (Bennett & Smithers 1968; Burnley 1992). These translations contain a significant number of loanwords.

It is evident that the Middle English loanwords, borrowed directly from Latin, gained admission through the written language—Latin was a spoken language only among ecclesiastics or people of learning (Timofeeva 2011a). For instance, Trevisa's translation of Bartholomaeus' *De Proprietatibus Rerum* includes a long list of words that were taken directly from the Latin source text. These words were not attested in earlier periods of English, as such indicating how such words were first borrowed. A similar case is illustrated in the biblical translations of Wycliffe and his associates (see Section 2.2.1). In their texts, one can identify a significant number of loanwords from Latin that were not previously attested in English. Many of these words re-appeared in the biblical retranslations that followed the Wycliffite translation (Dellit 1905; Baugh & Cable 2013).

In the 14th century, the new professionalism in the area of translation was represented clearly in Geoffrey Chaucer's work (c. 1340–c. 1400). Chaucer produced close translations of several works of Dante, Petrarch and Boccaccio from Italian, following a foreignization strategy, a translation of a part of de Lorris' and de Meun's *Roman de la Rose* from French, a translation of the French version (prepared by Renaud de Louens) of Albertano of Brescia's *Liber Consolationis et Consilii*, a translation of Boethius' *De Consolatione Philosophiae* (see below). Chaucer's *Troilus and Criseyde*—based on Boccaccio's *Il Filostrato*—includes close translation as well as free invention and parts from Boethius. It is generally agreed upon that Chaucer's translation of Boethius' *De Consolatione Philosophiae* is based both on the Latin original and a French translation, even though we do not have access to his French source (Ness & Duncan-Rose 1982). Caxton described Chaucer, when he published Chaucer's translation of Boethius' *De Consolatione Philosophiae*, as the "first translatour of this sayd boke into Englissh and enbelissher in making the sayd langage ornate and fayr" (Blake 1991: 121; see also Fehlauer 1908; Fischer 1979; Hoenen & Nauta, eds, 1997).

With respect to unsuccessful early translations, Kane (1951) comments on the Middle English *Romans of Partenay, or of Lusignen*: "[it is] not simply bad stylistically; it is impossible to read, for it is, properly speaking, not written in English [...]". However, the above translation included remarks from the translator on his methodology and purposes, which is not common in the case of other publications of translated books. The source text was the French *Le Roman de Mélusine, ou Histoire de Lusignan* by the poet Coudrette—written in the first years of the 15th century. The anonymous English translation was written in the Midland dialect. The translated text contains minor additions as a result of metric constraints.

Kane also comments on five examples of mistranslation, although some of them are probably due to manuscript errors, like "dardane" for "D'Ardane", with the interpretation 'in the Ardennes region' (F2728, E2488). Kane's, as well as Pearsall's (1977b) critique, are based on their claim that the translator intended to translate line for line and even word for word. Moreover, the translators preferred a literal translation of the French impersonal construction "y avoir" as 'there had', instead of 'there was' (Hosington 2006, 2015). A line-by-line rhyming translation should have met several constraints in terms of word order. As a result, even an incomprehensible text may appear. It is also worth noticing that some words, which, according to the OED and the MED, were first attested in *Partenay*, were borrowed into the translated text from the source text.

In the medieval period, the Catholic Church played a significant role in the production and authorization of translations, mainly from or into Latin. The Catholic Church held a negative attitude towards translations into the vernacular and often characterized the vernacular as a corrupt language and Latin as the norm. Translation into Latin was considered an important condition for the wide circulation of a book. However, translations into the vernacular contributed, to a major degree, to the emergence and consolidation of a national and literary consciousness in the Middle Ages and the Renaissance as well as in the 19th century. For instance, Bishop Bryan Walton observed in 1659 that the 1611 Bible (Authorized Version) "can stand comparison with any other European version" (Norton 1993: I.219). Translations also favored literary and national confidence in the Augustan period. Alexander Pope's *Imitations of Horace* (1734–1737), which contains the Latin source text and the English translation, presents an example of the new tendency. In contrast, translated texts from vernacular languages into English were never so important as translations from Latin. There was, however, a hierarchy of source languages, with French occupying a leading position in the later Middle Ages and after the Restoration.

Several patrons also became translators: Earl Rivers and the Earl of Worcester prepared translations, printed by Caxton; Elizabeth I produced translations from Greek and Latin, such as the translation of Boethius' *De Consolatione Philosophiae* in 1593, or translations of Horace's, Plutarch's and Euripides' works (Ellis & Oakley-Brown 2009). However, women translators or writers are in great minority: Elizabeth I (1533–1603) is a notable exception (Matthiessen 1931; Lathrop 1933; Benkert 2001).

Caxton's own translation of Raoul Fèvre's *History of Troy* (1475) is the earliest extant book printed in English by Caxton and Colard Mansion. Caxton also produced a translation of the French version of the Latin poem *The Aeneid* by Virgil (1490). With regard to his own translations, Caxton noted, in several cases, that his translations are close to the source text (Culpeper 2015). Caxton's texts have been identified as containing Latinate constructions and a large number of doublets, that is, pairs of words that include conjoined native and borrowed cognates. His style also involves anaphoric cohesive devices, such as anaphora and cataphora, through pronouns and clausal qualifiers, i.e. embedded clauses that describe what is expressed in their clausal head. This style, which Bornstein (1978) names "clergial style", can also be found earlier in Chaucer's translation from French (*Livre de Mellibee et de Prudence*, Tale of Melibee). The emergence of this style shows how significant an influence translations can have on the English prose (Workman 1940). Moreover, Caxton popularized the so called "clergial" or "curial" style, which became typical for the 15th century. Probably, Caxton acquired this type of style through his translations of French texts that were associated with the court of the Dukes of Burgundy. At least this is the claim of Bomstein (1978) who relates this style to the earlier Chaucer's translation of the *Livre de Mellibee et de Prudence*. Elements of this style can also be located in documents prepared by the English royal administration (Burnley 1986).

In circa 1440, Robert Parker prepared a translation of Palladius, which was commissioned and most likely corrected by Humphrey, Duke of Gloucester.

The project of the latter had as its aim to enrich English letters (Pearsall 1977a). In around 1470, Malory produced the *Morte D'Arthur*, which was partly a translation from French, partly an adaptation of an earlier English work, and partly an original work. It was published by William Caxton in 1485.

Many of the translations discussed above show clear impacts on the English literary language; even the literary model of the Middle English period is thought to have been based on foreign texts. The influence of foreign languages was greater in vocabulary, but it is also present in syntax in cases where the translations were kept close to the source text. In several instances, the development of the Middle English literary language can be described as an accommodation between foreign influences and native change (Blake 1992).

2.2.1 *Biblical vs. Non-biblical Translations in the History of English*

In this section, I discuss major landmarks of English translations: I present some remarks on a possible role of biblical and non-biblical translations in grammatical change in English, in a contrastive way. The aim of the two parts of the present section is to demonstrate similarities and differences of the type of influence that biblical and non-biblical translations can have in grammatical change in English.

2.2.1.1 Biblical Translations and Grammatical Change in English: An Overview of the Major Landmarks

Biblical translations into English appear to play a significant role in the diachrony of English because they form a typical trigger of written language contact involving a series of adaptations of texts which cover all periods of the diachrony of English. Biblical translations also offer a significant contribution to the development of the standardization of the English language (Burnet 1773–1792 [1967], II: 141, cf. also Partridge 1973; Strathearn 2011; Marsden & Matter 2012; Paget & Schaper 2013; Riches, ed., 2015; Cameron 2016; Kristmannsson 2019). For a complete list of all English translations of the Bible, see Chamberlin (1991).

The differences between the structure of English and the structure of the source languages, mainly Hebrew, has caused several challenges. The corpus of Old English biblical texts contains interlinear glosses, translations and free paraphrases of the Bible. Most of the Old English paraphrases of the Bible are poems with Germanic alliterative verses that mainly retell stories from the Old Testament. The Latin manuscripts of the Psalms and the Gospels include most of the interlinear glosses. Interlinear glossing is the most imitative translation type and probably the earliest type of translation. In the earliest manuscripts, English translational equivalents were provided above Latin words. In the 9th century, systematic glossing of the psalter into English appeared, first and foremost to assist monks in their understanding of basic texts for the practice of liturgy (Pulsiano 1995; Lendinara 2013, 2014; van Gelderen 2014). In this period, no one could challenge the priority of the source text (Stanton 2002): moreover, the translation was not an independent text, instead it accompanied the source text.

The biblical translations into Old English include the four Gospels (translated in the second half of the 10th century) and the first books of the Old Testament. All of them translate the Latin Vulgate, i.e., the translation of the Old and New Testament by Jerome. Alfred (871–899) was the leading person behind the earliest extant close translation of the Bible into English (Keynes & Lapidge 1983; Frantzen 1986; Marsden 2012; see also Sections 2.1.3 and 7.2 below). Alfred started his translational projects with a close translation of Exodus 20–23 (Frantzen 1986). Later, he translated the first fifty psalms. At the end of the 10th century, when Ælfric presented his first works as a homilist, there already existed a significant vernacular literary tradition in England that progressed *in parallel to the formal Latin tradition*. At the beginning of the 11th century, the English Hexateuch was composed, which included Ælfric's translations of *Genesis* 1–24:26, *Numbers* 13–26 and *Joshua*, as well as anonymous versions of *Genesis* 25–50, *Exodus, Leviticus, Numbers* 1–12, and *Deuteronomy* (Marsden 2008). Yet, in broad terms, there are limited direct translations of the Old Testament into Old English.

In the Middle Ages, the dominant language of the Church was Latin because England was a Catholic country. Religious translations from Latin—and, later, from Hebrew and Greek—occupied a significant position in the written contact between English and other languages. By the 13th century, English had undergone several significant changes in morphosyntax and the lexicon and, as a result, *the understanding of earlier translations was more difficult.* One of the earliest partial Middle English translations of the Old Testament are the translations of *Genesis* and *Exodus*, which were composed in rhyming couplets around 1250. These consist of 4,162 lines, surviving only in an early 14th-century manuscript (Morey 2000). Chapters 36, 38 and 48 are completely absent from *Genesis*, and a larger part is omitted in *Exodus*. The Middle English Metrical Paraphrase of the Old Testament was probably composed before the 15th century; it includes 18,372 lines in twelve-line stanzas and is retained in two mid-15th-century manuscripts (Livingston, ed., 2011; Morey 2000; Nevalainen 2008).

The first complete English translation of the Bible was prepared by an Oxford reform leader, John Wycliffe, about 1380–1383. Wycliffe's English translation of the Bible [Wycliffite Bible] from the Latin Vulgate was not authorized by the Church. The Wycliffite Bible was a collaborative translation—and several names have been associated with the publication of this translation, including John Wycliffe, John Purvey, Nicholas Hereford and John of Trevisa. The translation process probably started in the 1370s and the translated text is retained in approximately 250 manuscripts. Even though the circulation of this and other translations among the population was limited, biblical translations were used during religious services, were a tool for theology scholars, and constituted *influential texts* that might have triggered semi-natural change because of the *prestige* with which they are associated. The Wycliffite Bible has been considered one of the most significant factors in the development of a written standard, which emerged in the late Middle English period (Ellis & Oakley-Brown 2009).

Two versions of the Wycliffite Bible have survived: the earlier one from the early 1380s and the later one from after Wycliffe's death. The Earlier Version is extremely literal—similar to a glossing translation. It can be regarded as a faithful English continuation of the Latin Vulgate tradition which in turn is dependent on its source text. The Later Version, however, is less close to the source text (Dove 2007: 139–140; Marsden 2012).

The consequences of the religious reform that followed Henry VIII's break with Rome's Catholicism were realized with an explosion of biblical translations. Moreover, biblical translations were also connected to the rediscovery of Greek as a cultural language in Western Europe, a notion which had been lost during the Middle Ages. William Tyndale's translation of the New Testament (1525) used as source text for the first time the Greek original text (Desiderius Erasmus' 1516 edition of the Greek text). It is apparent that Cardinal Wolsey, a cardinal of the Catholic Church, condemned Tyndale's English translation and all new English terms introduced by Tyndale through his translation of Greek and Hebrew terms.

Tyndale's texts, translations and polemical texts, contain examples of syntactic archaisms (Canon 2016), that is, borrowings and re-introductions of obsolete forms from an earlier period of the language—what one would characterize as evidence of a type of *written contact with earlier forms of English*. One such example is the use of the early/archaic second person singular and plural pronouns in Tyndale's texts: the second person *plural* pronoun had begun to appear in *all*, singular and plural, contexts in Early Middle English. Tyndale used the verbal forms for second singular and plural number productively, as well as the distinction between the subject pronoun *ye* and the object pronoun *you*, following earlier texts. However, the first attestations of the nominative *you*, instead of *ye*, appeared in the 14th century and was productively used in the literary language by the 1540s.

Moreover, Tyndale used *modal preterites*, that is, past forms of modals with a hypothetical, future reference, in his translation. However, modal preterites had already been dispreferred, as opposed to modal auxiliary verbs, by the 16th century (3a vs. 3b).

(3) a. *If I **were to die** before I wake*
     b. *If I **should die** before I wake*

It appears that Tyndale avoided the modal constructions of the source text and preferred modal preterites in his translations as well as in all his other works, which include non-translated polemical texts. Canon (2016: 66) observes some aspects of Tyndale's preference in the following passage:

> His [Tyndale's] use of this particular modal preterite form is not only higher than that of other translators, it bucks the trend of a rapid decline in the use of such forms. [...] [M]y analysis of the subjunctive tokens in the polemical works revealed a much higher percentage of use of modal preterite inflections in the Tyndale texts than in the comparison corpus.

The result was an archaizing style that started to be connected to biblical registers from the 16th and 17th century and remained linked to these registers until today. Accordingly, several scholars have argued that Tyndale's preferences for archaic pronouns, word formations and syntactic constructions have marked English Christian discourse as well as the development of English (see also below 3.3; see Lavidas 2018a).

The revisions of Tyndale's translation have a long history, with Miles Coverdale's revision first appearing in 1535. In 1537, in Antwerp, John Rogers' translation of the Bible, based on both Tyndale's and Coverdale's translations, was published under the pseudonym of *John Matthew*. Coverdale prepared a new translation of the Bible, *The Great Bible*, which was published in 1539. Its title-page included a drawing in which Henry VIII hands copies of the Bible to Archbishops Cranmer and Cromwell, to distribute them to a crowd of people. The drawing clearly reflects the involvement of the Church and the State in the preparation and publication (authorization) of biblical translations (Wilson 1976; King 1982).

In 1560, a group of translators, Protestants who left England after Queen Mary's accession, published *the Geneva Bible*. This translation was reprinted until 1715 and was widely used. A new authorized version was published in 1568, *the Bishops' Bible*, which was a revision of the Great Bible, in order to counter

EARLY HISTORY OF TRANSLATIONS AND GRAMMATICAL CHANGE

the unauthorized but very popular Geneva Bible, which had a strong Puritan support. In the period 1582–1610, exiled Catholics also prepared a vernacular biblical translation, the Rheims-Douai version.

In 1604, King James I agreed with John Reynolds' proposal on the creation of a new translation (Kitagaki 1981; Wilson 1976). The Authorized Version of the Bible (1611) replaced Bishops' Bible. The history of the Authorized Version is reminiscent of the case of the Greek Septuagint: A committee of 54 scholars started the translation work in 1604 and published the translation in 1611. King James I and Bishop Bancroft commissioned six teams of translators to prepare the book—which was a revision rather than a new translation—according to a set of rules: traditional readings, and mainly those included in the Bishop's Bible, should be retained to a significant degree in the new translation. The Authorized Version and the Book of Common Prayer were spread all over England more than any other publication of this period; the first translation of the Book of Common Prayer into English is attested in 1549, was reissued after modifications in 1552 and was revised in 1662 (Butterworth 1941).

Some of the grammatical characteristics of the above biblical translations already deviated from the grammar of their period, including early forms, such as the second person singular pronoun *thou* (see Hogg & Denison 2006: 28), the nominative pronominal form *ye* and the third person singular verb suffix -*(e)th*. The Authorized Version mainly drew upon Tyndale's translation of the Greek New Testament (1525) and the Hebrew Pentateuch (1530), as well as upon Coverdale's translation of the remainder of the Old Testament (complete Bible 1535). The 1611 Bible appeared with different names, "King James Version" or "Authorized Version", because the authorization was connected to considerations of patronage and commission. Translations could also be authorized through reference to other earlier translations—this could lead to imitation of features of earlier translations as well (Ellis & Oakley-Brown 2009). See Chapter 3. The Authorized Version was not met with a very positive reaction when it was first published in 1611, in contrast to preference for the Geneva Bible during this period.

More recent translations were influenced to a larger degree by characteristics of the common language. The Revised Version (1881, 1885) made around 30,000 changes to the Authorized Version—many of which were due to improved textual resources, whereas the Revised Standard Version (1952) did not include some Biblical constructions, obsolescent words and morphosyntactic characteristics of Early Modern English. Moreover, the New Revised Standard Version (1989) did not contain some archaic terms and replaced, for instance, exclusive constructions of the text with inclusive ones, like *believers* instead of *brothers* (Kohnen 2012). The New English Bible (1970) met a severe critique and was characterized as "drab, imprecise, and unimaginative" (Partridge 1973; see also Hammond 1982). In addition to all of these translations, several other translations exist, for instance, translations prepared by individual authors: e.g., the translations of James Moffatt, John B. Phillips, Edgar J. Goodspeed, including Richard Challoner's (1749–1772) translation which contained major revisions of the text in the Catholic Rheims-Douai Bible.

As a consequence of this, a type of Biblical English has been recognized in the scholarship (cf. Kohnen 2012: 1047). The major lexical and morpho-syntactic characteristics of "Biblical English" concern the following archaic forms and characteristics: second person pronouns (*ye* vs. *you*; *thou* vs. *you*), the second and third person inflectional endings (*-st, -th*), plural forms of nouns (e.g., *brethren*), archaic past forms (e.g., *spake*), word orders that can be found in earlier periods (e.g., inversion with initial adverbials), lexical archaisms (e.g., *behold, forthwith*) (Crystal & Davy 1969).

The question that arises is whether these characteristics appeared beyond the religious domain. For instance, the Authorized Version has been considered a work with profound influence on the development of written English, Lowth (1979 [1775]), for instance, argues that the English of the Authorized Version is "the best standard" of English, and McGrath (2001) claims that the Authorized Version is a "landmark in the history of the English language" with an influence that "has been incalculable" (McArthur 1992). It has even been argued by Gör-lach (1999: 519) that the details of how the Bible affected the written standard has yet to be fully worked out. The King James/ Authorized Version probably affected the field of idiom and lexical resources, in particular. For instance, Nevalainen (1999) demonstrates a relation between the biblical influence and the development of personal metaphors: e.g., in the case of "Magdalene" as a term for 'a fallen woman reformed'.

The Authorized Version also includes the literal translation of many Hebrew words and phrases, which, then, became common words in contemporary English. It is worth noting that Kohnen (2012: 1048–1049; my emphasis) admits that a detailed corpus-based study of the King James/ Authorized Version as a significant parameter of the development of English is absent:

> [...] one could claim that there are no detailed and comprehensive, let alone corpus-based, studies of the *King James Bible as a factor in the history of English* or of the impact of "Biblical English" on the formation of Standard English. Apart from the studies mentioned above, we find only small-scale, scattered investigations, most of which are not interested in the larger picture of language history. It might be *a rewarding task* for a

substantial and comprehensive *corpus-based project* to find out whether the picture of the far-reaching influence can be supported.

One of the aims of the corpus study presented in Chapter 7 is indeed to cover aspects of the above-mentioned gap.

2.2.1.2   Non-biblical Translations and Grammatical Change in English

The Renaissance initiated a new interest in Latin and Greek that even led to the emergence of Neo-Latin or Renaissance Latin. In the same period, an increased interest in translations of classical works into English emerged. The revival of classical learning led to a new contact situation between English and Latin and a new period of borrowings, mainly mid-16th century—mid 17th century (cf., among many others, Venuti 2000, 2008; Vermeer 2000; Ellis, ed., 2008; Pade 2013). The new tendency for translations of classics resulted in a long list of new Latin loanwords. A parallel new trend supported the view that grammar-school pupils should become bilingual in Latin and English (Adamson 1999; Ellis & Oakley-Brown 2009; Miller 2012).

Early classicizers of the Renaissance re-produced characteristics of the style of Latin in their English—whereas later classicizers did not aim at imitation but at equivalence. The latter tendency required the usage of native means, with the purpose of a classical style and classical effects. Accordingly, Milton, for instance, imitated Horace's syntax, and Pope imitated Horace's tone. Chapman's *Iliad* (1598–1611) had to compete with Homer, and Pope's *Iliad* (1715–1720) also had to look at how Chapman translated the text. These facts again support the view that different phases of a diachrony of a language exist when it comes to written contact. In the first phase, written contact is found between the language represented in native/ non-translated texts and a foreign language, for instance, Latin or Greek. In the second phase, written contact is found between the language represented in native/ non-translated texts and an earlier form of the same language.

Most Greek loanwords were introduced indirectly into English through Latin or French, becoming loanwords through the study and translation of Greek documents, and thus through written contact. The ideas of the Renaissance also involved a kind of re-borrowing from Latin of words already borrowed from French in earlier stages. According to Minkova & Stockwell (2009: 50), written contact is a significant parameter for the development of English, in that, for instance, in Early Middle English more words were borrowed from a classical source through translating classical texts than directly from French.

Reactions against translations also hindered access to certain texts. The argumentation against translations at that time included concerns that, through translations into the vernacular language of the audience, the study of Latin and Greek would become more restricted and meet obstacles (Jones 1966; Nevalainen 2008; Ellis & Oakley-Brown 2009). In this respect, several scholars continued to produce texts in Latin—which were often translated into English later. For instance, in 1551 Ralph Robinson translated Thomas More's *Utopia*, written in 1516, and in 1610 Philemon Holland translated William Camden's *Britannia* in Latin, written in around 1585. Moreover, John Skelton wrote several books in Latin—but also translated Diodorus Siculus from Poggio's Latin translation.

The main properties of the translations from the end of the 17th century are mostly represented in the work of two important translators of that period: John Dryden and Alexander Pope—whereas the late 18th century was dominated by Alexander Tytler's translations. Dryden and Pope followed Chapman's early theoretical framework of translation process, as stated in his translation of the *Iliad*. According to Chapman, translations can be characterized as linguistic mimesis (1598—Preface of *Seaven Bookes of the Iliad*).

2.2.2 *Written Contact and Grammatical Change vs. Translation Effects in the History of English*

The contact between Latin and English is a clear example of *written language contact*. The contact with Latin did not result in a large number of loanwords, similarly to the contact with French in the Middle English period. In addition, the written contact with Latin was not a case of prolonged intense contact for the whole population, being confined to speakers who were competent in both languages, English and Latin (see Section 1.2).

Taylor (2008: 341) has correctly emphasized that any examination of Old English should take into consideration the possibility of this type of contact effect because many of the Old English prose texts were translations of Latin source texts. In this respect, Taylor argues that these properties are not really relevant for the structural history of the language, that is they are an artifact of the textual type, and do not represent any real change to the English language. I agree with Taylor and I, further, relate contact effects of translations to a type of semi-natural change in the native grammar (see Section 6).

The issue of translation effects, as can be evidenced in early translated texts, is directly relevant for the hypothesis of written contact-induced change. It is clear that translation effects should be different depending on the nature of the source text. Accordingly, one should be able to distinguish between biblical vs. non-biblical translation effects. A classical study on historical contact effects of translation focusing on the influence of Latin on English prepositional phrases with pronominal complements is Taylor (2008). Biblical Latin is mainly a head-

EARLY HISTORY OF TRANSLATIONS AND GRAMMATICAL CHANGE 47

initial language,[2] that is, in Biblical Latin the *head* precedes its complements. On the contrary, Old English shows variation between head-initial and head-final orders. Taylor distinguishes between direct *vs.* indirect translation effects, which in turn are related to the opposition between biblical *vs.* non-biblical translations. Direct vs. indirect translation effects derive straightforwardly from different strategies applied in the Old English translations of biblical and non-biblical texts. Direct effects of translation mainly appear in the case of glossing; they concern cases of reproduction of a matching construction in the target language when a particular construction is found in the original text. Indirect effects of translation reflect in reality a type of syntactic priming; the influence of a construction in the source text leads to a higher frequency of the particular construction in the target language even in cases where it is not attested in the source text (cf. among others, Hartsuiker & Westenberg 2000).

Old English showed variation in the case of prepositional phrases with pronominals: pronouns could appear to the right or to the left of prepositions. In Latin, however, the pronoun could *not* be found in the position preceding the preposition. Accordingly, in the case of translations from Latin, four types of data are available: In the same passage,

– English (target texts) and Latin (source texts) show a head-initial PP;
– English demonstrates a head-final PP, with the pronoun either immediately to the left or away from the preposition, while the Latin source text has a head-initial PP;
– English has a head-initial PP even though the Latin source text shows no PP;
– English has a head-final PP even in cases where the Latin source text shows no PP.

Taylor's data derive from the York-Toronto-Helsinki Parsed Corpus of Old English Prose (YCOE) (Taylor et al. 2003). Taylor (2008) has analyzed all cases of PPs in the English originals, all cases of PPs in short translations, and some samples of long translations. The Latin source for each PP in the translated text has also been located by Taylor. She demonstrates the contrast between direct and indirect translation effects with a quantitative study. A direct translation effect is evident for both biblical and non-biblical translations; in both biblical and non-biblical translations in passages involving a PP in the source language, the frequency of head-initial PPs is higher than in non-translations. An indirect translation effect can appear if there is no PP in the source text, as is evident

---

2 There is consensus that there is a process of change from head-finality to head-initiality from Latin to Romance: cf., among others, Ledgeway (2015).

TABLE 2.1   The frequency and weight of head-initial PPs with and without a PP in the source text, comparing non-translations with biblical and non-biblical translations

	%Preposition-Pronoun (head-initial PPs)	Weight
Non-translations	78.0	.411
Non-biblical translations No source PP	60.3	.342
Non-biblical translations Source PP	92.2	.796
Biblical translations No source PP	80.5	.595
Biblical translations Source PP	95.0	.808

TAYLOR 2008: 354; TABLE 14

from the distribution presented in Table 2.1. The contrast between the presence of a PP in the source text and the absence of a PP in the source text is statistically significant in the case of non-biblical translations but not in the case of biblical translations. According to Taylor, this indirect influence is a type of *priming effect*; the high frequency of head-initial order in the Latin source text leads the translator to use a higher frequency of head-initial orders in general in biblical translations, and not only in passages where there is a PP in the source text.

Taylor has indeed set the base for this type of analysis of contact, as well as having opened new directions in the research of written language contact. Taylor (2008: 356) clearly states that whether the same pattern and effect will reoccur with other constructions where Latin differs from Old English is an empirical question (see also Haeberli 2018 on object pronoun placement in Middle English and effects of contact in translation).

The possibility of borrowing from Latin into English has so far been examined mainly with regard to the accusativus-cum-infinitivo (AcI) construction with verbs of knowing, declaring and thinking (Fischer 1988, 1992, 1994, 2013;

Miller 2002; Mitchell 1985, among others). Other early studies on written contact between Latin and English include the following: Nunnally (1992) examined the Gospel of Matthew and concluded that the order of adnominal genitives in NPs was not affected by Latin. Kytö & Rissanen's (1993) investigation of the DET[erminer] POSS[essive] construction in English also showed that this construction did not correlate with the equivalent construction in Latin: even though this construction belonged to a high or Latinate English style, no translation effects could be found. Warner (1982) has argued that the *that-ne construction* in Middle English was also typical for a Latin-related register—and not a translation effect. Instead, Warner argued that *-ne* was a calque of Latin *quin* which did not depend on the Latin construction, occurring instead in non-translated texts. The above-mentioned studies provide evidence for the assumption that *different constructions are differentially affected by translation*. According to Taylor (2008: 356), this raises the question of the range of this variation and its relation to other linguistic and extralinguistic factors.

A scrutiny of earlier studies also reveals that most studies of the contact between English and Latin have focused on the following constructions in English where one can observe cases of possible influence:
– absolute constructions (ablativus absolutus),
– the nominativus-cum-infinitivo construction (NcI),
– the accusativus-cum-infinitivo construction (AcI),
– the passive infinitive.
However, as already observed in the case of other grammatical properties, these early studies have delivered mixed results on the degree of a potential influence from Latin.

It is only with regard to the influence of Latin on English absolute constructions and the NcI construction, which are mostly attested in translations that an agreement is found in the earlier scholarship (Fischer 1989; Kohnen 2003; Nagucka 2003; Los 2005; Timofeeva 2008, 2010, 2011b). On the contrary, various views have been raised in studies of the AcI and the passive infinitive constructions. Passive infinitives and AcI constructions are assumed to have had a different status than NcI and absolute constructions (Fischer 2013). Fischer (1991) has shown that passive infinitives were attested only following auxiliaries in Old English; in the Middle English period, they could be found rarely also with AcI and impersonals, but they were mostly found in direct translations from Latin.

Lightfoot (1981) had also concluded that Latin influence was at work in the extension of the AcI constructions to new classes of verbs. According to his view, a *new* rule in Middle English arose, permitting the deletion of CPs allowing subjects of infinitives to be governed by the matrix clause. According to Lightfoot, this new rule was the result of the translation of Latin AcI constructions into English. However, in a later study, Lightfoot (1991) argues that AcI in English were also the result of an internal development involving a change in the behavior of preposition *to*.

Observe that AcI constructions did not emerge in all Germanic languages (Fischer 2013). For instance, such constructions are not attested in Dutch or German, even though similar contact situations with Latin hold true for these languages as well (Krickau 1877, Fischer 1994).[3] Fischer argues here that the role of word order is significant for this development, in particular that older Germanic languages demonstrated SOV with verb second (V2) orders in main clauses; written tradition and standardization has led to the grammaticalization of the word order properties with different results in English (SVO order) and in Dutch or German (SOV order and verb second properties).

2.2.3   The Role of Retranslations in Diachronic Linguistic Studies

Multiple translations of the same text in different periods of the diachrony of English are of great value in the study of written contact—and, in particular, in the study of the relation between diachrony of translations and grammatical change (see also Section 2.2). According to Romaine (1985: 458), renderings of the same text in different periods can illustrate significant differences between the characteristics of different periods of English: Romaine shows that this type of comparison enables the researcher to keep genre and topic constant and to focus on the available lexicalization resources.

Romaine argues that Boethius' *De Consolatione Philosophiae* is a good example of a text that can be used in relevant comparisons (see also the corpus study presented in Sections 7.2 and 7.3 below). This text appeared in an Old English translation by King Alfred, in around 880 AD, in an Old High German translation by Notker 100 years later, and in four French translations in the 13th–14th centuries. One of these French translations, probably the one by Jean de Meun, was the model for Chaucer's Middle English translation in around 1300. Elizabeth I also translated Boethius' text in 1593. Hence, a comparison of Alfred's, Chaucer's and Elizabeth's translations covers a period as long as 700 years. However, Romaine (1985: 458) argues that a comparison of translations also presupposes several assumptions, such as the fact that word formation

---

3   But see also Barðdal & Eythórsson (2012) who point out that AcI exists with the relevant verb classes in both non-translated Old Icelandic texts and Gothic. The above remark suggests that the AcI construction was a Germanic inheritance, although for some reason, either not inherited into West Germanic or having changed in that branch.

rules (concerning her case studies) are optional devices which can be avoided/ exploited as a stylistic element.

Nevertheless, Romaine argues that this type of comparison is appropriate when it comes to a diachronic examination of word formation. Romaine investigates the productivity of -ness formations, in contrast to formations with the borrowed Romance -ity suffix, in the three English versions of Boethius' text mentioned above (Alfred's, Chaucer's and Elizabeth's translations). Her results show that: (i) Alfred had 87 forms with the Germanic -ness suffix; (ii) Chaucer used 59 -ness forms and 52 -ity forms, in general; (iii) 11 of the -ness forms attested in Alfred are also found in Chaucer; (iv) Elizabeth used both -ness and -ity suffixes 38 times; and (v) 18 of Elizabeth's -ity forms are also attested in Chaucer's version.

Thus, a type of continuity from Alfred to Elizabeth can be illustrated, for instance, in the case of the forms *sweetness* and *bitterness*. Figure 2.2 demonstrates the challenges involved in this type of comparison. For instance, Elizabeth used *doulcenes* in contexts where Alfred and Chaucer had *sweetness*. Or, for instance, Chaucer and Elizabeth could use *goodness* or *bounty* where Alfred had *godnes*.

Figure 2.2 from Romaine documents a significant case of change in lexical resources: First, loanwords like *stability* and *stable* are in a coexisting relation to native words like *steadfastness*. Moreover, suppletion may be the result of borrowing, like in the cases of *felicitie, dignitie, prosperitie*. In other cases, there is enrichment of lexicalization resources, for instance in the examples of *stableness* and *stability*. The lexical resources may also become less transparent or even reduced, as in the case of both Chaucer and Elizabeth's paraphrasis with -ness due to the loss of some words since Alfred's text. The above-mentioned changes in lexical resources resulted in a renewal of lexical fields through a type of relexification with foreign material.

Romaine (1985) also compares Boethius' translations to two translations of the *Polychronicon* which appeared between Chaucer's and Elizabeth's translations of Boethius. She finds that different strategies have been applied in the two translations; the unknown translator of the Polychronicon (15th century) preferred using many new words while, at the same time, the translator followed a literal translation of Latin into "Latinate-English".

Trevisa (14th century), in contrast, preferred native English words: he included 50 nouns with the suffix -ness, whereas the unknown translator only used 13; and Trevisa used seven forms with the -ity suffix in contrast to 44 forms of the other translation. According to Romaine, coexisting forms (*fragileness / fragility*) may emerge in later translations, as well as semantically related sets (*madness / insaneness / insanity*) and lexical pairs (*clearness / clarity*). For

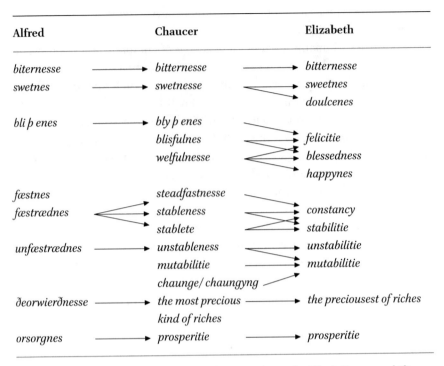

FIGURE 2.2　Lexical correspondences in Boethius' translations by Alfred, Chaucer and Elizabeth
ROMAINE 1985: 460

instance, Chaucer and Wycliffe included all these coexisting forms in their works productively: in Wycliffe's work, *bareyness* and *bareynte* and *feersness* and *feerste* are attested within the same text.

In this section I have focused on translations into English, with an emphasis on early phases of translation with the aim to test the main hypothesis advanced in this book on the role and status of written contact through translation in the history of English. More closely, I have explored the possibility of a relation existing between the diachrony of translations, and, in particular, of retranslations, and the diachrony of the language. I have also discussed the properties of different types of translations and how these can be related to possible written contact-induced changes or translation effects. In Part 2 (Chapter 7), I connect the discussion above to corpus surveys on English translations, through an examination of data related to aspects of voice and argument structure in biblical and non-biblical English retranslations. I then compare the corpus data from these English translations to data retrieved from non-translated texts. In this way, the data from the corpus surveys will complement the above theoretical discussion, indeed offering further insights into the approach advocated in this book (on corpus studies of oral contact, see Adamou 2016).

2.3   Greek in Written Contact: History of Early Translations

To reiterate my main hypothesis, retranslations do not reflect grammatical change: the grammatical characteristics of later retranslations do not follow grammatical change in a direct way, either in biblical or in non-biblical translations. This means newer translations may include innovative grammatical characteristics, but also an archaizing style obliterating actual changes. In this respect, retranslations illustrate an example of *grammatical multiglossia:* their grammatical characteristics, influenced by earlier texts and the source text, coexist with the grammatical characteristics that are also attested in innovative, contemporary non-translated texts. However, the coexistence of the two grammatical systems does not mean that the distribution of the grammatical characteristics in translations is due to chance. Conversely, the distribution of non-translated/native characteristics and translated characteristics (due to transfer) is systematic. Grammatical multiglossia is the result of a complex transfer from grammars of other languages, transfer from grammars of earlier periods, presence of innovated, retained/archaic and borrowed features.

The theoretical sections of this book (Chapters 2 and 3) aim at presenting a history of early translations into English and Greek and its interaction with grammatical change in English and Greek. In this manner, the theoretical part of the book sets the scene for the theoretical account of the role of early translations and retranslations. In Part 2, I introduce data from corpus surveys that add information on the relation between the diachrony of grammatical characteristics in retranslations and the diachrony of grammatical characteristics in non-translated texts. Recall that the analysis concerns cases of written contact through translations observed in English and Greek, and not cases of language contact in general. A history of language contact—even a history of early language contact—would probably require examination of data from one language only (and its contact with other languages). However, the investigation of written language contact through translation is strictly related to more than one language, the source and the target language—and a third language in the case of indirect translations. For this reason, I believe that a contrastive analysis of English and Greek can be of value in any examination of the history of early translations and their relation to grammatical change. Through

54   CHAPTER 2

the contrastive study of early translations, this main aim, the analysis of early
written contact, may be approached.

2.3.1 *Introduction. Translations in the History of Greek*

Early Greek translations occupy a central position in the histories of Greek and
have been regarded as directly related to several aspects of the development of
the Greek language. For instance, Horrocks (2014) refers to the following texts
that demonstrate significant landmarks of early translations into Greek:

– the moderately Atticizing—imitating the earlier, Ancient Greek Attic dialect
  —translation from Latin of Josephus' history *On the Jewish War* from the first
  century AD (on Atticism, see Section 4.3);
– the early Cypriot Greek translation of French legal texts in the *Assizes* from
  the 14th century;
– the Greek translation of *Apollonios* from Italian, which includes rhyming
  couplets published in Venice around 1525;
– the translation of Boccaccio's *Theseid*, from Italian into Greek. This text was
  probably prepared in the late 15th-early 16th century in Crete and published
  in Venice in 1529;
– the poem *The Old Knight* of early 15th century (without a title in the manuscript) from a French or Italian version of an 'Introduction' added to the
  romance *Guiron de Courtois* (*or Palamedes*); it belongs to the Arthurian cycle
  and does not show any relation to the Greek cultural tradition; and
– the translated (or adapted) romances from western source texts that closely
  followed the vernacular tradition to a higher degree than the non-translated
  romances. They were, however, more literary than, e.g., the language of
  the *Chronicle of the Morea*, the early 14th-century vernacular chronicle. For
  instance, the above characteristics (vernacular but also literary linguistic
  properties) are reflected in the translation of *Phlorios and Platzia-Phlora*,
  which is a late 14th-early 15th century version of an adaptation into Tuscan
  of a French original text (see, among others, Kakridis 1961 [1936]; Politis 1973;
  Koutsivitis 1994; Brock 2007; Lianeri & Zajko (eds) 2008, Lianeri 2014; di Leo
  2013).

The contact between Greek and Latin in late antiquity and between Greek
and Semitic languages in the period of Hellenistic-Roman Koine involves two
significant examples of written language contact in the diachrony of Greek.[4]
From the second century BC, there is a stable necessity for translations of Latin
texts into Greek; for instance, of Latin imperial letters or senate resolutions or

---

4 It is of significance for our study that the Hellenistic period is "the formative stage for what
   is ultimately Modern Greek" (Bubenik 2010). In addition, based on evidence from the Sep-

EARLY HISTORY OF TRANSLATIONS AND GRAMMATICAL CHANGE 55

laws. See, for example, the translation of the *Res gestae* into Greek, from the 1st century AD (Wigtil 1982; Bubenik 2010). Several errors in these texts have their source in the translation practice of word-for-word which was common in this period (Brixhe 2007; Brock 2007). For instance, in the *Res gestae*, the phrase (*sacerdotu*)*m quattuor amplissima colle*(*gia*) (*Res gestae* 9.1) 'by the four colleges of priests' was translated into Greek as follows: ἐκ τῆς συναρχίας τῶν τεσσάρων ἱερέων / *ek tês synarchías tôn tessárōn hieréōn* 'from the college of the four priests' (Wigtil 1982: 191). In addition, Brixhe (2007) claims that *periphrases* in Greek are probably influenced through the literal translation of Latin diathetic and aspectual periphrastic forms. Accordingly, he considers it quite possible that Latin contributed to the expansion of periphrases in Greek in late Hellenistic Greek.

2.3.2   *History of Translation and Language History: Later Developments in the Diachrony of Greek*

The early Byzantine period demonstrates significant examples of early translations in Greek context that mainly constitute translations of legal texts (Troianos & Velissaropoulou-Karakosta 1997). However, the history of translation theory in Greece started with Nikolaos Sofianos, according to Kakridis (1961 [1936]), as Sofianos was the first scholar to translate an Ancient Greek prose work into Modern Greek and to write theoretical texts about translation, as well as the first scholar to prepare a grammar of Modern Greek—even though his grammar was not published until 1870. His translation of Pseudo-Plutarch's *On the Education of Children* was published in 1544 in Venice. Sofianos regarded translation as a means of education and aimed at using a variety which could represent the naturalness of the target variety (Connolly & Bacopoulou-Halls 2011; on the development of translation theories, see, among many others, Goutsos, ed., 2001; Grammenidis & Floros 2019).

Between the 16th and the 19th century, a great variety of texts were translated into Greek. Interlingual translations into Greek involved a rich number of languages: among others, Latin, English, French, German, Italian, Russian and Arabic (Zaviras 1972). The list of translated works shows an important variety of religious and philosophical texts—mainly, (interlingual) translations of Cicero, Virgil, Shakespeare, Descartes, (intralingual) translations of Plato and Aristotle. Moreover, the main purpose of the first translations was to offer education to the subjugated Greeks.

---

tuagint and the New Testament as well as from Egyptian papyri, many scholars have argued that grammatical changes that appeared as Semitisms prevailed and accelerated in bilingual communities.

56   CHAPTER 2

Publications of translated literature into Greek increased impressively: the 16th century included only one publication; the 17th century five; the 18th century 57; the 19th century 3000; and during the first half of the 20th century 2500 publications (Kasinis 2005 [1998]: 14; Misiou 2014). Heptanesian poets, for instance, produced translations of Classical Greek works and foreign well-known books, to support the vernacular of their time, demotic Greek. Iakovos Polylas (1825-1896) considered translation a way to test the strength and features of a language.

2.3.3   *Greek Intralingual Translations and Their Characteristics*

An important number of writers started to use a demotic Greek variety in the 17th and 18th centuries—in accordance with new needs and growing readership. Their texts included religious works and histories, biblical anthologies and translations of the New Testament. Biblical translations into Modern Greek emerged as a necessity in Greece *later than in other European countries* (Remediaki 2013). Besides translation- and theological-related issues, biblical translations in Greek further received linguistic and national dimensions, after the establishment of the new Greek state. For instance, Constantinos Economos (1780–1857) and Neophytos Vamvas (1776–1866) expressed opposing approaches to the issue of biblical translations (Connolly & Bacopoulou-Halls 2011). Economos had the view that it is not possible to translate the Bible into Modern Greek, mainly because he believed that Modern Greek was vulgar. He also insisted that many Greeks could understand the language of the original text, and that, actually, not everyone should be able to read the Bible, to avoid false interpretation and heresy (Kakoulidi 1980; Manousakas 1986; Grammenidis & Floros 2019).

A debate on translations emerged in Greece from the end of the 18th century with a focus on the linguistic variety of translated text, that is, whether translations should be written in the archaic or demotic variety. The movement of demoticism initiated new dynamic directions for the area of translation (Mackridge 2010b; Rossoglou 2012). In the 20th century, the issue of publication of translations was incorporated in the *Language Question*.[5] See Section

---

5   On the Greek Language Question, see, among many others, Mackridge (2010a: 127):

   The Greek language controversy started when writers of the Greek Enlightenment began to argue about which variety of Greek was most suitable for educational and scholarly writing. The controversy had two dimensions. The first was the dispute between those who believed that Ancient Greek alone was suitable for such writing and those who believed that Modern Greek was appropriate. The second was the disagreement among proponents of the written use of the modern language as to which variety of it should be used. In these

EARLY HISTORY OF TRANSLATIONS AND GRAMMATICAL CHANGE 57

6.3 on diglossia and how written language contact is related to diglossia and grammatical change; see also Chapter 3 that includes a discussion on biblical translations and their role/ status in linguistic diachronies.

The debate on Greek translations of the Bible escalated in 1901 in the *Gospel Riots/Evangelika*, which followed Gospels' translation by Alexandros Pallis into Modern Greek. In 1901, *Akropolis*, an Athenian newspaper, published Alexandros Pallis' first passages of a demotic translation of the Gospels. Many members of the University of Athens considered the translation as an assault on the holy text and the Orthodox Church. The reactions against the translation led to violent demonstrations, attacks on the offices of the newspaper and a number of dead demonstrators, as the police opened fire (November 8th, 1901).

In 1903, the performance of Aeschylus' *Oresteia* in the demotic variety at the theater of Herodes Atticus triggered similar fights and debates as well as accusations of supporters of the demotic variety of treason. In November 1903, two people were killed during demonstrations, led by university students under the influence of Professor Mistriotis, demanding the cancellation of the theatrical performance of Sotiriadis' translation. The translation of classical works was seen as an attempt to disconnect the modern Greek from the ancient Greek culture and to separate modern Greece from its heritage—even though Modern Greek translations made the classical texts accessible to speakers of Modern Greek. However, these attempts of intralingual translation of religious—as well as Classical Greek—texts followed the model of translation of passages of the Old and New Testament by Ioannikios Kartanos in the 16th century (1536) and the Early Modern Greek translation of the New Testament by Maximos Kallipolitis in the 17th century.

I remind the reader that the hypothesis advanced in this book involves a parallelism between early contact with other languages (Latin and/ or Greek) through translation in the first periods of a written language, on the one hand, and influence of (that is, a type of contact with) earlier periods of the same language during later periods of a written language, on the other. The above parallelism justifies my decision to examine both interlingual (in the case of English, mainly, as well as in the case of the Greek Septuagint) and intralingual translations (across English and Greek). This involves a special emphasis on the distinction between biblical and non-biblical translations, their status, characteristics and role in the development of a language, following the conclusions of previous studies. In the case of biblical translations, the early history of

---

disputes Korais was on the side of the modern language, but he believed that it needed to be corrected in order to be usable for educational and scholarly purposes.

Cf. also (among many others) Beaton 1994; Mackridge 2009; Horrocks 2014: 438–470.

both intralingual and interlingual translations may provide us with significant insights into the relation between diachronic (re)translations and grammatical change.

Alexandros Pallis aimed at proving that demotic Greek/ the Modern Greek vernacular could also be used for "difficult" texts; therefore, he also translated Euripides, Thucydides, Shakespeare and Kant. Most studies refer to Pallis' translations of the *Gospels* and the *Iliad*. His translation of the *Iliad* also met opposing reactions: the starting point of his translation was his assumption that Homeric poems as popular creations should be turned into contemporary demotic folk songs, and that, accordingly, the translator should follow the characteristics of Greek demotic songs.

It appears that, in Greece, *intralingual translations*—that is, translations of earlier Greek texts into Modern Greek—have always attracted significant attention (see Chapter 4 on intralingual translations). This fact is related to (i) a desire to prove the continuity of Greek, rather than to produce a Modern Greek text, and (ii) the necessity to show that the modern language was able to serve as a vehicle for the ideas of the antiquity or the past in general (Connolly & Bacopoulou-Halls 2011; Remediaki 2013). Oikonomou & Aggelinara (1979) point out that 294 rhyming translations of Ancient Greek tragedies into Modern Greek were published until 1978, that 62 translations of tragedies of Aeschylus were published, 90 translations of Sophocles and 142 translations of Euripides (Maronitis 2001; Rossoglou 2012). The number of translators also significantly increased in the recent years from the 1980s—and the list of translators now includes names of some of the best writers, theatre directors and scholars: Phanis Kakridis, Giorgos Giatromanolakis, Pavlos Matessis, Costas Tachtsis, Dimitris Maronitis and Giorgos Chimonas, to mention only a few.

Regarding the approaches to translation practice in Greece, not many examples of theoretical discussions are found until 1768 when Evgenios Vulgaris explored basic questions on translation in his translation *On the Discord in the Polish Churches. Historical and Critical Essay; Translated from French into the Popular Greek Language, with Historical and Critical Notes*—published in Leipzig. Vulgaris stressed the necessity that the target text should be written in the current vernacular of the target audience—and that a native speaker should always check the translated text (Connolly & Bacopoulou-Halls 2011). Moreover, Katartzis (1730–1807) proposed that teaching of Ancient Greek should take place through Modern Greek translations of Ancient Greek as well as through Modern European texts.

In the same context, Adamantios Korais (1748–1833) dealt with *both* intra- and interlingual translations. He treated translation as a mean to enrich the target language, Modern Greek. In this respect, Korais contributed to the *Language Question* (see fn. 5 above) by promoting three important principles—which were served in his translations too:

- descendants should have access to the language of the ancients, to achieve access to a "storehouse of learning" and access to self-determination;
- the modern written language should follow the grammar of the contemporary oral language; and
- the modern oral language should be treated as the basis of all language use and should be "corrected" to a degree, as far as is possible (Beaton 1994; Connolly & Bacopoulou-Halls 2011).

Regarding more recent theoretical approaches to translation in the Greek context, one should mention Lorenzos Mavilis (1860–1912) who took the position that a translation should always be evaluated on the basis of its own coherence and appropriateness. Mavilis also stressed the influence of translated works on the development of the national language and of the literature of the nation. In more recent time, Giorgos Seferis (1900–1971) stated that he aimed to cleanse and enrich Greek through his translations, in order to make Greek functional to "bear" texts coming both from the literature of the West and the older Greek literature (1980: 241; in Connolly & Bacopoulou-Halls 2011).

Seferis distinguished between interlingual translations (his term: *antigraphi* 'copy') and intralingual translations (his term: *metagraphi* 'transcription'). He argued that intralingual translation into Modern Greek is not always simple or satisfactory even though less mediation is required for a Greek translator to access an Ancient Greek text, rather than for a translator who is not a speaker of Modern Greek. Moreover, Seferis proposed that the purpose of translation of ancient texts into Modern Greek should be to prove that Modern Greek also has the necessary resources. However, Seferis criticized translators who did not always attempt to enrich the modern language through material from the ancient language. In contrast, Elytis (1911–1996) suggested a new terminology of intralingual translation—"Modern Greek morfi/ form"—and of interlingual translation—"second writing/ defteri graphi".

In the following sections, I discuss in detail some aspects of the early history of translations into Greek, with an emphasis on intralingual retranslations. In this context, I examine the main characteristics and approaches to Biblical Greek. My main hypothesis is that there is also no direct relation between the diachrony of retranslations and grammatical change in the case of intralingual translations. Following earlier studies on written contact and translation effects, I distinguish between biblical and non-biblical translations and explore the different types of effects and possible changes in Greek due to written contact.

60 CHAPTER 2

2.3.4 The Case of Biblical Greek

2.3.4.1 Introduction

The Septuagint translation and the New Testament are both frequently characterized as "Biblical Koine Greek" texts. The term *Jewish Greek*, which refers to an ethnolect, is another term that is used but is not widely accepted in the scholarly community (Bubenik 2010). Accordingly, de Lange (2007) and Janse (2007) have also underlined the sociolinguistic as well as the regional features of these texts and supported the view that Biblical Koine Greek can mean "one particular regional variety or substandard of the Koine, i.e. the Syro-Palestinian Koine" (Janse 2007: 647). There is a consensus in the field that many characteristics of this regional variety can also be found in biblical texts. Jewish communities of Palestine and Syria were bilingual in Greek and Aramaic—and upper classes should have been multilingual with a knowledge of Hebrew as well (Bubenik 2010). Chapter 3 below provides a deeper discussion of the effect of biblical translations on grammatical change.

2.3.4.2 Semitisms in Biblical Greek

In this section, I present a brief overview of Biblical Greek and, in particular, of the Septuagint. The examination of the morphosyntactic *Semitisms* of Biblical Greek is a central aim of numerous studies. Blass, Debrunner & Funk (1961: 4) summarize the challenges of such studies in the following passage: "not everything which conforms to Semitic idiom is a Semitism, nor is everything which appears somewhere or sometime in Greek genuine Greek". Blass & Debrunner present a list of Semitisms and propose a distinction between interference from a spoken Jewish Greek and Semitisms as translation effects. Semitisms as translation effects concern examples of Semitisms that are universally accepted for the translated text of the Septuagint, or examples from the New Testament that are likely to be based on an Aramaic text. Accordingly, Maloney (1981), for instance, proposes a list of eight syntactic, five morphological and four true lexical Semitisms. Well-known examples of Semitism include the apodosis of a conditional with καί/ *kaí* 'and' (see Hebrew *wāw* consecutivum; Bubenik 2010) and the pleonastic use of a personal pronoun in relative clauses (Lavidas 2012). With regard to pleonastic pronouns, Biblical Koine Greek appears to follow the Semitic characteristic of a redundant use of the correlative pronoun αὐτός *autós* 'he', even though the relative pronoun in Greek marks all relevant categories expressed by the correlative pronoun, i.e., person, number, gender and case.

Another potential Semitism is the decrease in the presence of the dative case. Bortone (2010) documents the replacement of the dative by a PP and the co-presence of the new PP and the old dative, selected by the same verb, even

EARLY HISTORY OF TRANSLATIONS AND GRAMMATICAL CHANGE   61

in different paragraphs of the same Biblical Koine Greek text (see 4a vs. 4b, from Bortone 2010—on the dative in Koine Greek, see also Gianollo & Lavidas 2013).

(4)   a. Koine Greek New Testament; John 8:25[6]
      λαλῶ   ὑμῖν
      lalô   **hymîn**
      talk.1SG 2PL.DAT
      'I talk to you'

vs.

      b. Koine Greek New Testament; John 8:27
      λαλῶ   εἰς τὸν   κόσμον
      lalô   **eis tòn**   *kósmon*
      talk.1SG to ART.ACC.SG world.ACC
      'I talk to the world'

Moreover, there is an important decrease of the cases selected by the prepositions. Bortone (2010), for instance, shows that Mark's Gospel includes only two prepositions (ἐπί *epí* and παρά *pará*) that may govern all three cases. One should also note the frequent use of complex prepositions in Hellenistic Greek, both in Biblical and non-Biblical Hellenistic Greek (Krebs 1884: 5). For instance, the complex preposition *li=pnēy* 'in front of' (lit. 'in the face of') is attested with over a thousand examples in the Hebrew source text of the Septuagint (Bubenik 2010). Sollamo (1979: 13 ff.) argues that the Hebrew source text is responsible for the frequent use of polymorphemic prepositions in the Greek translation: ἔμπροσθεν *émprosthen* 84 occurrences, ἐναντίον *enantíon* 181 occurrences, ἐνώπιον *enópion*, 'lit.: in the eye/face of', 218 occurrences.

---

6 For the translations of the examples, I have adopted the versions reproduced in the Perseus Project with some modifications; for specific texts I have also used the following translations, also with modifications: the World English Bible [www.perseus.tufts.edu], the New International Version (2011) and the New English Translation of the Septuagint [ccat.sas.upenn.edu/nets/edition], in the case of biblical translations, and James Huddleston's translation (Chicago Homer: http://digital.library.northwestern.edu/homer/). I follow the Brill transliteration system for the Greek texts and add a broad phonological transcription only in the case of Modern Greek examples; for all other periods, I only offer transliteration. Moreover, for the sake of readability, glosses are limited to basic morphological information. Regarding abbreviations, I cite the early Greek texts and authors with the abbreviations used in the TLG and Liddell, Scott & Jones, and the early English texts with the abbreviations used in the Penn-Helsinki Corpus and OED when a text is not included in the Penn-Helsinki Corpus.

62

CHAPTER 2

TABLE 2.2   Formal translation correspondences between Biblical Greek and Hebrew and Aramaic

Biblical Koine		Hebrew/Aramaic
(i)	Present tense	Participles
	(Futuristic present)	(Participle of 'Futurum Instans')
	(Present with past sense)	(Participle of past action)
(ii)	Aorist	Perfect
	(Futuristic aorist)	('Prophetic' perfect and 'perf. confident.')
	(Aorist with present sense)	(Stative perfect)
(iii)	Future	Imperfect
	(with past sense)	(with past sense)
(iv)	Perfect	Derived conjugation verbs
	(Omnitemporal)	

THOMPSON 1985: 53

Thompson (1985) provides a list of formal translation correspondences in Table 2.2 between Hebrew and Aramaic, on the one hand, and Biblical Koine, on the other hand.

Much debate also concerns the origin of periphrastic forms in Biblical Koine, of the type shown in (5) below. Note, however, that in Biblical Koine the periphrasis of the auxiliary in the present with a present participle was not productive—not attested in many syntactic structures. In addition, the periphrasis of the auxiliary in the future with a present participle was not frequent either. This fact probably means that the periphrastic expression of the progressive aspect was not a fully grammaticalized category, which contrasts Biblical Koine with Late Hebrew and Aramaic (Bubenik 2010).

(5)   Koine Greek New Testament; Luke 13:10
      ἦν   διδάσκων
      ên   didáskōn
      was.3SG teach.PRTC.PRS.SG.NOM
      '[He] was teaching.'

However, according to Bubenik (2010, 2016), the progressive aspect in the Septuagint and the New Testament differed significantly from the progressive aspect in the other Hellenistic works: the source of difference may be found in the influence from the Semitic background of translators and authors of these texts. Observe that the same author could use both *ἦν διδάσκων ên didáskōn* [was.3SG teach.PRTC.PRS.SG.NOM] and *ἐδίδασκε edídaske* [teach.IMP.3SG]; the latter form was attested in educated registers which reflect Hellenistic literary texts; the former form was attested in the Christian vulgar variety or the colloquial variety of the Syro-Palestinian Koine (Bubenik 2010). In later stages of Greek, like Medieval Greek, the progressive construction expresses continuity but is lost in contemporary Greek—except for in the Tsakonian dialect.

In the present section, I have briefly discussed the main characteristics of Biblical Greek that can be the result of a transfer from the language of the source text (in the case of the Septuagint). In the following section (2.2.5), I provide a detailed presentation of the main characteristics of biblical translations into later Greek. I focus on the type of relation found between grammatical characteristics of diachronic (re-)translations and the development of these characteristics as reflected in non-translated texts. Most of the biblical translations discussed here are included in the corpus of translations used in the corpus surveys of Part 2 of this book.

2.3.5 *Biblical Translations into Later Greek*

2.3.5.1 Greek Biblical Translations: Brief Overview

The first translation of a biblical text into Greek is the interlingual translation of the Hebrew Old Testament into Koine Greek, the Septuagint (third century BC-first century AD; see Section 2.3.5.2). The Old Testament was translated by 72 Greek-speaking Jewish scholars from Hebrew to their contemporary Greek in the third century BC, as an initiative of king Ptolemy II Philadelphus (see also above). The Septuagint was also the source of influence and Old Testament quotations for writers of the New Testament. The translations of Theodotion in the second century AD, Aquila of Sinope also in the second century AD, Symmachus in the third century AD, and the Fragments of the Samareitikon/ Samaritan Pentateuch are other early Greek translations of the Hebrew Bible, which have survived only in a fragmentary form.

There is a significant temporal gap between (i) the first Greek intralingual biblical translations of the New Testament of the 16th and 17th century, on the one hand, and (ii) their source text, the Koine Greek New Testament (first century AD), and the first Greek interlingual biblical translation, the Septuagint (third century BC-first century AD), on the other hand. The Koine Greek New Testament is a non-translated work; most scholars agree on this—despite disagreement on the possibility that some passages may have appeared initially in Aramaic (Wellhausen 1903, 1911). It is written in the Koine Greek of the first century AD. The development of Greek made intralingual translations into later

Greek a necessity, for the understanding of the biblical text by speakers of Greek of the following centuries to be possible, although this necessity should have emerged much earlier than the 16th and 17th century. In a similar way, later translations of the Septuagint were also required for its understanding by the speakers of the subsequent generations. For instance, in 1543, Agapius of Crete translated the Psalms into his contemporary Greek.

The history of translations of the Koine Greek New Testament includes several important landmarks. Maximos Kallipolitis prepared a vernacular translation of the New Testament—with the support of the Patriarch Cyril I Lucaris of Constantinople—which was published in 1638 in Geneva. From the 18th century until the early 20th century, limited attempts of translations of the biblical texts include the following significant cases:

(i) In 1703, Seraphim of Mytilene's translation of the New Testament into Modern Greek was published in London by the English Society for the Propagation of the Gospel in Foreign Parts. This translation was condemned by Patriarch Gabriel III of Constantinople in 1704.

(ii) In 1833, Frangiskos Soavios published his translation of the Pentateuch and Joshua from Hebrew into Modern Greek.

(iii) In 1850, Neophytos Vamvas, Professor at the University of Athens, and his associates prepared a translation of the Old and New Testament into Katharevousa "purified" [archaized] Greek.

(iv) In 1901, Alexandros Pallis produced a Modern Greek translation of the Gospels. The publication of this translation in a newspaper instigated riots in Athens, known as Evangelika ("events/riots related to the Gospels"), with demonstrators accusing Alexandros Pallis of trying to dissolve the national and religious unity and of trying to "sell" Greece to Turks and Slavs (see above and Section 4.3).

On editions of the Bible translated into Modern Greek, see also, among many others, the classic study of Darlow & Moule (1911). See also Kakoulidi (1980); Delicostopoulos (1998); Kitromilides (2006); Scouteris & Belezos (2015).

After the first half of the 20th century, one can observe a significant increase in the number of biblical translations. In 1967, Vasilios Vellas and other Professors of the University of Athens translated the New Testament into simple Katharevousa/ "purified" [archaized] Greek, based on the *Textus Receptus*, that is, "the received standard text", with the support of the Greek Bible Society. In 1985, a translation into modern demotic, vernacular Greek, prepared by Professors of the Universities of Athens and Thessaloniki who worked on this translation from the mid-1960s, was published with the support of the Greek Bible Society. This translation was based on a critical text of the Koine Greek New Testament, which is a Byzantine paraphrasis of the original text (cf. Sec-

EARLY HISTORY OF TRANSLATIONS AND GRAMMATICAL CHANGE   65

tion 2.3.5.2). In 1994, Spyros Filos revised Vamvas' (1850) translation of the Bible into the modern demotic, vernacular language. In 1997, a translation of the Old and New Testament was published with the approval of the Orthodox Church of Greece, known as Today's Greek Version (TGV). This translation of the New Testament was first published in 1985.

Following the above overview, I now concentrate on the analysis of some significant cases of Greek biblical translations. My major aim is to explore the type of relation between the grammatical characteristics of Greek diachronic (re)translations and the development of these characteristics, as reflected in non-translated texts.

2.3.5.2 Major Landmarks of Biblical Translations into Greek: Their Position in the History of the Language

(i) The Septuagint and its effect

I start the detailed exploration of Greek biblical translations with the Septuagint, the early Greek translation of the Old Testament. There are three important parameters that one should keep in mind when working with the data of the Septuagint: (i) we do not have all required information on the Hebrew *Vorlage*, the source text of the Septuagint; (ii) we do not have the original target Greek text; (iii) we lack information about the translation technique. Scholars of the Septuagint usually start their work with the assumption that the *Vorlage* of the Greek text is the Masoretic Text (MT) and that the Greek text published in the critical editions is a good approximation of the Greek of the Old Testament. However, one should always be ready to deal with the possibility of a divergent Greek text or Hebrew source text (Porter 2000, 2013b, 2016b; Horrocks 2014).

The terminus ante quem of the translation of the Septuagint should be the second century BC with the composition of the Greek translational fragment of Deuteronomy. Several scholars have attempted to connect the Septuagint with the bilingual community of Jews who could understand both Greek and Hebrew (see Section 2.3.4). According to this hypothesis, the function of the Greek translation was interpretive: this means that the Greek translation was initially dependent of the Hebrew text, as it would offer an interpretation of the Hebrew text. The development of the Septuagint in later periods is related to the weaker understanding of Hebrew by the Greek-speaking Jews and the change of the Septuagint into an independent text, which was supposed to be read as a "normal" text and not as an interpretation of another text (Pace 1984; Olofsson 1988; Wasserstein & Wasserstein 2006; Naudé 2009).

The Greek of the Septuagint triggered debates already in Antiquity: Philo (1st century BC–1st century AD), for instance, praised the variety of the Septuagint to an extensive degree, but others expressed criticism based on criteria that relate to possible influence from other languages. A common approach of the modern period viewed the language of the Septuagint as a form of a Judaized Greek dialect or even as a type of Greek whose function was to express the Gospel.

In recent studies, there is consensus that the Greek of the Septuagint is diverse because the Septuagint contains books translated freely, books translated literally and books directly composed in Greek (Bons & Joosten [eds] 2016). Its register can be diverse, from representing a "vulgar" level of the language to representing a literary Koine. In addition, the "corpus" of the Septuagint includes texts from the third century BC as well as texts from later periods, even to the second century AD. The distinctness of the language of the Septuagint can be reflected in the influence of the Septuagint on later works. The term "Septuagintisms" in the Greek New Testament, and in other writings, provides evidence in favor of an important role of the variety of the Septuagint in that there is an obvious relation between the Septuagint and the origin of constructions and lexical items of later periods.

Jewish translations of the Old Testament into Greek, which show several connections with rabbinic interpretations of Scripture, also appeared after the acceptance and use of the Septuagint by Christianity. The new translations were triggered by a necessity to correct the Septuagint and bring it closer to the Hebrew source text and by the fact that the Septuagint was adopted by the Christian Church. The first translation was prepared by Aquila (130 AD), a Greek from Sinope of Pontus, who was converted to Judaism. His translation followed the rabbinic principle that all letters and symbols included in the text of the Old Testament are inspired by God. The translation of Theodotion from Ephesus (180 AD) into an elaborated Greek replaced the use of the Septuagint in the Christian Church, in the case of the book of Daniel. Symmachus prepared a new translation (210 AD), which was also used by Lucian of Samosata in his revision of the Septuagint (circa 312 AD). Symmachus' translation was free of literalism and appears to be a free translation. In Hexapla of Origen from Caesaria (240–245 AD), the so called fifth, sixth and seventh translations survived (Chastoupis 1981).

The revival of the debate of the Greek of the Septuagint began with Friedrich W. Sturz's work (1808) on the Alexandrian dialect—but complete examinations of this question did not occur until the mid of the 19th century (Aitken 2014a). Early studies supported an analysis of the Septuagint as reflecting a distinctive Jewish dialect because the text combines non-classical characteristics with a syntactic interference from Hebrew. Later studies have challenged the assumption of a Jewish dialect that was reflected in the grammar and lexicon of the Septuagint. It seems that the translators of the Septuagint had a knowledge of Classical and Late Biblical Hebrew through the study of Hebrew texts; they also had a knowledge of Aramaic, which was a spoken and written language in Ptolemaic Egypt, and were familiar with the vernacular Hebrew of Palestine.

It is often a complex task to distinguish the type of influence on the Septuagint text, as three possible sources of influence should be taken into account: Aramaic, spoken Hebrew, and literary Hebrew. This is shown by George (2010), who presents examples of Hebrew translation effects on the Septuagint in increased usage of pronouns, parataxis and non-native prepositional constructions.

Horrocks (2014: 106–108) distinguishes different types of translations between the various books of the Septuagint: the variety of the *Pentateuch* represents the natural contemporary Koine and *Lamentations* show mechanical literalness; *Tobit* (*Apocrypha*) reflects characteristics of a near-vernacular; *Esther* demonstrates many literary elements, whereas *4 Maccabees* can even be characterized as an Atticizing text (Pietersma 2002; Horrocks 2014: 106–108). Horrocks refers, for instance, to *3 Rgns 18:17–21* as an example of a passage with a normal Koine style and disagrees with the possibility that the Septuagint was written in a Jewish-Greek dialect (cf. also Swete 2003 [1902]; Evans 1999, 2001, 2005; Fernandez Marcos 2000; Porter 2013b, 2016b; Bons et al., eds, 2014; Bons & Joosten, eds, 2016).

In the present section, I examine various hypotheses of the variety of the Septuagint: this enables me to discuss significant aspects of earlier analyses of the Septuagint. The hypotheses of the Septuagint can be accounted for on the basis of my claim that the Septuagint constitutes a translation that reflects the coexistence of multiple grammars—a type of grammatical multiglossia—as well as contact and transfer of elements from one grammar to the other.

Even though authors of late antiquity may have recognized an Alexandrian dialect in the text of the Septuagint, they did not refer to any Jewish, or Christian or biblical, dialect. Such terminology was first used in the Renaissance with the conflict between the Hebraists who focused on the differences between the Septuagint and other Greek texts of the period, and the Purists who attempted to find similarities between Classical or Atticizing Greek and Biblical Greek (Aitken 2014a; Porter 2000, 2016b).

The origin of the conflict had a theological character; a Biblical Greek dialect can be authorized, and its usage can be justified through its relation with the religion (see also below). Biblical Greek—including both the Greek of the New Testament and the Greek of the Septuagint—has been considered a distinct type of Greek because of similarities between the language of the two biblical texts and of differences between the Greek of the Bible and the Greek of the classical writings. Thiersch (1841) prepared one of the first studies on Biblical Greek as a distinct type of Greek; his study focused on the Pentateuch, which he compared to Attic Greek. He concluded that Biblical Greek should be seen as including a large number of Hebraisms (Porter 2000, 2013a, b, 2016b; Porter & Carson, eds., 2015).

According to the *Hebraic/Jewish Greek Hypothesis*, the Greek of the Septuagint is different than the Greek of other Koine writings. The advocates of the *Hebraic/Jewish Greek Hypothesis* claim that the Jewish Greek of the Septuagint can be found in other Greek works written by Jews—including the New Testament; that is, a type of a Jewish Greek dialect existed (Porter 2013b, 2016b; Aitken 2014b). Gehman (1951) argues in favor of a Jewish-Greek jargon of the synagogues and Turner (1955) of a particular dialect.

Starting with Soisalon-Soininen, the Septuagint school of the University of Helsinki is associated with the examination of translation techniques. Sollamo, Aejmelaeus, Voitila and Sipilä have developed various approaches to the framework of the Septuagint school. In addition, other scholars have also followed a similar methodological perspective—for instance: Joosten, van der Kooij, Muraoka, Olofsson and Tov. According to their main hypothesis, each book of the Septuagint was produced, as a rule, by a single translator, at least in an initial phase of translation (Sollamo 1979).

The investigation of the translation techniques by the above scholars, among others, led to a division into three types of categories of translation: *free—literal—slavish*. Esther o′, Proverbs, Job, Isaiah, and Daniel o′, Pentateuch, in particular Exodus and Genesis, and Joshua have been considered as the freest translations. Ecclesiastes, 2 Esdras, Judges A and B, Jeremiah, Ezekiel, and the Kaige recension [KR] sections of 1–4Reigns have been shown to be the most slavish translations. The remaining parts of the Septuagint are literal—rather than slavish—translations.

Around 1895, the discovery of Greek documentary papyri in Egypt made several scholars argue in favor of significant similarities between the Greek of the papyri and the Greek of the Septuagint and the New Testament. For instance, differences in the Greek vocabulary of the Septuagint and the Classical Attic works could be accounted for through similar usages observed in the contemporary papyri. Deissmann was the first to emphasize the significance of the discovery of the Greek documentary papyri and inscriptions in Egypt in his *Bible Studies* (1895, 1897) and in his *Light from the Ancient East* (1908). Deissmann uses the term Hellenistic Greek to refer to the Greek of 300 BC–500/600 AD.

Deissman recognizes the character of the Septuagint as a translated work but he disagrees with the hypothesis of spoken or written Semitic Greek. He accepts that Hebraic or Semitic features exist in the Septuagint and that the morphosyntax of the language of the text is influenced by Semitic characteristics; however, for his analysis, the morphosyntax should be characterized as Hellenistic and not as Semitic (Porter 2016b). Deissmann was a leading figure in this new movement that considered both the Septuagint and the New Testament as reflecting the Greek of their period. For Deissmann, the Greek of these texts was the standard language of this period, with possible transfer from the oral language and the source text. Deissmann's conclusions support my *Hypothesis of Grammatical Multiglossia*: according to that view, contact between coexistent grammars can result in mixing/code-switching even in the same clause (see Part 2 and 6.3 below).

Histories of the Greek language composed from the early 20th century onward also support the hypothesis that the Septuagint represents the Koine Greek language. Even though the translation effects and the Semitic substrate were considered in earlier studies to be the source of the differences between the Greek of the Septuagint and the literary Greek (and one cannot deny that a close translation of a sacred text leads to the presence of Hebraisms), the language of contemporary documents from Egypt conclusively shows, however, that the Septuagint followed the ordinary written Greek of its period (Pietersma 2002; Horrocks 2014). For this reason, the Septuagint is indeed an important source of information about the development of the Greek in the Hellenistic period. The *Hellenistic/ Koine Greek Hypothesis* regarded Hellenistic Greek as being the result of the development of Greek in the post-classical period and as a single variety spoken and written through the Mediterranean. Accordingly, the Greek of the Septuagint did not constitute a unique case but a type of translational Greek and a form of Koine Greek. The Semitic influence led to a rise in frequency of constructions that are already attested in Koine Greek (Porter 2000, 2013a, b, 2016b).

A revival of the Koine Greek Hypothesis emerged in 1980 but it was probably a continuation of the early hypothesis; for instance, as has already been discussed above, many histories of Greek, written in the 20th century, still support the *Koine Greek Hypothesis*. However, one also observes an increase in the number of later studies arguing in favor of this hypothesis. Recent studies recognize the influence of the Semitic lexicon and morphosyntax on the Septuagint but only in relation to the fact that it was a translated work within the wider context of Hellenistic Greek (Joosten 2016). Porter (1989, 2000) argues that it is possible to identify common characteristics of translation Greek. Following a sociolinguistic approach, he claims that Deissmann's studies have shown that the Septuagint and the New Testament shared the code of Koine Greek (Porter prefers the concepts *code* and *text* instead of dialect and language). However, there are numerous manifestations of a code depending on various factors, such as register.

In the context of multilingualism of Alexandria, Koine Greek was the prestigious language, the lingua franca of the dominant classes. According to Porter (1989, 2000, 2013a), in such linguistic context, lexical transfer might occur from Hebrew to the primary language, Greek, for religious needs, but syntactic transfer should have the direction from the primary language, Greek, to the secondary language of the area, Hebrew. Horsley (1989) also applies concepts related to bilingualism—as well as diglossia, code-switching, interference to languages of the first century in Palestine. He makes a distinction between first languages and preferred languages, primary and secondary bilingualism, productive and receptive bilingualism (Porter 2013a). Horsley also examines Semitisms and concludes that the *Hypothesis of Jewish Greek* cannot be supported through any convincing linguistic framework.

A new debate concerns the contrast between the characteristics of the Septuagint as a literary language and its characteristics as a typical documentary language. The latter hypothesis is based on features that are typical of "chancery" Greek; that is, Greek constructions attested in documentary sources. Another term that was used instead of literary language is *educated Greek* (Porter 2013b, 2016b).[7] According to this view, the translators should not have been bilingual speakers or Jews with knowledge of Greek but literate enough to be able to use Greek. Memorization and copying of classical authors and Homer was a method included in the educational system of antiquity for learning how to write. According to the *Educated Greek Hypothesis*, the translators of the Septuagint were probably members of the class of the Ptolemaic bureaucracy. It follows then that the translation process and the style reflected in the Septuagint are quite similar to the translation process and style of other ancient translated texts. Moreover, if the above hypothesis is correct, the translation of the Septuagint appears to be relevant to the scribal context of Egypt, where the Greek language could offer social and political benefits. Accordingly, the Greek of the Septuagint can be described as a Ptolemaic variety of Greek rather than as a Jewish variety of Greek (see also Horrocks 2016; Muraoka 2016; Voitila 2016).

---

7 But cf. Joosten (2008) who rejects the hypothesis that the Septuagint translators should have studied Classical Greek texts and disagrees with the lists of literary vocabulary in the Septuagint.

(ii) Translations of the New Testament into later Greek: Maximos Kallipolitis

In this section, I present in detail characteristics of the *major early biblical translations into later Greek*, in an attempt to describe the context of written language contact and its role in the development of the language. The data also favor one of my main hypotheses that contact does not only concern different languages but also the transfer of grammatical characteristics from earlier periods of the same language, especially as evident in the case of written contact. Intralingual translations, and retranslations, can offer evidence of the above type of written contact between characteristics of earlier periods and characteristics of their contemporary language. In contrast, interlingual translation provides evidence for another type of written contact, the one between different languages.

Maximos Kallipolitis was an educated person, who studied in the Patriarchic Academy and, probably, in Italy; he was a student of Theophilos Korydalleus (see above, Section 2.3.5.1). He prepared the first complete translation of the New Testament into his contemporary spoken language, under the aegis of the Patriarch of Constantinople, Cyril I Lucaris (1572–1638). Maximos Kallipolitis worked on his translation from March 1629 and completed the translation in one year. The Patriarch examined the translation and probably modified some passages.

Due to several obstacles, the publication of the translation in two volumes was not possible until 1638, in Leiden or Geneva, after the death of Cyril I Lucaris and Maximos Kallipolitis.[8] It was in the same year, when the translation was published, that Cyril II Kontaris condemned Cyril I Lucaris and all contemporary trends towards Calvinist teachings. Copies of the translation arrived in Constantinople in 1645 when the situation was more favorable with Patriarch Parthenios II, a willing person to contribute to the spread of the translation to Constantinople and Smyrne (Vasileiadis 2013a, to-appear).

However, there were still important reactions from conservative circles. For instance, Meletios Sirigos (1590–1664), in a series of public sermons, demanded the condemn of the translation as a heretical text, and the Patriarch immediately stopped its further publication. In 1672, the Patriarch of Jerusalem also

---

8 Ἡ Καινὴ Διαθήκη τοῦ Κυρίου ἡμῶν Ἰησοῦ Χριστοῦ, δίγλωττος, ἐν ᾗ ἀντιπροσώπως τότε θεῖον πρωτότυπον καὶ ἡ ἀπαραλλάκτως ἐξ ἐκείνου εἰς ἁπλῆν διάλεκτον, διὰ τοῦ μακαρίτου κυρίου Μαξίμου τοῦ Καλλιουπολίτου γενομένη μετάφρασις ἅμα ἐτυπώθησαν ["New Testament of our Lord Jesus Christ, diglot, which publishes both the divine original text and its corresponding translation into a simple variety by Maximos Kallipotis, without any change"].

expressed a condemn against the translation. In 1703, Maximos Kallipolitis' translation was re-published in London after significant attempts and was corrected by Seraphim Mytilineos in 1704 with the support of the Anglican Church; the Orthodox Church banned its publication. In 1710, a revision of Seraphim's version was prepared by Anastasios Michail, with the support of the Royal Society of Prussia; this text was also used later by the British Bible Society in its publications. A ban against the acquisition and reading of this translation and its revisions reappeared in 1823 and 1836, with the Patriarch of Constantinople, Gregorius VI (cf. Vasileiadis 2013a).

A recent reprint of the 1638 edition was prepared by Emmanouil Kasdaglis and its first volume was published by MIET in 1995 and the second and third volumes in 1999 (see Section 8.1). Zoumpoulakis (2015), in an article in a newspaper (*To Vima*), claims that there is no Modern Greek translation of the Bible that had *an influential and formative role* as the Authorized Version or Luther's translation had for their communities. According to his view, *Maximos Kallipolitis' translation* could be the only translation that could have had such a role, but this translation was not circulated in reality because of the opposition of the Church; *Vamvas (and his collaborators') later translation* was widely read because Greek protestants used it as their Bible. Modern Greek biblical translations are fewer in number in comparison to translations into national languages of the West as well as in comparison to translations of Classical Greek works. Moreover, translations of Ancient Greek texts were prepared by major Modern Greek authors—but this is not the case with biblical translations, with only very few exceptions. In this respect, according to Zoumpoulakis (2015), it is evident that the first translation of the Old Testament from the Hebrew source text into Modern Greek was published only in 1997.

In this section, I have introduced the main properties of later Greek biblical translations. In the following section, I connect the later Greek biblical translations to a broader external context and history, and, in particular, to issues related to the authorization of biblical texts.

(iii) Translations of the New Testament into later Greek: Authorization

Debates on biblical translations as well as the concomitant conflicts stem from the significant question of authorization of translations of the Bible. The official Church is involved in the issue of authorization of biblical translations from the period of Maximos Kallipolitis' translation (1638), which was supported by Cyril I Lucaris. However, as already mentioned above, the official Church condemned the translation (for instance, the Patriarch of Jerusalem condemned the translation in 1672) and its "corrected" version by Seraphim

EARLY HISTORY OF TRANSLATIONS AND GRAMMATICAL CHANGE

Mytilineos, in the following decades; cf. the condemnation of this version by the Patriarch of Constantinople in 1704 (Panagopoulos 1995). In the 19th century, the British Bible Society managed to receive authorization of the revised version of Anastasios Michail by the Ecumenical Patriarch Cyril VI (1814). The British Bible Society promoted the official acceptance of Hilarion's [late Metropolitan of Turnovo] translation of the New Testament (1828) as well as Vamvas' translation. Hilarion's translation had the consensus of Patriarch Cyril VI and Patriarch Gregorius V but was condemned by the Holy Synod of the Greek Orthodox Church in 1823 (Vaporis 1975; Konstantinou 2012, Vasileiadis to-appear).

Vamvas' translation did not have the approval of the Church. It was published in 1850 but was condemned twice earlier by the Synod of the Ecumenical Patriarch. The reasons of condemn were related to accusations of undermining of the dogmatic tradition and of the value of the original language of the New Testament (Vasileiadis 2013a, b). Other reasons referred to the danger of the Protestant Church and of other religious reforms for the Orthodox Church. The danger—also triggered by the recent foundation of Protestant schools and publications of religious texts on the Protestant dogma—led to a ban of any new translation of the Bible (Vaporis 1975, 1984; Panagopoulos 1995).

Evangelika Riots related to the translation of the Gospel (in November 1901) were also considered as associated with an attempt of royalty to force new "foreign" ideas through new translations of the New Testament—for instance, through the translations by Ioulia Somaki and Alexandros Pallis. As already discussed above (Section 2.3.5.1), university students demonstrated against the translations—and against what was considered as connected with these translations—with violent consequences and the resignation of the government and the archbishop of Athens. Another result of these events was the addition of the following phrase to the Constitution of 1911 (article 2, paragraph 2):

> The text of the Holy Scripture should remain as it is, without any change —its rendering into other linguistic forms is not allowed without a previous approval of the Great Christian Church of Constantinople [*Το κείμενο των Αγίων Γραφών τηρείται αναλλοίωτον η εις άλλον γλωσσικόν τύπον απόδοσις τούτου άνευ της προηγουμένης εγκρίσεως και της εν Κωνσταντινουπόλει Μεγάλης του Χριστού Εκκλησίας απαγορεύεται απολύτως*].

The above article was included in all later versions of the Constitution, with an addition from 1927: "... *της αυτοκέφαλου Εκκλησίας της Ελλάδος* ... " '[without the previous approval] of the Autocephalous Church of Greece'.

In the decade of 1960, the United Bible Society re-discussed the issue of a new translation of the New Testament and assigned this work to four Professors of the Faculty of Theology at the University of Athens, without a previous consensus of the Ecumenical Patriarch and the Church of Greece. Their translation received an approval from the Church, even though their source text was not the text authorized by the Patriarchate but the Textus Receptus with additions from Nestle's edition (Vaporis 1994; Panagopoulos 1995; Porter & Pitts 2008).

This chapter has included a broad discussion of Greek intralingual translations, seen as a type of retranslation; moreover, I have discussed several aspects of the history of Greek biblical translations. In Chapter 3, I go onwards to analyzing the main characteristics of biblical translations in order to understand how they can form a significant corpus for an investigation of grammatical change. This also includes analyzing the role of translation in grammatical change, through contact between characteristics of translations and characteristics of the non-translated language.

CHAPTER 3

Biblical Translations

3.1 The Corpus of Biblical Translations: Source of Evidence of Grammatical Change

3.1.1 *Biblical Translations as a Corpus*

The earliest written biblical translation is the Septuagint, a Koine Greek translation of Hebrew Old Testament texts. The Old Testament is a collection of 39 books: most of them written in Hebrew; several passages were also written in Aramaic. The Christian Bible includes the above books and the New Testament—and in some traditions, the Deuterocanon as well. The New Testament includes 27 books, written in Koine Greek in the period between 50–100 AD. The Deuterocanon/Apocrypha were also written in Greek and are considered canonical, that is, authoritative, in the Roman Catholic and Orthodox Church (Zogbo 2009). The target audience of the Septuagint was primarily Greek-speaking Jews of the Graeco-Roman diaspora. According to the tradition behind this translation, the Septuagint was the result of a collaborative work of 72 Jewish scholars; for this reason, its name derives from the Latin *Septuaginta*, LXX, '70' (see 2.2.5.2).

The legend about the translation of the *Pentateuch* by 70 or 72 Jewish elders in the third century BC on the island of Pharos is the reason for the name of the translation even though the legend is related only to the first five books of the Old Testament (Letter of Aristeas 310–311; Philo's Life of Moses 2: 25–42). The translation project started under Ptolemy II of Egypt and took place during the third and second centuries BC in, or around, Alexandria. In the second century AD, the Jewish scholars, Aquila, Theodotion and Symmachus, prepared revised and new translations of the Septuagint (see 2.2.5). Moreover, the Old Testament Hebrew texts attracted the work of various scholars, but a basic standardization of these texts was not available until the 9th century. The standardized text, known as the Masoretic text (MT) became the source text of the major Christian and Jewish translations of the Old Testament. *Biblia Hebraica Stuttgartensia* is the complete edition of the text that was used as the source text of various translations of the Old Testament texts.

Regarding the New Testament text, the content of the New Testament was fixed by 367 AD under Athanasius, the bishop of Alexandria. The first translations of the New Testament include its translation into Latin, Coptic and Syriac. In 383 AD, Pope Damasus I commissioned Jerome to translate the whole

© KONINKLIJKE BRILL NV, LEIDEN, 2022 | DOI:10.1163/9789004503564_004

76 CHAPTER 3

Bible into Latin; Jerome's translation, known as the Vulgate, was completed by 406 AD. The Vulgate translation became the source text of numerous other translations: Armenian, Georgian, Ethiopic, Arabic, Persian, Gothic, Early English (see also Lampe, ed., 1969; Metzger 2001; Noss 2007; Wendland & Noss 2012; Porter et al. [eds] 2019. On the influence of Greek through biblical translations: see Tzitzilis 1999).

Biblical translations form a natural parallel corpus with an homogeneous pragmatic context. We should, however, keep in mind the theological restrictions posed on biblical translations and the restrictions due to the faithfulness of the translator. The above limitations create a challenge to the study and use of biblical translations as a source of data, providing evidence of *written language contact*: in particular, faithfulness as well as the tendency of translators to override the native characteristics of the target language constitute important factors in the formation of biblical translations (Gianollo 2011, cf. also Koltsiou-Nikita 2009).

Many of the first biblical texts were, in reality, interlinear translations of the Greek source text. This is, for instance, the case for the earliest Latin versions of the Bible, known as the Old Latin, which were probably interlinear translations of the Greek text (Plater & White 1926). Gianollo (2011) has examined DPs (Determiner Phrases) in the genitive in the Greek and the Latin New Testament and has argued that the similarities are due to translation techniques/strategies that are related to sacred texts but also the result of native "natural" changes in the Latin syntax. Gianollo's analysis is based on a quantificational comparative study of the four Gospels in the Greek and the Latin Vulgate text and on a comparison of the Vulgate data with earlier and contemporary Latin data which represent the new colloquial register.

According to Gianollo's conclusions, the translator perceived the genitive extraposition construction of the Greek text (e.g., *τοῦ δὲ Ἰησοῦ Χριστοῦ ἡ γέννησις / toû dè Iēsoû Khristoû hē génesis* 'the birth of Jesus Christ' [Mt 1:18]) as "alien" and reanalyzed it at the clausal level, while singling out the Greek clitic "ethical" genitives (e.g., *καὶ ἐπέχρισεν αὐτοῦ τὸν πηλὸν ἐπὶ τοὺς ὀφθαλμοὺς / kaì epékhrisen autoû tòn pēlòn epì toùs ophthalmoùs* 'and anointed the man's eyes with the clay' [Jn 9:6]).

Moreover, following a significant grammatical change that took place between Classical and Late Latin, Classical Latin showed variation between the position of the genitive before the noun/ head and the position of the genitive following the head noun, but in Late Latin, the genitive is attested following the head noun. Gianollo argues that the post-nominal positioning of the genitives was a real change in Latin (parameter resetting)—not a translation effect. Gianollo's main conclusion is that the translator, Jerome, did *not* follow the language of the source text in the case of "alien" constructions to his Latin native grammar. Jerome used similar constructions provided by his native grammar in the Latin Vulgate (cf. 2.1.1). However, he also applied the conservative register following the classical rhetorical tradition. As a result, a new Christian style was developed.

There is also a long tradition of using religious texts for cross-linguistic comparisons, for instance, based on the multilingual translations of the Lord's Prayer (see Adelung 1806–1817 [1970]). Both the Old and the New Testament have been translated into approximately 400 languages. In addition, there are 1,000 languages in which only the New Testament is translated (Cysouw & Wälchli 2007; Wälchli 2007). The use of parallel corpora for translational equivalents can be regarded as an alternative to the questionnaire method (Dahl 2007).

The following characteristics of biblical translations make them important parallel corpora in typological research (Dahl 2007):[1]

(i) The target languages are located in various and different places of the globe—and cover an important part of the world languages;

(ii) Many biblical translations are freely available on the Internet;

(iii) The Bible contains heterogeneous texts, belonging to different genres, including argumentative passages and passages of narratives;

(iv) Even though the biblical texts represent written language, they also contain passages that reflect natural, oral direct speech;

(v) Biblical texts are well prepared for inclusion in parallel corpora because of their partitioning into chapters and verses. Strong's Numbers (that is, annotations added to some biblical texts based on James Strong's [19th century] system—see below) can also offer word alignment, in the case of translations where they have been added;

(vi) In the case of translations of the New Testament, versions of the source text with morphological and lexical information are available. According to Dahl (2007), a parallel biblical corpus should be restricted—at least

---

1 De Vries (2007) has examined the challenge of textual multiplicity in biblical translations: in several cases, there is not one single source text—but different texts that have their own tradition. The period which constitutes the diachronic parameter, the location and the Christian Church are factors that determine the use of a different source text. This means that biblical translations cannot always be considered as directly equivalent. Moreover, inherent biases in all translational equivalents are related to the fact that these texts demonstrate features of written language as well as of standardized registers. Biblical translations also represent data of a specialized register.

at a first stage—to the New Testament: it is easier to examine one source language only, and there are also various morphosyntactically annotated versions of the source text.

An example of this type of studies shows how Strong's Numbers can facilitate the examination of the definite article in English translations (Dahl 2007; Cysouw et al. 2007). Under Strong's guidance, a concordance was compiled of the King James/ Authorized Version, the Hebrew Old Testament (the Masoretic text) and the Greek New Testament (the Textus Receptus). The concordance appeared in 1890 and was based on the list of all words that are attested in the Hebrew Old Testament and the Greek New Testament, which were given numbers according to their alphabetical order. The numbers were, then, added to the Authorized Version.

In a later stage, the same numbers, Strong's numbers, were also added to other biblical translations. Some words in the target text may have multiple Strong's Numbers, if multiple words of the Hebrew or the Greek text were translated as a single word in the target text. The invariable definite article is marked with Strong's Number 3588. The data indicate that the Koine Greek article is almost twice as frequent as the English definite article *the*. An obvious difference concerns the absence of definite articles before proper names in the English text. If one excludes proper names, the two languages use the definite article in quite similar percentages (Cysouw et al. 2007).

Word alignment can reveal which word in a target text is the most likely translation of a word in the source text. For this purpose, Dahl (2007) has used the T-score measure (Fung & Church 1994), which calculates the association between two items. A T-score measures the likelihood that the distribution of two items is not due to chance: A high T-score means that it is not likely that the two items are attested in their syntactic environments by chance. T-scores can be used without difficulties with invariant forms—as is the case of the Modern English definite article *the*. For example, Table 3.1 from Dahl includes the words from the Authorized Version that have the highest T-scores based on a comparison to the Greek definite article; Table 3.2 illustrates the results with regard to the French translation of Louis Segond.

Dahl has also investigated the future tense in biblical texts in a similar manner. New Testament Greek has a synthetic future, which makes a comparison to English translations which use auxiliaries a complex case. However, T-scores that indicate which words are attested most often in the same context show that the auxiliaries *shall* and *will* are the most frequent equivalents of the Greek synthetic future in most English biblical translations.

T-scores can also offer insights into the diachronic development of the above-mentioned auxiliaries in their function as future markers. The data from

TABLE 3.1 Comparison between the Greek definite article and its correspondent words in the *Authorized Version*

English	T-score
the	35.94
and	21.67
of	21.33

DAHL 2007: 178

TABLE 3.2 Comparison between the Greek definite article and its correspondent words in the *French Louis Segond translation*

French	T-score
la	16.86
le	16.79
de	15.97
qui	15.16
les	13.58

DAHL 2007: 179

the Wycliffite translation of the 14th century in Table 3.3 from Dahl (2007) demonstrate that the highest T-scores concern forms of the auxiliary *shall*. In the Authorized Version and recent translations, *shall* is still very productive as a translational equivalent of the synthetic Greek future, but *will* also appears to be productive in contrast to the data in the Wycliffe translation. In translations of the 21st century, *will* is the most productive equivalent of the Greek future and there is a clear decline in the usage of *shall*.

However, if one only examines the frequency of *will* and *shall* in English translations, without a contrastive perspective as above, one does not take into consideration the function of the auxiliaries or the aspect of translational equivalents.

Cysouw et al. (2007) have developed an automatic alignment method that enables the extraction of data from a corpus of pairs of words that are associated. According to their model, *co-occurrence* is the joint occurrence of

TABLE 3.3   Greek future tense and T-scores in *English biblical translations*

Wycliffe (14th century)		Tyndale (16th century)		King James' version (1611)		World English bible (2000+)	
schal	24.89	*shall*	23.67	*shall*	29.18	*shall*	4.03
schalt	8.63	*shalbe*	13.79	*shalt*	8.95		
schulen	18.98	*shalt*	8.10				
shal	6.77						
shalt	2.38						
will	–	*will*	13.86	*will*	16.62	*will*	25.65

DAHL 2007: 180

words in a defined part of a text, e.g., in a window of words, a sentence or a whole text. Cysouw et al.'s measure calculates the likelihood of co-occurrence of two words. Co-occurrences with multilingual (sentence-aligned) parallel texts enable conclusions, through a statistical analysis, on translational equivalents. Cysouw et al. have measured significant co-occurrences between words from different languages, so-called "trans-cooccurrences", based on sentence translation pairs.

The main assumption of this type of study is that if a linguistic form of a source language is translated into the same form in a target language in most of the instances, then, this form of the target language should be the highest ranked trans-occurrence of the particular translational equivalence. All other forms that may appear as translations have lower significance values and are alternative translations. That is, there are other possibilities of translating the particular form; the most prominent translational equivalent appears with the highest value and is followed by translations with lower values. According to this methodology, two biblical texts should be merged into a bilingual text, to measure the trans-co-occurrences. The verses are also merged to bilingual sentences, as in the examples (6a, b) from Cysouw et al. (2007) which includes the English/ Authorized Version and the German/ Luther's version. Each word has a language-identifying tag, for the automatic distinction of languages to be possible.

(6)   a.   Genesis 1:2 [@en: English; @de: German]
           And the earth was without form, and void; and darkness was upon the
           face of the deep. And the Spirit of God moved upon the face of the
           waters. Und die Erde war wüst und leer, und es war finster auf der Tiefe;
           und der Geist Gottes schwebte auf dem Wasser.

b. And@en the@en earth@en was@en without@en form@en and@en void@en and@en darkness@en was@en upon@en the@en face@en of@en the@en deep@en And@en the@en Spirit@en of@en God@en moved@en upon@en the@en face@en of@en the@en waters@en Und@de die@de Erde@de war@de wüst@de und@de leer@de und@de es@de war@de finster@de auf@de der@de Tiefe@de und@de der@de Geist@de Gottes@de schwebte@de auf@de dem@de Wasser@de (Cysouw et al. 2007).

Cysouw et al. (2007) also use Strong's Numbers (annotations added to some biblical texts based on James Strong's [19th-century] system—see above), for an evaluation of their algorithm.

Recall that the main aim of the present book is to describe the early history of English and Greek translations, with an emphasis on a possible relation between the diachrony of translations—in the form of diachronic retranslations—and the diachrony of the language. In this way, as well as through its contrastive character, the present study contributes in a different way than previous studies which have also had Kroch's (1989, 2001) and Roeper's (1999, 2016) hypothesis on syntactic diglossia and universal bilingualism as a starting point (see Chapters 1 and 6). Accordingly, a prerequisite of my discussion and analysis is that grammatical change would not have been plausible unless language contact is involved. Therefore, on my view, it is important to be able to distinguish between various types of contact: not only (oral or written) contact with other languages or dialects, but also contact with earlier periods of the same language or with grammatical characteristics of translated texts of the same language.

3.1.2   *Biblical Translations: The Parameter of Intralingual Translations*

The role of intralingual biblical translations has been examined less thoroughly in previous studies, but there is still a consensus in the field that intralingual biblical translations may also reflect instances of grammatical change, because they can be related to the need for (a new) translation for linguistic reasons, among other factors. Intralingual translations—which refer to target texts written in later periods of the source language (cf. Chapter 4)—demonstrate various types of change, when compared to their source text. These changes mainly concern either linguistic aspects or the content of the text. The changes in content—which do not constitute a part of the present study—involve omission, addition or restructuring of parts of the source text. Changes in the linguistic form may involve syntactic and lexical changes (Screnock 2018); see Table 3.4.

TABLE 3.4   Types of change in intralingual translations

Content changes	Linguistic changes
Additions	Lexical
Restructuring	Syntactic
Omission	

SCRENOCK 2018: 527

The discussion of intralingual translations started with Roman Jakobson in 1959 (see Chapter 4 below). Jakobson (1959: 261) defined intralingual translations as "an interpretation of verbal signs by means of other signs of the same language". Other terms have also been used, such as *paraphrasing* or *rewording*. Several scholars have emphasized the similarities between intralingual and interlingual translations; Steiner (1975), for instance, argues that both types of translation use the same mechanisms of transfer between the source and the target text. Moreover, according to Zethsen (2009), changes in syntactic constructions in the case of intralingual translations are mainly connected to the historical gap between the source and the target texts: changes in the syntax of the target texts in intralingual translations make the texts more contemporary (Zethsen 2009: 804; Remediaki 2013). Zethsen also distinguishes between additions that are *explanations* or *explications*, as well as between *subjective* and *objective* additions: for instance, an objective addition may enhance understanding of the text—whereas a subjective addition makes the text become more "alive". The aim of grammatical modifications in the case of intralingual translations is to "transfer the source text into an everyday language rather than an archaic or formal language" (Zethsen 2009: 805).

Screnock (2018) modifies Zethsen's model and adds more categories to the proposed typology of motivations for changes in intralingual translations. Four types of motivation refer to the potential differences between the audience of the target text and the source text in time or culture. Three motivations for change in the target text derive from parameters related to the linguistic knowledge of the audience. Several motivations concern potential differences in perceptions of norms: the audience may have different cultural, social, religious norms than the audience of the source text. Accordingly, the intralingual translation can be defined as a transfer of meaning from a source to a target text through changes in the language and content triggered by a potential distance between the audience of the source text and the audience of the target text in (linguistic) knowledge or norms (Screnock 2018).

Part 2 of this book demonstrates—on the basis of empirical studies—how biblical (intralingual) translations can form a valuable corpus that can answer questions that are related to diachronic (re)translations and their role and position in the development of grammatical characteristics. The following section presents details on the other potentially important role of biblical translations, that is, biblical translations as triggering grammatical change.

3.2 Biblical Translations as Factor of Grammatical Change

Several studies have aimed at demonstrating the role of biblical translations in grammatical change. The fact that biblical texts have been translated into a high number of languages and in many different periods of their diachronies have facilitated hypotheses of contact-induced change and spread of grammatical characteristics to various other languages.

Drinka (2011, 2017), for instance, connects the spread of syntactic and stylistic characteristics of the New Testament, and in particular of the periphrastic perfect and progressive constructions, to the model of the Koine Greek text and its subsequent translations. Moreover, Drinka argues that the periphrastic progressive of New Testament Greek demonstrates an increased productivity following the model of the Septuagint. This construction was later borrowed into the Latin Vulgate and was attested in Christian Latin works frequently. Amenta (2003) also claims that the periphrastic progressive construction functioned as a symbol of membership in the Christian community.

According to the above-mentioned hypothesis, the periphrastic progressive construction was transferred through the Latin Vulgate to the European written tradition. The presence of similar constructions in Gothic and Old Church Slavonic was also considered to follow from their property of being a "sacral stamp" (Psaltes 1913), that is, linguistic characteristics that mark the membership in the Christian literature (Drinka 2011, 2017).[2] The periphrastic perfect also became more productive—but to a lower degree. Drinka concludes that, in this respect, the influence of Greek and Biblical Hebrew on the development of stylistic and syntactic properties of eastern and western European languages was significant: the progressive marked the *Christian accent* and was borrowed through translations into several languages; the perfect affected western European languages but only indirectly via Latin.

---

2 Cf. also Mohrmann (1959, 1961–1977) and the so-called Nijmegen school.

Drinka argues that Koine Greek was the model which the Gothic, Latin, Old Church Slavonic and other translations attempted to imitate. The result was what Psaltes (1913) named "sacral stamp". According to the above-mentioned hypothesis, the influence of the "sacral stamp" was initially transferred from Hebrew to the Greek New Testament through the Greek Septuagint, and, later, through the Greek New Testament to Latin, Gothic and Old Church Slavonic (Drinka 2011). More specifically, the direction of influence was from the Septuagint, the literal translation of the Hebrew Bible, to Luke who adopted the archaic style of the Septuagint. Wifstrand (2005: 42) claims that, through the features that Luke borrowed from the Septuagint, Luke created "an aura of sacred history" and made his text appear as the fulfillment of the Old Testament. Luke relied on the Greek of the Septuagint as a model—and not directly on the Hebrew text. In this respect, he used forms that did not appear any longer more in his contemporary Koine Greek language. Wifstrand (2005: 38), for instance, observes that ὅδε *hóde* in the Greek New Testament is a demonstrative pronoun only in the passage in (7a) and in the construction τάδε λέγει *táde légei* '[He] says these things' in Revelation. A Septuagint model can be traced in examples of the Septuagint that include the pronoun ὅδε *hóde*, as in the example in (7b).

(7)   a.   Koine Greek New Testament; Luke 10:39
　　　καὶ   τῇδε　　　　ἦν　　　　ἀδελφὴ　　　καλουμένη
　　　kaì   *têide*　　　　*hên*　　　*adelphḕ*　　*kalouménē*
　　　and this-one.DAT was.3SG sister.NOM.SG call.MP.PRTC NOM.SG
　　　μαριάμ
　　　mariám
　　　Mary.NOM
　　　'She had a sister called Mary.' (lit. 'to this one was a sister called Mary.')

　　　b.   LXX; Genesis 25:24
　　　καὶ   τῇδε　　　　ἦν　　　　δίδυμα　　　ἐν   τῇ
　　　kaì   *têide*　　　　*ên*　　　*dídyma*　　*en   têi*
　　　and this-one.DAT was.3SG twin.NOM.PL in ART.DAT.SG
　　　κοιλίᾳ　　　　αὐτῆς
　　　koilíai　　　　*autês*
　　　womb.DAT.SG her
　　　'There were twins in her womb.' (lit. 'to this one were twins in her womb.')

BIBLICAL TRANSLATIONS

According to Drinka (2011: 47; fn. 9), English translations also involve a "sacral stamp" of a different type:

> Note that English, too, partakes of the "sacral stamp", in elevating these familiar lines by means of archaic language, such as that found in the King James version: "My soul doth magnify the Lord/And my spirit hath rejoiced in God my Saviour."

To conclude, in this section, I have presented earlier studies which attempt to locate effects of biblical translations that may have influenced the development of grammatical characteristics of target languages. In the following section, I discuss examples of how a corpus of English biblical translations can reveal the relation between grammatical change and the development of grammatical characteristics in diachronic (re)translations.

3.3 English Biblical Translations: Examples of Corpus-Based Surveys

Previous studies have shown how a biblical corpus can serve as a source of evidence for the development of grammatical constructions and lexical features. In this section, I present the results of two relevant corpus studies, one dealing with changes in a morphosyntactic construction and one examining changes in lexical meaning. Various examples of the construction of *forbid* with a *that-clause* are attested in the diachrony of English. This construction was quite frequent before the late Middle English period (Iyeiri 2003) but is now fossilized in the pattern illustrated in (8).

(8) New English Bible; Genesis 44:17
   Joseph answered, 'God forbid that I should do such a thing!'

Iyeiri (2003) examines why *God forbid that* ... is still retained in English even though *that*-clauses cannot appear productively after *forbid* in other contexts (without "God" as the subject). The latest example of a *that-clause* selected by *forbid* is presented in (9), attested on the front matter of the Authorized Version (1611).

(9) Authorized Version; Front matter
   *We know that Sixtus Quintus expresly forbiddeth, **that** any varietie of readings of their vulgar edition, should be put in the margine ...*

The construction under investigation, *God forbid that* ..., is attested in the *Wycliffite Bible*, where it was equivalent of the Latin *absit* and had the function of an interjection, as is shown in (10a–b). *God forbid* was followed by *that*-clauses in other biblical translations; it was productively used in the other translations as an interjection as well, as is shown in (11).

(10) a. Vulgate; Romans 7:7
   *quid ergo dicemus? lex peccatum est? **absit**,*
   'What shall we say, then? Is the law sinful? Certainly not.'

b. John Wycliffe; Romans 7:7
   *The lawe is synne? **God forbede**.*

(11) William Tyndale; Genesis 4:7
   ***God forbydd that** thy servauntes shulde doo so*

God forbid that can be distinguished from other usages of *forbid* based on several characteristics: some of them are associated with the status of the former construction as a fixed phrase in translation. One such instance is the *expletive negation*—which is found in subordinate clauses selected by adversative verbs, such as *doubt, deny, forbid* in early English. This expletive negation turns out to be absent from the construction *God forbid* (Iyeiri 2003); see the examples in (12a, b).

(12) a. **Expletive negation:**
   Great Bible; Isaiah 5:6
   *I will also forbyd the cloudes that they shall **not** rayne vpon it*

b. ***God forbid:***
   Miles Coverdale; 1 Maccabees 9:10
   *And Iudas sayde: **God forbyd**, that we shulde fle from them*
   (Iyeiri 2003)

God forbid that is attested in fixed phrases where the complementizer directly followed the main verb. In other contexts, *forbid* and the *that*-clause could be separated by an indirect object or by other elements. Moreover, *God forbid* did not appear with non-finite complements—in contrast to *forbid* which could select non-finite complements, with an increased frequency from the late Middle English period.

In a similar manner, the English translations of the New Testament can provide evidence, for instance, of differences between the conceptual world of Modern English and 17th-century English, and may also reveal important aspects in historical semantics. For example, according to Wierzbicka (2006, 2012), a comparison of English biblical translations uncovers a change in language use, where faith, truth and certainty are replaced by doubt, facts and evidence. Wierzbicka associates a change from *verily* to *truly* in the text of translations to the fact that *verily* became archaic by the mid of the 20th century. According to Bromhead (2009), for instance, the Authorized Version includes both *verily* and *truly*. The non-usage of *verily* marks the end of a period that underscored faith, truth and certainty and the transition to a language that emphasizes doubts and empirical aspects (Wierzbicka 2006, 2012). The transition can also be seen in the change in the meaning of the verb *suppose*. Note that *truly* was also replaced in later translations by expressions marking a higher degree of uncertainty, such as *probably* and the new *I suppose*, or *really* and *in fact* (Wierzbicka 2012).

In addition, according to Wierzbicka (2006, 2012), the shift away from orality in English discourse led to a shift from spoken to written style in biblical English translations. It has been argued that Modern English discourse shows a lower degree of orality than the discourse of other European languages. For instance, the New King James Version (1982), which was otherwise compiled with the aim to remain close to the King James Version/ Authorized Version, did not retain the repetition of *verily*—which is reminiscent of a Hebraic *cognate object construction* (see Gianollo & Lavidas 2013 on the function of focused adverbials, such as the adverbial *verily*). The New King James Version preferred the expression *most assuredly, I say to you*, which clearly demonstrates the results of a tendency against orality (Wierzbicka 2006, 2012).

Moreover, the Authorized Version and the New Revised Standard Version reflect different assumptions on interpersonal relations. For instance, the two translations differ in the way they present Paul's attitude to his addressees (Wierzbicka 2012). In this respect, the New Revised Standard Version replaced phrases such as *I beseech you* of the Authorized Version with modern phrases such as *I urge you, I appeal to you*. In a similar way, the New Revised Standard Version replaced the verb *command* with *direct*, as well as the verb *exhort* with *urge*, as in (13a, b).

(13) a. New Revised Standard Version [NRSV]; 1 Corinthians 1:10
    *Now I **appeal** to you, brothers and sisters*

   b. King James/ Authorized Version; 1 Corinthians 1:10
    *... I **beseech** you, brethren*
    (Wierzbicka 2012: 440)

All the above-mentioned changes are related to a significant increase in the productivity of speech act verbs in Modern English. Wierzbicka proposes that the development of these verbs is associated with aspects of cultural history: For instance, the loss of performative constructions, such as *I pray you* or *I beg you* (meaning 'I ask you'), and the rise of the interrogative phrases *could you do it?* are related to the rise of the "value of personal autonomy". The new speech act verbs, *urge, suggest, appeal, direct, insist*, as well as the extension of causative constructions, manifest similar developments (Wierzbicka 2006: Ch. 6).

The above-described tendencies are also related to the process of incorporation of writing into the modern English culture. The development of numerous speech act verbs and the use of a part of them performatively, for instance: *I object, I argue, I suggest*, emphasizes the written character of Modern English. This written character of Modern English can also be evidenced by the fact that new speech act verbs appear in the New Revised Standard Version (mainly) and the Revised Standard Version, in contrast to what is attested in the Authorized Version. This tendency differentiates English from other European languages that did not show a similar development in their modern biblical translations (Wierzbicka 2006, 2012, see also Parsons & Hanks 2001).

The above-mentioned changes can be accounted for as involving in a broad tendency towards a [+written character] of English or as a gradual predominance of a written English variety on the language in general. In many cases of diglossia or multiglossia which also involve predominance of *written character-istics* and *archaisms*, one may observe the emergence of a "mixed" language too: the recent example of purified Greek/ *katharevusa*, vernacular Greek/ *dimotiki* and "mixed" Greek evidences the emergence and development of these varieties. "Mixed" languages, in general, are of significance with regard to my main hypothesis: the coexistence of grammars and the contact between the coexistent grammars, even in the same speaker, is apparent in the presence of "mixed" varieties/languages—as reflected in "mixed" grammatical characteristics—even with the same speaker.

My main hypothesis is the following: *in any account of grammatical change, we should take into consideration the contact between parallel grammars and transfer (change) in each of the parallel grammars due to the above-mentioned contact*; starting with Kroch's (1989, 2001) and Roeper's (1999, 2016) idea of parallel antagonistic grammars (in cases of transitional periods) and universal bilingualism, I claim that any explanation of grammatical change should involve parallel coexistent, in-contact grammars that allow transfer of grammatical properties from one coexistent grammar to the other. I name the above-described situation *grammatical multiglossia*. In the following chapter, I focus on examples of intralinguistic translations and their characteristics: I compare intralinguistic and interlinguistic translations and show how and when language contact is also involved in cases of intralinguistic translations.

CHAPTER 4

Intralingual Translations: Two Directions—to the Past or to the Present

4.1 Introduction

Jakobson (1959) distinguishes three types of translations: (i) *intralingual translation or rewording*: the same language is involved in the source and target language; (ii) *interlingual translation or translation proper*: the target is different than the source language; (iii) *intersemiotic translation or transmutation*: this involves non-verbal sign systems.[1]

Intralingual translation, which is directly related to the diachrony of a language, describes the transfer of a text within one language due to the fact that the development of this language can be divided into two or more periods, for instance, ancient and modern. Translation can make communication between these periods of the diachrony of the language possible (Maronitis 1997, 2001; Mossop 2016).

Intralingual translation has inherited problems and dilemmas from interlingual translation: studies on intralingual translation refer to the issue of (un)translatability of classical and sacred tests, or to the issue of a (non-)antagonistic relation between the target and source languages, among others. Both Steiner (1975) and Even-Zohar (1990) suggest that any linguistic problem that is implicit in interlingual translation is already implicit in all relevant intralingual discourse. However, in general, intralingual translation is less thoroughly researched (Baker 2009 / 1998: xvii; Zethsen 2009).

According to the polysystem theory and analyses of literary translation (Shavit 1986; Even-Zohar 1990; Weissbrod 1998, 2004), translation is a type

---

1 See Jakobson (1959: 232):

   We distinguish three ways of interpreting a verbal sign: it may be translated into other signs of the same language, into another language, or into another, nonverbal system of symbols. These three kinds of translation are to be differently labeled:

   1. Intralingual translation or rewording is an interpretation of verbal signs by means of other signs of the same language.
   2. Interlingual translation or translation proper is an interpretation of verbal signs by means of some other language.
   3. Intersemiotic translation or transmutation is an interpretation of verbal signs by means of signs of nonverbal sign systems.

© KONINKLIJKE BRILL NV, LEIDEN, 2022 | DOI:10.1163/9789004503564_005

of transfer and the main focus of the relevant research should be on the transfer from one culture to another. Weissbrod (2004) argues that transfer is the same mechanism in all types of translation. In the case of intralingual translation, the source text can be written in an earlier period of the same language—and, hence, the translation is *purely intralingual*, or the source text can be both the original text, written in another language, and earlier (translated) versions written in the same language. In such cases, the translation involves characteristics of both an intralingual and an interlingual translation.

In Part 2 of this book, which contains a discussion of corpus surveys of English and Greek biblical and non-biblical translations, I include many similar cases of translations where the source text can be an original text, for instance, in Greek or Latin, but also earlier translated versions of an original text. Hence, it is evident that (re)translations can be the result of a complex process that involves many factors.

4.2 Intralingual Translations as Evidence of Grammatical Change

As already stated, the aims of the present book are twofold; I analyze the development of grammatical characteristics of (re)translations, recognizing two significant directions and areas of research:

(i) Translations seen as a source of grammatical change—even though, my hypothesis is that the relation between grammatical change and translations is a complex one that involves multiple parallel grammars and contact and transfer between these grammars.

(ii) Translations also seen as evidence of grammatical change (cf., among others, Muchnik 2003; Hatim & Munday 2004; Thim-Mabrey 2006; Denton 2007).

I follow these twofold aims and directions of research, both in the case of exploration of interlingual and intralingual translations.

Several studies on intralingual translation refer to modern versions of classical literary works but recently also even to newer versions of, for instance, medical documents that have a lay readership as target. However, Mossop (2016) underlines that *dialect rewording* or updating of a text is a case of intralingual translation in contrast to texts prepared for lay readerships based on a source text. For instance, a translation of a Shakespearean work into Modern English is an example of a dialect rewording, as shown in (14) below, here cited from Mossop (2016: 5–6).

(14) **Translation**; Twelfth Night: A Verse Translation, Translated by Kent Rich-
mond, Full Measure Press, 2004
I sense a decent man inside you, captain.
And although nature often hides what's foul
Behind a lovely wall, I can have faith
That you, sir, have a mind that matches well
This fair and outward character I see.
Source; *Twelfth Night*, Act 1, Scene 2 (written about 1600-1602)
There is a fair behavior in thee, captain;
And though that nature with a beauteous wall
Doth oft close in pollution, yet of thee
I will believe thou hast a mind that suits
With this thy fair and outward character.

The above example presents a case of intralingual translation: the target text is
written in a different variety than the source text. Most L1 speakers of Modern
English cannot understand the passage in the source text or may misunder-
stand some of its aspects. The important question that arises concerns whether
the process of translation and the translated texts in the case of intralingual
rewording and interlingual translation differ from each other (see also above,
Section 2.3.5). Mossop (2016) uses the parallelism of translations with monolingual and bilingual speakers to show that there should be no additional mechanisms in the case of one or the other type of translation: as bilinguals may
switch languages, monolingual speakers may switch registers (Paradis 1998).
Accordingly, bilinguals can translate from the one language they speak to the
other—and, in a similar way, monolinguals can paraphrase a clause from one
register into another. There is no necessity, then, to assume additional neural
mechanisms that are specific to bilinguals (Paradis 1998: 422–423).

4.3 Types of Greek Intralingual Translations

(i) Intralingual translations in the context of Greek antiquity, Byzantium and Atticism

The necessity for intralingual translations emerges when the language of a literary work becomes non-understandable due to its early linguistic features or its
intense dialectic character. Already in the classical era, this need took the form
of interpretive comments on difficult words. One clear example is the passage
from Aristophanes' *Daitaleis*, where a person, probably the father, asks another,

probably his son, for an explanation of difficult Homeric words (*Ομήρου γλώτ-τας / Homérou glóttas*), referring to non-understandable passages from the *Iliad* and the *Odyssey* (Polkas 2006).

Plato in *Respublica* also presents examples of paraphrases of passages in the *Iliad*, whereas Democritus comments on idiomatisms and archaisms in the epic works in his text *On Homer, or on Correct Diction and Words* [*Περί Ὁμήρου ἢ Ὀρθοεπείης καὶ γλωσσέων / Perì Homérou è orthoepeíēs kaì glōsséōn*]. Accordingly, the first evidence of intralingual translations can be seen in the spread of annotations, notes and exegetical works, as well as in later dictionaries. All these types of intralingual translations were met with disapproval by the Atticism movement, which clearly distinguished between the prestige of Ancient Greek and, especially, the Attic dialect, as the early model of language, and the vernacular language of the period (see Montanari 1991; Remediaki 2013; Lianeri 2014).

In the Hellenistic period, philologists of Alexandria, following the Atticism movement, did not favor translations but included interpretations and comments on rare words in their work: for instance, Philitas of Cos and Simias of Rhodes (ca. 300 BC) prepared collections of epic and regional dialectal glosses. Moreover, Aristophanes of Byzantium wrote on *Περὶ τῶν ὑποπτευομένων μὴ εἰρῆ-σθαι τοῖς παλαιοῖς* [*Perì tôn hypopteuoménōn mè eirêsthai toîs palaioîs* 'About the words that we suspect our ancestors did not use'] and Crates of Mallos on Attic glosses (Kakridis 1971; Polkas 2006).

Atticism did not favor translations in Byzantium either. The idea of imitation of Ancient Greek models determined the production of written texts of the period. In this respect, Byzantine scholars continued the tradition of Alexandrian scholars and replaced other translation practices with imitation and copying and, less frequently, with paraphrases. Among others, Quintus of Smyrna, 4th cent., in his work *The Posthomerica—or sequel to Homer*, [*Τα μεθ' Ὅμηρον ἢ Παραλειπόμενα του Ομήρου*], an epic work in 14 books and 8,769 exameter verses, attempted to complete Homer's *Iliad* and to connect the *Iliad* with the *Odyssey*. Michael Psellos, 11th cent., prepared a paraphrase of the *Iliad* in prose. Ioannes Tzetzes, 12th cent., in his works *Events before Homer, Events in Homer, and Events after Homer* [*Τὰ πρὸ Ὁμήρου, Τὰ Ὁμήρου, Τὰ μεθ' Ὅμηρον*], *Theogony* [*Θεογονία*] and *Verse-Chronicle* [*Ἔμμετρη Χρονικὴ Βίβλος*] included paraphrases with allegoric interpretations of myths and metrical comments (Polkas 2006).

Hence, Atticism did not allow the translation of Ancient Greek works into later Greek but also required the translation of later Greek texts into Ancient Greek. Further relevant examples are the following: Apollinarius of Laodicea (310–390) adapted the New Testament in the form of Platonic dialogues.

Empress Eudocia (400–460) translated the Old Testament books into Homeric Greek verses. Nonnos, 5th cent., translated the Gospel of John into Homeric Greek, and Symeon Metaphrastes, 10th cent., added archaic elements to lives of saints and to books of martyrs, which were originally written in the vernacular variety (Varmazis 2006).

However, the opposite tendency is also attested in various cases and early texts were translated into the vernacular language. In the late Byzantine and late Medieval-early Modern Greek period,[2] when grammatical change resulted in further differences between Ancient Greek and the spoken language of the period, several paraphrases of histories and chronographies appeared. A characteristic example is Manuel Chartophylax' translation of Flavius Josephus' *Antiquities of the Jews* and *War of the Jews* (probably in the 16th cent.; Polkas 2006). Manuel Chartophylax is also considered to be the translator of Zonaras' Chronicle. Moreover, during the last Byzantine centuries, Paleologean scholars attempted to translate ancient texts into a "simpler" language as a part of their philological activities: among others, Maximos Planoudes, Manuel Moschopoulos, Demetrios Triklinios, Theodoros Metochites belong to this group of scholars (Varmazis 2006).

After the fall of Constantinople, the influence of the Italian Renaissance—through the immigrants to Venice, following the model of European scholars who translated classical texts into their new national languages—changed the status of the vernacular language and resulted in translations of important ancient Greek works: these translations include Nikolaos Loukanis' translation of the *Iliad* (1526) and Nikolaos Sofianos' translation of (Pseudo-)Plutarch's *On the Training of Children* (1544) (Varmazis 2006; Maronitis 2008). The latter translation is the first translation of an Ancient Greek prose work into Modern Greek. Note that it was written by the author of the first Grammar of Modern Greek (cf. 2.2.2 and, among many others, Lauxtermann 2020). Other intralingual translations from the same period include Zenos' translation of *Batrachomyomachia/ Battle of the frogs and mice* [Βατραχομυομαχία] (1539) and Andronikos Noukios' translation of Aesop's fables (1543).

Within the context of religious humanism, which started with the Patriarch Cyril I Lucaris, Ioannikios Kartanos prepared The Old and New Testament in 1536 which is a translation of an Italian source text in most of its parts (Kakoulidi-Panou & Karantzola 2000) and Maximos Kallipolitis produced a translation of the New Testament (see Section 2.3.5). Kartanos' translation was considered as a heretical work but it was welcomed by readers and indeed

---

2 For a detailed analysis of the grammar of Early Modern Greek, see Holton et al. (2019).

initiated further translations of the Bible (Varmazis 2006; Maronitis 2008). In this respect, Kartanos started, and Cyril I Lucaris completed, the so called "ecclesiastical demoticism" or religious humanism—a movement that made important clerics appreciate the vernacular language of the period (see Section 2.3.5.2).

In the following decades, the interest in translation of classical texts increased, with the indicative examples of Dimitrios Katartzis (1730–1807) and Adamantios Korais (1748–1833). On the contrary, supporters of the archaism at the University of Athens and the Church again rejected in an extreme manner the emerging practice of intralingual translation of classical and religious/sacred works (Maronitis 2008). As already discussed above, examples of reaction against intralingual translations include the violent events related to Pallis' translations, that caused the *Evangelika* in 1901, and to Sotiriadis' translations, that caused the *Orestiaka* in 1903. The term *Evangelika* refers to the violent demonstrations, which claimed human lives, against Alexandros Pallis' translation of the New Testament (section 2.3.3). The term *Orestiaka* refers to similar reactions against a theatrical performance of Aeschylus' Oresteia in Georgios Sotiriadis' mixed-language translation.

(ii) Atticism. The opposite direction: Translations into earlier varieties

The overview of intralingual translation above provides evidence that Atticizing texts are probably the clearest example of a translation into the opposite direction, i.e. into an earlier variety of the language. Atticism refers to a movement of imitation of the language of Classical Athens that had a significant influence in particular in the second century AD.[3] Atticistic dictionaries retain characteristics that reflect, for instance, an archaizing pronunciation of Greek, which is in some cases conservative and in other cases even artificial. For instance, the distinctive vowel length is lost in the second century AD but appears in several Atticistic dictionaries. Linguistic Atticism reached its highest significance in the second century AD. Phrynichus and Moeris, in particular, prepared books of guidance on how to use the Classical Attic variety. Atticists proposed the re-introduction of the lost dual number, the optative mood, the use of the conjunction *hópōs* 'that', as a "replacement" of *hína*, and a more productive use of the middle voice (Kim 2010; Horrocks 2014: 99 ff.; Vessella

---

3 Schmid (1887–1897) was a pioneer in the analysis of Atticism; similar studies appeared recently again with, among others, Swain (1996), Whitmarsh (2005: 41–54), Kim (2010) and Bons & Joosten, eds, (2016).

2014, 2018, among others). Atticists have been characterized as "imitators" (von Wilamowitz-Möllendorff 1900), "a museum of fossils" (van Groningen 1965) and "antiquarians" (Horrocks 2014).

Atticism is an example of a diglossia situation (Ferguson 1959), because it is related to high and low registers which are used for different societal functions—in formal vs. colloquial contexts—and represent "moderately distinct" varieties of the same language (Kim 2010; see also above, 4.3 (i)). The differences between the two varieties can be traced if one compares Atticizing authors and characteristics of the Atticizing variety, as described in the second century Attic lexica, to texts which are written in the spoken Koine.

Atticism increased its influence during the second and third century AD, up to the period of the Second Sophistic (see, among others, the Atticists of the Second Sophistic period: Aelius Aristides, Herodes Atticus, Philostratus). By the second century AD, the tendency of imitation of Classical Attic had changed into a fully developed purist movement. Earlier studies have attempted to account for this change by referring to the influence of individuals, mainly, the influence of the Augustan grammarian Apollodorus and Herodes Atticus (Schmid 1887–1897; von Wilamowitz-Möllendorff 1900). However, recent studies support the idea of a gradual development of the movement during the first century AD (Swain 1996; Schmitz 1997). In the second century AD, a negative proscription of any post-classical or non-Attic element was dominant, whereas the Language Question became a central debate.

According to Horrocks (2014), Atticist writers did not try to recreate the Classical Attic dialect, but they used, and supported, a written style that was based on resources from the past (cf. also Lee 2013; Horrocks 2014: 141). The diglossia context of Hellenistic Greek resulted in a literary variety of Koine which was quite controversial: it was located *between* a "diluted variety of classical Attic" (Horrocks 2014: 96) and a literary version of Koine. Recall that, according to the main hypotheses of this book, grammars do not only coexist but there is also contact between grammars and transfer of grammatical properties from one grammar to the other, which in turn may also result in grammatical code-switching or mixing (see Section 6.2 below).

In the same period, one may observe the coexistence of Polybius' and Diodorus Siculus' language variety with the informal varieties found in private documents in papyri, namely the bureaucratic variety of chancelleries and varieties of scientific prose. Polybius shows many characteristics that are similar to the ones of technical prose—such as the productive presence of nominalizations (Adams 2013; Horrocks 2014; Bubenik & Crespo 2013). However, Polybius should be considered as a moderate Atticist, especially with regard to the use of the optative and the perfect and future participles. Related to this, Bubenik &

Crespo (2013) represent the status of the Greek language of the Roman period through a sociolinguistic pyramid where:

(i) the high variety is related to the literary standards of the 'pure' Attic, as used by the Atticists;

(ii) several more informal varieties of Koine could be found below this level: the language of the privileged classes, attested in scientific prose or administrative documents, reflects the 'high register'. The language of the less educated people of lower classes, attested in Christian works, private texts and papyri, represents the 'low register';

(iii) local dialects of the post-Christian centuries are located below the middle level, at the bottom of the sociolinguistic pyramid.

'Colloquial' literature (e.g., Epictetus' works and the New Testament) represents the 'low register' of Koine; it was written by speakers without a higher education. Norden (1958) suggests that the instances where Luke does not follow Mark's text first and foremost involve passages where Mark uses a construction or a word that was disfavored by the Atticists. Wifstrand (2005), however, rejects the idea that Luke tried to make his text more Attic in such cases. According to Wifstrand, not all of Luke's changes had the purpose to increase the classical features of the text. Moreover, it is anachronistic to name Luke as an Atticist—because the Atticist movement was not established until the 2nd century AD. The reason is probably Luke's cultivated written style, which stands in a stark contrast to Mark's style which represents the popular spoken variety. The educated written variety used by Luke is the one that directly continues the variety of the standard Hellenistic prose without any elements of classicism (Adams 2013).

Christian writers and Apostolic Fathers of the period of the 1st and 2nd century AD used the New Testament as their model. On the contrary, early on the higher clergy stopped using the low status variety of Hellenistic Greek, the one attested in the early Christian literature and in the New Testament, because they felt it important to use a variety acceptable to the educated pagans, who were now among the people listening to the teaching of Christianity (Adams 2013; Bubenik & Crespo 2013). In the 4th century AD, the Great Fathers of the eastern churches, Basil of Caesarea, Gregory of Nazianzus, Gregory of Nyssa, and John Chrysostom were using 'pure' Attic in their dogmatic and exegetic Christian works. In this manner, the morphosyntactic diglossia was strengthened and entered dynamically into the medieval linguistic situation of Byzantium.

As a part of practice of later/ Byzantine Atticism, saints' lives and martyrologies were translated into a higher status variety/ register—for instance, by Symeon Metaphrastes during the second half of the 10th century—and chronicles were written in a more learned variety of Greek. However, even Byzantine Atticists did not consider their work as Classical Attic writing but only as a part of a continuous classical tradition. For instance, Thomas Magister in the 14th century, who was an Atticist grammarian of a late period, continued the early tradition of Atticists and assisted Byzantine writers in their attempt to produce a language variety which had similarities with the Classical Attic variety (Horrocks 2014: 99 ff.; Adams 2013; Lee 2013).

Atticistic texts, and any attempt of translation into an earlier period of the language, illustrate—to an extreme degree—how speakers of a language can have negative attitudes towards grammatical change and may thus attempt to incorporate grammatical characteristics of an earlier period in their texts. In the following section (4.4), I briefly demonstrate how intralingual translations are related to retranslations; retranslations that appear in different periods translate a source text written in another language but are also based on, and influenced by, earlier translations of the source text into earlier forms of the same language. For intralingual translations, there is no source text in another language, and translations of this type are influenced by earlier translations of the text into the same language.

4.4 Retranslations and Their Relation to Intralingual Translations

(i) The Retranslation Hypothesis

Reasons for retranslations can be traced to the observation that translations "age", and this fact creates the need for new translations. Retranslations and revisions of biblical translations demonstrate how the vocabulary and the grammar represented in the translations become archaic and obsolete. For instance, Nevalainen (1999: 348) argues that the period of Early Modern English is long enough for even prestigious vocabulary to become obsolete and archaic.

According to Koskinen & Paloposki's *Retranslation Hypothesis*, first translations are more domesticating than retranslations (Koskinen & Paloposki 2003, 2010, 2015; Paloposki & Koskinen 2004, 2010). That is, first translations can be described as naturalization of the source text, a kind of introduction that integrates the source texts' culture into the target languages' culture (Bensimon 1990; see also Koskinen & Paloposki 2003 and Brownlie 2006.).[4] Later

---

4 According to Gürçağlar (2009: 233):
    The 'retranslation hypothesis' originated in an article written by the French translation

translations can, however, maintain the cultural distance. A first translation is more assimilating and attempts to reduce the otherness, whereas retranslations "would mark a *return* to the source-text" (Gambier 1994: 414; on retranslations, see, among many others, Du-Nour 1995; Kujamäki 2001; Oittinen 2002; Lefevere 2016). Moreover, according to Paloposki & Koskinen, the assimilating properties of first translations create the need for a source-oriented translation. Counter-examples, however, are related to second translations that appear to be more source-oriented than first translations.

Other scholars have argued that domesticating translations are only related to a characteristic of a certain phase in translated literature, and, therefore, one cannot support a basis for a hypothesis on common characteristics of retranslations (cf. Chesterman 2000). In addition, based on Lopes' (2006) and Kujamäki's (2001) findings, it appears that the strong version of the *Retranslation Hypothesis* does not suffice to cover the differences between retranslations. Rather, to account for retranslations, one should also examine translatorial styles and audiences, as well as general changes in translation norms. That is, not only the time or the order of publication form important factors for the characteristics of the retranslations, but also different audiences and translators constitute significant factors.

Marketing potential can also be another factor relevant for the need for retranslations (Gambier 1994; Vanderschelden 2000; Ballard 2000). However, a significant starting point in several studies on retranslation is the widespread idea that classics or great books "need" retranslation. Vanderschelden (2000: 1) argues that it is always a matter of time before a literary translation is replaced by a new one. Collombat (2004) also connects the tendency for retranslations to (i) translators' increased awareness of their task; and (ii) the *Narrative Theory*, according to which each translation can be seen as one version of one original text.

The contrast between reprints and retranslations is another important aspect of this discussion. This contrast is also linked to the costs of a retranslation, as well as to the choices of what to retranslate and what to reprint. The preferences depend on different profiles of publishers at different times, but young

---

scholar Antoine Berman in a special issue of the journal *Palimpsestes*. Speaking strictly of literary retranslations, Berman argued that translation is an 'incomplete' act and that it can only strive for completion through retranslations (1990: 1). The kind of completion Berman had in mind concerned the success of a translation in getting closer to the source text and in representing the encounter between the translator and the language of the original (ibid.: 3).

publishing houses without the stock to re-print tend to prefer the option of retranslation. It appears, therefore, that retranslations are inevitable to a certain degree (Weissbrod 2004).

I would like to stress here that I do not support the view which considers time as being the only factor for retranslations. Nevertheless, my aim is to evaluate the role of the parameter of time and its effects, among all other parameters. In other words, my aim is to identify the exact role of time and how the grammatical characteristics of different periods, are reflected in (re)translations.

(ii) Retranslations: The case of Boethius' *De Consolatione Philosophiae*

Nevalainen (2006: 24) presents the main features of *retranslations of Boethius' De Consolatione Philosophiae*: according to her, the fact that several retranslations of this work appeared within a period of two centuries may reflect a rapid pace of language change. Nevalainen also points out other possible reasons that may have triggered the retranslations, such as the Renaissance interest in classical texts and the introduction of the printing press. In Part 2, I discuss the results of my corpus surveys that examine Boethius' retranslations. See Sections 7.2 and 7.3.

Three Early Modern English translations of Boethius' *De Consolatione Philosophiae* are included in the Helsinki Corpus [HC]. See (15a–c) from Nevalainen (2006).

(15) a. Helsinki Corpus; George Colville (trans.), *Boethius*, 1556: 68
      Hetherto it suffyseth that I haue shewed the maner and forme, of false
      felicite or blessednes, which if thou beholdeste perfetlye, it restythe
      to declare from henceforthe, whyche is the very true felicitie.
      BOE: Truelye I do se, that ryches cannot be satisfied with suffysaunce,
      nor power wyth kyngedomes, nor reuerence with dygnities, not
      glory with nobilitie or gentles, nor myrth with pleasures.
    b. Helsinki Corpus; Elizabeth I (trans.), *Boethius*, 1593: 57–58
      'Hitherto hit sufficeth to shewe the forme of gileful felicitie, wiche if
      you Clirely beholde, the ordar than must be to shewe you the true.'
      'Yea I se,' quoth I, 'that ynough suffiseth not riches, nor Power kingdomes,
      nor honor dignities, nor glory the prising, nor Joy the pleasure.'
    c. Helsinki Corpus; Richard Preston (trans.), *Boethius*, 1695: 124
      Let it suffice that I have hitherto described the Form of counterfeit
      Happiness: So that if thou considerest well, my Method will lead me
      to give to thee a perfect Draught of the true.
      Boet. I now see plainly that Men cannot arrive at a full Satisfaction by

> *Riches, nor at Power by enjoying Principalities or Kingdoms, nor at*
> *Esteem and Reverence by the Accession of Dignities, nor at Nobility*
> *by Glory, nor at true Joy by carnal Pleasures.*
> (Nevalainen 2006: 25)

According to the passages in (15), a number of words are attested in all three translations, for instance, *riches*, *power*, *kingdoms*, *dignities*, *glory*, and *pleasure(s)*. However, there are differences in lexical preferences in several instances. For example, in Colville's translation, *felicite* or *blessednes* are used, in Elizabeth's translation *felicitie* is used, while in Preston's translation the word *happiness* is used in the same context (Partridge 1973; Nevalainen 2006).

Native English words are derived with the ending -*ness*, while the word *felicity* with the suffix -*ity* is a Middle English loanword from French (see Section 7.4). Elizabeth uses *felicity* in her translation and only rarely *blessedness* and *happiness*. This shows that there is a gradual replacement of *blessedness*, with a religious origin, by *felicity*, as the equivalent of the Latin *felicitas* (see also Fischer 1979; Koivisto-Alanko 1997; Rissanen 1997; Breul 1999; Aschenbrenner 2014; Kaylor 2015).

Nevalainen (2006) provides another example of a comparison of retranslations which is based on the characteristics of negation in two translations of Boethius' text: namely Chaucer's 14th century's and Richard Preston's 17th century's version. With regard to negation, Chaucer uses *ne*, *not* and *no* in passages where Preston prefers the negative coordinating conjunction *neither ... nor* and the non-assertive *any*, as is shown in (16a–b) from Nevalainen (2006): 112.

(16) a. Helsinki Corpus; Geoffrey Chaucer (transl.), *Boethius*, 1380s: 433.C2
   *Thanne is sovereyn good the somme and the cause of al that oughte ben desired; forwhy thilke thing that withholdeth **no** good in itselve, **ne** semblance of good, it **ne** mai **not** wel in **no** manere be desired **ne** requerid.*

   b. Helsinki Corpus; Richard Preston (transl.), *Boethius*, 1695: 139
   *Good then, is the Cause why all things are desired; for that which **neither** in Reality **nor** Shew doth retain **any** thing of Good, is by **no** means to be desired [...]*

In Chapter 4, I presented the main characteristics of intralingual translations and how they are related to the diachrony of language. Moreover, I discussed the similarities and differences between intralingual and interlingual translations. Intralingual translations can function as evidence of grammatical change (Section 4.2), similarly to the way retranslations of a foreign source text can offer data on grammatical change. I examined the main types of Greek intralingual translations (Section 4.3) and significant examples of intralingual translations in the Greek antiquity and Byzantium. In addition, Atticism provides examples of the opposite direction, that is intralingual translations into earlier varieties of Greek. I further analyzed the main similarities between retranslations and intralingual translations and the *Retranslation Hypothesis* that compares the first translation of a foreign text to its later translations into the same target language (Section 4.4). Nevalainen (2006) offers a classic study on the comparison of English retranslations of the same source text. In the following chapter (Chapter 5), I present further examples of changes in the history of English being examined in previous studies as related to (re)translations: (re)translations provide evidence of the particular changes, or, in other cases, written language contact through translation has been considered as having triggered the particular changes.

CHAPTER 5

Examples of Studies on Grammatical Change in English through Translations

5.1 Introduction

In this chapter, I discuss indicative examples—and not an exhaustive presentation—of changes in the diachrony of English being analyzed in previous studies as related to (re)translations. According to these studies, (re)translations provide evidence of the changes described below (Section 5.2) or, in other cases, the particular changes have been analyzed as a result of written language contact through translation (Section 5.3). The examples in this chapter derive only from studies on English because there are no studies focusing on the diachronic aspects of written language contact in Greek. My data in Part 2 of this book attempt to cover this gap.

5.2 Translations and Multilingualism in the History of English

Several studies have examined infinitives in the history of English in relation to translations and influence from other languages—in particular, Latin (cf. 2.1.2). The rise of the accusativus-cum-infinitivo (AcI) constructions with the causative *(ge)dōn* 'do, make'—see the example in (17a)—and the rise of the *to*-INF(infinitive) construction with *(ge)dōn*—see the example in (17b)—have also been considered in earlier studies both as resulting from Latin influence, and as development of native English (Timofeeva 2010, 2011b).

(17) a. ÆCHom i [Ælfric's Catholic Homilies I] 468.21
    *þu dydest minne broðer his god **forlætan***
    you did   my.ACC brother his god forsake.INF
    'You made my brother forsake his god.'

   b. ChronE [Anglo-Saxon Chronicle E (Peterborough Chronicle)] 1128.10
    *He dide ðone king **to understanden***

Analyses that favor a Latin influence base their argumentation on evidence from Old English translations, which used the construction *(ge)dōn + infini-*

© KONINKLIJKE BRILL NV, LEIDEN, 2022 | DOI:10.1163/9789004503564_006

tive to translate the Latin AcI constructions with the causative *facere* 'make'. However, analyses that support an explanation related to the development of English (internal change) have located the source of the rise of this construction in the argument structure of *(ge)dōn*. The latter verb could be used (i) as a three-place verb with *to*-VP complements and a 'give/ grant' interpretation (cf. Vázquez-González & Barðdal 2019: 610), and (ii) as a two-place verb with *AcI* and *that*-clauses and a 'make' interpretation.

Timofeeva (2010, 2011b) presents a detailed analysis of the development of these constructions in English. She compares Old English translations to their Latin source, and finds all possible translations of the *facere-AcI* constructions into Old English. She also collects all occurrences of the constructions under examination in non-translated texts and in the *Dictionary of Old English Corpus* (*DOEC*) (all attestations of *(ge)dōn*). In addition, she conducts corpus surveys in the electronic database of the *Fontes Anglo-Saxonici* [A Register of Written Sources Used by Authors in Anglo-Saxon England—https://www.st-andrews .ac.uk/~cr30/Mercian/Fontes]. Timofeeva (2010) shows that an intermediate category of texts are neither typical translations, in that they do not refer to one particular source text, nor are they original Old English texts, as they exhibit similarities to Latin texts. Timofeeva documents that the construction *(ge)dōn* + *AcI* followed Latin in broad terms.

However, Timofeeva questions the use of the term "syntactic borrowing" here because of the type of contact between English and Latin in the Old English period when oral contact between Latin and English was limited. The acquisition of literary competence in Latin (as L2) concerned only people who could acquire Latin through studying, copying or glossing Latin texts. Even though L2 Latin could be promoted through school, it was still restricted to religion (Timofeeva 2010, 2011b). According to Timofeeva, this fact can have as a consequence that the results of language contact are only restricted in the lexical domain—whereas grammatical borrowing does not appear to be very plausible. Hence, a Latin effect on causative constructions should mainly be confined to the small group of bilingual speakers of Latin and English; it can also influence other communities of speakers but to a limited degree.

Timofeeva's explanation is based on Heine & Kuteva's (2005) approach to syntactic borrowing. According to Heine & Kuteva's model (see also Section 1.3), syntactic borrowing should be analyzed as a process of grammatical replication that includes several stages. Contact-induced grammaticalization is related to frequency and context factors in its earlier stages. In the first stages, when the replica unit is pragmatically marked, the term *use pattern*— and not *category*—should be used. *Contact situations* make *replicated/ new use patterns*—as well as *native minor use patterns*—less marked and, therefore, more frequent. Accordingly, for Timofeeva, the contrast between categorial structures and discourse-based structures is important for the examination of Old English. With written contact, the translation-induced grammaticalization is triggered through mechanisms of grammatical replication and results in *new translation patterns*, which will or will not lead to the rise of *full-fledged categories*.

Koller (1998) underscores the contrast between use patterns and category patterns in his work on the role of translation in the diachrony of German. According to his analysis, the influence of translation can be located both in changes in the linguistic system (*Systeminnovationen*) and in changes in particular registers, in either the norm or the style (see also above, Section 1.2.2). Accordingly, changes in norm and style, that is, new minor use patterns, can also develop into changes in the system, that is, into new categories.

Earlier studies have shown that, for the rise of a new category, both contact-induced and translation-induced innovations require prolonged and intense contact or a long and continuous translation tradition. As discussed above, it seems that these prerequisites hold true for the development of the Old English (*ge*)*dōn* + *AcI* construction only to a limited degree. Timofeeva (2011b) suggests that the above observations (by Heine & Kuteva) can explain glosses, translations and written Old English, if analyzed as *translation patterns that changed into minor use patterns*. However, Timofeeva rejects the hypothesis of further development in the domain of categories (system of the language).

According to Heine & Kuteva (2005), if some speakers regularly translate category "Mx" of the source language with category "Rx" of the target language, these two languages show a *translational equivalence*. However, this type of equivalence is not related to the structure of the categories (see also Section 1.2). In other words, the translational equivalence is not necessarily linked to a structural equivalence between Rx and Mx. According to Timofeeva's (2011b) study, *facere* + *AcI* had several translation equivalents in Old English:

(i)   (*ge*)*don*-AcI;
(ii) (*ge*)*don-that*-clause;
(iii) *hatan/ lǣtan*-AcI;
(iv) morphological causatives.

A repeated and frequent translation of the same Mx may result in a translation use pattern, that is, in a new convention. The new pattern may spread from translated to original texts that belong to the same register or text type. Timofeeva (2011b) considers this type of spread very plausible for the situation of Old English because most of the text types of Old English imitated the corresponding text types of Latin. She argues that early Old English—except for the case of glosses—showed a preference for the (*ge*)*dōn-that*-clause construction; in late Old English, both (*ge*)*don-that*-clause and (*ge*)*don*-AcI constructions were attested in texts that had characteristics of both translations and native Old English texts.

In this respect, Timofeeva (2011b) proposes a *translation-induced interference* approach, instead of a syntactic borrowing analysis: Old English speakers learned the construction/category *facere*+AcI of Latin through reading and translating Latin texts. They produced two translational equivalents for this construction/category: (*ge*)*don-that*-clause and (*ge*)*don*+AcI. These translational equivalents changed into translation patterns in a later stage.

5.3 Grammatical Characteristics and the Effect of Other Languages in the Diachrony of English

The following grammatical characteristics and constructions have also been examined in earlier studies in direct connection to (re)translations in the history of English.

(*i*) *Agreement and morphosyntax*
Variation in the usage of suffixes -*th* and -*s* could appear in the 16th century in the same text. For instance, this is the case with Elizabeth's translation of *Boethius* (circa 1590), as presented in (18) from Lass (1999: 162–163).

(18) Elizabeth's *Boethius*; Book 0, Prose IX; Pemberton 1899
   *He that seek**ith** riches by shunning penury, nothing car**ith** for powre, he chos**ith** rather to be meane & base, and withdrawe**s** him from many naturall delytes ... But that waye, he hath not ynogh, who leue**s** to haue, & greue**s** in woe, whom neerenes ouerthrowe**s** & obscurenes hyde**s**. He that only desyre**s** to be able, he throwe**s** away riches, despis**ith** pleasures, nought esteem**s** honour nor glory that powre want**ith**.*

According to Lass (1999: 163 ff.) in a sample of the above translation (Proses IV, VI, IX–XII), the results show 68.8 % of presence of the suffix -*s* in contrast to 31.2 % of presence of -*th*. The verbs *have* and *do* manifest a different distribution: there are 10 usages of *hath* and only one of *has*, whereas *doth* is found in all 16 occurrences of third singular uses of 'do'. It appears that the new -*s* was frequent but had not yet replaced the old -*th*. The verbs *do* and *have* followed this tendency with a delay.

Accordingly, it appears that the grammatical properties of translated texts may function, in some periods, similarly to grammatical properties of earlier forms of the language, which are more accepted or prestigious, and are in contact with the contemporary grammar of the language. In this respect, translation leads to a type of diglossia—which shows that language always develops through coexistence of parallel grammars and contact between parallel grammars. Hence, in cases where diglossia and contact do not involve an earlier variety of the same language, they may still involve grammatical characteristics of translated texts.

Early English provides examples of contact between a "translated language" and the contemporary language; in the history of Greek, as documented in the available surviving texts, the examples of contact between the earlier forms of the language and the contemporary language prevail, whereas, in cases like with the Atticism movement, the opposite direction is also possible, the translated language includes a significant number of earlier characteristics rather than many instances of newer forms or constructions.

(*ii*) Datives

An influence from French, where the indirect object is marked by a preposition, can explain characteristics that appear, for instance, in the *Aȝenbite of Inwit*, completed in 1340, by Dan Michel of Northgate, a Benedictine monk. *Aȝenbite* shows signs of transfer from French even in its syntax and is a rather close translation of the French source text. However, there is no agreement among scholars on how significant the French influence was on the spoken language regarding the change in the *to-datives* (Allen 1999: 214–215).

(*iii*) Passives

Furthermore, an examination of the scientific text *The Cyrurgie of Guy de Chauliac* (14th century) indicates a higher frequency of passives than actives in this text, which can also be explained through the fact that this text is a translation from Latin (Kytö 1991). This text has been described as far removed from the typical English characteristics of this period (Donner 1986).

(*iv*) Word order

Pintzuk (2005) also examines the influence of Latin source texts on the object position in Old English translations. Her hypothesis is that target texts would show a higher frequency of OV orders than non-translated Old English texts in instances where there is a close translation of the source text. Pintzuk's analysis is a multivariate analysis investigating the influence of Latin on I-final structures (where the verb follows its complements), as one of the possible factors that may have a significant effect on the position of positive nominal objects in Old English clauses with auxiliary verbs. On the contrary, according to Pintzuk's results, clause type and date of composition are factors that may favor I-initial clauses; the length of the object as well as the case of the object can favor either I-initial or I-final clauses.

Wood (2007) shows how the possessive-first construction differentiates from the *demonstrative-first construction* on the basis of a comparison between versions C (Corpus Christi College, Cambridge 322) and H (Bodleian Library, Hatton 76 fols. 1–54) of Pope Gregory's *Dialogues*. Bishop Wærferth of Worcester translated the C version in the 9th century from Latin into English. H is a revision written 100–150 years later with modifications in syntax, vocabulary, and spelling (cf., among others, Yerkes 1982).

(*v*)   *Auxiliaries*

In the domain of auxiliary verbs, it has been argued that the contrast between *will* for volitionally marked future and *shall* for unmarked future has its basis in the Wycliffite biblical translation (see, among others, Strang 1970). However, the above explanation may refer only to a part of the characteristics of these verbs and only to an aspect of their development. According to Rissanen (1985), for instance, *will* developed in colloquial language as an example of a change from below,[1] and later than *shall*.

Moreover, several studies have supported a causative origin of *do*. According to this hypothesis, the causative use of *do* first appears in translations from Latin or in formal and literary contexts. In addition, Terasawa (1985) compares eight biblical translations, from the *West Saxon Gospels* to the *New English Bible*, as a part of his exploration of the development of the causative *make*. The verb *make* developed a use involving three-place construction, that is, an agentive causative—in addition to the initial two-place construction that was purely causative.

Several studies have also shown that perfects of deponents in Latin source texts were often translated with progressives in Old English (Wülfing 1894/1897). The above observation has been considered an evidence in favor of a Latin influence on the English progressive (Denison 1993; Mair & Leech 2006). Jespersen (1940:177) uses biblical translations from various stages of the English diachrony as parallel historical corpora: among other features, he shows a significant increase in the presence of progressives from late Middle English onwards.

---

1 Labov characterized change from below as "systematic changes that appear first in the vernacular and represent the operation of internal, linguistic factors"; it concerns changes that occur below the level of social awareness (Labov 1994: 78).

A similar case is the usage of the progressive to translate the Latin construction ESSE + future participle. According to Mosse (1938) the progressive emerged in interlinear glossing to replace Latin forms that did not have a corresponding form in Old English. For instance, it replaced:

(i) the perfect tense of deponent verbs;
(ii) ESSE 'be' + future participle;
(iii) the appositive present participle;
(iv) ESSE 'be' + present participle.

The English constructions that replaced the Latin ones became a characteristic of a learned translation style and retained their status until the 20th century. The influence of the Vulgate (see Sections 2.1.1 and 3.3), with the frequent use of the construction ESSE + present participle, resulted in a presence of the progressive in the *West Saxon Gospels* as a *calque* of the Latin construction. However, for Nickel (1966), the progressive was not frequent before the late Middle English period, and, therefore, the role of interlinear translations and glosses in the rise of the progressive has probably been exaggerated.

Scheffer (1975: 131–273) also argues that, even though the progressive is common in translations from Latin and not frequent in poetry, this is not proof of a Latin origin. Scheffer's comparison concerns progressives in the early Wærferth's translation of *Gregory's Dialogues* to progressives in the later version. His argument against the Latin influence is based on the fact that source texts may include frequent progressive-inducing forms that are not translated with a progressive in the Old English texts, and that progressives in Old English can be used in several contexts independently of Latin. Scheffer's conclusion is that the progressive was a native construction reinforced by translations from Latin in written Old English (Kilpiö 1989).

CHAPTER 6

From *Syntactic Diglossia* and *Universal Bilingualism* to What Diachronic Translations Can Tell Us about *Grammatical Multiglossia*

6.1   A Theoretical Proposal: *Grammatical Multiglossia*

Grammatical change can be seen as the result of a failure in the transmission of grammar across time. Even though there is no consensus on whether failure in the transmission of grammar is the only source of grammatical change, most would agree that it is one of the most important reasons of change indeed. The failure of transmission of grammar can be triggered by the type of evidence available to the learner or by the age of the learner, for instance, in the context of language contact and change through L2 acquisition (Kroch 1989, 2001). There is a consensus, even in different theoretical models, that language contact is a significant actuating force for grammatical change.[1] For instance, one of the most well-known examples of grammatical change through contact concerns the loss of the infinitive in the Balkan languages (cf., among others, Joseph 1983a). This example derives from a genetically diverse Sprachbund, where Greek, various Slavic languages, a Romance language and Albanian were in contact for centuries. In the case of English diachrony, Middle English, for instance, demonstrates significant contact effects between native English and Scandinavian, caused through the Viking invasions of the 9th and 10th centuries. There is, though, a debate about the exact type of influence of the Scandinavian dialects on English (Jespersen 1962 [1905]; Thomason & Kaufman 1988; Kroch, Taylor & Ringe 2000—Emonds & Faarlund 2014).

In contrast, two significant challenges to theories of grammar have their source in historical linguistic data: the first one concerns the (apparent) optionality of grammatical rules and features; the other one relates to instances of gradualness in grammatical change. Gradualness appears to be a significant challenge to linguistic theories in several cases of change, such as in the well-

---

1   Cf. Longobardi (2001) who assumes in his *Inertial Theory* that grammatical change must have its causes in external factors because, in any other case, it should, ideally, not happen at all. Weerman (1993) and Kroch & Taylor (1997: 318) also support the view that the source of grammatical change can be located in the input children may receive from L2 learners "with an imperfect command" of the L2.

© KONINKLIJKE BRILL NV, LEIDEN, 2022 | DOI:10.1163/9789004503564_007

known example of the emergence of the auxiliary *do* in English. Other examples of gradualness in earlier studies concern the loss of verb second (V2 / a requirement that the verb should be in second position) in English (Kroch 1989), and the change from verb-final to verb-medial word order in Old English and Ancient Greek (Taylor 1994, Pintzuk 1995). According to van Kemenade (2007), grammatical change is characterized through gradualness, diffuseness and optionality.

Kroch (1989; 2001) proposes a model of grammar competition, according to which transition stages reflect the coexistence of more than one grammar—*syntactic diglossia*—and a competition between these grammars, namely the *Competing Grammars Hypothesis* or the *Hypothesis of Internalized Diglossia*. Whereas competing constructions can be different depending on the social register, *the vernacular* slowly prevails and forces the conservative variety out of use. For instance, based on data on the presence of *do*-support between 1400 and 1750 (Ellegård 1953), Kroch shows that there is grammar competition between a grammar in which the finite verb moves to I/ Aux and a competing grammar with *do*-support.[2]

The idea of syntactic diglossia, that is, the hypothesis that the language of individuals and speech communities reflect several systems of grammar, with minimal lexical and phonological variation, is related to approaches to code-switching. Weinreich et al. (1968) treat examples that can be recognized as instances of syntactic diglossia and code-switching as cases of *orderly differentiation*, that is, variation in both a single grammatical system and in coexistent systems of dialects or languages in contact. Examples of competing grammars appear, for instance, in studies by Kroch (1989) and Santorini (1993), involving change in word order in Yiddish. Pintzuk (1991) also presents a similar analysis of change in word order in English, whereas Taylor (1994) develops a competing grammars analysis of changes in word order between Homeric and Classical Greek. Another example of word order change, the loss of verb second in Spanish, has been analyzed as a result of competing grammars by Fontana (1993).

Several studies, starting with Kroch (1989), have argued in favor of a constant rate of replacement of one grammar by another. The transition of change shows a *Constant Rate Effect*—which, according to Kroch (1989: 205), is related to the fact that an advancing form "jumps from zero to some small positive value in a temporal discontinuity"; the initial small positive value is the point of actua-

---

2   See Biberauer & Roberts (2005) for an alternative analysis—see also below.

tion. In terms of parameters, the transition of change corresponds to the spread of a new parameter setting. In Universal Grammar (which is identified with the properties that are available in all human languages), parameters limit the number of choices that a learner has to make and, therefore, account for systematic grammatical variation between languages. In other words, parameters indicate the availability of certain options and the setting of parameters determines the core-grammar of a language.

The Constant Rate Effect represents a generalization about this transition of change: that is, if a single parameter is involved in the change and the mix of the opposed settings slowly changes in a speech community, one expects that the rate of change (loss or replacement, etc.) should be the same in all contexts that are affected by the change. The Constant Rate Effect links parametric change to grammar competition and introduces a quantitative character into the study of grammatical change. Kroch's analysis is based on the idea of actual speakers in specific circumstances (Kroch 1989)—instead of the concept of an ideal speaker and a homogeneous speech community (Chomsky 1965). Accordingly, for instance, speakers of 15th century Northern English or of 21st century Cypriot Greek may use several dialects besides the literary standard of English of the 15th century or the Standard Greek of the 21st century: a single speech community does not feature only one grammatical system. The above idea logically leads to the concept of competing grammars.

Based on a similar perspective, Niyogi & Berwick (1997) propose a model of dynamic systems, according to which learners do not always acquire all properties of the target grammar: as a result, a group of speakers may acquire the new parameter setting, and another group of speakers may acquire the old parameter setting, and the population of speakers is mixed in these terms. Their model assumes that the competing parameter settings are located in different speakers; therefore, the quantitative character of grammatical change cannot be found in the individual but in the population.

According to Kroch, however, the variation that derives from the different parameter settings can be found across texts and within the same texts as well. To account for this variation, we need to allow, in Kroch's terms, for "syntactic diglossia within individual authors" in periods of grammatical change (Kroch 2001: 722). For Kroch, *individual speakers* choose between diglossic grammars at a characteristic average rate: this rate concerns entire speech communities and changes because one of the grammars slowly prevails and the other grammar stops being used (Kroch 1989, 2001). Furthermore, according to Kroch, every speaker acquires both settings of parameters when a community of speakers becomes diglossic. Kroch (2001: 722) argues that, in cases of diglossic communities, the choice of which criterion of well-formedness to apply in a particular clause falls in the domain of performance—it should not be an issue for grammatical theory.

Learners can acquire diglossic competence; even though the way they achieve the diglossic acquisition should be an important issue for language acquisition studies (Kroch 1989, 2001). Note, however, that even balanced bilinguals have always demonstrated evidence of presence of a dominant language in various experiments. This observation holds true even in cases of early language acquisition of two languages, where the one language appears to control certain characteristics of language processing, which, therefore, leads to a preference for this language in neutral contexts for both languages.

With historical data, we are restricted to the characteristics of the written language. In Kroch's terms, the forms in competition in situations of syntactic diglossia may represent a contrast between *a conservative literary* and *an innovative vernacular language.* The vernacular language is used in a significant frequency, has a psycholinguistic advantage and prevails over the literary language even in written texts.

However, I claim that *coexistence* of more than one alternative grammatical rule and characteristics in the same period—and even in the same speaker—is possible, and it is *not the case that competition of alternative rules is available only in transitional periods*: I call this alternative proposal the *Hypothesis of Grammatical Multiglossia.* The *Hypothesis of Grammatical Multiglossia* starts from and modifies Kroch's proposal of syntactic diglossia. Roberts (2007) also disagrees with the view that coexistence of various grammars should not be peaceful and argues that the presence of native bilinguals can be used as an argument for the peaceful coexistence of multiple grammars.

The examples of *competing grammars in the case of written contact,* observed in early translations, can add significant evidence to the above debate and can support the presence of types of syntactic diglossia in cases where competing or coexistent grammars may play a role. Syntactic diglossia indicates that a speaker may have competence in more than one grammar; the lexica and the phonologies of each system can be similar, but the two grammars are different in the value of one parameter at least—and they are, therefore, distinct grammars (Kroch 1989, 2001). True bilinguals clearly evidence the presence of two distinct grammatical systems in a single individual speaker.

Thus, in this book, these observations are placed into a *historical perspective* with *added evidence from the area of historical translations.* Parallel grammars in case of syntactic diglossia are not different from syntactic variants in a monolingual speaker (Martinet—Introduction to Weinreich (1979 [1953]: vii)). Similar remarks have been made by Paradis (2004: 187) who considers *translation between two languages* and *paraphrasing in a single language as parallel pro-*

cesses. Even though translation seems to be ephemeral, one can argue that new elements that appear in translations can really diffuse in a population because of their *prestigious character* and the fact that *translations can be influential and trigger semi-natural changes* (but different types of translations [biblical, non-biblical, etc.] can be influential in different periods—see Sections 1.2 and 2.1.1; and see below on semi-natural changes).

As seen above, competing forms in syntactic diglossia represent a contrast between a conservative literary variety and an innovative vernacular variety (Kroch 2001: 723). An innovative grammar reflects a "more native" grammar than the prestige or "conservative" variety; the latter is "acquired a bit later in life" (Kroch 2001: 723). This perspective implies the existence of similarities between syntactic diglossia and other forms of bilingualism or diglossia. Diglossia refers to the case of two distinct grammars that are appropriate for a different range of sociolinguistic functions: in this respect, diglossia can concern a contrast between a low variety, related to informal contexts, and a high variety, connected with formal situations (Ferguson 1959; Weinreich et al. 1968).

As mentioned above, several studies on the history of English syntax (in particular) have demonstrated changes related to characteristics of *parallel grammars*. For instance, Pintzuk (2002) analyzes the Old English contrast between AuxOV and OVAux as a result of competing grammars, shown in (19a, b). Pintzuk's explanation is based on an analysis of (19a) as generated with head-initial TP (IP in her terms; auxiliaries precede their verbal complements)—whereas, in (19b), the structure involves a head-final TP (auxiliaries follow their verbal complements). A single text, the translation of Gregory the Great's *Cura Pastoralis* by Alfred, in the late 9th century, contains both structures. This is in accord with Kroch's assumption that competing grammars can be found in a single author as well as in a single text.

(19) a. CP [Cura Pastoralis] 52.2

  *He   ne **mæg** his agene **aberan**.*
  3SG.NOM.MASC NEG can his own support
  'He cannot support his own.'

 b. CP [Cura Pastoralis] 22.21–22

  *hu he   his agene unðeawas **ongietan wille***
  how 3SG.NOM.MASC his own faults perceive will
  'how he will perceive his own faults'

Moreover, Roeper (1999, 2016) argues that all speakers show characteristics of a degree of bilingualism: all speakers are bilingual or multilingual due to the fact that they use parts of more than one grammar, and, mainly, when these parts are connected to lexical items.[3] Roeper's (1999, 2016) hypothesis on Universal Bilingualism follows Kroch's perspective on syntactic diglossia (see also Amaral & Roeper 2014, Liceras 2014). Roeper (1999: 169–170) proposes that even if there is a difference in a single rule, one has to postulate two grammars and bilingualism because single grammars cannot have contradictory rules. In this respect, one should also mention Yang (2002) who, among others, combines Universal Grammar and statistical learning and argues that different grammars can be in competition and variability of speakers' competence can be the result of a probabilistic combination of multiple grammars (Yang 2002: 26–33). Both Roeper and Yang propose that learners must test possible grammars against the input. Roeper also suggests that social factors can influence language variation within the same speaker.[4]

Arguments in favor of syntactic diglossia also derive from studies on L2 acquisition. L2 acquisition studies, and, in particular, studies on different types of L2 acquisition, provide information on the way learners are able to acquire diglossic competence—in contrast, for instance, to Roberts' (2007) disagreement—and the way learners are able to achieve diglossic competence.

6.2   Historical Grammatical Multiglossia, L2 and Bilingualism

(i)   On Kroch (1994, 2001) and the role of L2 in grammatical change

In the present section, I demonstrate the way that L2 acquisition can be related to Kroch's approach and how earlier L2 acquisition studies have been based on Kroch's analysis to account for aspects of L2 acquisition. As seen above, the aim of the *Competing Grammars Hypothesis* or the *Hypothesis of Internalized Diglossia* is to explain the optionality that appears in grammars in periods of parametric change (Kroch 1994, 2001; Pintzuk 2006). According to this hypothesis, learners internalize more than one representation in periods of significant

---

3   But cf. Muysken (2014) who rejects Roeper's proposal.

4   On an opposite view that does not recognize more than one grammar within the same speaker, but only one grammar with variation, see Adger (2006, 2007, 2016). For Adger, intra-speaker variation is the result of the underspecification on the mapping between syntactic information and forms. Recall that Borer (1984) has also proposed that inflectional morphology, for instance, is stored in the lexicon (cf. also Chomsky's 1995, 2005) and, according to this approach, one should expect interlanguage variation due to the characteristics of inflectional morphology.

changes—but see above on my *Hypothesis of Grammatical Multiglossia* (cf. also Sections 6.3 and 6.4)—because of an ambiguity in the input.

An important challenge to any attempt of explanation of grammatical change derives from examples of protracted or slow changes. In addition, cases that show optionality between an old and a new option also cause problems to accounts of grammatical change. According to the main assumption of Generative Grammar, grammars do not tolerate optionality. As discussed in Section 6.1 above, the *Competing Grammars Hypothesis* manages to respect the above assumption by claiming that learners can internalize more than one grammar. Regarding syntactic change, Kroch (1994: 180) argues the following:

> Syntactic change proceeds via competition between grammatically incompatible options which substitute for one another in usage.

According to my *Hypothesis of Grammatical Multiglossia* (see also Section 6.4), however, both internalized multiglossia and multiglossia in a language community should be possible: we agree with Kroch with respect to internalized parallel grammars—but we also follow other analyses in that we recognize multiglossia in community too. However, whenever I refer to *internalized diglossia/ multiglossia*, I follow Kroch's analysis; other approaches to diglossia do not accept internalized diglossia in a speaker but only in the community of speakers.

First (L1A) and second language acquisition (L2A) studies have supported explanations on variability that show great similarities to the *Competing Grammars Hypothesis* (Zobl & Liceras 2005; Liceras 2014). For instance, it has been shown that conflicting data may lead to conflicting analyses by the learner (Hankamer 1977). The learner settles on one analysis eventually, after several possible analyses of the input (Verrips 1994). Parametric variability in L2A has also been shown to arise from coexisting grammatical representations (Montrul 1998, Robertson & Sorace 1999). In addition, the *Competing Grammars Hypothesis* can account for another important characteristic of L2 (Selinker 1972): the recessive grammar need not be completely lost and can be accessed long after it has been replaced. Several studies on L2 acquisition have been carried out with the aim at showing that parallel grammars affect L2 acquisition in a similar way they affect the diachrony of a language. The direction of the above-mentioned research is from the remarks on diachrony to L2, and not the opposite.

Observe that changes in L2 mirror changes in the historical development of languages, and the order of changes in L2 appears to be similarly scheduled: for instance, grammars lose verb-raising in a top-down sequencing following the hierarchy of functional projections (CP/TP/VP) (Zobl & Liceras 2005). Parallel paths in L2 and diachrony support the view of internalized diglossia.

(ii)   Historical language contact and bilingualism

There is a long tradition of explanations of grammatical change related to bilingual speakers. Weinreich (1979 [1953]), for instance, locates the source of contact-induced change in bilingual speakers who possess two linguistic systems. Other scholars have also argued in favor of a correlation between contact-induced change and bilingualism even though they have supported the view that bilinguals cannot possess two linguistic systems (Matras 2010, see also the volume edited by Pahta et al. [2018]). Transfer of elements from one language into another, in the case of an individual speaker, however, can easily show that partial (at least) competence in two languages is possible (Winford 2003; Hickey 2012).

Code-switching, where bilinguals alternate between varieties within the same speech situation (Winford 2003; Tsiplakou 2009, 2014; Consani 2013) can also be seen as source of borrowing in the case of transfer of elements within an individual speaker.[5] There is no consensus of the characteristics of bilingualism required for code-switching, when it can be source of borrowing, and on the number of speakers who should be involved in code-switching. Some researchers have argued that the required number of speakers for code-switching to trigger borrowing can be small, but it should concern high-status speakers. The presence of high-status speakers could, therefore, explain an easy spread of the borrowed material throughout the community. Prestigious translations, written by high-status translators, can be related to successful borrowing and transfer of grammatical characteristics of source text languages.

Further arguments in favor of *grammatical multiglossia* derive from the study of diglossia—and the relation of diglossia to grammatical change: studies on diglossia favor a hypothesis of coexistence of varieties or coexistent systems even *in non-transitional periods*.

---

5   On historical bilingualism and the case of Latin, see Adams (2003). On bilingualism in the context of historical English, see also Timofeeva & Ingham (2018) and Wright (2018). On ancient bilingualism in the Greek context, see, among others, Janse (2002) and Rochette (2013).

6.3 Historical Grammatical Multiglossia and Ferguson's Diglossia

We claim that the investigation of typical cases of diglossia and the analysis of what, traditionally, is considered as diglossia can provide rich insights into the development of parallel grammars—and, in particular, to the role of translations in contact and development of grammars. The study of typical cases of diglossia adds arguments in favor of a type of grammatical diglossia/ multiglossia, which predicts coexistence and contact between parallel grammars, *even in non-transitional periods.*

In his classic study on diglossia, Ferguson (1959: 326) states that an explanation of the coexistence of two varieties of the same language in the same speech community with different functions is required for a better understanding of historical linguistic problems. Ferguson also claims that examining diglossia is significant for an analysis of language change (1959: 340). He provides the following detailed definition of diglossia (1959: 336):

> DIGLOSSIA is a relatively stable language situation in which, in addition to the primary dialects of the language (which may include a standard or regional standards), there is a very divergent, highly codified (often grammatically more complex) superposed variety, the vehicle of a large and respected body of written literature, either of an earlier period or in another speech community, which is learned largely by formal education and is used for most written and formal spoken purposes but is not used by any sector of the community for ordinary conversation.

My view of *coexistent (not only opposing)* grammatical multiglossia is closely related to Ferguson's approach to diglossia as a *stable coexistence* of two varieties—and not only for a transitional period. Diglossia can emerge in various conditions and can have various sources. According to my hypothesis, *written contact* with other languages, as reflected in translated texts, produced under the influence of a source text, as well as characteristics of earlier periods of the same language may constitute plausible sources of diglossia.

Diglossia is not unstable; on the contrary, diglossia may persist for several centuries. Intermediate forms of the language that attempt to resolve diglossia may be relatively unstable or uncodified at the first stages. Diglossia can also be resolved with the borrowing of lexical items from a high prestige variety to a low prestige variety (Ferguson 1959). For instance, in the case of Greek, a mixed language was used from the first stages by the majority of the press. Ferguson (1959) describes diglossia in Greek, which has long roots—but is fully developed at the beginning of the 19th century, with the emergence of a literary language that was based on many characteristics of previous periods of literary Greek. Borrowing of words from a high prestige variety can also be attested in the case of *learned borrowings* from Latin into Romance languages.

More recently, Snow (2013) proposed three subtypes of diglossia, as related to historical parameters:

(i) 'Traditional diglossia', which refers to diglossia situations in pre-modern communities; it concerns the existence of *a sacred language as a high prestige variety* and is evidenced in the examples of Latin, Sanskrit, Classical Chinese, Classical Arabic;

(ii) Revived diglossia, which concerns examples of revival of ancient languages—in some cases in colonial conditions (see the example of Atticism in Section 4.3);

(iii) Modern diglossia, which refers to modern standard languages that form a high prestige variety, in contrast to modern non-standard languages.

In the case of traditional diglossia, the high prestige variety is a 'sacred language' (Snow 2013). The high prestige variety can also have the form of a classical or a literary language (demonstrating a literary tradition). Revived diglossia is related to the diachrony of Greek, which was also one of the languages examined in Ferguson's (1959) classic study. Greek provides an example of a new prestige variety, *katharevusa*, which emerged in the early 1800s based on characteristics of the grammar and vocabulary of earlier periods.

Modern diglossia can be illustrated, for instance, with German-speaking parts of Switzerland, where the high prestige variety, High German, is a modern high standard—not a sacred or an ancient language (Snow 2013). In the example of German-speaking parts of Switzerland, the standard language of another nation-state has been accepted as the high prestige variety.

An example related to an aspect of the history of diglossia can be found in the development of Latin and the emergent Romance languages. Latin was still used for certain occasions of formal speech—and definitely for writing— in parallel to the emergent Romance languages. The vernacular of the new Romance dialects was used for everyday communication; but Latin was the language of literature and religion (Ferguson 1959).

According to Jespersen (1946: 39), the most significant phenomenon of the development of languages is the emergence of national common languages. For example, it has been argued in several studies that the Protestant Reformation affected the valorization and standardization of vernaculars of northern Europe: the reinforcement of the vernaculars was achieved with the realization that vernacular could express the Bible without any alternation in the content (Linn 2013). It is not a coincidence that the first grammar of German (*Teutsche Grammatica* by Valentin Ickelsamer, *c.* 1500–1541) appeared in the same year as the biblical translation of Luther. Even though it was more a guide to usage rather than a typical grammar, it should have been triggered through the emergence of confidence in the possible status of German as a literary variety.

The later grammars—the first proper grammar, *Teutsch Grammatick oder Sprach-Kunst* by Laurentius Albertus (*c.* 1540–1585) as well as the successful grammar of the 16th century *Grammatica Germanicæ Linguæ* of 1578 by Johannes Clajus (1535–1592)—used Luther as their model (Linn 2013). The production of the Bible in a vernacular language chronologically parallels the emergence of grammar books in other countries: for instance, the first study of the Dutch grammar (*Twe-spraack van de Nederduitsche Letterkunst*) from 1584 by Hendrik Spiegel (1549–1612) was the result of a similar movement of linguistic confidence in Dutch, which was also responsible for the first compete Dutch translation of the Bible. Therefore, Linn (2013) concludes in favor of the existence of a significant relation between *biblical translations and the process of standardization*—alongside with the religious issues of Protestant Reformation.

Weiß (2001, 2005a) proposes that languages be distinguished into *first and second order natural languages*, N1 and N2 languages, based on the assumption that the presence/ absence of L1 acquisition constitutes a criterion of naturalness of languages. N1 languages have native speakers and are acquired as L1s while N2 languages are not acquired as L1s. *Standard languages* can be characterized as N2 languages *at the periods when* they are not acquired as L1s. Dialects are N1 languages at all times, they are always transmitted through L1 acquisition.

In a similar way, Emonds (1986) characterizes sentences such as the example in (20a) as "grammatically deviant prestige constructions". The second conjunct of a conjoined subject is marked with the accusative case in English, as in the example in (20b)—but, according to the correct usage, (20a) is preferred with the second conjunct in the nominative case.

(20) a. *Our landlord and **we** very often disagree.*
 b. *Our landlord and **us** very often disagree.*

According to Emonds (1986: 235), constructions such as the one illustrated in the example in (20a) are not part of a dialect acquired and spoken as a native language, but rather part of the prestige or standard usage, which is an "extragrammatical deviation", imposed in certain, especially written, forms of language, through cultural institutions.

Sobin (1997) names these rules "grammatical viruses": they are parasitic on the generative system (Lasnik & Sobin 2000: 352); therefore, they form a special part of the competence of adults. Besides prescriptivism, *literacy* is also considered a source of grammatical inconsistency in cases of languages with non-natural characteristics. The hypothesis about the role of literacy is related to the fact that standard languages are originally exclusively *written languages* (Weiß 1998, 2001)—and we should add the fact of their *translated written character* in their first periods, in many cases.

According to Weiß too, a major source of such developments can be traced to *borrowing induced by language contact*. Haspelmath (1997: 213) has also considered this type of change as a superficial change resulting from system-external sociolinguistic factors—rather than as a deep change in the system. The above discussion provides evidence of how diachronic, dialectological and comparative studies may reveal cases of semi-natural grammatical change. Modern standard languages include both natural and artificial characteristics and constructions. The reconstruction of linguistic diachronies and the synchronic investigation of languages need to take into consideration semi-natural characteristics as well. Languages include core constructions (which follow the principles), idiosyncratic constructions and semi-natural constructions—even though the above types of constructions may overlap to a degree (Weiß 1998, 2001).

It is evident that *parallel* first and second order natural grammars can have various different forms—translated vs. non-translated, archaic vs. innovative, among others—and their presence can be triggered by various reasons. In learned contexts, borrowing creates parallel morphosyntactic subsystems, which are present together with the native morphosyntactic subsystem, in a type of code-switching or a mixed language. Borrowed forms can create a morphosyntactic subsystem—parallel to the native morphological paradigms and syntactic constructions. For instance, this is the case of English plurals with Latin and Greek base: *phenomen-on* vs. *phenomen-a*. Kossmann (2010, 2013) names the above tendency: *parallel system borrowing*. Parallel system borrowing appears very frequently in *learned contexts*, in European languages with Greek or Latin forms or in languages of the Muslim world with Arabic forms.

Most of the examples of parallel system borrowing in the literature concern nouns; however, there are also examples of other forms not related to nominal morphology. For instance, Ghomara Berber, spoken in northwestern Morocco (Mourigh 2016, among many others) is a variety that developed inflectional parallel systems. In this language, all paradigms show parallel systems with Arabic forms. For instance, paradigms such as nominal marking of plural, adjectival agreement, pronominal forms and verbal inflection, are involved in the parallel systems. Verbal parallel systems are not related only to inflection. For example, object clitics of Arabic are used with verbs bearing Arabic inflection, whereas object clitics of Berber are used with verbs bearing Berber inflection (Mourigh 2016, among many others).

Borrowed inflection functions in a different way from the native inflection: this leads to creation of morphosyntactic or categorial subsystems (Kossmann 2008). An example of categorial different subsystems derives from Cypriot Arabic. According to Newton (1964), Cypriot Arabic marks case in Greek loanwords but not in native Arabic nominals (Kossmann 2008). Note that if a language has parallel systems, the borrowed material *may spread* and can be found even in lexical items not related to the borrowed element historically. However, at a first stage, the extension of the borrowed elements affects only foreign lexical items. At a later stage, it may also affect native lexical items: for instance, in Yiddish, the Hebrew masculine plural suffix can also be used with Germanic words (Katz 1987). Therefore, the spread of borrowed material is not necessarily a change related to language contact with a foreign language, as parallel systems, if existing in a language, belong to the system of the same language and their characteristics spread like other features of the language. Their original relation to language contact does not make the process of spread different from other cases of spread (for example, through analogy).

6.4 Historical Grammatical Multiglossia as Related to (Semi-)natural Change

Based on the above discussion, what I propose is that *coexisting—and not only competing—grammatical multiglossia* has a significant role in the diachrony of languages: the *Hypothesis of Grammatical Multiglossia* recognizes the role of diglossia of individuals in grammatical change, similarly to Kroch's syntactic diglossia, and is also inspired by Ferguson's analysis of classic diglossia that reveals the role of earlier forms of the language, as well as of other languages, in coexistent and stable parallel systems. Multiglossia, the stable coexistence of parallel grammars, affects the development of languages because it triggers various contexts of contact. Standardization, as related to standard written languages, constitutes one of the significant examples of cases of coexisting multiglossia (see Ferguson 1959 and above).

As already discussed above, standard varieties may include *artificial syntactic constructions*, which do not absolutely follow the principles of the Faculty of Language, that is, principles related to the biological endowment of language, which is universal and shared among humans. Chomsky (1995: 51) claims that at least standard languages are "partially invented" and "may even violate the principles of languages". Standard languages are not entirely subject to L1 acquisition: instruction is involved in a part of the linguistic knowledge of adult speakers. The distinction between natural and non-natural languages is related to the issue of language acquisition, that is, a language is natural if it is acquired as a native language, if it is "acquired by its users without special instruction as a normal part of the process of maturation and socialization" (Lyons 1999: 1).

Languages that are subject to L1 acquisition can be characterized as *first order natural* or *N1 languages*; in this respect, standard languages can be named as *second order natural* or *N2 languages* (Weiß 1998, 2001, see 6.3). Accordingly, grammatical change can also be distinguished into two basic types: *natural and semi-natural grammatical change* (Weiß 1998, 2001). Below I discuss the characteristics and examples of semi-natural grammatical change.

We recognize similar characteristics of development also in languages with *long written tradition*, such as in Greek: in these languages, however, the contact was steady with *earlier forms of the language*, and the artificial or second order natural grammar mainly had its source in earlier forms of the same language. In the case of English, even though Contemporary English is subject to L1 acquisition, it still contains inconsistent characteristics, that is, irregular properties which one would not expect on the basis of the overall organization of the grammar, partly differentiating the standard language from dialects. The above-mentioned fact shows how the requirement of a cooperation between theoretical linguistics and sociolinguistics constitutes a strong necessity for the diachronic examination of any language (Weiß 2004; Sitaridou 2014, 2016, 2022).

In another example, Standard German emerged as a written language in the 14th–15th century. However, until the 19th century, Standard German was hardly used in colloquial speech. Until the second half of the 20th century, Standard German was not acquired as a first language (Durrell 1999). This means that the standard variety did not have native speakers for around 500 years. The same is also true for the situation in other European countries. For instance, the Netherlands (Marle 1997) and other European countries had *only a written standard and oral dialects* until the 19th century (Weiß 1998, 2001).

However, standard varieties may be related to a type of native competence even in early times. For instance, speakers who used written Standard German in the 18th century had first acquired dialects as native languages before learning written Standard German. In this respect, the development of standard varieties is indirectly related to L1 acquisition because the new standard and the dialects are *interrelated varieties*— the standard language mainly contains the characteristics of one, or more, dialects, which are recognized as the "correct" forms of the language—even though they are not identical. In contrast, standard languages show characteristics that are not connected only with native grammatical change, because originally they were not subject to L1 acquisition only. Accordingly, standard languages are exceptional in that they are not acquired as L1 languages for a particular period of time (that is, during the period of establishment of the rules of the standard language). A once artificial language, in that it was once constructed to a degree by norms, offers primary linguistic data to children, who acquire the contemporary standard language as a natural language (Weiß 1998, 2001).

In this respect, standardization, a process related to *semi-natural grammatical change*, differs from natural grammatical changes in that

(i)   it stops or prevents natural grammatical change, and it preserves early characteristics of languages;

(ii) it creates artificial structures (Weiß 2001).

For instance, the survival of the *adnominal genitive case* in Standard High German is an example of a semi-natural grammatical development. In contrast to Standard High German, adnominal genitive case was lost in German dialects and in typologically close languages (English, Dutch, Yiddish). Hence, according to the above assumptions, (a) *artificial* syntactic characteristics exist; and (b) artificial syntactic characteristics affect the primary linguistic data when the standard languages are subject to L1 acquisition.

An example from the history of English concerns data demonstrating that only the standard variety allows the pattern given in (21), whereas English dialects show different characteristics.

(21) Do not tolerate a second negation if simple sentence negation is intended. (Weiß 2001)

This pattern of negation, found in the standard language, reflects an example of artificial characteristics if put in the relevant diachronic context and if one takes the development of dialects into consideration. For instance, the standard variety follows a rule that is attested in earlier periods of the dialects and has clearly changed in all dialects. In this respect, I argue that a dialect constitutes the (first order) natural grammar of the speakers, and parallel second order natural grammars can have the form of a standardized grammar—or be reflected in translations, with transfer from another language, or in case of intralingual translations, with transfer from an earlier period of the same language.

Following Weiß' perspective, I claim that standard languages are N2 or second order native languages because they start as *exclusively written translated and written non-translated languages* and secondarily as *learned languages*—and not as acquired L1s. Modern standard languages still contain artificial and non-natural constructions of the type labeled as "grammatical viruses" or "grammatically deviant prestige constructions". Constructions which were maintained due to prescriptive rules demonstrate different characteristics than constructions which are shaped through grammatical change triggered by internal factors (Weiß 1998, 2001, 2004). Evidence of whether a particular grammatical retention or change is due to external factors or the process of standardization through instruction—and not to L1 acquisition—can be derived from the study of dialects. For example, the absence of articles with proper nouns in Standard German, as opposed to in the dialects, may have various sources. One of the sources can be that the standard language preserves an older stage where proper nouns appear without articles.

Theoretical linguistics has ignored normative forces and pressure for a long time. However, there are examples of analyses that recognize the role of the normative pressure: Emonds (1979), Schütze (2001) on accusative subjects, Sobin (1997), Lasnik & Sobin (2000) on grammatical viruses, van Gelderen (2004) on grammaticalization. Kroch's approach is in absolute agreement with Weiß' N1-N2 model; in the context of historical linguistics, the possibility that some texts of earlier periods do not reflect a native competence has been recognized by Kroch (2001), among others, who supports the idea of a syntactic diglossia within individual authors; according to Kroch one of the *diglossic variants* is more native than the other (Kroch 2001: 723; see above 6.1 and 6.2). Kroch's model mainly supports the view of a *competition* of competences, which is responsible for the grammatical characteristics attested in the texts.

However, according to Weiß, it is possible that neither competence prevails which means *stable coexistence of parallel grammars*, according to my *Hypothesis of Grammatical Multiglossia*—and certain constructions are hybrid. For instance, examples of the type found in (22a) from German, which can be found up to the 18th century, demonstrates characteristics of combination of a prenominal dative, as in (22b), and an adnominal genitive, as in (22c); Weiß 2005b.

(22) a. *des   Herrn   sein Brief*
     ART.GEN master his letter

  b. ***dem***   *Herrn   sein Brief*
     ART.DAT master his letter

c. ***des***   *Herrn*   *Brief*
ART.GEN master letter
'The master's letter'

The construction with the dative case in (22b) is part of the N1 dialectal or vernacular competence; the construction with the genitive in (22c) is part of the N2 standard competence. Hence, examples like those in (22a) can be considered as the result of *mixing* of both constructions and not as a reflection of any linguistic competence. My hypothesis is that there is not only mixing of different languages (as shown in Alexiadou 2017, among others), but also mixing of different parallel grammars of the same language (see Sections 6.1, 6.3 as well as Section 1.2 and the discussion of corpus surveys in Sections 7 and 8).

The variation in *historical texts* is not due to different parameter settings in all cases (see Roberts 2007)—but may demonstrate different hybrid forms. One can, therefore, expect the existence of a type of interlanguage grammars, that is, a type of L2 learners' grammars which undergo development, known from L2 acquisition (Ritchie & Bhatia 1996). *Translated texts* are also the best candidates to reflect such *interlanguage grammars*. In addition, many authors have probably acquired a partial competence of *writing*: their texts neither reflect their L1 competence nor the standard grammar of the period (Weiß 1998, 2001); instead, their texts may represent the output of an interlanguage grammar.

PART 2

Data: English and Greek Translations and Grammatical Change

∵

CHAPTER 7

English Data

7.1 Introduction

The central hypothesis of this study can be described as follows: If one examines the development of the grammar as reflected in translated texts through the example of retranslation of the same source text, one will observe that the diachrony of translated texts does not display the changing characteristics and the continuity that can be found in the diachrony witnessed by non-translated texts. Hence, the diachrony of retranslations does not reflect the well-known cases of change attested in the diachrony of non-translated texts.

I argue that later retranslations do not exhibit instances of change according to the overall grammatical change, i.e., according to the examples of grammatical change reflected in non-translated texts—either in the case of non-biblical translations or in the case of biblical translations. However, translations provide us with evidence of the status and role of grammatical multiglossia, i.e., of the various systems of grammar which coexist in all periods: these systems of grammar reveal contact between each other and transfer from one to the other.

The *quantitative data* to be discussed in this chapter serve the broad research questions proposed here.[1] The data from the corpus surveys mainly concern morphosyntactic phenomena related to voice and argument structure in English and Greek. The following section includes a brief discussion of the major phenomena that are examined in these corpus studies, from a diachronic point of view. This means that the purpose of the presentation in this section is, on the one hand, to provide insights into the diachronic development of the features under examination, to make it possible to identify the characteristics of the texts of the corpus in the course of the relevant development, and, on the other hand, to discuss the chronology of emergence of particular characteristics in the overall diachrony of the language.

---

1 Note that the aim is to uncover quantitative tendencies in the development of grammatical characteristics as attested in specialized corpora. I leave the question of more sophisticated statistical analyses open for future research. For readability reasons, reasons of space and to make the presentation less complicated, the tables only provide relative frequencies.

© KONINKLIJKE BRILL NV, LEIDEN, 2022 | DOI:10.1163/9789004503564_009

130   CHAPTER 7

7.2   Voice, Argument Structure and Transitivity in English Biblical
       Diachronic Retranslations

(i)   The development of voice and argument structure in English

The following discussion of the development of voice and argument structure
in English is mainly based on data in Lavidas (2009). Starting with the morphological marking of voice, I observe two major types of change in transitivity
alternations in the history of English (see also Section 7.3 on the development
of cases and voice in English). These two are: (a) Morphological syncretism
of the causative and anticausative due to changes in the morphology of the
causative; (b) Morphological syncretism of the causative and anticausative due
to changes in the morphology of the anticausative. I now discuss each of these
in turn.

(a)   *Morphological syncretism of the causative and anticausative due to changes*
       in the morphology of the causative

With *causative* and *anticausative*, I refer to the following constructions: a causative construction includes an agent or cause in the subject position and a
patient in the direct object position; an anticausative construction includes
a patient in the subject position. Verbs participating in these constructions
express a change-of-state meaning. Most of change-of-state verbs alternate, i.e.:
they can participate in both causative and anticausative constructions, e.g., the
verb *break* in Modern English:

       I broke the vase (causative)—*The vase broke* (anticausative).

Among many others, see Kulikov 1998, 2011a, b; Cennamo et al. 2015; Hock 2019;
Barðdal et al. 2020.
     Several examples of apparent causativizations or anticausativizations—
that is, new-innovative causative/ transitive or anticausative/ intransitive use
of an earlier form that was attested only in anticausative/ intransitive or
causative/ transitive constructions, respectively—are in reality the result of
a morphophonological change in English. The morphological change led to
a merger of causative and anticausative forms (i.e., it led to a merger of
earlier specialized forms that were used only in causative or anticausative
constructions). In other words, a morphophonological change led to verbs
showing no formal differentiation when used as causatives or anticausatives,
i.e., it led to labile types. This means that one does not find evidence for an

ENGLISH DATA

innovative causative or anticausative construction in this case, but a significant morphophonological change and merger of the causative (specialized form attested in causative constructions) with the anticausative form (specialized form attested in anticausative constructions).

In most cases, the causative form became the same as the anticausative (Möhlig & Klages 2002): the causative form lost its additional formal characteristics (prefixes, suffixes) that differentiated it from the anticausative form, and appeared with the same form as the anticausative.

The historical development briefly described above took place according to the following diachronic path: Old English retained traces of the Proto-Germanic distinction between primary/ inchoative/ anticausative or strong stative and secondary/ weak causative types, as seen in (23a) below. Old English neutralized the productive in Proto-Germanic morphophonological alternation of the type *meltan* (anticausative)—*mieltan* (causative). Furthermore, Middle English texts provide evidence of a merger of the primary/ inchoative/ anticausative and secondary/ causative type: the causative form changed to become the same with the anticausative, which prevailed in this way (Visser 1963–1973: §131). A parallel development is related to the loss of the causative prefixes *ge-* and *be-* in the Middle English period (Krahe & Meid 1969: 37). The prefix *ge-*, for instance, was a causativizing morpheme, its presence resulted in a causative interpretation in Old English, as shown in (23b).

(23) a. *sincan* 'to sink'   *sencean* 'to cause to sink'
    meltan 'to melt'   *mieltan* 'to cause to melt'
    brinnan/ beornan 'to burn'   *bærnan* 'to cause sth. to burn'
                        (Visser 1963–1973: §131)
    b. *feallan* 'to come down'   *gefeallan* 'to bring sth. down'
    hwîtian 'to be/ become white'   *gehwîtian* 'to make sth. white'
    minsian 'to diminish/ get smaller' *geminsian* 'to make sth. smaller'
                (Visser 1963–1973: §134; Kastovsky 1992: 380)

The examples in (24) demonstrate that the prefix *ge-* could be used almost freely to derive causative constructions based on an unprefixed root that was used in anticausative constructions. As a result, the semantic domain of transmission of light, for instance, could include several causative types—besides the large number of anticausatives. A similar role was also played by the prefix *be-*, which could derive causative verbal types; for instance: *flow* 'to roll'— *beflowan* 'to overflow'.

(24) *scinan* 'to emit light/ be shining'   *gescinan* 'to make sth. emit light/ be shining'

    bierhtan 'to shine brightly'   *gebierhtan* 'to make sth. shine brightly'
    beorhtian 'to become brightly'   *gebeorhtian* 'to make sth. become brightly'

(Díaz Vera 2000: 28)

The productive use of these prefixes was lost in Early Middle English—according to Visser (1963–1973), due to reasons related to morphophonological changes;[2] this resulted in the emergence of verbs that could be used in causative and anticausative constructions without any formal difference (labile verbs).

(*b*)   *Morphological syncretism of the causative and anticausative due to changes in the morphology of the anticausative*

Table 7.1 demonstrates examples of anticausatives that acquired the same form as the corresponding causatives as a later development. However, there are instances—though not productive at all—where the morphophonological differences between the causative and the anticausative were not lost, such as with *licgean—lecgean, feallan—fellan* (*lie—lay, fall—fell*). However, the verb *openian* 'open' is an example of a verb that is used in causative and anticausative constructions without any formal change as early as Old English. Note that, in this case, there is no consensus whether the anticausative or the causative construction is earlier; most cognate verbs of other Germanic languages also use identical forms both in the causative and anticausative constructions (see examples in 25).

(25) **Old Saxon**   *opanon* 'to make sth. be open / become open'
    Old High German   *offanõn* 'to make sth. be open, be known / become open'

(Heidermanns 1993: 640)

Another relevant development concerns the loss of the reflexive pronoun that could mark intransitives/ anticausatives in Old English. Only very few intransitives could be attested with and also without a reflexive pronoun in the period of Middle and Early Modern English, as seen in (26a–b) (Mustanoja 1960: 431).

---

2   On argument structure and the contact between Middle English and French, see Trips & Stein (2019).

ENGLISH DATA

TABLE 7.1   Anticausatives acquiring the same form as the causatives in various periods of English

Early Middle English *fill* (< Old English *fyll*)	
Middle English	
circa 1200	*drye(n)* 'to dry up' (< Old English *drygan*: adjective *dry*)
Middle English	
14th century	*close(n)* (< Old English *clysan* / Middle English *closen*: *close* < Old Frisian *clos*—adjective)
Modern English	
18th century	*clean* (from adjective *clean*)

BASED ON DATA FROM KRAHE & MEID 1969

(26) a. Chaucer, The Canterbury Tales: The Knight's Tale (CT I), 1691 [1: 1693]
       *he **rideth hym** ful right*
       'Then, sharply he did veer off to the right.'
   b. Chaucer, The Canterbury Tales: The Knight's Tale (CT I), 968 [1: 970]
       *No neer Atthenes wolde he go ne **ride***
       'He did not want to go or ride any nearer to Athens.'

In several instances, intransitives are attested with a reflexive pronoun in Early English but without a reflexive pronoun in the 16th–17th century, such as in the case of the verbs *cure, hide, shape, sell* (Hermodsson 1952: 65; Visser 1963–1973: § 145). This new tendency of dropping the reflexive pronoun also led to a merger of the causative and the anticausative. In a parallel development, the presence of the reflexive pronoun began to express an emotional involvement of the subject in the described event, as in (27a) vs. (27b) (on emotional involvement in ditransitive constructions, see Barðdal et al 2011).

(27) a. An Elizabethan in 1582: the diary of Richard Madox, 84
       *I **prepared my self** to be redye*
   b. The trial of Sir Nicholas Throckmorton, 66 Cii
       *So the Frenchmen **prepared** to interrupt his arrival*

In the present section, I have discussed general diachronic tendencies in English where verbs in causative and anticausative constructions are attested with the same form in later stages. The result of the morphological merger of verbal forms of both constructions can have various reasons, as observed above. In the following section, I describe the research methodology of my corpus surveys, which are based on word lists, i.e., lists of verbs meaning change-of-state. The corpus surveys trace the development of various parameters in translated and non-translated texts, in a comparative manner, in several periods of the history of English.

(ii) Methodology of study and word lists

The first set of corpus studies examines English translations, with the Latin Vulgate or the Koine Greek New Testament as source texts, as well as some intralingual translations and retranslations. In the case of early and late English biblical translations, even though most of the English texts are translations of a Latin translation, or retranslations based on earlier English translations, characteristics of interlingual translation of the Greek source text can always be valid because the Greek source text could have influenced the translated text in the case of later translations as well.

The first set of phenomena examined in the present corpus studies are connected to the area of argument structure and voice. In all the corpus studies, I have also included data from the diachrony of non-translated English, as a basis for comparison. Accordingly, I have tested whether the observed tendencies in the translated texts are a result of translation effects or of the overall development of the language. The quantitative evidence is derived mainly from the following translations of the biblical texts:

– English Standard Version (21st century),
– English Revised Version (19th century);
– Authorized Version (17th century);
– Tyndale's translation (16th century);
– Wycliffe's translation (14th century).

All data from the above-mentioned texts are also compared to their direct—especially, for Tyndale's translation—or indirect source text of the Koine Greek New Testament.

The corpus searches involve examination of a list of selected verbal meanings—based on a word list, which derives from studies on voice and argument structure, mainly from Lavidas (2009) and Lavidas et al. (2012). The data from the source text, the Koine Greek text of the New Testament, constitute the starting point of the selection of the verbal meanings in the word list. Table 7.2 includes the verbal meanings as they appear in the Koine Greek text. The studies that introduce the methodology of word lists are mainly the following: Haspelmath (1993), Haspelmath et al. (2014), Nichols et al. (2004), Grünthal & Nichols (2016), Nichols (2017, 2018).

As discussed below, the word list of the present study is not derived from the above-mentioned studies in all its details but is mainly based on verbs attested

ENGLISH DATA   135

TABLE 7.2   Word list for the corpus surveys on voice and argument structure

Main list of verbal meanings

'boil'	'grow'
'clean'	'melt'
'close'	'rot'
'dry'	'tear'
'heal'	

Additional list of verbal meanings; for corpus surveys with low number of results based on the main list of verbs

'anger'	'finish'
'become sick'	'get born'
'become strong'	'heighten'
'blind'	'die'
'break'	'open'
'burn'	'overflow'
'change'	'reinforce'
'darken'	'reveal'
'decrease'	'scatter'
'destroy'	'split'
'empty'	'spread'
'enlighten'	'stop'
'enrage'	'strengthen'
'fatten up'	'subside'
'fill'	

in the source text of the Koine Greek New Testament: I have started with all meanings mentioned in previous studies of word lists; I have, then, searched for these in the text of the Koine Greek New Testament; moreover, on the basis of the results regarding the most frequent verbs expressing a change-of-state meaning in the text of the Koine Greek New Testament, I have compiled the word list which contains the verbal meanings investigated. Table 7.3 includes the abbreviations of the divisions of the time periods used in the corpus surveys (according to the Penn Parsed Corpora of Historical English).

The corpus surveys provide quantitative evidence on numerous questions. With regard to all of the selected verbs that express a change-of-state meaning, I have examined the relative frequencies of the following features:

TABLE 7.3   Chronologies/ Divisions of the time periods and abbreviations used in the corpus surveys (according to the Penn Parsed Corpora of Historical English)

M1	1150–1250
M2	1250–1350
M3	1350–1420
E1	1500–1569
E2	1570–1639
E3	1640–1710
B1	1700–1769
B2	1770–1839
B3	1840–1914

i.   the relative frequencies of active *vs.* passive/ non-active voice forms;
ii. the relative frequency of (active *vs.* passive/ non-active) voice forms of the particular verbs in anticausative constructions;
iii. the relative frequency of active voice forms when used in anticausative *vs.* transitive constructions;
iv. the relative frequency of (active *vs.* passive/ non-active) voice forms of these verbs when used with an animate subject and when used with an inanimate subject.

Furthermore, I have investigated the distribution of

a.   transitive *vs.* anticausative constructions, and
b.   animate *vs.* inanimate subjects of verbs in transitive and anticausative constructions.

7.2.1   *English Diachronic (Re)translations of the New Testament*

(i)   Parameters of morphological expression of voice

The first part of the corpus survey examines English translations of the New Testament. I focus on phenomena of voice and argument structure. The main aim of the quantitative analysis in the present section is a comparative one: that is, to compare relevant features of early and later English translations. Moreover, with regard to each of the parameters under examination, data from the Koine Greek New Testament, the source text of Tyndale's translation and of late English translations, provide a comparative basis for further conclusions.

ENGLISH DATA

All data are evaluated against the basic tendencies of the same phenomena in the English diachrony as evidenced in non-translated texts (cf. also Walser 2016).

The present section contains a systematic presentation and discussion of the results of the corpus surveys. As described in Section 7.2, all quantitative data involve particular verbal meanings in a word list and not all verbs and verbal meanings attested in the corpus (see the list of meanings and criteria of choice above in Table 7.2). I first discuss data on the distribution of active and non-active morphological expression of voice derived from the corpus of English translations of the New Testament. I choose the term "non-active" to describe the unmarked form in the intransitive construction, following the relevant literature on unmarked vs. marked expressions of transitive and intransitive constructions, i.e., transitivity alternations, and on lability.

Lability concerns cases where the unmarked form is used both in the transitive and intransitive construction (see Kitazume 1996; Kulikov 1998, 2003; Lavidas 2004, 2007; Letuchiy 2010; Kulikov & Lavidas 2013). This means that the aim is to contrast *"labile"-active voice forms* of intransitives, which are unmarked in that they are the same as the verbal forms used in the transitive constructions, with non-labile/ non-active voice forms of intransitives, which differ from the form used in the transitive construction. The term *non-active forms* refers to forms that are different than the one used in the transitive construction, i.e. they are different than the unmarked forms.

In English, this would mean a passive—periphrastic or non-periphrastic, depending on the period—or a reflexive form, with a personal or a reflexive pronoun, depending on the period. In the case of the Koine Greek source text, non-active refers to middle/ passive, in the aorist and future, or mediopassive verbal suffixes, in all other tenses, in contrast to the active suffixes. The decision to use this terminology is directly related to the theoretical discussion and analysis of lability. Following this decision, it will be possible to unify many different types of non-active voice forms.

The main aim of the quantitative analysis in this section is to compare the features under examination in early and later English translations, whereas data from the Koine Greek text of the New Testament can provide a comparative basis for further analysis related to the source text. In the case of translations, the results show a slightly higher percentage of active forms, that is, of the unmarked form of the selected verbs in all English translations, in comparison to the Koine Greek source text; the differences in frequency between active or non-active forms in the data from Koine Greek are not significant (Figure 7.1).[3]

CHAPTER 7

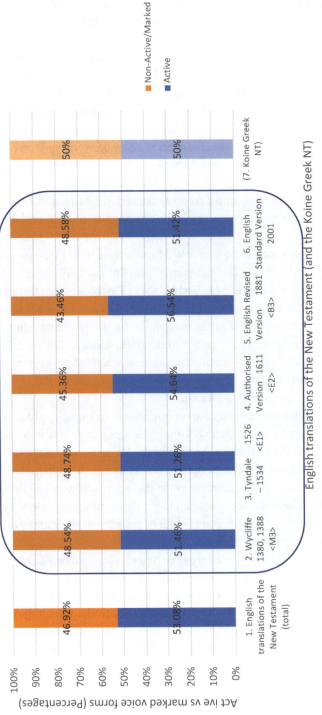

FIGURE 7.1 Active vs. non-active/marked voice forms in the corpus of English translations of the New Testament (and the Koine Greek NT) (See the list of selected verbal meanings: Table 7.2)

ENGLISH DATA

A clear variation may be observed between the translated texts, a higher frequency of non-active forms of the verbs under examination is found in the translated texts of the Authorized Version and the English Revised Version, in comparison to the other English translations. The other three translations exhibit similar percentages: the non-active forms are attested with the following percentages: 51.42 % (English Standard Version), 51.26 % (Tyndale), 51.46 % (Wycliffe).

Figure 7.2 displays the results of the distribution of morphology expressing voice in anticausatives, i.e., verbs in anticausative constructions, in the translations of the corpus; in other words, I examine the morphological expression of voice of the selected verbs in anticausative constructions. There is no doubt that the Koine Greek text shows a clear preference for non-active anticausatives; however, the difference between active and non-active/ marked forms in the English translations is not significant. The distribution of voice forms in anticausative constructions is similar in the Wycliffite translation, Tyndale's translation and the English Standard Version.

A higher percentage of anticausatives with non-active/ marked forms is attested in the English Revised Version and the Authorized Version. The differences between the Koine Greek text and the English translations are related to cross-linguistic differences involving characteristics of the morphological expression of voice in English and Greek and the productivity of non-active/ marked forms in Greek in the period of the New Testament, in contrast to the active forms of Late Middle and Early and Late Modern English (see 7.1(i)); on the development of Greek voice, see 8.1 (i).

The distribution of active forms in anticausative *vs.* transitive constructions in the translations is given in Figure 7.3. In relation to all statistical findings, note that most of the data derive from passages that are parallel, since most translations use the verbs under examination in the same sentences.

---

3 In the present corpus studies, the texts of the Penn Parsed Corpora of Historical English are used. On details about the editions, see: https://www.ling.upenn.edu/hist-corpora/PPCME2 -RELEASE-4/index.html;

  https://www.ling.upenn.edu/hist-corpora/PPCEME-RELEASE-3/index.html;

  https://www.ling.upenn.edu/hist-corpora/PPCMBE2-RELEASE-1/index.html [last access: May 7, 2020].

  With regard to the English Standard Version, the following edition is included: Packer, J.I. (ed.). 2001. *The Holy Bible, English Standard Version. Containing the Old and New Testaments.* Wheaton, Illinois: Crossway Bibles. In the Greek part of the corpus study, the texts of the TLG corpus are used [Thesaurus Linguae Graecae Digital Library. Ed. by Maria C. Pantelia. http://stephanus.tlg.uci.edu]: With regard to the Koine Greek New Testament, the following edition is used: Aland, K., M. Black, C.M. Martini, B.M. Metzger & A. Wikgren. 1968. *The Greek New Testament, 2nd edn.* Stuttgart: Württemberg Bible Society (Thesaurus Linguae Graecae [TLG]).

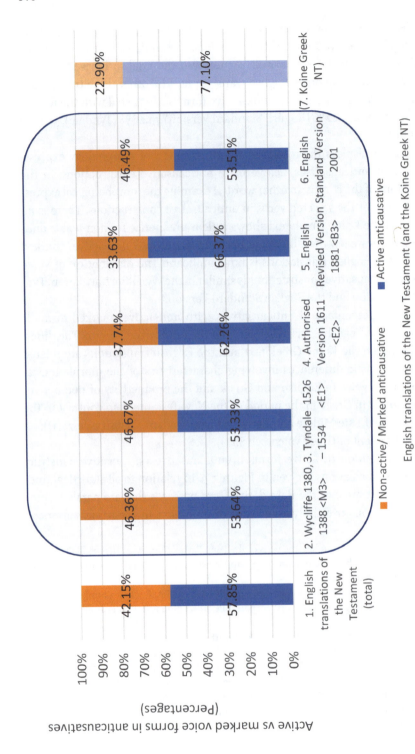

FIGURE 7.2 Distribution of voice forms in anticausative constructions in the corpus of English translations of the New Testament (and the Koine Greek NT) English translations of the New Testament (See the list of selected verbal meanings: Table 7.2)

ENGLISH DATA

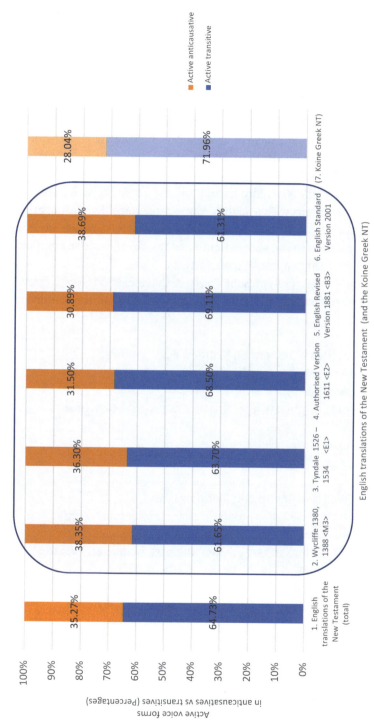

FIGURE 7.3 Active voice forms in transitive and anticausative constructions in the corpus of English translations of the New Testament (See the list of selected verbal meanings: Table 7.2)

However, this not always the case and this was not necessarily the aim of the present study. Instead, the goal here was broader, to investigate and compare the voice and transitivity characteristics of the verbs of my list in the texts under examination—and not only in parallel passages.

All English translations of the study show a clear preference for unmarked (active) forms in transitive constructions. However, the percentage of active forms in transitive constructions in the English translations of the New Testament is lower than the percentage of active forms in transitive constructions in the Koine Greek text; English translations of the New Testament (average percentage): 64.75% vs. Koine Greek New Testament: 71.69%. In the English Standard Version and the Wycliffite translation, the active forms are attested in transitive constructions with a slightly lower percentage than in the other English translations. Observe that there is also a preference for active forms in transitive constructions in the above-mentioned translated texts, in comparison to active forms in anticausative constructions.

The examples in (28a)–(28l) present a passage that includes the verb "grow" in the Greek source text, and the same passage in the English translations of the corpus.[4]

(28) a. Koine Greek New Testament; Matthew 6:28

καταμάθετε τὰ κρίνα τοῦ ἀγροῦ πῶς
katamáthete tà krína toû agroû pôs
consider.2PL ART.NOM lilies.NOM ART.GEN field.GEN how

αὐξάνουσιν
auxánousin
grow.ACT.3PL

b. Koine Greek New Testament; Matthew 13:32

ὅταν δὲ αὐξηθῇ μεῖζον τῶν λαχάνων ἐστὶν
*hótan dè **auxēthêi** meîzon tôn lachánōn estìn*
when PRT grow.PASS.3SG greater ART.GEN herbs.GEN be.3SG

c. Wycliffe; Matthew 6:28
*Biholde ye the lilies of the feeld, how thei **wexen**.*

---

4 Among many others, see Bruce (1970: 14) on the Wycliffite translation, Su Fang Ng's (2001: 320) on Tyndale's translation, Price & Ryrie (2004: 119) on the Authorized Version, Bullough (1953: 463) on the English Revised Version, Strathearn (2011: 245–246) on the English Standard Version, and Horrocks (2014: 147) on the Koine Greek New Testament.

ENGLISH DATA

d. Wycliffe; Matthew 13:32
*but whanne it **hath woxen**, it is the moste of alle wortis*

e. Tyndale; Matthew 6:28
*Considre ye lylies of ye felde how they **growe**.*

f. Tyndale; Matthew 13:32
*But when it **is groune** it is the greatest amoge yerbes*

g. Authorized Version; Matthew 6:28
*Consider the lillies of the field, how they **grow***

h. Authorized Version; Matthew 13:32
*but when it **is growen**, it is the greatest among herbes*

i. English Revised Version; Matthew 6:28
*Consider the lilies of the field, how they **grow***

j. English Revised Version; Matthew 13:32
*but when it **is grown**, it is greater than the herbs*

k. English Standard Version; Matthew 6:28
*Consider the lilies of the field, how they **grow***

l. English Standard Version; Matthew 13:32
*but when it **has grown** it is larger than all the garden plants*

The examples in (29a)–(29f) present a passage that includes the verb "close" in the Greek source text, and the same passage in the English translations of the corpus.

Matthew 25:10

(29) a. Koine Greek New Testament
καὶ   ἐκλείσθη   ἡ   θύρα
kaì   ekleísthē   hē   thýra
and   shut.PASS.3SG   ART.NOM   door.NOM

b. Wycliffe
*and the yate **was schit**.*

144 CHAPTER 7

   c. Tyndale
     *the gate **was shett vp***

   d. Authorized Version
     *and the doore **was shut.***

   e. English Revised Version
     *and the door **was shut.***

   f. English Standard Version
     *and the door **was shut.***

The examples in (30a)–(30l) present a passage that includes the verb "open" in the Greek source text, and the same passage in the English translations of the corpus.

(30) a. Koine Greek New Testament; Matthew 20:33
     Κύριε   ἵνα   ἀνοιγῶσιν   οἱ   ὀφθαλμοί
     Kýrie   *hína*   ***anoigôsin***   *hoi*   *ophthalmoí*
     Lord.VOC that open.ACT.3PL ART.NOM eyes.NOM

   b. Koine Greek New Testament; Matthew 3:16
     καὶ ἰδοὺ   ἠνεῴχθησαν   αὐτῷ   οἱ   οὐρανοί
     kaì idoù   ***ēneóichthēsan***   *autôi*   *hoi*   *ouranoí*
     and behold opened.PASS.3PL 3SG.DAT ART.NOM heavens.NOM

   c. Wycliffe; Matthew 20:33
     *Thei seien to him, Lord, that oure iyen **be opened.***

   d. Wycliffe; Matthew 3:16
     *heuenes **weren openyd** to hym*

   e. Tyndale; Matthew 20:33
     *They sayd to him: Lorde that oure eyes maye **be opened.***

   f. Tyndale; Matthew 3:16
     *And lo heue **was ope** over hym*

   g. Authorized Version; Matthew 20:33
     *They say vnto him, Lord, that our eyes may **be opened.***

ENGLISH DATA

h. Authorized Version; Matthew 3:16
   the *heauens **were opened** vnto him*

i. English Revised Version; Matthew 20:33
   *They say unto him, Lord, that our eyes may **be opened**.*

j. English Revised Version; Matthew 3:16
   *the heavens **were opened** unto him*

k. English Standard Version; Matthew 20:33
   *They said to him, "Lord, let our eyes **be opened**."*

l. English Standard Version; Matthew 3:16
   *the heavens **were opened** to him*

Figure 7.4 displays data on the relation between the distribution of voice forms and animacy in the biblical retranslations. Regarding animate subjects, all English translations of the New Testament show similar characteristics and a clear contrast between the frequent active forms with animate subjects and the less frequent non-active/ marked forms with animate subjects. The above-mentioned clear contrast is not attested in the data from the Koine Greek source text, where non-active/ marked forms with animate subjects are more frequent than in the English translations of the New Testament—even though again less frequent than the active forms with animate subjects.

The characteristics of inanimate subjects and the distribution of voice forms appear to be different between the texts of the corpus: one observes significant variation between the texts in this case. Inanimate subjects are attested in constructions with non-active/ marked voice forms in most cases in the text of the Authorized Version and the English Revised Version: these two texts demonstrate similar characteristics with respect to this factor, in contrast to the other texts. This means that the Authorized Version and the English Revised Version follow the tendency found in the Koine Greek source text for high percentages of inanimates with marked forms (non-actives), in contrast to the other English translations of the New Testament. Tyndale's translation, the Wycliffite translation, and to a lower degree, the English Standard Version exhibit high frequency of active forms even with inanimate subjects.

Moreover, Figure 7.5 demonstrates a preference for animate subjects with the verbal meanings of our study both in the English translations of the New Testament and the Koine Greek text. The Koine Greek text illustrates a higher percentage for animate subjects with the verbs under examination than the

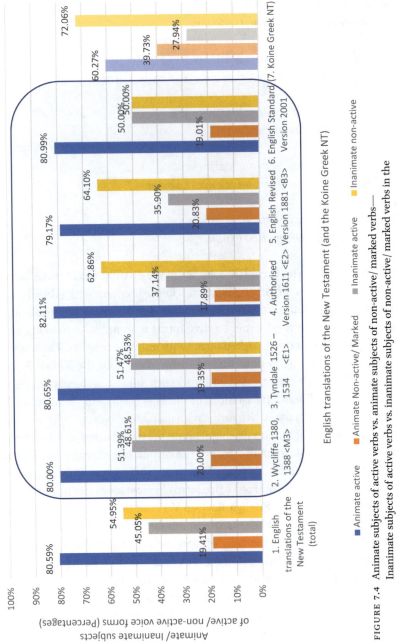

FIGURE 7.4 Animate subjects of active verbs vs. animate subjects of non-active/ marked verbs—Inanimate subjects of active verbs vs. inanimate subjects of non-active/ marked verbs in the corpus of English translations of the New Testament (See the list of selected verbal meanings: Table 7.2)

ENGLISH DATA

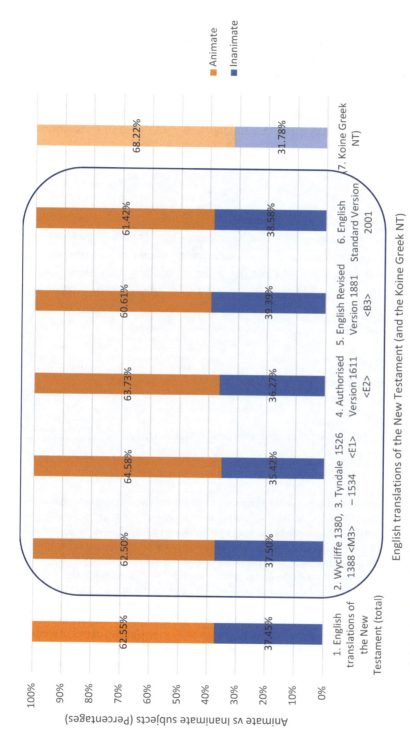

FIGURE 7.5 Animate vs. inanimate subjects in the corpus of English translations of the New Testament (and the Koine Greek NT) (See the list of selected verbal meanings: Table 7.2)

148   CHAPTER 7

other texts of the corpus. All English translations demonstrate similar percentages—and there is no difference between them. As expected, the results provide evidence in favor of a similar lexical conceptual structure (LCS) of the selected verbs in the various examined texts.[5] The high frequency of animate subjects can be seen as an evidence in favor of two-place predicates.[6]

The examples in (31a)–(31f) present a passage that includes the verb "close" in the Greek source text, and the same passage in the English translations of the corpus.

Luke 4:25

(31) a. Koine Greek New Testament

ὅτε   ἐκλείσθη   ὁ   οὐρανὸς   ἐπὶ ἔτη   τρία καὶ
hóte   ekleísthē   ho   ouranòs   epì été   tría kaì
when shut.PASS.3SG ART.NOM heaven.NOM for years three and
μῆνας   ἕξ.
mênas   héx.
months six

b. Wycliffe
*whanne heuene **was closid** thre yeer and sixe monethis*

c. Tyndale
*when hevyn **was shet** thre yeres and syxe monethes*

---

5 The lexical conceptual structure (LCS) refers to the linguistic representation of semantic and syntactic properties of lexical items and the regularities between the sets of these properties (Hale & Laughren 1983; Guerssel et al. 1985; Hale & Keyser 1986, 1987, 1988; Jackendoff 1988, 1993; Levin & Rappaport 1986, 1995, 2005; Grimshaw 1990; Levin 1993; Rappaport et al. 1993). See Levin & Rappaport Hovan (2019: 145):

LCSs are a form of predicate decomposition intended to capture those facets of verb meaning which determine grammatical behavior, particularly in the realm of argument realization. Research on LCSs and the structured representations that are their descendants has contributed to our understanding of the nature of verb meaning and the relation between verb syntax and semantics. This research has shown the importance of semantic representations that distinguish between root and event structure, as well as the importance of the architecture of the event structure to the determination of grammatical behavior. Furthermore, such developments have led some researchers to propose that representations of verb meaning should be syntactically instantiated.

6 Two-place predicates ascribe a property to the subject and *take two arguments* (two referential expressions associated with theta-roles).

ENGLISH DATA

d. Authorized Version
*when the heauen **was shut vp** three yeres and sixe moneths*

e. English Revised Version
*when the heaven **was shut up** three years and six months.*

f. English Standard Version
*when the heavens **were shut up** three years and six months.*

The examples in (32a)–(32f) present a passage that includes the verb "stop" in the Greek source text, and the same passage in the English translations of the corpus.

Acts 5:42

(32) a. Koine Greek New Testament
οὐκ ἐπαύοντο διδάσκοντες
*ouk **epaúonto** didáskontes*
NEG ceased.3PL teach.PRTC.NOM

b. Wycliffe
*thei **ceessiden** [...] to teche*

c. Tyndale
*they **ceased** not teachinge*

d. Authorized Version
*they **ceased** not to teach*

e. English Revised Version
*they **ceased** not to teach*

f. English Standard Version
*they did not **cease** teaching*

(ii) Comparison to the overall diachronic tendencies of non-translated texts

In this section, I evaluate the results of the corpus survey, which was discussed in (i), through a comparison to the overall diachronic tendencies in the history

150   CHAPTER 7

of English, on the basis of non-translated texts. The data here concern the same
verbal meanings as the ones examined in the case study of the translations of
the corpus. I investigate their characteristics in the corpus of non-translated
texts included in the *Penn Parsed Corpora of Historical English* (Kroch & Taylor
2000; Kroch et al. 2004; Kroch et al. 2016).[7]

I compare the results concerning the selected verbs in the English biblical
translations to the overall diachronic tendencies evidenced in non-translated
texts. First, I test the hypothesis of a change in the distribution of active vs. non-
active/marked morphological expression of voice, which may have affected the
frequencies of active and non-active forms in translations. The data from the
non-translated texts included in the Penn Parsed Corpora of Historical English
reflect stability in the presence of active and non-active forms in all periods
(Figure 7.6). If one compares the translations of the same text, one observes
differences—a type of development—in the grammatical characteristics of
the translations of the same source text. This type of development is evident
mainly when the diachrony of non-translated texts does not show a similar
change.

In an analogous manner to the distribution of active vs. non-active/marked
forms in non-translated texts, the morphological expression of voice in anticausative constructions appears to be similar in all examined periods. Middle English anticausatives and Early and Late Modern English anticausatives
exhibit the same overall tendency for a preference for unmarked (active) forms
(Figure 7.7). With respect to the frequencies of transitive and anticausative
constructions with active forms, the distribution is similar in all periods: there
are no statistically significant differences between the various periods, with a
preference for active anticausatives in all periods. However, note that the percentage of active transitive (i.e., active forms in transitive constructions) vs.
active anticausatives (i.e., active forms in anticausative constructions) depends
on idiosyncratic characteristics of the texts included in the corpus, and the
tendency is not clear. In other words, according to the data, some periods do
not show a difference in the preference for transitives or anticausatives (Figure 7.8).

---

7   On the York-Toronto-Helsinki Parsed Corpus, cf. Pintzuk & Plug (2002); Taylor et al. (2003).

ENGLISH DATA

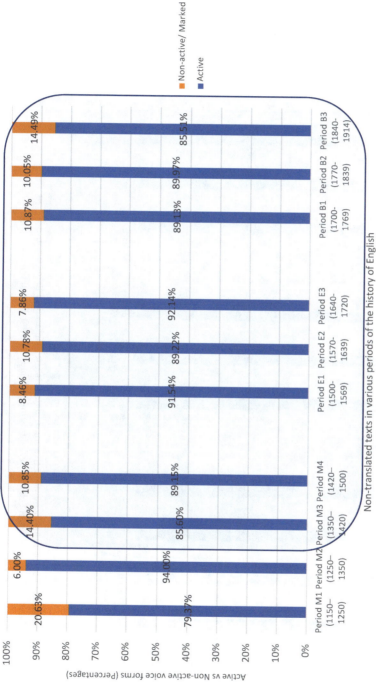

FIGURE 7.6 Distribution of active vs. non-active/ marked voice forms in the diachrony of English non-translated texts (See the list of selected verbal meanings: Table 7.2); Penn Parsed Corpora of Historical English

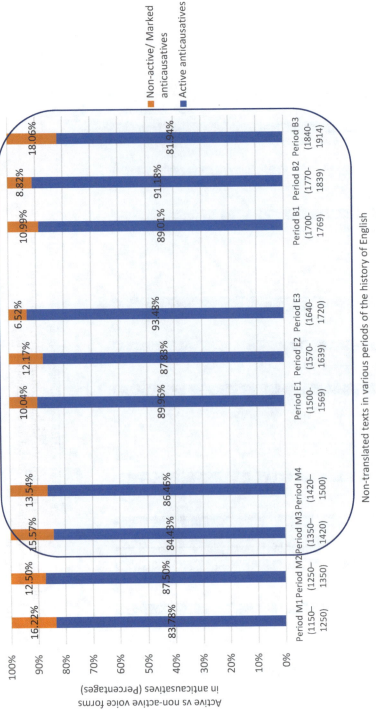

FIGURE 7.7 Distribution of voice forms in anticausative constructions in the diachrony of English non-translated texts (See the list of selected verbal meanings: Table 7.2); Penn Parsed Corpora of Historical English

ENGLISH DATA

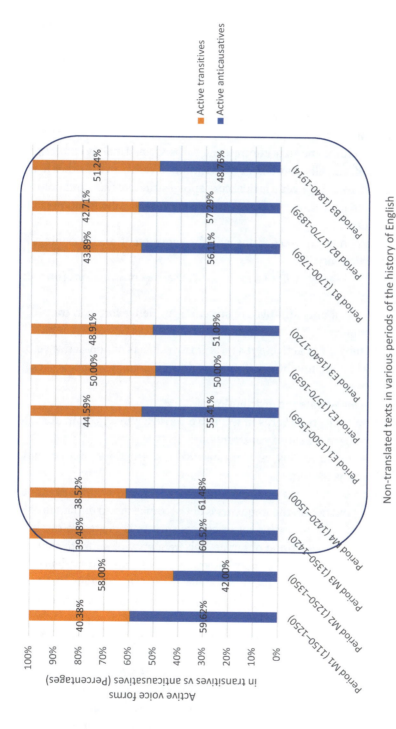

FIGURE 7.8 Transitive and anticausative constructions with active voice forms in the diachrony of English non-translated texts (See the list of selected verbal meanings: Table 7.2); Penn Parsed Corpora of Historical English

154

(iii) Voice and argument structure. Detailed case studies of particular verbs

The second set of corpus studies explores the selected verbs separately and compares the characteristics of their lexical conceptual structure on the basis of the relative frequency of the voice forms and the argument structure patterns. The word list of the present corpus survey includes the following verbs: 'grow' vs. 'dry' vs. 'heal' vs. 'tear' vs. 'clean' vs. 'close'. According to their lexical conceptual structure, one may contrast the verbs 'clean' (mainly) and 'close', on the one hand, and all the other above-mentioned verbs, on the other hand: the analysis of 'clean' involves a lexical conceptual structure that contains two sub-events. Thus, I examine the relative frequencies and the distribution of the following features:

(i) active *vs.* non-active voice forms with the above-mentioned meanings in all constructions;

(ii) active *vs.* non-active voice forms in anticausative constructions (on anticausatives, see 7.1);

(iii) active forms in anticausative constructions *vs.* active forms in transitive constructions;

(iv) animate subjects of active verbs *vs.* animate subjects of non-active verbs, as well as inanimate subjects of active verbs *vs.* inanimate subjects of non-active verbs.

Furthermore, I investigate the distribution of:

(i) inanimate subjects of verbs in transitive constructions *vs.* animate subjects of verbs in transitive constructions;

(ii) transitive constructions *vs.* anticausative constructions, that include verbs in any voice form.

Figures 7.9–7.14 present data on the frequencies of the verbs under examination separately (and not on the frequencies of the overall group of the selected verbs). The starting point of this set of corpus surveys is related to the lexical conceptual structure: if one observes high frequency of animate subjects with a verb, regardless its voice morphology, this constitutes an evidence for a two-place predicate. On the contrary, one expects lower frequency of transitive constructions and of animate subjects in the case of one-place predicates.

The verb "grow" demonstrates no difference either between the English translations of the New Testament under examination or between the Greek source text and the English translations of the New Testament (see Figures 7.9 and 7.10). The verb "grow" is attested with active forms in anticausative constructions in all texts of the corpus. Regarding animacy, there is no difference between the frequencies of animate and inanimate subjects *in any of the texts.*

ENGLISH DATA

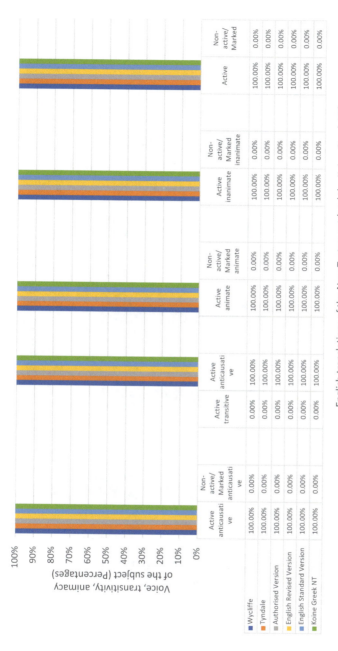

FIGURE 7.9 Voice, transitivity and subject animacy: The verb "grow" in the corpus of English translations of the New Testament

Note: Note that (non-)active (in)animate refers to constructions with (in)animate subjects and (non-)active voice forms. I follow a similar strategy in the usage of all terms here. "Grow" is attested with active morphology in anticausative constructions, both with animate and inanimate subjects, in all translations and the Koine Greek New Testament.

English translations of the New Testament (and the Koine Greek NT)

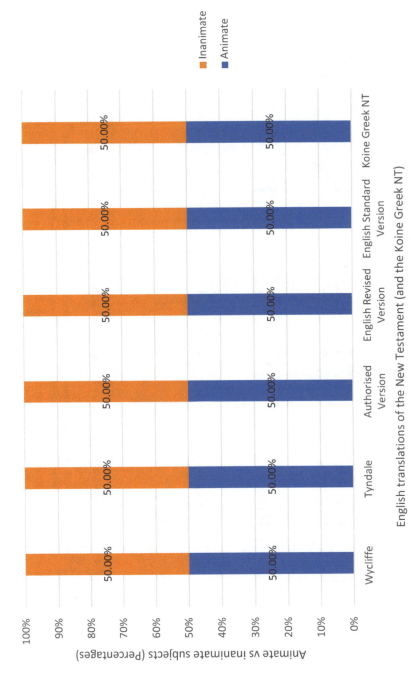

FIGURE 7.10　Animate vs. inanimate subjects: The verb "grow" in the corpus of English translations of the New Testament

ENGLISH DATA

The verb "dry" exhibits variation between its attestations in the English translations of the New Testament and the Koine Greek source text (Figures 7.11 and 7.12). It is attested with active forms in anticausative constructions in the English translations of the New Testament, but with non-active forms in anticausative constructions in the Koine Greek text. It presents similar characteristics in all English translations of the New Testament in that its active forms are found mainly in anticausative rather than in transitive constructions, in contrast to the Koine Greek text. Active forms are also more frequent than non-active forms in all constructions in all English translations of the New Testament, in contrast to the Koine Greek text.

In addition, inanimate subjects appear in constructions with active voice forms rather than with non-active forms in all English translations, in contrast to the Koine Greek text. The only significant difference between the English translations of the New Testament concerns the data on animate subjects with active forms in the Authorized Version. For instance, the results of the Pearson chi-square test are statistically significant for the comparison between animate subjects with active forms in Tyndale's translation and in the Authorized Version (χ^2=10.526, p<.05), with an effect size of φ=.229, which is a small effect size [Pearson chi-square test; exact significance]. Furthermore, the characteristics of the lexical conceptual structure of this verb appear to be similar in all texts of the corpus—including the Koine Greek text—as evidenced from an absolute predominance of inanimate subjects, irrespective of morphological expression of voice.

The data on the verb "heal" are similar to those on the verb "grow" in that there is no difference between the English translations and between the translations and the Koine Greek source text (Figures 7.13 and 7.14). The verb is attested with active forms in transitive constructions, and its subject is animate. According to the data, its subject is animate in all examples, and the verb "heal" appears to have a different lexical conceptual structure than the verb "dry".

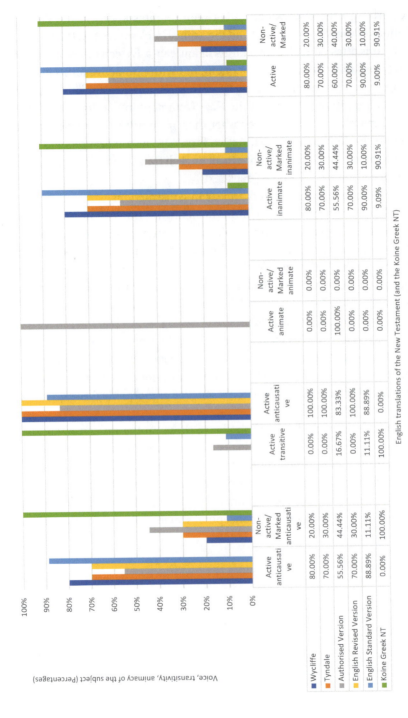

FIGURE 7.11   Voice, transitivity and subject animacy: The verb "dry" in the corpus of English translations of the New Testament

ENGLISH DATA 159

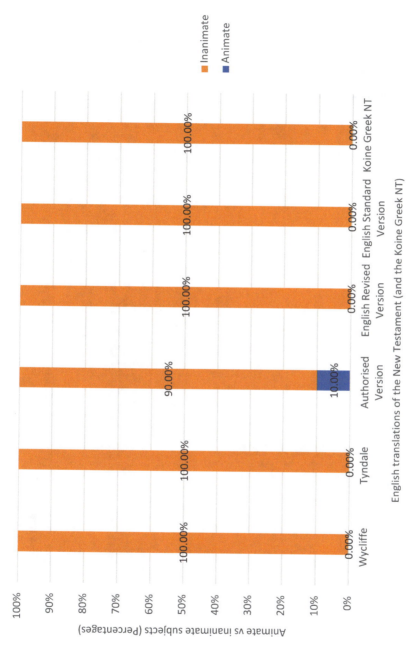

FIGURE 7.12 Animate vs. inanimate subjects: The verb "dry" in the corpus of English translations of the New Testament

160   CHAPTER 7

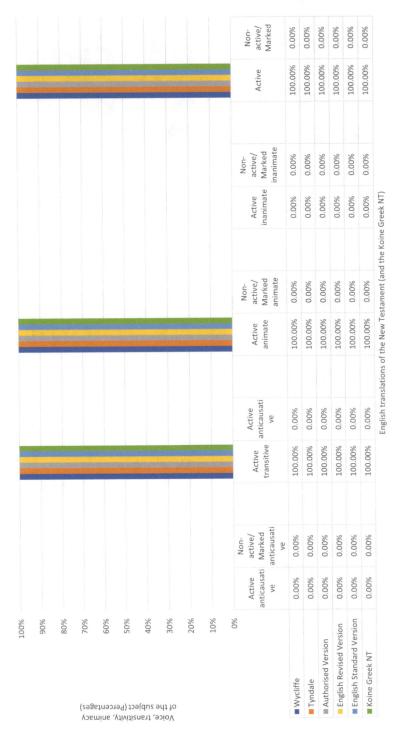

FIGURE 7.13 Voice, transitivity and subject animacy: The verb "heal" in the corpus of English translations of the New Testament

ENGLISH DATA

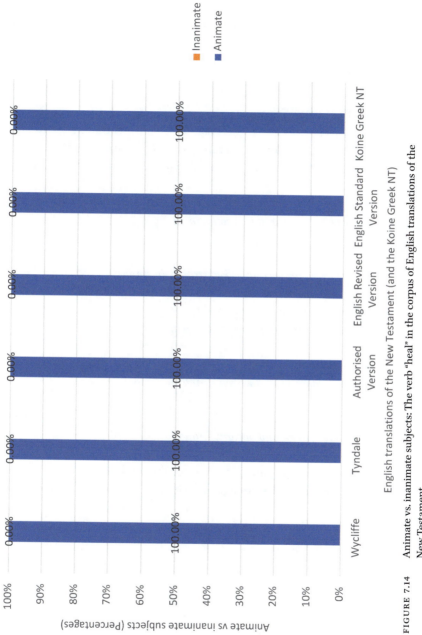

FIGURE 7.14 Animate vs. inanimate subjects: The verb "heal" in the corpus of English translations of the New Testament

162 CHAPTER 7

The examples in (33a)–(33f) present a passage that includes the verb "grow" in the Greek source text, and the same passage in the English translations of the corpus.

Luke 2:40

(33) a. Koine Greek New Testament

Τὸ δὲ παιδίον ηὔξανεν καὶ ἐκραταιοῦτο
tò dè paidíon ēúxanen kai ekrataioûto
ART.NOM PRT child.NOM grew.ACT.3SG and became-strong.3SG

b. Wycliffe
*And the child **wexe**, and was coumfortid*

c. Tyndale
*And the chylde **grewe** and wexed stronde in sprete*

d. Authorized Version
*And the child **grew**, and waxed strong in spirit*

e. English Revised Version
*And the child **grew**, and waxed strong*

f. English Standard Version
*And the child **grew** and became strong*

The examples in (34a)–(34f) present a passage that includes the verb "dry" in the Greek source text, and the same passage in the English translations of the corpus.

Mark 5:29

(34) a. Koine Greek New Testament

καὶ εὐθὺς ἐξηράνθη ἡ πηγὴ τοῦ
kai euthỳs exēránthē hē pēgè toû
and immediately dried.PASS.3SG ART.NOM fountain.NOM ART.GEN
αἵματος αὐτῆς
haímatos autês
blood.GEN her

ENGLISH DATA

163

    b. Wycliffe

      *And anoon the welle of hir blood **was dried vp***

    c. Tyndale

      *And streyght waye her foutayne of bloude **was dryed vp***

    d. Authorized Version

      *And straightway the fountaine of her blood **was dried vp***

    e. English Revised Version

      *And straightway the fountain of her blood **was dried up***

    f. English Standard Version

      *And immediately the flow of blood **dried up***

The examples in (35a)–(35f) present a passage that includes the verb "heal" in the Greek source text, and the same passage in the English translations of the corpus.

Matthew 8:7

(35) a. Koine Greek New Testament

      Ϗαὶ᾽ λέγει   αὐτῷ,   Ἐγὼ   ἐλθὼν,   θεραπεύσω
      *Ϗaì' légei   autôi,   Egò   elthòn,   **therapeúsō***
      and say.3SG 3SG.DAT 1SG.NOM come.PRTC.NOM heal.FUT.1SG
      αὐτόν.
      autón.
      3SG.ACC

    b. Wycliffe

      *And Jhesus seide to him, Y schal come, and schal **heele** him.*

    c. Tyndale

      *And Iesus sayd vnto hym: I will come and **heale** him.*

    d. Authorized Version

      *And Iesus saith vnto him, I will come, and **heale** him.*

    e. English Revised Version

      *And he saith unto him, I will come and **heal** him.*

f. English Standard Version
*And he said to him, "I will come and **heal him.**"*

The data on the verb "tear" present a contrast between Tyndale's translation and the Authorized Version (to a lesser degree) on the one hand, and all other English translations and the Koine Greek source text, on the other hand (Figure 7.15). In all other texts than Tyndale's translation and the Authorized Version, "tear" is attested with non-active forms in anticausative constructions with inanimate subjects. Tyndale's text and the Authorized Version contain examples of active anticausatives (i.e., anticausative constructions with active verbs).

Moreover, in Tyndale's translation, "tear" is attested with active forms in half of the examples. With respect to the lexical conceptual structure, all texts show a preference for inanimate subjects with "tear" (Figure 7.16). A significant percentage [33.33%] of animate subjects is found only in the Koine Greek text. For instance, the results of the Pearson chi-square test are statistically significant for the comparison between animate subjects in the Koine Greek text and the English Standard Version (χ^2=7.401, p<.05), with an effect size of φ=.192, which is a small effect size [Pearson chi-square test; exact significance].

The verb "clean" shows similar characteristics in all English translations and the Koine Greek text. It is attested in anticausative constructions with non-active forms, its active forms are found only in transitive constructions, the non-active forms have inanimate subjects, and the distribution of active and non-active voice forms shows slightly more frequent presence of non-active forms in all texts of the corpus (Figure 7.17). The only observed difference concerns a tendency in the Koine Greek text in favor of animate subjects in the case of constructions with active voice forms, in contrast to the data from the English biblical translations that do not indicate any significant difference in terms of animacy. For instance, the results of the Pearson chi-square test are statistically significant for the comparison between animate subjects with active forms in the Koine Greek text and Tyndale's translation (χ^2=5.717, p<.05), with an effect size of φ=.169, which is a small effect size [Pearson chi-square test; exact significance].

The verb "clean" appears to have the same lexical conceptual structure in all English biblical translations, which is demonstrated in the preference for animate subjects, if one examines all attestations of the verb "clean" irrespective of morphological expression of voice (Figure 7.18). The Koine Greek text shows similar characteristics but with a higher percentage of inanimate subjects, if compared to the English translations.

ENGLISH DATA

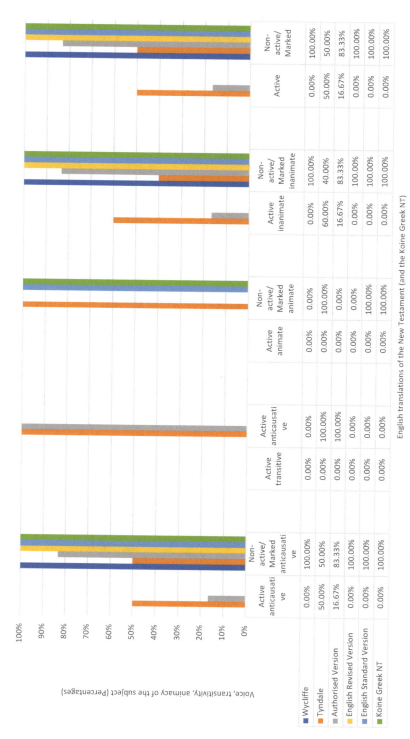

FIGURE 7.15 Voice, transitivity and subject animacy: The verb "tear" in the corpus of English translations of the New Testament

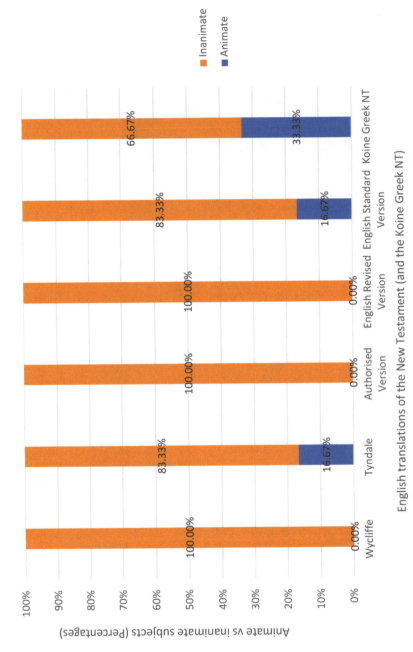

FIGURE 7.16 Animate vs. inanimate subjects: The verb "tear" in the corpus of English translations of the New Testament

ENGLISH DATA

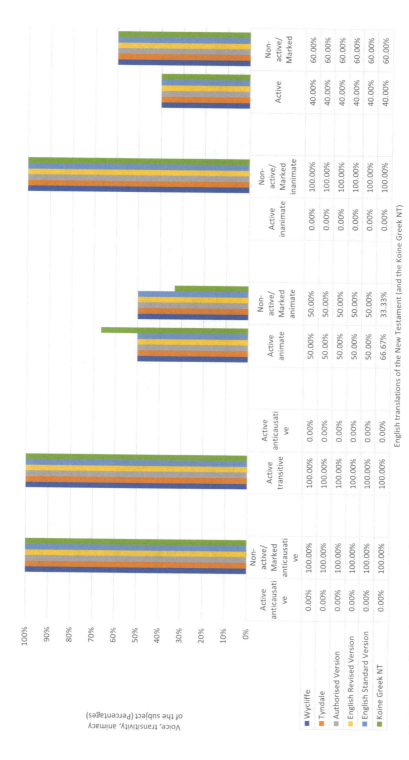

FIGURE 7.17 Voice, transitivity and subject animacy: The verb "clean" in the corpus of English translations of the New Testament

168   CHAPTER 7

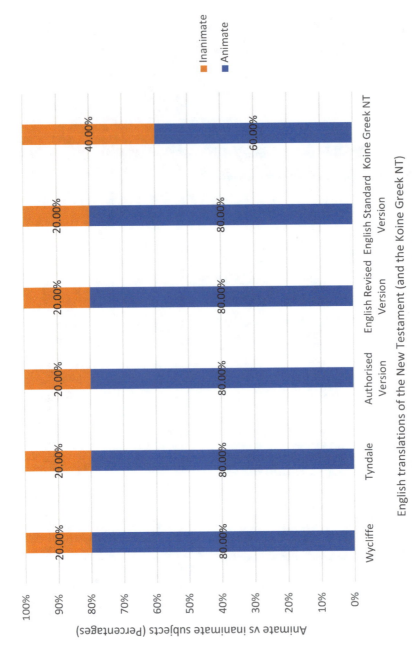

FIGURE 7.18   Animate vs. inanimate subjects: The verb "clean" in the corpus of English translations of the New Testament

ENGLISH DATA   169

The verb "close" displays an identical picture with the verb "heal" in terms
of presence of similar characteristics in all texts of the corpus, that is, one does
not observe important differences between the texts of the corpus (Figure 7.19).
However, "close" is attested with inanimate subjects in contrast to "heal", which
should reflect a different lexical conceptual structure. The verb "close" is found
only with non-active forms in anticausative constructions in the corpus, and
its subject is inanimate in all cases (Figure 7.20).

The examples in (36a)–(36f) present a passage that includes the verb "tear"
in the Greek source text, and the same passage in the English translations of
the corpus.

Matthew 27:51

(36) a. Koine Greek New Testament
τὸ   καταπέτασμα τοῦ   ναοῦ   ἐσχίσθη   ἀπ'
tò   *katapétasma toû*   *naoû*   ***eschísthē***   *ap'*
ART.NOM curtain.NOM ART.GEN temple.GEN tore.PASS.3SG from
ἄνωθεν ἕως κάτω,   εἰς δύο
ánōthen héōs kátō,   eis dýo
top-from to   bottom in two

b. Wycliffe
*the veil of the temple **was to-rent** in twey parties, fro the hiest to the low-*
est.

c. Tyndale
*the vayle of the temple dyd **rent** in twayne from ye toppe to the bottome*

d. Authorized Version
*the vaile of the Temple **was rent** in twaine, from the top to the bottome*

e. English Revised Version
*the veil of the temple **was rent** in twain from the top to the bottom*

f. English Standard Version
*the curtain of the temple **was torn** in two, from top to bottom.*

The examples in (37a)–(37f) present a passage that includes the verb "clean" in
the Greek source text, and the same passage in the English translations of the
corpus.

170 CHAPTER 7

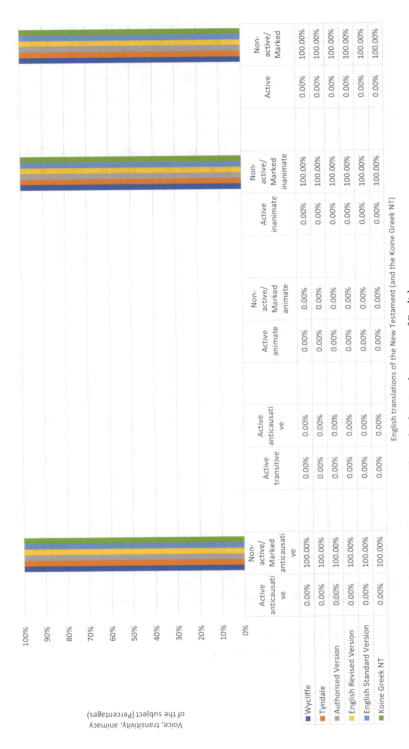

FIGURE 7.19 Voice, transitivity and subject animacy: The verb "close" in the corpus of English translations of the New Testament

ENGLISH DATA 171

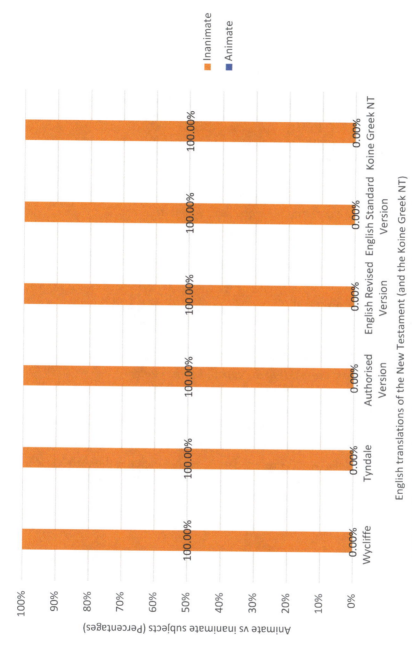

FIGURE 7.20 Animate vs. inanimate subjects: The verb "close" in the corpus of English translations of the New Testament

172 CHAPTER 7

Matthew 23:26

(37) a. Koine Greek New Testament

καθάρισον πρῶτον τὸ ἐντὸς τοῦ ποτηρίου καὶ
kathárison *prôton* *tò* *entòs* *toû* *potēríou* *kaì*
cleanse.IMP.2SG first ART.ACC inside ART.GEN cup.GEN and

τῆς παροψίδος
tês *paropsídos*
ART.GEN plate.GEN

  b. Wycliffe
    clense *the cuppe and the plater with ynneforth*

  c. Tyndale
    clense *fyrst the outsyde of the cup and platter*

  d. Authorized Version
    cleanse *first that which is within the cup and platter*

  e. English Revised Version
    cleanse *first the inside of the cup and of the platter*

  f. English Standard Version
    First **clean** *the inside of the cup and the plate*

The examples in (38a)–(38f) present a passage that includes the verb "close" in the Greek source text, and the same passage in the English translations of the corpus.

Acts 21:30

(38) a. Koine Greek New Testament

καὶ εὐθέως ἐκλείσθησαν αἱ θύραι.
kaì *euthéōs* *ekleísthēsan* *hai* *thýrai*
and straightway shut.PASS.3PL ART.NOM gates.NOM

  b. Wycliffe
    and anoon the yatis **weren closid.**

  c. Tyndale
    and forthwith the dores **were shut** *to.*

ENGLISH DATA

d. Authorized Version
   *and forthwith the doores **were shut.***

e. English Revised Version
   *and straightway the doors **were shut.***

f. English Standard Version
   *and at once the gates **were shut.***

The first corpus survey examined characteristics of voice and argument structure in English biblical translations prepared in different periods. The following section adds data from non-biblical English diachronic retranslations (that is, translations of the same source text from different periods) in a contrastive manner. The main hypothesis is that diachronic retranslations

(i)   do not reflect changes attested in non-translated texts of the same period, and

(ii)   demonstrate transfer from non-translated texts through a type of contact (Chapter 6).

In broad terms, English demonstrates continuity of grammatical characteristics of voice and argument structure, as seen in non-translated texts. However, this continuity cannot be found in the retranslations of the biblical texts, which show differences in various grammatical characteristics, through a complex transfer from the source texts—the Latin translation used as a source text and the Greek source text—and from non-translated texts of their period.

7.3   Voice and Transitivity in English Diachronic Biblical vs. Non-biblical Translations

(i)   Major changes in the English voice system and transitivity

The second set of phenomena that I examine through a corpus study of English retranslations is related to case and voice. In order to locate the position of my data in the overall diachronic tendencies in English, I briefly present the development of the syntactic phenomena under examination (see also Section 7.2 on the development of transitives/ causatives and intransitives/ anticausatives). Most parts of the present discussion are based on Fischer et al. (2017). Starting with data on *Case*, note that two of the major changes are related to the genitive case (see Table 7.4). The genitive case has shown a decrease in its use and has been replaced in most of its functions by Preposition

TABLE 7.4 Overview of changes in case form and function in the history of English

Changes in case form and function:	Old English	Middle English	Modern English
genitive	various functions	genitive case for subjective/ possessive	same
dative	various functions/ PP sporadic	*of-phrase* elsewhere	
accusative	main function: direct object	increase in *to-phrase*	

FISCHER ET AL. 2017: 4

Phrases introduced with the preposition *of* (Mustanoja 1960: 75—Rosenbach 2003, 2004). According to several studies, the new construction with the preposition *of* was probably influenced by French constructions with *de*.

The genitive suffix -(*e*)*s* stopped showing characteristics of a typical case suffix in the course of the Middle English period: the link between the case suffix and the noun became less close (Allen 2008: 152 ff.). For instance, in later Middle English, the -*es* form could be added to a Preposition Phrase following the head noun, as in (39).

(39) Chaucer, BD [Book of the Duchess] 168
in the god of slepes heyr
'the god of sleep's heir' (Fischer et al. 2017: 87)

Note that the Old English genitive marked several functions; on the contrary, the Middle English genitive was restricted to a few functions only, such as to the subjective and the possessive function—whereas the partitive and the objective function became extremely less frequent (Allen 2008). As a recent development the *s-genitive* extended to non-possessives in phrases such as "*the schoolbook's content*"—which probably is a 20th-century development (Fischer et al. 2017).

With regard to the development of the *passive* in English, the ambiguity between Present-Day English adjectival constructions and passives with the verb *be* reflects the diachronic development from adjectival to *be-passive*. There is consensus that the periphrastic passive has already emerged in Old English (Fischer et al. 2017—Denison 1993; Warner 1993, 1997). The *be-passive* underwent several further changes in the periods after Old English, especially with

ENGLISH DATA

TABLE 7.5   Overview of changes in voice-system in the history of English

Changes in voice-system:	Old English	Middle English	Modern English
passive form	*beon/weorðan* + (inflected) past participle	BE + uninflected past participle	same; new *GET* passive
indirect passive	absent	developing	(fully) present
prepositional passive	absent	developing	(fully) present
passive infinitive	only after modal verbs	after full verbs, with some nouns and adjectives	same

FISCHER ET AL. 2017: 4

the new prepositional passives (where the object of a preposition is promoted to subject) and indirect passives (where the indirect object is promoted to subject) and the extension of the passive to infinitives. Old English could also mark the passive construction with the auxiliary *weorðan* (see Table 7.5). The same verb could be used as a copula in Old English with the meaning of 'become'. This auxiliary is lost in later periods—in contrast to a totally different development of its cognates in other West Germanic languages. A Scandinavian influence has been proposed as a reason for the loss of the passive auxiliary.

In Present-Day English, three types of passives can be distinguished, according to the position of the derived subject in the corresponding transitive construction: direct passives (the direct object is promoted to subject of the passivized verb), indirect passives (the indirect object is promoted to subject) and prepositional passives (the object of a preposition is promoted to subject), as shown in (40) from Fischer et al. (2017). Only the direct passive construction is attested in Old English; as mentioned above, the indirect passive and the prepositional passive constructions emerged in the period of Middle English. For instance, the indirect passive can be found in texts by the end of the 14th century. Most studies consider the spread of the new indirect passive as extremely slow. In addition, it has been argued that certain verbs can be found in the new indirect passive construction quite earlier than other verbs. The prepositional passives appear around 1200, probably favored by a change in word order.

However, a passive structure was also lost in the diachrony of English: verbs that took objects in other cases that the accusative case could form passives in Old English, as shown in (41) with the verb *help*. In such instances, the subject

176 CHAPTER 7

is empty in the passive construction, and the only argument is marked with the dative both in the passive and the transitive construction. This type of passive construction disappeared in the course of the Middle English period.

(40) a. *He was arrested.* direct passive
b. *He was given a reprimand.* indirect passive
c. *This was frowned upon.* prepositional passive

(41) ÆCHom.II [Ælfric's Catholic Homilies: The second series (Godden 1979)], 39.1 293.178
and wæs ða **geholpen** *ðam unscyldigum huse*
and was then helped ART.DAT innocent house.DAT
'And then the innocent house was helped/ was given help.' (Fischer et al. 2017: 151)

With regard to the mediopassive or middle construction of Present-Day English, where the agent is suppressed and the direct object becomes the subject without the introduction of a passive auxiliary, as in the examples in (42a–b), from Fischer et al. (2017: 152), this construction is attested in Early Modern English but appears with significant frequency only in the last 200 years. The emergence and spread of the mediopassive/ middle construction can be connected to the presence in various periods of the history of English of causative-anticausative verbs that can be used in transitive and intransitive constructions without any formal change (42c)—see also 7.1: (i). Other explanations involve a tendency of transitives to acquire an intransitive use in the Middle English period and a change in information structure with the increasing preference for subjects to express old information.

(42) a. *This car drives like a dream.*
b. *This book won't sell.*
c. *The potatoes grew/ they grew potatoes.*
Fischer et al. (2017: 152)

Another important change in passives is related to passive infinitives, which, according to Fischer (1991), were grammatical only after modal verbs in Old English—but not with the verb *be*, or as adjuncts to an NP, or as adjectives or as subjects. Mainly in translations from Latin, the passive infinitives could also be found in AcI [accusativus-cum-infinitivo] constructions and after impersonal verbs (on control infinitives in Germanic, see, among others, Barðdal & Eythórsson 2007). The above-mentioned constructions, which were not avail-

ENGLISH DATA

able in Old English non-translated texts, became grammatical constructions in the course of the Middle English period (Timofeeva 2010; Fischer et al. 2017); see also Section 5.2.

(ii) Boethius

The corpus survey of the present section follows the same methodology—and is related to the same parameters—as my first corpus survey on English biblical translations (see Section 7.2.1). The data concern cases of complex interlingual translations and retranslations: I compare early and late English biblical translations as well as retranslations of Boethius' text *De Consolatione Philosophiae* "Consolation of Philosophy". The Roman Christian philosopher Anicius Manlius Severinus Boethius is the author of the largely Neoplatonic (5-books) work *De Consolatione Philosophiae* (sixth century AD). The work *De Consolatione Philosophiae*, which was an extremely well-known and widely read book in medieval times, includes prose and poetry (see also Section 4.4). Philosophy in this work is presented as a woman who converts Boethius, a prisoner, to the notion of Good. According to her teaching, humans have free will and there are no obstacles to divine foreknowledge and order. Reparation and reward beyond death consoles the prisoner Boethius. In this respect, Boethius transmits the main Platonic doctrines to the medieval communities. Several translations of the Latin work appeared in early vernacular literatures: For example, King Alfred's English translation of the ninth century, Chaucer's translation of the 14th century, and Elizabeth I's translation of the 16th century.[8]

The corpus studies of the current section investigate characteristics of argument structure. All the data are evaluated against evidence from non-translated texts of English of the same periods, which provides insights into the diachronic development of the phenomena under examination. All data presented in the present section (Boethius' translations—biblical translations—non-translated texts) derive from *the Penn Parsed Corpora of Historical English* (Kroch & Taylor 2000; Kroch et al. 2004; Kroch et al. 2016). On details about the editions, see: https://www.ling.upenn.edu/hist-corpora/PPCME2-RELEASE-4/index.html; https://www.ling.upenn.edu/hist-corpora/PPCEME-RELEASE-3/index.html; https://www.ling.upenn.edu/hist-corpora/PPCMBE2-RELEASE-1/index.html [last access: May 7, 2020].

---

8 Maximos Planoudes (1255–1305), a Byzantine scholar and writer, also translated *the Consolation of Philosophy* into the Byzantine Greek of the 13th century. With respect to other target languages, cf., for example, the 11th century German translation of Notker Labeo and the 13th century French translation of Jean de Meun.

7.3.1 *Corpus Survey*

(i) Transitives vs. intransitives in English biblical vs. non-biblical translations

The corpus surveys of the present section refer to features related to important aspects of transitivity and argument structure which show diachronic change, cross-linguistically, according to previous studies. A further restriction on the present corpus surveys is posited by the available corpora annotations: for instance, most of the corpora do not include annotation of null objects (drop of objects). Following the discussion of the above-mentioned factors, I investigate the relative frequency of the following features:

(i)   verbs with overt objects *vs.* verbs without an object in main clauses;
(ii)   pronoun objects vs. noun objects;
(iii)   active vs. non-active voice forms.

The corpus survey is based on a list of selected verbal meanings (on word lists, see Haspelmath 1993, Haspelmath et al. 2014, Nichols et al. 2004, Grünthal & Nichols 2016, Nichols 2017, 2018), derived from studies on voice and argument structure, mainly from Lavidas (2009) and Lavidas et al. (2012); see also 7.1 above. The data from the biblical source text, the Koine Greek text of the New Testament, constitute the starting point for the selection of the verbal meanings. Table 7.6, which repeats Table 7.2, includes the verbs as appear in the Koine Greek text. Table 7.7 lists the abbreviations of the time periods used in my corpus surveys, following the Penn Parsed Corpora of Historical English.

The first study aims at examining verbal transitivity and overt direct objects in biblical and non-biblical retranslations. All biblical translations of the corpus demonstrate similar results with respect to the presence of overt direct objects, with the exception of the Middle English text of the Wycliffite translation (third sub-period of the Middle English period) (Figure 7.21).[9] The non-biblical translations of the corpus also present similar relative frequencies regarding the contrast between constructions with overt direct objects and intransitive constructions (Figure 7.22). Only the 19th-century translation of Henry Rosher James shows a higher relative frequency of intransitive constructions in contrast to the other English translations of Boethius' text. In the case of transitivity and overt direct objects, the overall diachronic development, as evidenced in non-translated texts, does not demonstrate any kind of significant change (Figure 7.23).

---

9   Among many others, see Norton (1985: 515) on Purver's (1764) translation and Marlowe (2001) on Newcome's (1796) and Ellicott et al.'s (1881) translations.

ENGLISH DATA

179

TABLE 7.6 Word list for the corpus surveys on voice and argument structure (it repeats Table 7.2)

Main list of verbal meanings

'boil'	'grow'
'clean'	'melt'
'close'	'rot'
'dry'	'tear'
'heal'	

Additional list of verbal meanings; for corpus surveys with low number of results based on the main list of verbs

'anger'	'finish'
'become sick'	'get born'
'become strong'	'heighten'
'blind'	'die'
'break'	'open'
'burn'	'overflow'
'change'	'reinforce'
'darken'	'reveal'
'decrease'	'scatter'
'destroy'	'split'
'empty'	'spread'
'enlighten'	'stop'
'enrage'	'strengthen'
'fatten up'	'subside'
'fill'	

TABLE 7.7 Chronologies/ Divisions of the time periods and abbreviations used in the corpus surveys, following the Penn Parsed Corpora of Historical English: M3-E3

M3	1350–1420
E1	1500–1569
E2	1570–1639
E3	1640–1710

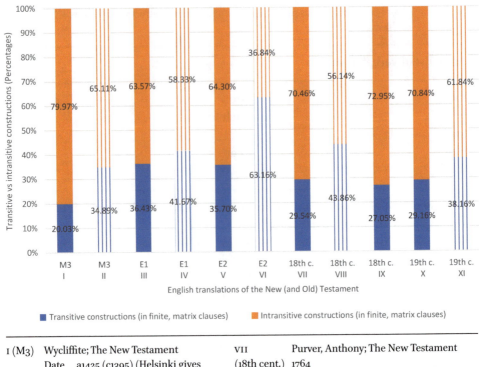

I (M3)	Wycliffite; The New Testament Date a1425 (c1395) (Helsinki gives c1388?)	VII (18th cent.)	Purver, Anthony; The New Testament 1764
II (M3)	Wycliffite; The Old Testament a1425 (a1382)	VIII (18th cent.)	Purver, Anthony; The Old Testament 1764
III (E1)	Tyndale, William; The New Testament 1534	IX (18th cent.)	Newcome, William; The New Testament 1796
IV (E1)	Tyndale, William; The Old Testament 1530	X (19th cent.)	Ellicott, Charles John et al.; The New Testament 1881 (published 1885)
V (E2)	Authorized Version; The New Testament 1611	XI (19th cent.)	English Old Testament Revisers 1885
VI (E2)	Authorized Version; The Old Testament 1611		

FIGURE 7.21 Transitive vs. intransitive constructions in finite, matrix clauses in the corpus of English biblical translations (See the list of selected verbal meanings: Table 7.6). See also Appendix 2 (i) for details on the sample included in the corpus

ENGLISH DATA

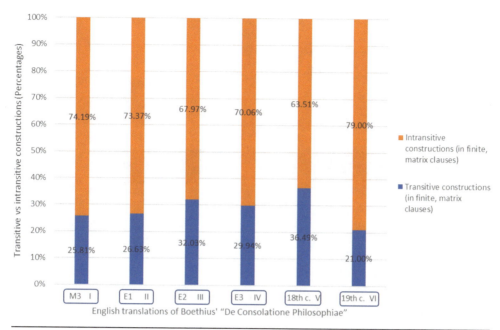

I (M3)	Chaucer	IV (E3)	Richard Graham, 1st viscount Preston
	Date ?a1425 (c1380)		1695
II (E1)	Colville, George	V	Ridpath, Philip
	1556	(18th cent.)	1785
III (E2)	Tudor, Elizabeth I	VI	James, Henry Rosher
	1593	(19th cent.)	1897

FIGURE 7.22 Transitive vs. intransitive constructions in finite, matrix clauses in the corpus of English translations of Boethius' *De Consolatione Philosophiae* (See the list of selected verbal meanings: Table 7.6). See Appendix 2 (ii) for details on the sample included in the corpus

This means that, in this case, stable characteristics and continuity are also represented to a degree in the English, biblical and non-biblical, translations prepared in different periods.

In the present study, I do not discuss the details of a comparison between the characteristics of the translated texts and the characteristics of the source text as appear in the corresponding passages of Boethius' Latin text. I am aware that such comparison—not included in the aims of the present book and left open for future research—can reveal further significant aspects of the ways that the translated texts reflect similar or different characteristics and strategies than the source texts in the same passage. The present study mainly aims at a comparison between the various translations/ diachronic retranslations. This means that I mainly focus on the examination of the "parallel diachrony"

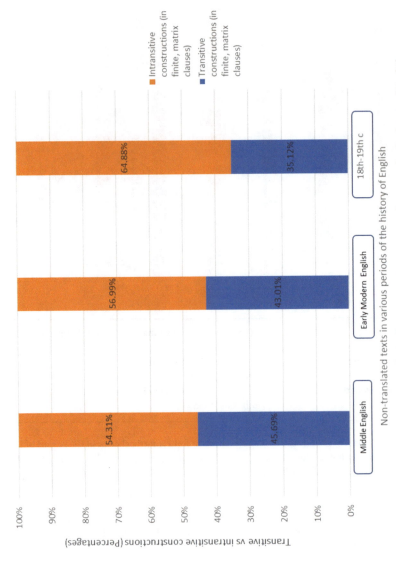

FIGURE 7.23 Transitive vs. intransitive constructions in finite, matrix clauses in the diachrony of English non-translated texts. (See the list of selected verbal meanings: Table 7.6); Penn Parsed Corpora of Historical English

of the translated texts and not on the transfer of characteristics of the source text. A comparison with the source text is not a main aim of the present study: for examples of such comparison, see Lavidas (2019a). However, a comparison of diachronic retranslations with the diachrony of non-translated texts and a study of the changes reflected in the non-translated texts are included in the main aims of my study.

(ii) English biblical vs. non-biblical (diachronic re)translations: Transitivity/ Object nouns vs. pronouns

The second set of corpus searches investigates the relative frequency of object pronouns and object nouns in the historical corpus of English biblical and non-biblical translations. In the case of biblical translations, the translations of the New Testament of all periods show similar relative frequencies of object pronouns and object nouns. The retranslations of the Old Testament also demonstrate similar results, without any significant difference (Figure 7.24). The sub-corpus of non-biblical translations presents similar relative frequencies of object pronouns and object nouns with a statistically significant preference for object nouns; the 19th-century translation is the only exception (Figure 7.25). For instance, the results of the Pearson chi-square test are statistically significant for the comparison between object pronouns and object nouns in the translation of Elizabeth I (χ^2=68.914, p<.05), with an effect size of φ=.587, which is a medium effect size [Pearson chi-square test; exact significance].

The 19th-century translation of Boethius' text does not demonstrate significant differences in the relative frequency of object pronouns and object nouns. Note that the 19th-century translation of Boethius does not follow the overall diachronic characteristics found in the data from the non-translated texts, which clearly indicate a rise in the presence of object nouns, from the Middle English to the Early and Late Modern English period (Figure 7.26). Hence, the English biblical and non-biblical translations may manifest stability or even the reverse direction of tendencies than the direction of the overall grammatical change observed in non-translated texts. Accordingly, I argue that retranslations do not directly reflect instances of grammatical change, which are represented in non-translated texts; in this respect, they form a parallel diachrony and constitute an example of the proposed multiglossia that predicts the coexistence of multiple input and multiple grammars (see Chapter 6). Multiple grammars are in contact and transfer from the one to the other is possible.

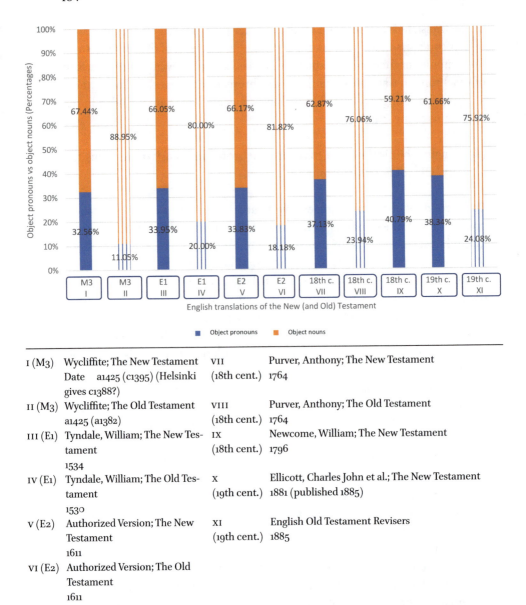

I (M3)	Wycliffite; The New Testament Date a1425 (c1395) (Helsinki gives c1388?)	VII (18th cent.)	Purver, Anthony; The New Testament 1764
II (M3)	Wycliffite; The Old Testament a1425 (a1382)	VIII (18th cent.)	Purver, Anthony; The Old Testament 1764
III (E1)	Tyndale, William; The New Testament 1534	IX (18th cent.)	Newcome, William; The New Testament 1796
IV (E1)	Tyndale, William; The Old Testament 1530	X (19th cent.)	Ellicott, Charles John et al.; The New Testament 1881 (published 1885)
V (E2)	Authorized Version; The New Testament 1611	XI (19th cent.)	English Old Testament Revisers 1885
VI (E2)	Authorized Version; The Old Testament 1611		

FIGURE 7.24   Object pronouns vs. object nouns in the corpus of English biblical translations. (See the list of selected verbal meanings: Table 7.6). See Appendix 2 (i) for details on the sample included in the corpus

ENGLISH DATA 185

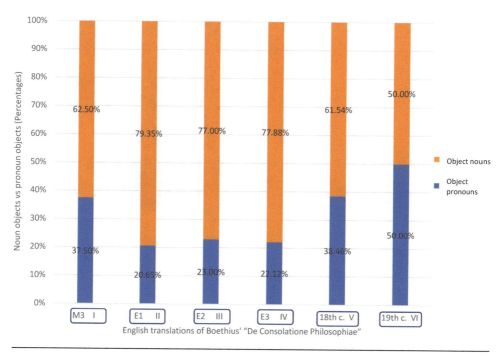

I	Chaucer	IV	Richard Graham, 1st viscount Preston
(M3)	Date ?a1425 (c1380)	(E3)	1695
II	Colville, George	V	Ridpath, Philip
(E1)	1556	(18th cent.)	1785
III	Tudor, Elizabeth I	VI	James, Henry Rosher
(E2)	1593	(19th cent.)	1897

FIGURE 7.25   Object pronouns vs. object nouns in the corpus of English translations of Boethius' *De Consolatione Philosophiae*. (See the list of selected verbal meanings: Table 7.6). See Appendix 2 (ii) for details on the sample included in the corpus

(iii) English biblical *vs.* non-biblical (diachronic re)translations: Voice

The relative frequency of non-active/ marked formations in the English biblical translations is similar in all translations of the present corpus, with only few exceptions (Figure 7.27). The data from the diachronic English biblical retranslations do not reflect a type of grammatical change: one does not observe a relevant grammatical change from the early to the late versions—but stability between the various translations. It appears that the relative frequency of non-actives is not significantly different in the texts of the corpus, demonstrating again that biblical translations do not exhibit significant differences between their early and later versions in the relative frequencies of core grammatical characteristics.

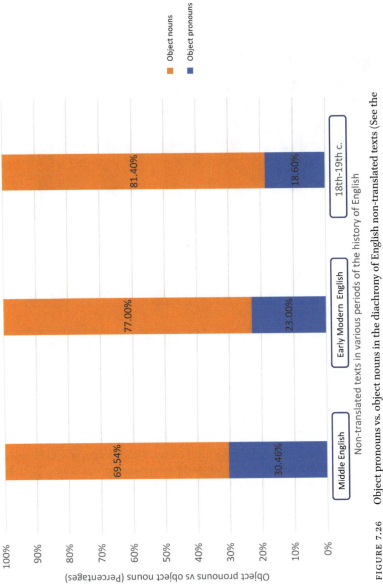

FIGURE 7.26 Object pronouns vs. object nouns in the diachrony of English non-translated texts (See the list of selected verbal meanings: Table 7.6); Penn Parsed Corpora of Historical English

ENGLISH DATA

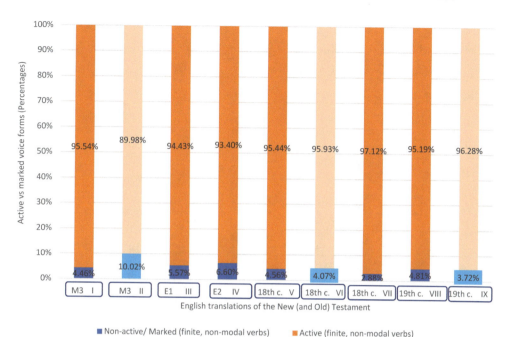

I (M3)	Wycliffite; The New Testament Date a1425 (c1395) (Helsinki gives c1388?)	VI (18th cent.)	Purver, Anthony; The Old Testament 1764
II (M3)	Wycliffite; The Old Testament a1425 (a1382)	VII (18th cent.)	Newcome, William; The New Testament 1796
III (E1)	Tyndale, William; The New Testament 1534	VIII (19th cent.)	Ellicott, Charles John et al.; The New Testament 1881 (published 1885)
IV (E2)	Authorized Version; The New Testament 1611	IX (19th cent.)	English Old Testament Revisers 1885
V (18th cent.)	Purver, Anthony; The New Testament 1764		

FIGURE 7.27   Active vs. marked voice forms in the corpus of English biblical translations. (See the list of selected verbal meanings: Table 7.6). See Appendix 2 (i) for details on the sample included in the corpus

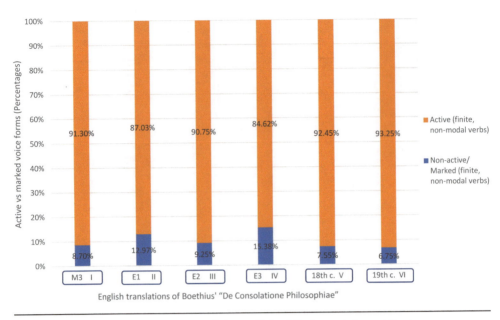

I (M3)	Chaucer	IV (E3)	Richard Graham, 1st viscount Preston
	Date ?a1425 (c1380)		1695
II (E1)	Colville, George	V	Ridpath, Philip
	1556	(18th cent.)	1785
III (E2)	Tudor, Elizabeth I	VI	James, Henry Rosher
	1593	(19th cent.)	1897

FIGURE 7.28 Active vs. marked voice forms in the corpus of English translations of Boethius' *De Consolatione Philosophiae* (See the list of selected verbal meanings: Table 7.6). See Appendix 2 (ii) for details on the sample included in the corpus

On the contrary, the diachronic retranslations appear to share basic grammatical characteristics. In the case of the diachronic retranslations of Boethius' text, the non-active voice forms have a similar distribution in all texts (Figure 7.28). Only the translated texts of the 18th and the late 19th century show a statistically significant different relative frequency of non-active forms, which cannot be easily related to the diachrony of retranslations and the characteristics of their period. For instance, the results of the Pearson chi-square test are statistically significant for the comparison between non-active voice forms in the E3 (Early Modern English; subperiod: 1640–1710) and the 18th-century translation (χ^2=6.536, p<.05), with an effect size of φ=.181, which is a small effect size [Pearson chi-square test; exact significance].

An examination of the distribution of active *vs.* non-active voice forms in all non-translated texts of the Penn Parsed Corpora of Historical English reveals

ENGLISH DATA

stability in the presence of active and non-active forms in all periods (Figure 7.29). Again, the development of the non-translated texts is not directly reflected in the biblical or non-biblical translations. The above observation is directly related to the main proposal of the present study, the *Hypothesis of Grammatical Multiglossia*: various systems of grammar of the same language may exist; in a similar way, various parallel "diachronies" of the same language exist.

In the present section, I added data from diachronic English non-biblical retranslations and examined the development of grammatical characteristics again related to transitivity and voice. Even though non-biblical retranslations do not demonstrate the same picture as diachronic biblical retranslations, they present differences between them that contrasts the stability observed in non-translated texts, similarly to biblical retranslations. The differences are due to transfer from the source text and earlier texts, reflecting a type of written contact.

In the following section, I discuss a different type of study, a corpus-driven study that focuses on word-formation morphology but again on the basis of data from English biblical and non-biblical diachronic retranslations, that is retranslations from different periods of the history of English. Through a document classification approach, I test how written language contact works and how grammatical characteristics of earlier and late periods as well as characteristics of other languages and of the same language coexist and can be found to be in contact even in non-transitional periods.

7.4 English Biblical vs. Non-biblical Diachronic Retranslations: Borrowing of Word-Formation Morphology

In order to test (i) how written language contact works and (ii) the hypothesis that translations do not follow the development of grammar evidenced in non-translated texts, I conducted a different type of corpus study, which I discuss in the present section. The starting point of the present corpus search is Romaine's claim (1985: 452) that "the suffix *-ity* [...] makes its appearance in 14th–15th-century loanwords from French, and later, in loanwords from Latin." See also Gardner (2014). Following Taavitsainen & Schneider (2018), I answer the following questions in the present section: (a) *Can borrowing of derivational morphology, as it appears in English translations, be detected by means of Document Classification?* (b) *Can the characteristics of borrowing from the medieval period be detected in Early Modern English texts?*

In the present section, I examine the development of borrowing of word-formation morphology in diachronic retranslations. I compare translations of

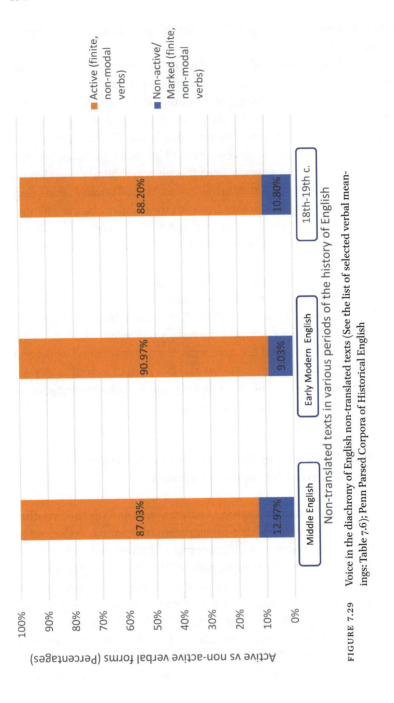

FIGURE 7.29 Voice in the diachrony of English non-translated texts in various periods of the history of English (See the list of selected verbal meanings: Table 7.6); Penn Parsed Corpora of Historical English

ENGLISH DATA

TABLE 7.8   The corpus: English translations of the Latin text of Boethius' *De Consolatione Philosophiae* and English translations of the New Testament

Sub-corpus I: English translations of the Latin text of Boethius' De Consolatione Philosophiae

Alfred's translation (9th–10th century)
Chaucer's translation (14th century; probably also based on a French translation)
George Colville's translation (16th century)
Elizabeth I's translation (16th century)
Richard Preston's translation (17th century; 1695)
Philip Ridpath's translation (18th century; 1785)

Sub-corpus II: English translations of the New Testament

Wycliffe's translation (14th century)
Tyndale's translation (16th century; based on the Koine Greek source text)
Authorized Version (17th century)
Purver's translation (18th century; 1764)
Newcome's translation (18th century; 1796)
English Revised Version (1881)
English Standard Version (2001)

the Latin text of Boethius' *De Consolatione Philosophiae* from different periods of English and translations of the New Testament into English. See Table 7.8.

According to my main hypothesis, the word formation patterns should also reflect grammar competition and *grammar coexistence*: transitional periods—but not only transitional periods (see Chapter 6)—demonstrate the *coexistence* of more than one grammar and a competition between these grammars (Kroch 1989, 2001). Grammar competition and coexistence are represented, for instance, in coexistent forms that appear in later translations, e.g., *fragileness/fragility*, and with semantically related sets, e.g., *madness/insaneness/insanity* (Romaine 1985). The diachronic perspective may provide information on the details of the *coexistence of parallel grammars*. Romaine (1985) also argues that the comparison of translations constitutes an appropriate approach to a diachronic examination of word formation. However, she has based her similar study only on the frequency of any noun in -*ness* and -*ity*: see Table 7.9.

TABLE 7.9 *-ness* and *-ity* formations in Alfred's, Chaucer's and Elizabeth's translations of Boethius' *De Consolatione Philosophiae*: data from Romaine 1985

Translation	Alfred	Chaucer	Elizabeth
-ness* vs. *-ity			
-ness formations	100%	53%	50%
newer *-ity formations*	-	47%	50%

Based on a machine learning approach through document classification (Mayfield & Rosé 2010, 2013), I locate *which features are the most characteristic* of the class of texts that are translations from Latin (the features with the highest weights in a logistic regression are the most characteristic for the class), and *to which degree early translations differ* from later translations and from non-translated texts. According to the aims of the document classification approach, the characteristic features of each class of documents—e.g., translated *vs.* non-translated, early translations *vs.* later retranslations, and early non-translated texts *vs.* later non-translated texts—should be automatically learned from the manually classified documents in a corpus-driven way. Document classification can derive significant results that show in a data-driven fashion which words are *the most indicative, i.e. typical of which category.*

I examine the derivational suffixes of Middle English with a different starting point than in my other corpus surveys: the derivational suffixes of Middle English have been considered as belonging to different types on the basis of their origin. Previous studies have described in detail the role of the French and Latin influence in the development of derivation of Middle English: see Dalton-Puffer (1992, 1997 2011) and Gardner (2011, 2014). Zbierska-Sawala (1989, 1991) and Ciszek (2004, 2012) investigate derivation in Early Middle English, and Rodríguez-Puente (2020) the development of *-ity* and *-ness* in Early Modern English. Trips' (2009, 2014) studies have a larger diachronic scope.

Many of the Old English derivational suffixes for abstract nouns, for instance, *-dom, -hede* [*-hade*, etc], *-lac* [*-lec*, etc], *-ness, -ship, -ung* [*-ing*, etc], were active in Middle English. In Middle English, Romance suffixes with similar functions were also added to the vocabulary of the language: e.g., *-acy, -age, -al, -aunce* (*-ence*, etc), *-(a)cioun* (*-ation*, etc), *-(e)rie, -ite, -ment* (van Gelderen 2014—cf. also Trips & Stein 2008). Accordingly, several Germanic and Romance suffixes could be synonymous: See Table 7.10 (van Gelderen 2014).

ENGLISH DATA

TABLE 7.10 Synonymous Germanic and Romance suffixes in Middle English

Germanic	Latin/ French
-dom/-hood (e.g., freedom)	*-ite* (e.g., liberty)
-hood (e.g., boyhood)	*-ence* (e.g., adolescence)
-ful (e.g., sinful)	*-al* (e.g., national)
-ing (e.g., beginning)	*-ment* (e.g., commencement)
-ship (e.g., worship)	*-ation* (e.g., adoration)

VAN GELDEREN 2014: 133

I base my study mainly on data collected through the *LightSide* program (Mayfield & Penstein Rosé 2010, 2013). Document classification can assist us in collecting rich sets of weighted lexical features (Taavitsainen & Schneider 2018). According to the document classification methodology, documents should be divided into binary classes of relevant *vs.* irrelevant types for an information retrieval task.[10] Words in the documents have the status of discriminators between the classes, whereas their syntactic context is not taken into consideration in this case. Document classification is a data-driven approach: the data are the main factor for the formation of hypotheses and analysis. Accordingly, document classification may reveal patterns not observed in past studies.

Moreover, I use algorithms with the aim of combining the relevant features: through a logistic regression, each feature can receive the optimal weight. Features with high weights in the results are features that are typical for the class, they discriminate well (they are good discriminators), for instance, between translated and non-translated texts. On the contrary, features with low weights are features that do not discriminate well. The data that I present here concern diachronic retranslations; I have collected them through logistic regression, setting a rare threshold of 5 for my surveys.

Table 7.11 presents chronologies and abbreviations related to the present corpus survey. Table 7.12 includes all details on the accuracy data according to the

---

10   A sophisticated quantitative analysis and an application of other methodologies of document classification are not an aim of the present book. Cf., for instance, Mikros (2006, 2007). I acknowledge that, if one adds the perspective of sophisticated quantitative analyses, other important directions of research may open, and significant new conclusions can be reached. Given the overall scope of the present book, I leave further alternative directions of quantitative analyses open for future studies (see fn. 1).

TABLE 7.11 Chronologies/ Divisions of the time periods and abbreviations used in the document classification study, following the Penn Parsed Corpora of Historical English: M3-E3 (it repeats Table 7.7)

M3	1350–1420
E1	1500–1569
E2	1570–1639
E3	1640–1710

machine learning approach as well as the results of document classification. The accuracy is high in most of the examples: over 95% in many cases, over 90% in the majority of the cases, with only few exceptions.

The present section introduced the basic aims and research methodology that I follow in my document classification corpus survey. In the following section, I discuss the results of three case studies focusing on nouns that bear Germanic vs. Latin/ French derivational suffixes and are good discriminators of English translations of Boethius' *De Consolatione Philosophiae* and of English biblical translations. The case studies of the corpus-driven part show the way early native and late borrowed derivational suffixes coexist in translations and non-translations of various periods—and *not only in transitional periods*. The results confirm the hypothesis of a *peaceful coexistence* of multilingual systems of grammar and of *transfer* of elements from the one to the other system—that is, of contact between these systems.

7.4.1 *Corpus Survey*

7.4.1.1   Case study I: Old English suffix *-ness* vs. the innovative Romance suffix *-itie* (/-ity)

In the present section, I discuss the results of a corpus-driven survey that investigates the borrowing of derivational morphology in the history of English. The hypothesis is that other grammatical characteristics than argument structure/ transitivity and voice should also support the same conclusion that translations do not reflect changes attested in non-translated texts directly. Borrowed and non-borrowed grammatical characteristics coexist even in later, non-transitional periods. I discuss the data from the document classification survey on the basis of three examples of comparison of derivational suffixes according to the relevant literature.

ENGLISH DATA

TABLE 7.12 Accuracy data (machine learning approach and document classification)

Boethius' translations

M3 vs. E1 translation
Accuracy 0.96
E1 vs. E2 translation
Accuracy 0.955
E2 vs. E3 translation
Accuracy 0.944
E3 vs. 1785 translation
Accuracy 0.907
1785 vs. 1897 translation
Accuracy 0.897

Boethius' translation vs. non-translated texts of the same period

M3 (14th-century) translation vs. M3 (14th-century) non-translation
Accuracy 0.98

New Testament

M3 vs. E1 translation
Accuracy 0.991
E1 vs. E2 translation
Accuracy 0.934
E2 vs. 1764 translation
Accuracy 0.95
1764 vs. 1796 translation
Accuracy 0.925
1796 vs. 1881 translation
Accuracy 0.895

Translation of the New Testament vs. non-translated texts of the same period

E1 (16th-century) translation of the New Testament vs. E1 (16th-century) non-translation
Accuracy 0.974

TABLE 7.13 *-ity* vs. *-ness* with nouns that are good discriminators in Chaucer's (14th-century) vs. Elizabeth's (16th-century) translation of Boethius' *De Consolatione Philosophiae*

Chaucer's translation		Elizabeth's translation	
Feature	Feature weight[a]	Feature	Feature weight
blisfulnesse	0.8639	vniuersalitie	0.4255
wikkidnesse	0.5515	dignitie	0.4131
wrecchidnesse	0.4111	felicitie	0.3994
schrewednesse	0.3350	nobilitie	0.3832
unselynesse	0.3193	blessedness	0.2744
symplicite	0.2484	seueritie	0.1866
welefulnesse	0.2223	happynes	0.1847
adversitie	0.1928	darknes	0.1828
swetnesse	0.1848	stabilitie	0.1747
lightnesse	0.1773	affinitie	0.1395
dyvinite	0.1645		
necessite	0.1296		

a On the methodology of working with feature weights, see, among others, Taavitsainen & Schneider (2018).

Following Romaine's (1985) remarks (see also Romaine 1983, 2005, Esteban-Segura 2011, among others), in Table 7.13 I compare the feature weight of the Old English suffix *-ness* vs. the innovative Romance suffix *-itie(/-ity)*,[11] that is, the degree according to which the relevant features are indicators of the translated vs. non-translated texts under examination. In Chaucer's translation, nouns with *-ness* still appear with a high feature weight. Elizabeth's later translation demonstrates the opposite results: nouns in *-itie* are attributed a higher feature weight than nouns in *-ness*. However, in both translations, nouns in *-itie* and *-ness* can be found in the list of nouns that are indicative of the particular text. It is evident that an alternative way of examining the patterns of borrowing reflected in translations could investigate only the relevant suffixes and their presence—and not the nouns bearing these suffixes. I leave this type of study open for future research because Romaine's remarks constitute the starting point of my examination; moreover, I follow the methodology of previous studies of document classification, and, therefore, I focus on the presence of nouns

---

11 With all attested orthographies.

ENGLISH DATA

with these suffixes in translations and not on the morphemes and their morphological context. Most importantly, the present type of investigation results in high accuracy numbers.

In Tables 7.14–7.16, I extend the above study to other early and later translations of Boethius' *De Consolatione Philosophiae*. I present indicative results of the suffixes *-ness* vs. *-itie* with nouns that are good discriminators of the particular texts (early vs. later translations). The grey color in the tables indicates that the feature weight is close to zero, which means that the particular feature is a good discriminator of both texts under examination. Here I discuss only a part of the results, that is, the most significant results regarding the contrast between early and later translations and word formation.

Table 7.14 illustrates that the suffix *-ity* appears in the list of nouns with high weight feature that are good discriminators of the E1 [16th-century] translation only, that is, of Colville's translation. On the contrary, the suffix *-ness* can be found both with nouns that are good discriminators of the E1 [16th-century] and with nouns that are good discriminators of the M3 [14th-century] translation, that is, of Chaucer's translation. Table 7.15 includes the results from a comparison between translated and non-translated texts of the same period (M3 subperiod of the Penn Parsed Corpora of Historical English), in terms of feature weight in a document classification analysis of word derivation suffixes. The *-ness* suffixes are mainly attested with nouns that are good discriminators of the 14th-century translated text.

On the contrary, the *-ity* suffixes are attested both with nouns that are good discriminators of the 14th-century non-translated text and the 14th-century translated text. The differences in the distribution of the suffixes are probably due to idiosyncratic characteristics of the selected non-translated text. In the case of biblical translations, nouns with the Romance suffix *-ity/ itie* are absent from the list of good discriminators in the case of both early and later translation. Moreover, nouns in *-ness* are good discriminators only of the late translation (Table 7.16).

Accordingly, the overall conclusion is in the same direction as the conclusion derived from the other types of corpus surveys: the data show a parallel development of the new word-formation suffixes in a grammatical system that coexists with the grammatical system of non-translated texts. In particular, the example of the early *vs.* later translated document classification study demonstrates a significant delay in the emergence of nouns in *-itie/ -ity* as good discriminators of translations, and especially in the case of biblical translations. The development of the new derivational suffix as attested in later retranslations is not reflected in a document classification/ logistic regression comparison between early and later translated texts and between translated and non-translated texts.

198 CHAPTER 7

TABLE 7.14   *-ity* vs. *-ness* with nouns that are good discriminators of the 14th-century (Chaucer's) vs. the 16th-century (Colville's) translation of Boethius' *De Consolatione Philosophiae*

Text	Features (discriminators)	Feature weight	Text	Features (discriminators)	Feature weight
14th-century translation	blisfulnesse wikkidnesse wrecchidnesse	1.221569214 0.857682021 0.532793914	16th-century translation	goodnes syckenes blyssednes	0.643323595 0.62443179 0.112176611
	–			felicitie prosperitie simplicitie aduersitie puritie	0.748893929 0.7366119 0.449386911 0.391012862 0.330160421

TABLE 7.15   *-ity* vs. *-ness* with nouns that are good discriminators of the 14th-century (Chaucer's) translation of Boethius' *De Consolatione Philosophiae* [sample] and of the 14th-century non-translated text [Purvey's General Prologue to the Bible; date: a1450 (a1397); genre: religious treatise]

Text	Features (discriminators)	Feature Weight	Text	Features (discriminators)	Feature Weight
14th-century translation	blisfulnesse wikkidnesse wrecchidnesse	1.091024178 1.052534751 0.474038199	14th-century non-translated text	rightfulnesse	0.063792765
	prosperite	0.122371089		charite autorite	0.61898095 0.365205807

ENGLISH DATA 199

TABLE 7.16 *-ity* vs. *-ness* with nouns that are good discriminators between the 14th-century (Wycliffe's) and the 16th-century (Tyndale's) translation of the New Testament

Text	Features (discriminators)	Feature Weight	Text	Features (discriminators)	Feature Weight
14th-century translation of the New Testament (Wycliffe)	derknessis	0.011263	16th-century translation of the New Testament (Tyndale)	wyldernes witnesses	0.52014 0.11701
	Ø (= absence of nouns in *-ity* in the list of good discriminators for the particular text)			Ø (= absence of nouns in *-ity* in the list of good discriminators for the particular text)	

7.4.1.2 Case study II: Synonymous Germanic (Old English) and Romance derivational suffixes

The starting point of the second example of a document classification survey concerns synonymous Germanic (Old English) and Romance derivational suffixes. Table 7.17 from van Gelderen (2014) presents examples of synonymous Germanic and Romance derivational suffixes.

The data from the second survey consist of unigram features, in a similar manner to the above data. They are sorted by weight; they present in a data-driven way which words are typical of which category, that is, which words are the most indicative of the particular type of text, in the case of early *vs.* later translations—translated *vs.* non-translated text. Tables 7.18 and 7.19 show which words appear higher in the list of good discriminators of the M3 / 14th-century translation if compared to the E1 / 16th-century translation of Boethius' text, as well as of the E1 translation if compared to the M3 translation, that is, in the case of reverse comparison (Table 7.18). Regarding the derivational suffixes under examination, only words with the Romance *-e(a)nce* (and *-ment*, to a degree) have a high feature weight in the Middle and Early Modern English translations. The Germanic derivational suffixes—included in the above list of synonymous suffixes—are absent from the list of good discriminators (Table 7.19).

In the case of the comparison of the E3 translation (1695 translation) to the 1785 translation of Boethius' text, it appears that the lists of good discriminators of both translations include nouns with Old English suffixes, e.g. *-dom, -ful, -ing, -ship*, as well as with Romance suffixes, e.g. *-ity, -e(a)nce, -ation, -ment*

TABLE 7.17 Synonymous Germanic and Romance suffixes in Middle English. It repeats Table 7.10

Germanic	Latin/ French
-dom/ -hood (e.g., freedom)	*-ite* (e.g., liberty)
-hood (e.g., boyhood)	*-ence* (e.g., adolescence)
-ful (e.g., sinful)	*-al* (e.g., national)
-ing (e.g., beginning)	*-ment* (e.g., commencement)
-ship (e.g., worship)	*-ation* (e.g., adoration)

VAN GELDEREN 2014: 133

TABLE 7.18 List of good discriminators of the 14th-century (Chaucer's) translation if compared to the 16th-century (Colville's) translation

14th-century (Chaucer's) translation (vs. 16th-century [Colville's] translation)

Feature	Feature weight
thilke	2.080102
ne	1.939726
ben	1.935346
alle	1.488744
thei	1.440026
yif	1.364062
thise	1.280733
thane	1.22972
whiche	1.223872
blisfulnesse	1.221569
schrewes	1.209415
hem	1.198464
wel	1.1922

ENGLISH DATA

TABLE 7.19 Romance vs. Germanic derivational suffixes [of Table 7.17] in the list of good discriminators of the 14th-century (Chaucer's) translation if compared to the 16th-century (Colville's) translation

Text	Features (discriminators)	Feature Weight	Text	Features (discriminators)	Feature Weight
14th-century translation	purveaunce reverence suffisaunce	0.564692 0.549386 0.121241	16th-century translation	prouydence ordynaunce	0.19994 0.18376
	torment	0.590634		ponishment	0.46878

(Table 7.20). However, the number of nouns with a Romance suffix that are good discriminators of the texts under examination is significantly larger than the number of nouns with an Old English suffix. A Pearson chi-square test was performed to assess the relation between the nouns that are good discriminators of the texts under examination and their nominal suffixes of different origin. The results are statistically significant for the comparison between the number of nouns with a Romance suffix and the number of nouns with an Old English suffix (χ^2=51.613, p<.05), with an effect size of φ=.645, which is a large effect size [Pearson chi-square test; exact significance].

As far as the contrast between translated and non-translated texts of the M3 period and the derivational suffixes under examination are concerned, the following suffixes are attested in the list of nouns that are good discriminators of the particular texts: the Old English -dom, -ful, -ing, mainly in the non-translated text, vs. the Romance -ity and -e(a)nce, in both the translated and the non-translated text. The number of nouns with a Romance suffix that are good discriminators of the texts under examination is again significantly larger than the number of nouns with an Old English suffix that are good discriminators (Table 7.21). A Pearson chi-square test was performed to assess the nouns that are good discriminators of the texts under examination and their nominal suffixes of different origin. The results are statistically significant for the comparison between the number of nouns with a Romance suffix and the number of nouns with an Old English suffix (χ^2=2.841, p<.05), with an effect size of φ=.294, which is a medium effect size [Pearson chi-square test; exact significance].

TABLE 7.20 Romance vs. Germanic derivational suffixes [of Table 7.17] in the list of good discriminators of the 1695 (Preston's) translation if compared to the 1785 (Ridpath's) translation

Text	Features (discriminators)	Feature weight	Text	Features (discriminators)	Feature weight
1695 translation	deceitful	0.408402	1785 translation	wisdom	0.18417
	beautiful	0.232679			
				hurtful	0.61935
	understanding	0.26127		powerful	0.29571
	friendship	0.664176		reasoning	0.59578
				blessings	0.28774
	nobility	0.887746			
	qualities	0.823484		unity	0.7753
	simplicity	0.379237		felicity	0.75284
	necessity	0.33951		calamities	0.50343
				authority	0.49587
	reverence	0.504023		reality	0.44127
	abundance	0.439753		divinity	0.36817
	consequence	0.023439		providence	0.71646
				indigence	0.53954
	natural	0.754078		importance	0.48232
				intelligence	0.48131
	punishments	0.850383		existence	0.47131
	government	0.710695		remembrance	0.44227
				assistance	0.40076
				reputation	0.56692
				participation	0.54443
				duration	0.03646
				perpetual	0.59372
				chastisement	0.69228
				arguments	0.64859
				enjoyments	0.30093

ENGLISH DATA

203

TABLE 7.21 Derivational suffixes [of Table 7.17] in the list of good discriminators of the 14th-century translated text (Chaucer's translation [sample]) if compared to the 14th-century non-translated text (Purvey's text; General Prologue)

Text	Features (discriminators)	Feature weight	Text	Features (discriminators)	Feature weight
14th-century translation	prosperite	0.122371	14th-century non-translated text	fredom	0.10897
				wisdom	0.08765
	purveaunce	0.988111			
	reverence	0.651975		faithful	0.04759
	suffisaunce	0.417159			
				vndirstonding	0.42493
				translating	0.33032
				teching	0.06219
				charite	0.61898
				autorite	0.36521
				veniaunce	0.23514
				penaunce	0.08252
				literal	0.61594
				comaundementis	0.20181
				comaundement	0.14821

TABLE 7.22 Romance vs. Germanic derivational suffixes [of Table 7.17] in the list of good discriminators of the 1611 translation of the New Testament (Authorized Version) if compared to the 1764 (Purver's) translation of the New Testament

Text	Features (discriminators)	Feature weight	Text	Features (discriminators)	Feature weight
1611 translation of the New Testament	preaching	0.416706	1764 translation of the New Testament	kingdom	0.51355
	notwithstanding	0.353449		everlasting	0.55097
	authority	0.263479		excepting	0.20255
				teaching	0.1818
	generation	0.101765		beginning	0.15923
				fasting	0.01463
				worship	0.15376
				repentance	0.23015
				commandment	0.33914
				garments	0.22399
				judgment	0.04042
				salvation	0.05855

In the case of biblical translations, the results appear to be similar to the ones of the comparison between early and later non-biblical translations. For example, if one compares the E2 translation (1611 translation—Authorized Version) to the 1764 translation of the New Testament, the Old English suffixes -*dom*, -*ing*, -*ship* and the Romance suffixes -*ity*, -*e(a)nce*, -*ation*, -*ment* are attested in the list of nouns that are good discriminators of these texts—and, in particular, of the 1764 translation (Table 7.22). The overall picture of both biblical and non-biblical translations is as follows: mainly, the Old English suffixes -*dom*, -*ing* (vs. the Romance suffixes -*ity*, -*e(a)nce*, -*ation*) are derivational suffixes of nouns that are good discriminators of the texts under examination. There is, however, a significant difference between the number of nouns with a Romance suffix and the number of nouns with an Old English suffix that are good discriminators of the examined texts, in particular, in the non-biblical translations.

ENGLISH DATA

7.4.1.3   Case study III: Romance vs. Germanic derivational suffixes in the
           list of good discriminators of translations

The third example of document classification survey examines the contrast
between

a.   the Middle English translations and the 18th-century translations of the
      corpus, and

b.   the Early Modern English translations and the Middle English transla-
      tions of the corpus.

Table 7.23 presents the accuracy numbers, which are over 95% in all cases.
Regarding the non-biblical translations, for example, the Old English suffixes
-dom, -ful, -ing, -ship and the Romance suffixes *-ity, -e(a)nce, -ation, -al, -ment*
are again attested with nouns that are discriminators between the texts under
examination, if one compares the Middle English (14th-century) translation
to the 18th-century translations. The number of nouns with a Romance suffix,
that are discriminators between the various examined texts, remarkably differs
from the number of nouns that bear an Old English suffix (Table 7.24).

   With regard to the data from the New Testament translations, if one compares the Middle English (14th-century) translation to the 18th-century translations of the corpus, one observes that the Old English suffixes *-dom, -ing,
-ship* and the Romance suffixes *-ment* (and *-ity* and -ation) are attested again
with nouns that are good discriminators of the 18th-century translations (Table
7.25). The overall conclusion is as follows: the Old English suffixes under examination are still discriminators of late—both non-biblical and New Testament
translations—translations. However, the number of nouns that bear a Romance suffix and are discriminators between the texts under examination is
clearly larger than the number of nouns with a Germanic derivational suffix
that are discriminators between the texts that I have examined.

206 CHAPTER 7

TABLE 7.23 Accuracy numbers (document classification): (i) Middle English vs. Early Modern English translations of the corpus; (ii) Middle English vs. 18th-century translations of the corpus

Non-biblical translations: translations of Boethius' *De Consolatione Philosophiae*

14th-century (Middle English) translation vs. 16th-/17th-century (Early Modern English) translations	Accuracy 0.96
14th-century (Middle English) translation vs. 18th-century translations	Accuracy 0.988

New Testament translations

14th-century (Middle English) translation vs. 16th-/17th-century (Early Modern English) translations	Accuracy 0.992
14th-century (Middle English) translation vs. 18th-century translations	Accuracy 0.995

TABLE 7.24 Non-biblical translations: Romance vs. Germanic derivational suffixes [of Table 7.17] in the list of good discriminators of the 14th-century (Middle English) translation if compared to the 18th-century translations of Boethius' *De Consolatione Philosophiae*

Text	Features (discriminators)	Feature weight	Text	Features (discriminators)	Feature weight
14th-century (Middle English) translation	reverence purveaunce	0.655159 0.618374	18th-century translations	wisdom	0.46537
				powerful	0.4281
				beautiful	0.06838
				useful	0.03057
				willing	0.02414
				felicity	0.58739
				simplicity	0.54296
				adversity	0.31989
				dignity	0.30672
				unity	0.30268
				qualities	0.07942

ENGLISH DATA

207

TABLE 7.24 Non-biblical translations: Romance vs. Germanic derivational suffixes [of Table 7.17] *(cont.)*

Text	Features (discriminators)	Feature weight	Text	Features (discriminators)	Feature weight
				immortality	0.04693
				mutability	0.03521
				providence	0.6639
				intelligence	0.26561
				difference	0.04318
				presence	0.03412
				innocence	0.00356
				universal	0.03911
				perpetual	0.03741
				duration	0.14438
				foundation	0.03784
				punishment	0.45697
				arguments	0.26556
				chastisement	0.24155
				government	0.06207
				resentment	0.0371

TABLE 7.25 New Testament translations: Romance vs. Germanic derivational suffixes [of Table 7.17] in the list of good discriminators of the 14th-century (Middle English) New Testament translation if compared to the 18th-century New Testament translations of the corpus

Text	Features (discriminators)	Feature weight	Text	Features (discriminators)	Feature weight
14th-century translations	–		18th-century translations	kingdom	0.14768
				everlasting	0.35488
				beginning	0.20215
				signifying	0.08062
				teaching	0.05985
				excepting	0.05454
				notwithstanding	0.03884
				willing	0.02671
				worship	0.16888
				authority	0.03788
				ointment	0.30193
				judgement	0.10015
				commandments	0.05495
				commandment	0.03763
				garments	0.02748
				garment	0.02404
				preparation	0.09972
				salvation	0.01781

7.4.2 Concluding Remarks

According to the main results derived from the surveys based on document classification and logistic regression, diachronic retranslations, that is, translations of the same text in different periods of the history of a language, do not display contact-induced changes or the new grammar directly. They manifest a parallel grammatical system, that is, a different grammatical system that includes instances of transfer from the source texts. The parallel grammatical system of translated texts is in contact with the grammatical system of non-translated, native texts and affects it and is affected by it. It is evident that diachronic retranslations of the same text provide us with significant information on the relation between the parallel "diachronies" of translated and non-translated texts. Romaine (1985, 1998) also argues that translations of the same text in different periods can reflect important changes in the vocabulary of the language. However, my claim is different than Romaine's view: diachronic retranslations do not reflect grammatical change but "multiglossia", coexistence of parallel grammars, and contact/ transfer between the parallel grammars even in the same synchrony.

The data from the English biblical and non-biblical diachronic retranslations have confirmed the hypothesis that diachronic retranslations do not follow changes represented in non-translated texts. Grammatical characteristics in translated texts demonstrate *a peaceful coexistence of native and borrowed elements even in non-transitional periods* and a *contact* between translated and non-translated characteristics, which is possible through the written language contact. For instance, non-translated texts show continuity of the basic characteristics of argument structure/ transitivity and voice, whereas translated texts may demonstrate differences in argument structure/ transitivity and voice between translations prepared in different periods. The following chapter focuses on Greek data on argument structure/ transitivity and voice because the diachrony of Greek shows significant changes in transitivity and voice.

CHAPTER 8

Greek Data

8.1 Greek Diachronic Retranslations of the New Testament: Voice and Argument Structure

(i) Methodology of research and word lists

In a similar fashion to the surveys on English (Chapter 7), I analyze character-istics related to argument structure and voice of Greek. The data derive from biblical translations as well as from diachronic intralingual retranslations. The present section also includes data from another domain of grammar, which were derived through a corpus-driven survey, similarly to the case studies I presented for English. The corpus-driven part of the present study investigates paraphrases/ intralingual translations of texts in later periods and examples of phrase matching, where the translator retains a phrase of the original text and modifies only one characteristic. The latter methodology of phrase match-ing, an example of a corpus-driven survey, can complete my conclusions in a similar way that the survey of document classification did for the diachronic English data. In the case of the Greek data, I conduct a quantitative analysis of data from intralingual translations, retranslations as well as interlingual trans-lations.

I compare early and late Greek biblical translations, which, mainly, consti-tute retranslations of the original Koine Greek source text. Moreover, in my examination of late translations, I examine both data from passages where the same verbal root is used in the translation as in the Koine Greek text of the New Testament, and data from passages where a different verbal root is used in the translation than in the source text. In this decision, I follow the methodology of studies that use *word lists*: Haspelmath (1993), Haspelmath et al. (2014), Nichols et al. (2004), Grünthal & Nichols (2016), Nichols (2017, 2018); see Section 7.2. I also compare these data to data from the other biblical text, the Septuagint, to trace further tendencies, in relation to my generalizations. I evaluate all quanti-tative evidence derived from the corpus surveys on translated texts against the development of the relevant features in the diachrony of non-translated texts. The latter data are mainly based on Lavidas et al. (2012).

I examine the selected list of verbs in the following texts: Koine Greek New Testament (*1st century AD*), Septuagint (*3rd–2nd centuries BC*), Kallipolitis' New Testament (*17th century*), Vamvas' New Testament (*19th century*), and Today's

© KONINKLIJKE BRILL NV, LEIDEN, 2022 | DOI:10.1163/9789004503564_010

GREEK DATA   211

Greek Version (TGV) (*20th century*). See Appendix 1 (1) for further information on the texts of the corpus. My corpus survey examines *a list of selected
meanings* chosen based on their semantic features and their morphology. All
verbs denote change of state and belong to the class of verbs that can bear two
voice morphologies ("ditipias"—"with two forms") in Present-Day Greek (see
Table 8.1).

(ii)   Corpus survey

I conduct two main types of corpus surveys. The first type concerns all selected
verbs as one group of verbs and the distribution of features of voice morphology and argument structure. The second type investigates the distribution of
the features under examination in the verbs separately, attempting to compare
classes of verbs and to reach conclusions on the role of the lexical conceptual
structure. Regarding the corpus study of all selected verbs as one group, I analyze the relative frequencies of the following features:
(i)   the distribution of active *vs.* non-active (mediopassive) voice morphology
        in all constructions;
(ii)   the distribution of active *vs.* non-active voice morphology in the anti-
        causative construction;
(iii)   the distribution of anticausative *vs.* transitive constructions, with verbs
        bearing active voice morphology;
(iv)   the distribution of active *vs.* non-active voice morphology of verbs with
        animate subjects—and active *vs.* non-active voice morphology of verbs
        with inanimate subjects.
The corpus searches also aim at investigating the distribution of the relative
frequencies of the following features:
(i)   active *vs.* non-active voice morphology in transitive constructions;
(ii)   animate *vs.* inanimate subjects in the case of transitive constructions;
(iii)   active and non-active transitives *vs.* active and non-active anticausatives.
I compare the above tendencies to the diachrony of these features in non-
translated Greek texts. The purpose of the latter comparison is to test whether
the generalizations based on the data from the translated texts are related
to the overall diachrony of Greek or reflect properties of the translated texts
and their retranslations. The data from the diachrony of non-translated texts
is mainly based on Lavidas et al. (2012) and include information on the distribution of voice morphology in the case of the verbs *katharizo* 'clean', *klino*
'open'—*stegnono* 'dry', *vrazo* 'boil', *sapizo* 'rotten', *liono* 'melt'. I examine the relative frequencies of active *vs.* non-active voice morphology of these verbs as well
as the distribution of active *vs.* non-active only in anticausative constructions.

TABLE 8.1   Word list for the corpus surveys on voice and argument structure (it repeats
            Table 7.2)

Main list of verbal meanings

'boil'	'grow'
'clean'	'melt'
'close'	'rot'
'dry'	'tear'
'heal'	

Additional list of verbal meanings; for corpus surveys with low number of results based on the main list of verbs

'anger'	'finish'
'become sick'	'get born'
'become strong'	'heighten'
'blind'	'die'
'break'	'open'
'burn'	'overflow'
'change'	'reinforce'
'darken'	'reveal'
'decrease'	'scatter'
'destroy'	'split'
'empty'	'spread'
'enlighten'	'stop'
'enrage'	'strengthen'
'fatten up'	'subside'
'fill'	

Moreover, I test the hypothesis that the parameter of lexical conceptual structure plays a significant role in the distribution of voice morphology, through an investigation of the relative frequencies of anticausative *vs.* transitive constructions with active verbs (that is, verbs bearing active voice morphology). I also investigate the factor of animacy of subjects in the diachronic development of these verbs. The data are based on Lavidas et al. (2012), but I also include additional quantitative data. The additional figures present data on the above verbs as one class of verbs, that is, they include data on the development of all these verbs as one verbal class, and not only as separate verbs, or

GREEK DATA   213

only related to the lexical conceptual structure factor. The figures also include
data on the distribution of the following parameters:

(i)   active *vs.* non-active voice morphology;
(ii)   active *vs.* non-active voice morphology only in anticausative construc-
       tions;
(iii) transitives *vs.* anticausatives, only with active voice morphology;
(iv)   active *vs.* non-active voice morphology with animate and inanimate sub-
       jects.

(iii) The development of voice and argument structure in Greek

In this section, I briefly discuss the diachrony of the Greek voice morphology. I base my discussion mainly on data from Lavidas et al. (2012). If one
contrasts Present-Day Greek and Ancient Greek voice morphology of verbs in
anticausative constructions, one observes the following significant differences.
Present-Day Greek has three verbal classes that can be used in an anticausative
construction and have an anticausative reading:

(i)   verbs with active voice morphology (e.g., *eklise* closed-ACT);
(ii)   verbs that can appear with active and non-active voice morphology (e.g.,
       lerose/ lerothike got-dirtied-ACT/ NACT);
(iii) verbs with non-active voice morphology (e.g., *skistike* got-torn-NACT);
       see (43a)–(43c).

(43) a. *To*   παράθυρο   έκλεισε   (από   τον   αέρα)
        To   *paráthyro*   *ékleise*   (*apó   ton   aéra*)
        To   *parathiro*   *eklise*   (*apo   ton   aera*)
        ART.NOM window.NOM closed.ACT.3SG (by   ART.ACC wind.ACC)
        'The window closed (by the wind).'

     b. *Ta*   παιχνίδια   λέρωσαν/ λερώθηκαν   από την   μπογιά
        Ta   *paichnídia*   *lérōsan/ lerốthēkan*   *apó tēn*   *mpogiá*
        Ta   *pehnidia*   *lerosan/ lerothikan*   *apo tin*   *boja*
        ART.NOM toys.NOM   dirtied.ACT/ NACT.3PL by   ART.ACC paint.ACC
        'The toys became dirty from the paint.'

     c. *H*   τέντα   σκίστηκε   από   τον   αέρα
        Ē   *ténta*   *skístēke*   *apó   ton*   *aéra*
        I   *tenda*   *skistike*   *apo   ton*   *aera*
        ART.NOM tent.NOM tore.NACT.3SG by   ART.ACC wind.ACC
        'The tent got torn by the wind.'

The first verbal class includes verbs of internally- (*sapise* 'rotted') and externally-caused (*eklise* 'closed') change of state, whereas the second and the third class only externally-caused change of state verbs (*katharise* 'cleaned'—*afksithike* 'increased') (among others, Theophanopoulou-Kontou 1983–1984, 2004, Tsimpli 1989, 2006, Alexiadou & Anagnostopoulou 2004, Roussou 2009, Alexiadou 2010). The verbs of the third class show similar morphological characteristics to the Ancient Greek verbs, in that they do not use active voice suffixes or alternation between non-active and active suffixes in anticausative constructions (Lavidas 2009).[1] All in all, anticausatives in Present-Day Greek can be distinguished in terms of voice morphology (only active; optionality between active and non-active; only non-active) as well as in terms of lexical conceptual structure: only externally-caused change of state verbs belong to the second and the third "morphological" class; internally-caused change of state verbs belong to the first "morphological" class of verbs. The diachronic development of all classes of anticausatives is related to an early stage that exclusively demonstrated non-active anticausatives, and to later stages that showed a clear increase in the presence of active voice morphology. Other developments concern changes in the verbal stem or parallel use of different verbal stems and, then, predominance of one of the stems, e.g. *vrasso/vratto → vrazo* 'boil', *tékō/tékomai → liono* 'melt', or loss of prefixed forms.

Accordingly, one may hypothesize a relation between change in non-active forms of anticausative constructions, on the one hand, and different lexical conceptual structure of the particular verbs, which concerns the contrast between one-place predicates and two-place predicates, on the other hand (Levin 1993, Levin & Rappaport Hovav 1995, 2005). However, even in Present-Day Greek, *klino* 'close', for instance, is an externally-caused change of state verb that bears only active morphology in anticausative constructions, and *sapizo* 'rot' is an internally-caused change of state verb that also bears only active morphology in anticausative constructions.

My conclusions on the lexical conceptual structure can be based on two factors: subject animacy and frequency of transitive constructions. Internally-caused verbs/ one-place predicates show a preference for inanimate subjects, irrespective of voice morphology, whereas externally-caused verbs/ two-place predicates prefer animate subjects only when they bear active voice morphology. One-place predicates are less frequent in transitive constructions than two-place predicates.

---

1 On middle voice in the Greek New Testament, see also Kmetko (2018). On voice in the aorist, cf. Tronci (2018).

GREEK DATA   215

TABLE 8.2   Voice morphology in Ancient Greek

Voice morphology in Ancient Greek

a.	All three classes of Modern Greek anticausatives	Non active
		(i) *ἐτάκην etákēn, ἐτήχθην etéchthēn* (passive) 'melted'
		(ii) *ἐκαθηράμην ekathērámēn* (middle), *ἐκαθάρθην ekathárthēn* (passive) 'cleaned'
		(iii) *ηὐξήθην ēuxéthēn* (passive) 'increased'
b.	Transitives	Both active and non-active (non-active with self-beneficient interpretation)
		παρασκευάζω *ναῦν*
		paraskeuázō *naûn*
		prepare.ACT.1SG ship.ACC
		'I prepare a ship.'
		παρασκευάζομαι *ναῦν*
		paraskeuázomai *naûn*
		prepare.NACT.1SG ship.ACC
		'I prepare a ship for myself.'
c.	Causatives	Only active
d.	Passives	Non-active (few instances of active)
e.	Reflexives	Non-active

FOLLOWING LAVIDAS ET AL. 2012: 392

As already mentioned, voice morphology in Ancient Greek had the following characteristics: verbs bore non-active (middle or passive) morphology in anticausative constructions and active morphology in causative constructions. In general, the system of voice morphology in Ancient Greek was complex in having middle/ mediopassive suffixes in all tenses and additional passive suffixes only in the future and aorist. Moreover, middle/ mediopassive voice forms could be used in passive constructions, and passive voice forms are attested in non-passive constructions as well; that is, in anticausative or even in transitive, auto-benefactive constructions. Ancient Greek non-active forms marked the derived subject or internal argument displacement—with anticausatives, reflexives, passives, auto-benefactive transitives—and were not related to the absence/ presence of an external argument (see Table 8.2).

8.1.1 *Data*

The present corpus survey examines *a list of selected meanings* chosen on the basis of their semantic features and their morphology, developing a methodology that first appears in Lavidas et al.'s (2012) study of Greek anticausatives. All verbs denote change of state and belong to the class of verbs that can bear two voice morphologies in Present-Day Greek, described in relevant studies on Greek morphosyntax as verbs *διτυπίας/ ditipias* "with two forms". The subcorpus used in the present study includes various Greek retranslations from different periods. The first complete intralingual translations of the Koine Greek New Testament and of the Septuagint Greek translation of the Old Testament were prepared from the 17th-century onwards—see Section 2.3.5—and, for this reason, the examination of intralingual retranslations does not concern any earlier work than the ones of the 17th-century.

In Figure 8.1, I present the distribution of voice morphology of the particular verbs (see the list of verbs in Table 8.1) in the source text of the Koine Greek New Testament and the 17th-, 18th- and 19th-century Greek translations of the New Testament.[2] For purposes of comparison with the other biblical text, I take into consideration the distribution of voice morphology in the Septuagint as well. The Koine Greek New Testament does not show a significant difference in the distribution of the active vs. the non-active voice morphology. A similar distribution re-appears only in Kallipolitis' translation and only with respect to the list of verbs that retain the same stem also used in the Koine Greek source text.

As already mentioned, I also examine the characteristics of voice morphology and argument structure of verbs that have a different verbal stem and replaced the verbs used in the source text. In most of the translated texts, there is a slight preference for active voice morphology. There is only one case where the non-active voice morphology shows a higher percentage than the active, and this case concerns verbs with a different verbal stem—than the one attested in the source text—in Vamvas' translation. These verbs demonstrate a preference for the non-active form. The Septuagint—together with the Present-Day Greek New Testament—show the highest percentage of presence of active forms (Figure 8.1).

As far as the distribution of voice morphology in anticausative constructions is concerned (Figure 8.2), the Koine Greek New Testament demonstrates a significantly high percentage of non-active voice forms. A Pearson chi-square test was performed to assess the relation between active vs. non-active

---

2 Among many others, see Horrocks (2014: 106) on the Septuagint and Vasileiadis (to-appear) on Kallipolitis, Vamvas and the Today's Greek Version.

GREEK DATA 217

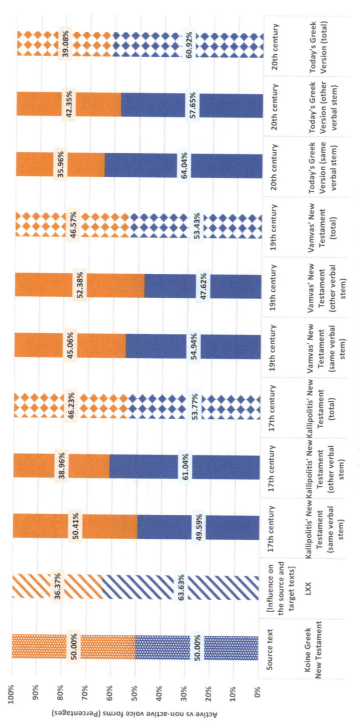

FIGURE 8.1 Distribution of voice morphology in the corpus of later Greek translations of the New Testament (See the list of selected verbal meanings: Table 8.1).

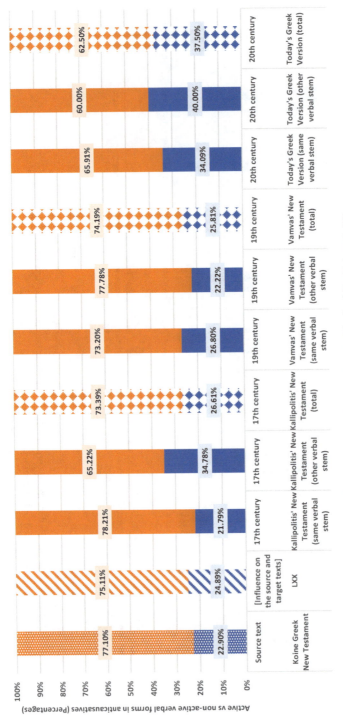

FIGURE 8.2 Distribution of voice morphology of verbs in anticausative constructions in the corpus of later Greek translations of the New Testament (See the list of selected verbal meanings: Table 8.1).

GREEK DATA 219

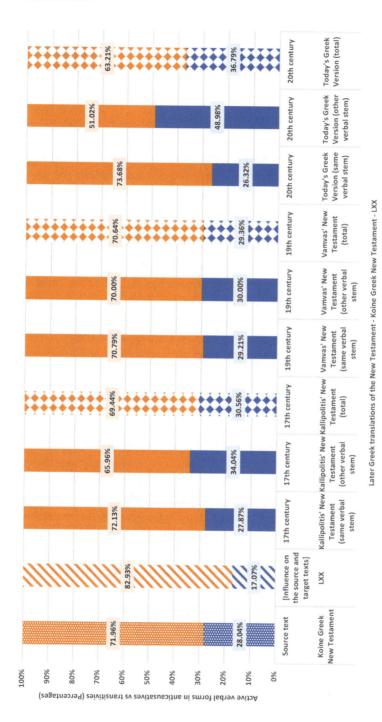

FIGURE 8.3 Distribution of active morphology of verbs in anticausative vs. transitive constructions in the corpus of later Greek translations of the New Testament (See the list of selected verbal meanings: Table 8.1)

anticausatives and the different texts and periods. The results are statistically significant for the comparison between active and non-active anticausatives in the Koine Greek text (χ^2=58.753, p<.05), with a large effect size of φ=.542 [Pearson chi-square test; exact significance]. The Septuagint shows a similar distribution.

Moreover, similarly to the source text, all Greek translations demonstrate high percentage of non-active anticausatives when the same verbal stem—that the source text uses—is attested but also when the verbal stem is replaced with another stem of similar meaning. The Today's Greek Version shows the highest frequency of active anticausatives (40%)—when a different verbal stem is used than the one of the source text—and, in this respect, is close to the tendency that appears in non-translated texts of Present-Day Greek.

One observes a similar picture in the case of the relative frequency of active forms in anticausative and transitive constructions (Figure 8.3). All later Greek translations show high percentage of active transitives (i.e., of active verbs in transitive constructions) in contrast to active anticausatives (i.e., to active verbs in anticausative constructions), in a similar way to the Koine Greek source text. The lowest percentage of active transitives is attested in the Today's Greek Version when different verbal stems are used. Note that there is a significant difference in this text between active transitives with the same verbal stems as the one attested in the Koine Greek text and active transitives with different verbal stems.

A Pearson chi-square test was performed to assess the relation between verbal stems of the active transitives (same *vs.* different than the verbal stems of the source text) and the different texts. The results are statistically significant for the comparison between active transitives in the Today's Greek Version with the same verbal stem as the one attested in the Koine Greek text and active transitives with a different verbal stem (χ^2=10.937, p<.05), with a small effect size of φ=.234 [Pearson chi-square test; exact significance]. The Septuagint presents the opposite tendency than the Today's Greek Version, with different verbal stems. It demonstrates the highest percentage of active transitives if compared to all texts included in the corpus.

The examples in (44a–e) "grow" in the Koine Greek source text, and the same passage in later Greek translations of the corpus (and an example with the same verb in the LXX).

GREEK DATA 221

Luke 1:80

(44) a. Koine Greek New Testament

τὸ   δὲ   παιδίον   ηὔξανεν   καὶ ἐκραταιοῦτο
tò   dè   paidíon   ēúxanen   kaì ekrataioûto
ART.NOM PRT child.NOM grew.ACT.3SG and became-strong.3SG

b. Kallipolitis

καὶ τὸ   παιδίον   ηὔξαν⟨ε⟩   καὶ ἐδυναμώνετον
kaì tò   paidíon   ēúxan⟨e⟩   kaì edynamóneton
and ART.NOM child.NOM grew.ACT.3SG and became-strong.3SG
τῷ   πνεύματι
tôi   pneúmati
ART.DAT spirit.DAT

c. Vamvas

Τὸ   δε   παιδίον   ηύξανε   καὶ εδυναμούτο
To   de   paidíon   ēúxane   kai edynamoúto
ART.NOM PRT child.NOM grew.ACT.3SG and became-strong.3SG
κατά το   πνεύμα
katá to   pneúma
in   ART.ACC spirit.ACC

d. Today's Greek Version (TGV): with a different stem

Τὸ   παιδί μεγάλωνε   καὶ τὸ   πνεύμα   του
To   paidí megálōne   kai to   pneúma   tou
to   pedhi meghalone ke   to   pnevma   tu
ART.NOM child.NOM grew.ACT.3SG and ART.NOM spirit.NOM his
δυνάμωνε
dynámōne
dhinamone
became-strong.3SG
'And the child grew and became strong in spirit.'

LXX

(44) e. Genesis 25:27

Ηὐξήθησαν   δὲ   οἱ   νεανίσκοι
ēuxéthēsan   dè   hoi   neanískoi
grew.PASS.3PL PRT ART.PL boys.NOM
'The boys grew up.'

222 CHAPTER 8

The examples in (45a–e) "close" in the Koine Greek source text, and the same passage in later Greek translations of the corpus (and an example with the same verb in the LXX).

Matthew 25:10

(45) a. Koine Greek New Testament
καὶ ἐκλείσθη ἡ θύρα
kaì ekleísthē hē thýra
and shut.PASS.3SG ART.NOM gate.NOM

    b. Kallipolitis
καὶ ἐσφαλίσθη ἡ πόρτα
kaì esphalísthē hē pórta
and shut.PASS.3SG ART.NOM door.NOM

    c. Vamvas
και εκλείσθη η θύρα
kai ekleísthē ē thýra
and shut.PASS.3SG ART.NOM gate.NOM

    d. Today's Greek Version (TGV)
και ἔκλεισε η πόρτα
kai ékleise ē pórta
ke eklise i porta
and shut.ACT.3SG ART.NOM door.NOM
'And the door was shut.'

LXX

(45) e. Isaiah 60:11
αἱ πύλαι σου [...] οὐ κλεισθήσονται
hai pýlai sou [...] ou kleisthḗsontai
ART.NOM gates.NOM your NEG shut.FUT.PASS.3PL

The examples in (46a–e) "open" in the Koine Greek source text, and the same passage in later Greek translations of the corpus (and an example with the same verb in the LXX).

GREEK DATA

223

John 9:26

(46) a. Koine Greek New Testament

πῶς ἤνοιξέν σου τοὺς ὀφθαλμούς;
pôs *énoixén* *sou* *toùs* *ophthalmoús?*
how opened.ACT.3SG 2SG.GEN ART.ACC eyes.ACC

b. Kallipolitis

Πῶς ἄνοιξε τὰ μάτια σου;
Pôs *ánoixe* *tà* *mátia* *sou?*
how opened.ACT.3SG ART.ACC eyes.ACC your

c. Vamvas

πώς ἤνοιξε τούς οφθαλμούς σου;
pós *énoixe* *toús* *ophthalmoús* *sou?*
how opened.ACT.3SG ART.ACC eyes.ACC your

d. Today's Greek Version (TGV)

Πώς σου άνοιξε τα μάτια;
Pós *sou* *ánoixe* *ta* *mátia?*
Pos *su* *anixe* *ta* *matia?*
how 2SG.GEN opened.ACT.3SG ART.ACC eyes.ACC
'How did He open your eyes?'

LXX

(46) e. Jeremiah 27:25

ἤνοιξεν κύριος τὸν θησαυρὸν αὐτοῦ
énoixen *kýrios* *tòn* *thēsauròn* *autoû*
opened.ACT.3SG Lord.NOM ACC.SG armory.ACC his
'The Lord has opened his armory.'

The Koine Greek source text and its later Greek translations, as well as in the Septuagint, show a similar distribution of active and non-active voice morphology with animate subjects (Figure 8.4). There is a clear preference for active voice forms with animate subjects. This preference is stronger in the Today's Greek Version when the same verbal stems are used, whereas there is no significant difference in the distribution of active vs. non-active forms in Vamvas' text when different verbal stems are used than in the source Koine Greek text. With inanimate subjects, one observes the opposite tendency and clear pref-

224　　　　　　　　　　　　　　　　　　　　　　　　　　　　　　　　　　　CHAPTER 8

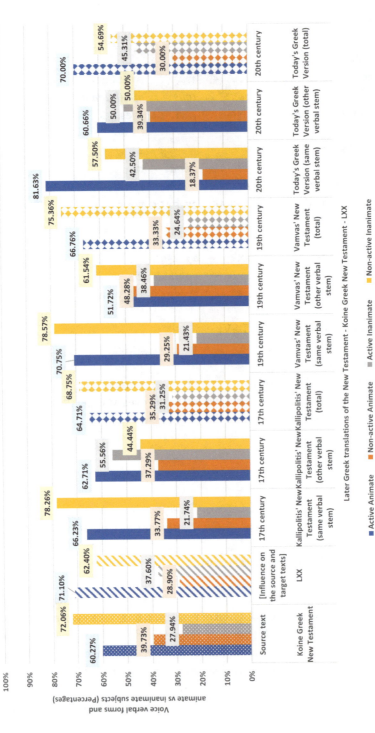

FIGURE 8.4　Distribution of voice morphology of verbs with animate and inanimate subjects in the corpus of later Greek translations of the New Testament (See the list of selected verbal meanings: Table 8.1)

GREEK DATA

erence for non-active forms in all texts of the corpus, except for the text of Kallipolitis, with verbs of different verbal stems, where inanimate subjects are attested with verbs that bear active voice morphology. The Today's Greek Version does not demonstrate a significant difference in the distribution of active and non-active forms, when different verbal stems are used than the ones of the source text, and differs from the Koine Greek source text.

I also examine the distribution of animate and inanimate subjects with the verbs of the word list irrespective of their voice morphology. The distribution of animate—inanimate subjects is also related to the lexical conceptual structure of the verbs (Figure 8.5—see (ii) below, for the results regarding each verb separately). The results show a clear preference for animate subjects (68.22%) in the data from the Koine Greek source text. In the Septuagint, the relative frequency of animate subjects is even higher (86.04%). All later Greek translations demonstrate similar tendencies even in the case of verbal stems that are different from the verbal stems of the source text.

I claim that the similarities in the results are related to the common semantic characteristics of the verbs under examination. In other words, the results demonstrate features related to common lexical conceptual structural characteristics of the verbs, rather than to a development of grammatical characteristics. The lexical conceptual structure of the selected verbs appears to remain stable in the diachronic retranslations under examination.

The only exception concerns the lower relative percentage (55.06%) of animate subjects in the Today's Greek Version, when the same verbal stem is used (as the one attested in the source text). However, the latter translation also shows a preference for animate subjects with the verbs under examination in all cases, with all types of stems (similar and different stems than the stems of the source text). When a different verbal stem is used in the Today's Greek Version, the percentage of animate subjects is 71.76%, which yields a similar relative frequency with that of the source text (63.22%) if one takes into consideration all verbs of the word list irrespective of their stem.

The examples in (47a–e) "close" in the Koine Greek source text, and the same passage in later Greek translations of the corpus (and an example with the same verb in the LXX).

Matthew 23:14

(47) a. Koine Greek New Testament

ὅτι	κλείετε	τὴν	βασιλείαν	τῶν	οὐρανῶν
hóti	*kleíete*	*tền*	*basileían*	*tôn*	*ouranôn*
that	shut.ACT.2PL	ART.ACC	kingdom.ACC	ART.GEN	heaven.GEN

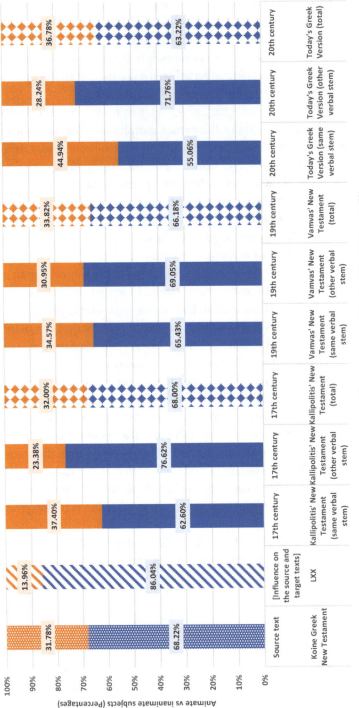

FIGURE 8.5 Distribution of animate vs. inanimate subjects in the corpus of later Greek translations of the New Testament (See the list of selected verbal meanings: Table 8.1)

GREEK DATA   227

b. Kallipolitis

διατì	κλείετε	τὴν	βασιλείαν	τῶν	οὐρανῶν
diatì	*kleíete*	*tèn*	*basileían*	*tôn*	*ouranôn*
because	shut.ACT.2PL	ART.ACC	kingdom.ACC	ART.GEN	heaven.GEN

c. Vamvas

διότι	κλείετε	την	βασιλείαν	των	ουρανών
dióti	*kleíete*	*tēn*	*basileían*	*tōn*	*ouranón*
because	shut.ACT.2PL	ART.ACC	kingdom.ACC	ART.GEN	heaven.GEN

d. Today's Greek Version (TGV)

γιατί	κλείνετε	στους	ανθρώπους	το	δρόμο
giatí	*kleínete*	*stous*	*anthrópous*	*to*	*drómo*
jati	*klinete*	*stus*	*anthropus*	*to*	*dhromo*
because	shut.ACT.2PL	to-ART.ACC	people.ACC	ART.ACC	road.ACC

για τη	βασιλεία	των	ουρανών
gia tē	*basileía*	*tōn*	*ouranón*
ja ti	*vasilia*	*ton*	*uranon*
for	ART.ACC kingdom.ACC	ART.GEN	heaven.GEN

'For you shut up the kingdom of heaven against men.'

LXX

(47) e. 2 Chronicles 28:24

καὶ	ἔκλεισεν	τὰς	θύρας
kaì	*ékleisen*	*tàs*	*thýras*
and	shut.ACT.3SG	ART.ACC	doors.ACC

'He shut the doors.'

The examples in (48a–e) "stop" in the Koine Greek source text, and the same passage in later Greek translations of the corpus (and an example with the same verb in the LXX).

Acts 5:42

(48) a. Koine Greek New Testament

[...]	οὐκ	ἐπαύοντο	διδάσκοντες
[...]	*ouk*	*epaúonto*	*didáskontes*
	NEG	stopped.MP.3PL	teach.PRTC.NOM

228 CHAPTER 8

b. Kallipolitis

[...] δεν ἔπαυαν   νὰ διδάσκουν
[...] den épauan   nà didáskoun
        NEG stopped.ACT.3PL PRT teach.3PL

c. Vamvas

[...] δεν ἔπαυον   διδάσκοντες
[...] den épauon   didáskontes
            NEG stopped.ACT.3PL teach.PRTC.NOM

d. Today's Greek Version (TGV)

[...] δε σταματούσαν   να διδάσκουν
[...] de stamatoúsan   na didáskoun
[...] dhe stamatusan   na dhidhaskun
        NEG stopped.ACT.3PL PRT teach.3PL
'They never stopped teaching.'

LXX

(48) e. 1Maccabees 11:50

καὶ παυσάσθωσαν   οἱ   Ἰουδαῖοι πολεμοῦντες
kaì pausásthōsan   hoi   Ioudaîoi polemoûntes
and ceased.PASS.IMP.3PL ART.NOM Jews.NOM fight.PRTC.NOM
'And let the Jews cease from assaulting [us and the city].'

In the present section, I presented the results of corpus surveys examining voice and argument structure in diachronic Greek biblical retranslations, that is, in biblical retranslations prepared in different centuries. I compared these results to the distribution of the same grammatical characteristics in the Koine Greek source text and the Greek translation of the other biblical text, the Septuagint. My hypothesis is that the grammatical characteristics represented in the diachronic Greek retranslations—even in the biblical retranslations—do not directly follow changes in grammar represented in non-translated texts written in different periods of the history of Greek. The aim of the following section is to test the hypothesis by examining diachronic tendencies related to voice and argument structure in Greek non-translated texts of various periods.

(i) Greek biblical translations *vs.* diachronic tendencies observed in non-translated texts

I compare the results discussed above to the development of the same grammatical characteristics in the Greek diachrony of non-translated texts. The data from non-translated texts are mainly based on corpus surveys in Lavidas (2009) and Lavidas et al. (2012). I distinguish between two verbal classes, which I have examined in the diachronic sub-corpus of translated texts, (see below (ii)): the verbal classes are related to a contrast between verbs meaning "clean" and "close" and all other verbs of the word list. The verbs "clean" and "close" display characteristics of a different lexical conceptual structure from the other verbs of the word list as evidenced by the fact that these verbs are mainly transitive when they bear active morphology (see Figure 8.11). The diachronic distribution of active *vs.* non-active voice morphology in the sub-corpus of non-translated texts appears to be similar for all lexical conceptual structures, both for two- and one-place predicates. This means that one observes an increase of the active forms of all relevant verbal classes and a decrease of the non-active forms (Figures 8.6–8.7).

There is no statistically significant difference between the verbal classes with respect to their diachronic tendencies: two-place predicates have slightly higher relative frequencies of active forms in later periods (99.59%) than one-place predicates (99.58%). If one compares Figures 8.6 and 8.7, which include data on the diachronic distribution of active and non-active voice morphology in non-translated texts, to the data from later Greek biblical translations (Figure 8.1), it is evident that later Greek translations, after Kallipolitis' translation, also show a preference for active forms. Kallipolitis' translation is similar to the Koine Greek source text—non-active forms are attested with a frequency of 50.41%—but the percentage of non-active forms steadily drops in all other translations, decreasing to 45.06% in Vamvas' translation and to 35.96% in the Today's Greek Version.

The data on the diachronic tendency of voice morphology of verbs in anticausative constructions in non-translated texts display a clear increase in the relative frequency of active forms, irrespective of the lexical conceptual structure of the verbs under examination (Figures 8.8–8.9). The later translations of Vamvas and the Today's Greek Version follow the above-mentioned tendency to a degree; however, this does not hold true for Kallipolitis' translation, which even shows a higher percentage of non-active anticausatives than the Koine Greek source text does. Note that, when a different verbal stem is used than the one attested in the source text, in Kallipolitis' translation and in the Today's Greek Version, but not in Vamvas' translation, the frequency of active

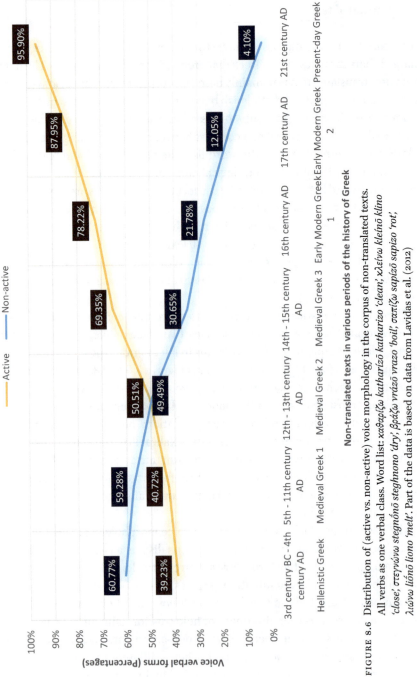

FIGURE 8.6 Distribution of (active vs. non-active) voice morphology in the corpus of non-translated texts. All verbs as one verbal class. Word list: καθαρίζω katharizō katharízo 'clean'; κλείνω kleinō klíno 'close'; στεγνώνω stegnōnō steghnono 'dry'; βράζω vrázō vrázo 'boil'; σαπίζω sapízō sapízo 'rot'; λιώνω liōnō liono 'melt'. Part of the data is based on data from Lavidas et al. (2012)

GREEK DATA

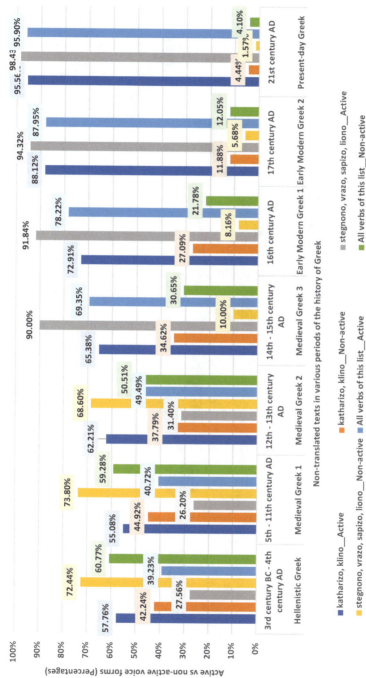

FIGURE 8.7 Distribution of (active vs. non-active) voice morphology in the corpus of non-translated texts. Word list: καθαρίζω katharízō katharizo 'clean'; κλείνω kleínō klino 'close'; στεγνώνω stegnónō steghnono 'dry'; βράζω vrázō vrazo 'boil'; σαπίζω sapízō sapizo 'rot'; λιώνω liónō liono 'melt'. Part of the data is based on data from Lavidas et al. (2012)

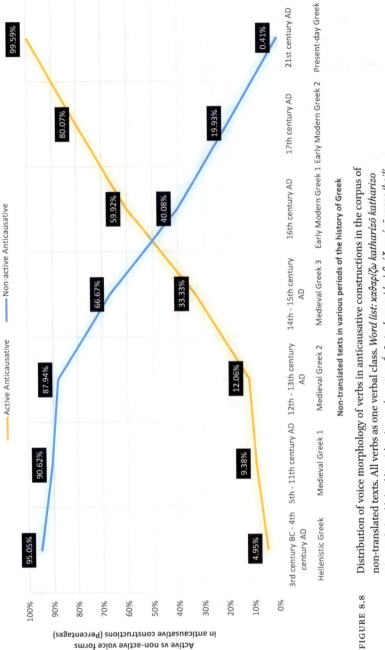

FIGURE 8.8   Distribution of voice morphology of verbs in anticausative constructions in the corpus of non-translated texts. All verbs as one verbal class. *Word list: καθαρίζω kleínō katharizō* 'clean'; κλείνω kleínō klīno 'close'; στεγνώνω stegnónō steghnono 'dry'; βράζω vrázō vrazo 'boil'; σαπίζω sapízō sapizo 'rot'; λιώνω liónō liono 'melt'. Part of the data is based on data from Lavidas et al. (2012)

GREEK DATA 233

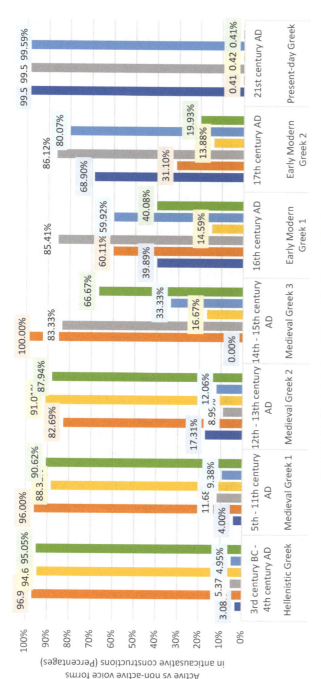

FIGURE 8.9 Distribution of voice morphology of verbs in anticausative constructions in the corpus of non-translated texts. Word list: καθαρίζω katharízō katharizo 'clean'; κλείνω kleínō klino 'close'; στεγνώνω stegnónō steghnono 'dry'; βράζω vrázō vrazo 'boil'; σαπίζω sapízō sapizo 'rot'; λιώνω liónō liono 'melt'. Part of the data is based on data from Lavidas et al. (2012)

234 CHAPTER 8

anticausatives is higher than in the Koine Greek source text—following the diachronic tendency observed in the data from non-translated texts (see above: Figure 8.2). When the same verbal stem is used as in the source text, both Vamvas' translation and the Today's Greek Version reflect the overall tendency of active anticausatives, but not Kallipolitis' translation.

With regard to the distribution of active transitives and active anticausatives, the overall tendency in non-translated texts (if one examines all verbs as one group) demonstrates a predominance of active transitives in early texts and no significant difference between active transitives and active anticausatives in Present-Day Greek, with increase of active anticausatives and decrease of active transitives in later periods (Figures 8.10–8.11). A Pearson chi-square test was performed to assess the relation between active transitives and active anticausatives and the different texts and periods. The results are statistically significant for the comparison between active transitives and active anticausatives in early texts. For instance, the results are statistically significant for the comparison between active transitives and active anticausatives in the period of Medieval Greek II and the verbs *katharizo, klino* (χ^2=138.378, p<.05), with an effect size of φ=.832, which is a large effect size [Pearson chi-square test; exact significance].[3] If one distinguishes between two- and one-predicate verbs, the lexical conceptual structure appears to play an important role in the overall tendency. Both classes of verbs started with similar relative frequencies in early Greek. However, two-predicate verbs acquired a distribution that did not exhibit a significant difference between active transitives and active anticausatives, with a slight preference for active transitives in later stages.

On the contrary, one-predicate verbs exhibit a significant change from a predominance of active transitives in Koine Greek, with a relative frequency of 86.28%, to a predominance of active anticausatives in Present-Day Greek, with a relative frequency of 84.93%. A Pearson chi-square test was performed to assess the relation between active transitives or anticausatives and one- / two-predicate verbs and the different—source and target—texts and periods. The results are statistically significant for the comparison between active

---

3 I refer to the following periods, time spans and registers: Homeric Greek, 8th century BC; Classical Greek, 5th century BC–4th century BC; (Hellenistic-Roman) Koine Greek, 3rd century BC–3rd century AD: Biblical (early and middle postclassical) Greek: (i) Septuagint, 3rd century BC–2nd century BC (early post-classical Greek) and (ii) New Testament, 1st century AD (middle post-classical Greek);

Non-biblical (early and middle post-classical) Greek, as represented, for instance, in the texts by (i) Polybius (early post-classical Greek), 3rd–2nd century BC and (ii) Epictetus (middle post-classical Greek), 1st–2nd century AD (Lavidas 2019a). On transliteration, translations and editions, see fn. 6 (Chapter 2).

GREEK DATA

FIGURE 8.10 Active voice forms in anticausative and transitive constructions in the corpus of non-translated texts. All verbs as one verbal class. Word list: καθαρίζω katharizō katharizo 'clean', κλείνω kleínō klino 'close', στεγνώνω stegnónō steghnono 'dry', βράζω vrázō vrazo 'boil', σαπίζω sapízō sapizo 'rot', λιώνω liónō liono 'melt'. Part of the data is based on data from Lavidas et al. (2012)

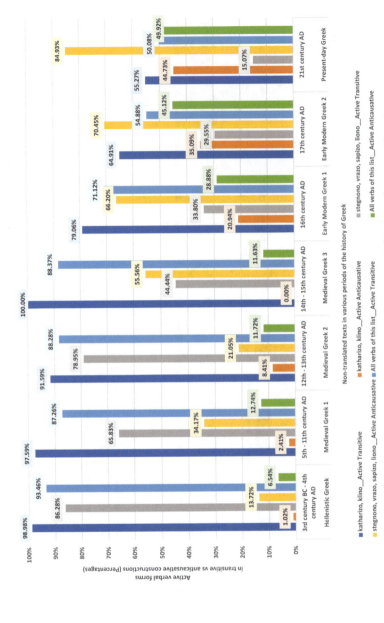

FIGURE 8.11 Active voice forms in anticausative and transitive constructions in the corpus of non-translated texts. Word list: καθαρίζω katharízō katharizo 'clean'; κλείνω kleínō klino 'close'; στεγνώνω stegnṓnō steghnono 'dry'; βράζω vrázō vrazo 'boil'; σαπίζω sapízō sapizo 'rot'; λιώνω liṓnō liono 'melt'. Part of the data is based on data from Lavidas et al. (2012)

GREEK DATA 237

transitives and active anticausative of one-predicate verbs (χ^2=101.436, p<.05), with a large effect size of φ=.712 [Pearson chi-square test; exact significance].

The sub-corpus of later Greek biblical translations does not show a similar tendency, except for the verbal stems that are different from the ones of the source text. In this case, active anticausatives are attested with a frequency of 34.04% in Kallipolitis' text, 30% in Vamvas' translation and 48.98% in the Today's Greek Version, whereas active anticausatives in the Koine Greek source text show a percentage of 28.04% (see above: Figure 8.3). In this respect, later Greek translations are clearly influenced by the source text and do not follow the overall tendency observed in non-translated texts—except for the case of the Today's Greek Version only.

Examples: (Active vs. non-active) voice morphology in the corpus of non-translated texts.

(49) a. Hellenistic Greek

Plutarchus Biogr. et Phil. Aetia physica (911c–919e) (1st–2nd cent. AD). Stephanus page 915 section B line 3.

τὰ	τῶν	ἀλιέων	σήπεται	δίκτυα
tà	*tôn*	*haliéōn*	*sépetai*	*díktya*
ART.NOM	ART.GEN	fishermen.GEN	rot.MP.3SG	nets.NOM

'[…] fishermen's nets rot [more in winter than in summer].'

b. Present-day Greek

το	τυρί	σάπισε	και	αλλοιώθηκε
to	*tyrí*	*sápise*	*kai*	*alloióthēke*
to	*tiri*	*sapise*	*ke*	*aliothike*
ART.NOM	cheese.NOM	rotted.ACT.3SG	and	infected.3SG

'The cheese got rotten and infected.'

Examples: (Active vs. non-active) voice morphology in the corpus of non-translated texts.

(50) a. Hellenistic Greek

Marcus Aurelius Antoninus Imperator Phil. *Τὰ εἰς ἑαυτόν* "Meditations" (2nd cent. AD). Book 3 chapter 16 section 2 line 1.

ἐπειδὰν	κλείσωσι	τὰς	θύρας
epeidàn	*kleísōsi*	*tàs*	*thýras*
because	closed.ACT.SUBJ.3PL	ART.ACC	gates.ACC

'because they were closing the gates.'

238   CHAPTER 8

b. Medieval Greek
Nicetas Stethatus Theol. et Hagiogr. Vita Simeonis Novi Theologici (11th cent. AD). Section 25 line 8.

ἔκλειεν	ἑαυτῷ	τὰς	θύρας
ékleien	*heautôi*	*tàs*	*thýras*
closed.ACT.3SG	himself.DAT	ART.ACC	gates.ACC

'He was closing the gates, so he could stay alone.'

c. Early Modern Greek
Franciscus SCUFUS Ὁ Γραμματοφόρος (17th cent. AD). Epistle 139 line 8.

νὰ	**κλείσουν**	πρῶτα τὰ	ὄμματα
nà	***kleísoun***	*prôta tà*	*ómmata*
PRT	close.ACT.3PL	first ART.ACC	eyes.ACC

'so that his eyes close first'

d. Present-day Greek

ἔκλεισε	με	δύναμη	την	πόρτα	και	ἔφυγε
ékleise	*me*	*dýnamē*	*tēn*	*pórta*	*kai*	*éphyge*
eklise	*me*	*dhinami*	*tin*	*porta*	*ke*	*efighe*
closed.ACT.3SG	with	force		ART.ACC	door.ACC	and left.3SG

'He closed the door with force and left.'

Examples: Voice morphology of verbs in anticausative constructions in the corpus of non-translated texts

(51) a. Hellenistic Greek
Achilles Tatius Scr. Erot. Leucippe et Clitophon (2nd cent. AD). Book 2 chapter 19 section 3 line 3.

θύρα	δὲ	ἐν	ἀρχῇ	τοῦ	στενωποῦ	μία
thýra	*dè*	*en*	*archêi*	*toû*	*stenōpoû*	*mía*
gate.NOM	PRT	in	beginning	ART.GEN	narrow-part.GEN	one.NOM

ἐκλείετο.
ekleíeto.
closed.MP.3SG

'A gate was shut where the narrow part started.'

GREEK DATA 239

b. Medieval Greek
Paulus Monembasiensis Scr. Eccl. Narrationes (10th cent. AD). Narration 5 line 13.

καὶ	πάλιν	αὐτομάτως	ἐκλείσθησαν	αἱ	θύραι
kaì	pálin	automátōs	ekleísthēsan	hai	thýrai
and	again	by-itself	closed.PASS.3PL	ART.NOM	gates.NOM

'And the gates were again closed by themselves.'

c. Present-day Greek

η	πόρτα	έκλεισε	ξαφνικά
ē	pórta	ékleise	xafniká
i	porta	eklise	ksafnika
ART.NOM	door.NOM	closed.ACT.3SG	suddenly

'The door closed suddenly.'

Examples: Active voice forms in anticausative and transitive constructions in the corpus of non-translated texts.

(52) a. Hellenistic Greek
Plutarchus Aratus (1st–2nd cent. AD). Chapter 24 section 6.

τὰ	μέρη	τοῦ	σώματος [...]	ἀτροφεῖ	καὶ
tà	mérē	toû	sṓmatos [...]	atropheî	kaì
ART.NOM	parts.NOM	ART.GEN	body.GEN	waste-away.3SG	and

σήπεται
sḗpetai
rot.MP.3SG

'The parts of the body [...] waste away and rot.'

b. Present-day Greek

το	φυτό	σάπισε	με	το	πολύ
to	phytó	sápise	me	to	polý
to	fito	sapise	me	to	poli
ART.NOM	plant.NOM	rotted.ACT.3SG	with	ART.ACC	much.ACC

νερό
neró
nero
water.ACC

'The plant got rotten with too much water.'

240   CHAPTER 8

The relative frequency of the non-active voice morphology significantly drops in the diachrony of non-translated texts both in the case of animate and inanimate subjects (Figure 8.12). A Pearson chi-square test was performed to assess the relation between non-active morphology and animacy of the subject and the different texts and periods. The results are statistically significant for the comparison between non-active verbs with inanimate subjects in the sub-periods of Medieval Greek II and III (χ^2=44.348, p<.05), with a large effect size of φ=.471 [Pearson chi-square test; exact significance]. Non-active forms with inanimate subjects show higher percentage than active forms with inanimate subjects in Koine Greek but decrease to a frequency of 4.79% in Present-Day Greek. Non-active forms with an animate subject drop from 30.06% in Koine Greek to 3.32% in Present-Day Greek.

The opposite tendency is observed in the case of active forms and animate and inanimate subjects. Active forms with inanimate subjects show the most significant increase and a frequency of 95.21% in Present-Day Greek, whereas they demonstrate a frequency of 24.34% in Koine Greek—in contrast to the non-active forms with inanimate subjects, which are attested with a frequency of 75.66%. A Pearson chi-square test was performed to assess the relation between active forms and animacy of the subject and the different texts and periods. The results are statistically significant for the comparison between active forms with inanimate subjects in Koine Greek and Present-Day Greek (χ^2=104.443, p<.05), with a small effect size of φ=.723 [Pearson chi-square test; exact significance]. Animate subjects with active voice forms rise from 69.94% in Koine Greek to 96.68% in Present-Day Greek. The later Greek biblical translations follow the overall tendency only in the case of verbs of the same stem. Non-active forms with animate subjects drop from 39.75% in the Koine Greek source text to 33.77% in Kallipolitis' text, to 29.25% in Vamvas' translation, to 18.37% in the Today's Greek Version (see above: Figure 8.4).

One observes a similar distribution in the case of inanimate subjects with non-active forms but only when the same verbal stem is used as the one used in the source text. The different development of verbs using the stem attested in the source text demonstrates that verbal stems in translated texts play a significant role in the way that the translated texts show similar or different characteristics than the source texts.

With respect to active voice forms with animate subjects, all translated texts follow the overall tendency for high relative percentages of actives with animate subjects in later periods—except for Vamvas' text when different verbal stems are used. Vamvas' text presents a frequency of 51.72% of animate subjects with active forms (see above: Figure 8.4). The active voice forms with inanimate subjects follow the diachrony of non-translated texts and become less frequent,

GREEK DATA

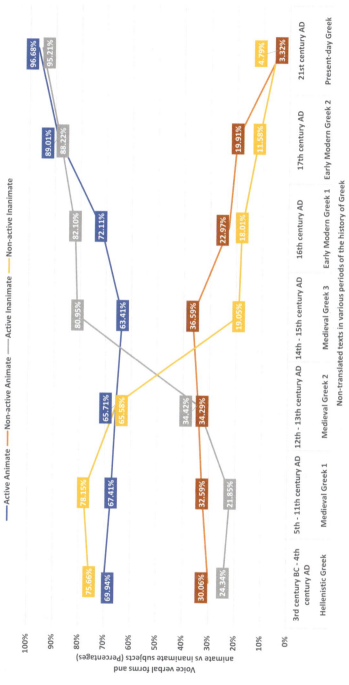

FIGURE 8.12 Distribution of active and non-active voice morphology with animate subjects in the corpus of non-translated texts. See the list of selected verbal meanings: καθαρίζω *katharizō* *katharizo* 'clean'; κλείνω *kleinō klino* 'close'; στεγνώνω *stegnónō steghnono* 'dry'; βράζω *vrázō vrazo* 'boil'; σαπίζω *sapízō sapizo* 'rot'; λιώνω *liónō liono* 'melt'. Part of the data is based on data from Lavidas et al. (2012)

242   CHAPTER 8

in particular when used with verbs with the same verbal stems as the one found in the source text. However, a different distribution can be found in the Today's Greek Version.

Examples: Active and non-active voice morphology with animate subjects in the corpus of non-translated texts.

(53) a. Hellenistic Greek
Strabo Geogr. Geographica (1st cent. BC–1st cent. AD). Book 15 chapter 1 section 42 line 8.

κλείουσι   *τὴν*   *εἴσοδον*   *λάθρᾳ*
kleíousi   *tền*   *eísodon*   *láthrai*
close.ACT.3PL ART.ACC entrance.ACC secretly
'They close the entrance secretly.'

b. Medieval Greek
BELLUM TROIANUM Epic. Ὁ Πόλεμος τῆς Τρωάδος (13th–14th cent. AD). Line 13461.

τὰς   *πόρτας*   *τοὺς*   *ἐκλεῖσαν*
tàs   *pórtas*   *toùs*   *ekleîsan*
ART.ACC doors.ACC 3PL.ACC closed.ACT.3PL
'They closed the doors against them.'

c. Early Modern Greek
Marinus Tzanes BUNIALES Poeta Ὁ Κρητικὸς Πόλεμος [Cretan War] (17th cent. AD). Chapter 2 section 120 line 44.

μὲ   *χῶμα*   *νὰ*   *τοὺς*   *κλείσει.*
mè   *chôma*   *nà*   *toùs*   *kleísei*
with soil   PRT 3PL.ACC close.ACT.3SG
'... to close/ cover them with soil.'

d. Present-day Greek

O   *Γιάννης*   *ἔκλεισε*   *την*   *πόρτα*   *ξαφνικά*
O   *Giánnēs*   *ékleise*   *tēn*   *pórta*   *xafniká*
O   *Janis*   *eklise*   *tin*   *porta*   *ksafnika*
ART.NOM Janis.NOM closed.ACT.3SG ART.ACC door.ACC suddenly
'Janis closed the door suddenly.'

Figure 8.13 includes information on the diachrony of verbs belonging to the class of two-place predicates. The data show a clear drop in the frequency of their non-active forms and a clear increase in the frequency of their active

GREEK DATA 243

FIGURE 8.13 Distribution of voice morphology in the corpus of non-translated texts. Word list: καθαρίζω katharízō katharízo 'clean'; κλείνω kleínō klíno 'close'. Part of the data is based on data from Lavidas et al. (2012)

244 CHAPTER 8

forms. One-place predicates demonstrate the same type of development: that is, increase in the frequency of their active forms and decrease in the frequency of their non-active forms (Figure 8.14). However, the above-mentioned change affects one-place predicates in an earlier period than it affects two-place predicates.

Examples: Voice morphology in the corpus of non-translated texts.

(54) a. Hellenistic Greek
Galenus Med. De compositione medicamentorum secundum locos libri x (2nd cent. AD). Volume 13 page 325 line 9.

μέχρις οὗ	***καθαρίσῃ***		*τὴν*	*κύστιν*
méchris hoû	***katharísēi***		*tền*	*kýstin*
until	cleanse.ACT.AOR.SUBJ.3SG	ART.ACC	bladder.ACC

'until it cleans the bladder.'

b. Medieval Greek
BELLUM TROIANUM Epic. Ὁ Πόλεμος τῆς Τρωάδος (13th–14th cent. AD). Line 5530.

ἄνεμος,	*τὴν*	*βρόμαν*	***καθαρίζει.***
ánemos,	*tền*	*bróman*	***katharízei.***
wind.NOM	ART.ACC	dirt.ACC	clean.ACT.3SG

'The wind cleans the dirt.'

c. Early Modern Greek
FABULAE CRETENSES Comic. et Fab. Στάθης (16th–17th cent. AD). Part 2 line 340.

δρόσος [...]	***καθάρισε***	*τὲς*	*δυσκολιές*
drósos [...]	***kathárise***	*tès*	*dyskoliés*
dew.NOM	cleaned.ACT.3SG	ART.ACC	difficulties.ACC

'Dew [...] cleaned away the difficulties.'

d. Present-day Greek

O	*Γιάννης*	***καθάρισε***	*το*	*δωμάτιό*	*του*
O	*Giánnēs*	***kathárise***	*to*	*dōmátió*	*tou*
O	*Janis*	***katharise***	*to*	*domatio*	*tu*
ART.NOM	Janis.NOM	cleaned.ACT.3SG	ART.ACC	room.ACC	his

χτες
chtes
htes
yesterday

'Janis cleaned his room yesterday.'

GREEK DATA

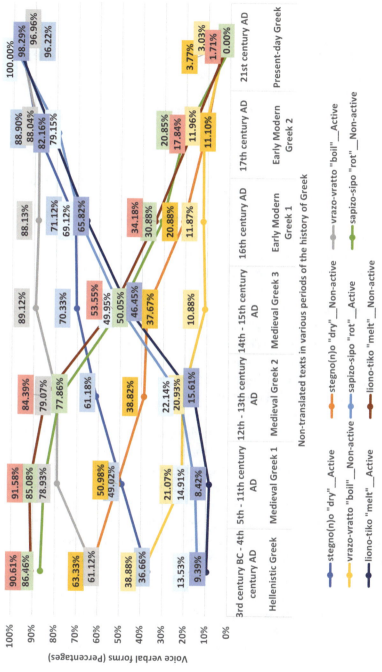

FIGURE 8.14 Distribution of voice morphology in the corpus of non-translated texts. Word list: στεγνώνω stegnónō steghnono 'dry'; βράζω vrázō vrazo 'boil', σαπίζω sapízō sapizo 'rot', λιώνω liónō liono 'melt'. Part of the data is based on data from Lavidas et al. (2012)

246   CHAPTER 8

Examples: Voice morphology in the corpus of non-translated texts.

(55) a. Hellenistic Greek
          ARCHIGENES Med. Fragmenta (1st–2nd cent. AD). Page 24 line 27.
          βρᾶσον   ὁμοῦ   πάντα
          brâson   *homoû*   *pánta*
          boil.ACT.IMP.2SG together   everything.ACC
          'Boil everything together.'

      b. Early Modern Greek
          GEORGIUS CHORTATZES Trag. vel Comic. Katzurbos (16th–17th
          cent. AD). Prolog-act 1 scene 1 line 76
          τούτή   'ναι [...] τὴν   καρδιά   μου βράζει
          toúté   *'nai* [...] *tèn* *kardiá* *mou* **brázei**
          this.NOM.FEM be.3SG ART.ACC heart.ACC my   boil.ACT.3SG
          'She ... makes my heart 'boil'.'

      c. Present-day Greek
          To   φαγητό   ἔβρασε   πολύ γρήγορα
          To   *phagētó* **ébrase**   *polý grḗgora*
          To   *faghito* **evrase**   *poli ghrighora*
          ART.NOM food.NOM boiled.ACT.3SG very fast
          'The food was boiled very fast.'

The results of the corpus surveys on the development of voice and argument
structure in non-translated texts written in different periods revealed a different picture than the one described in the case of English. One observes a
significant change related to an increase in active anticausatives (that is, verbs
with active voice morphology in anticausative constructions). On the contrary,
the English data do not demonstrate a relevant significant change. Translated
texts do not reflect either the stability of the examined grammatical characteristics, in the case of English, or the change, in the case of Greek. The grammatical characteristics of diachronic Greek retranslations do not directly follow
the relevant changes attested in non-translated texts. They appear to show a
more complicated picture, which probably derives from transfer of characteristics of the source texts, transfer of characteristics of earlier texts as well as
from transfer of grammatical characteristics of non-translated texts of the same
period.

GREEK DATA 247

(ii) Greek translations of the New Testament: Voice and argument structure. Detailed case studies of particular verbs; the factor of the lexical conceptual structure

The second type of corpus survey focuses on each of the verbs of the word list separately, to provide evidence on the role of the lexical conceptual structure. The following verbal meanings are included in the relevant corpus searches: *afxano* 'grow' vs. *anigo* 'open' vs. *therapevo* 'heal'—vs. *katharizo* 'clean' vs. *klino* 'close'. The lexical conceptual structure refers to the contrast between verbs such as *katharizo* 'clean' (mainly) and *klino* 'close', on the one hand, and all other verbs of the list, on the other hand. The verb *clean*, for instance, has been analyzed as a verb that has a lexical conceptual structure that includes two events and is attested mainly in transitive constructions (Lavidas et al. 2012).

I test the quantitative evidence from translated texts prepared in various periods against the overall tendency observed in the Greek diachrony of non-translated texts. In the present study, I base my conclusions on the contrast between the quantitative analysis of the verbs *katharizo* 'clean' (mainly) and *klino* 'close', which appear in transitive constructions with active voice morphology, and all other verbs described above and included in Lavidas et al. (2012).[4] I examine the following relative frequencies:

(i) the contrast between active *vs.* non-active voice morphology in all constructions;

(ii) the distribution of active *vs.* non-active voice morphology in anticausative constructions;

(iii) the contrast between anticausative and transitive constructions, with verbs bearing active voice morphology; and

(iv) the contrast between active and non-active voice morphology, with animate and inanimate subjects.

Moreover, I include the following factors in my examination—in a similar way as in all corpus surveys of the present study:

(i) the distribution of active *vs.* non-active verbs in transitive constructions;

(ii) the relative frequencies of transitives with inanimate and animate subjects; and

(iii) the contrast between active and non-active transitives and active and non-active anticausatives.

---

4 See Figure 8.15 below, with data on active anticausatives *vs.* active transitives.

248   CHAPTER 8

I compare the above-mentioned types of quantitative data to the overall tendencies observed in the diachrony of non-translated texts (in particular, in relation to the verbal classes *katharizo* 'clean'—*klino* 'close' vs. all other verbs of the word list).

In the present section, I discuss data derived from the biblical Greek translations concerning the verbs of the word list separately. First, I examine the verb *afxano* 'grow', which is attested with active forms in the Koine Greek source text (Figure 8.15). All later translations display a similar distribution as the source text, and *afxano* 'grow' bears active voice morphology in all cases. Only the text of the Septuagint appears to follow the characteristics of pre-Koine Greek and contains examples where the verb bears active and non-active voice morphology without any statistically significant difference. The same holds true for the distribution of voice morphology of the verb *afxano* 'grow' in anticausative constructions. All texts of the corpus, except for the Septuagint, present a similar distribution of voice forms and include active anticausatives only (i.e., active voice forms in anticausative constructions).[5]

The data from non-translated texts exhibit different tendencies than the tendencies attested in the corpus survey investigating the animate and inanimate subjects and the distribution of voice morphology in translated biblical texts. However, only the Septuagint shows different relative frequencies than the other texts belonging to later periods, in this case too. The later biblical Greek translations demonstrate similar characteristics to the Koine Greek source text.

The data from the various translations on animate and inanimate subjects, irrespective of the verbal voice morphology, indicate that *afxano* 'grow' in Kallipolitis' and Vamvas' texts is attested with animate and inanimate subjects in a similar way as in the source text. In the Today's Greek Version, however, *megalono*, which replaces *afxano*, is attested only with inanimate subjects (Figure 8.16). It is of significance that the differences related to lexical conceptual structure features do not affect the distribution of voice morphology, and the voice morphology of the verb *megalono* 'grow' in the Today's Greek Version presents the same characteristics as it does in the other translations.

---

5 I provide explanations on the terms used (for instance, active anticausatives etc.) in many parts of the book because there is no consensus on the terminology in the relevant literature, which depends on the theoretical model.

GREEK DATA 249

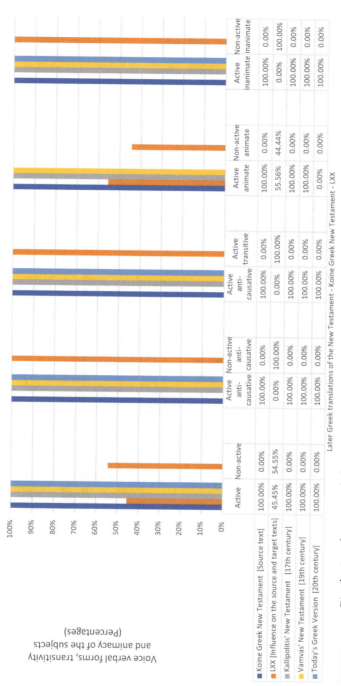

FIGURE 8.15 Distribution of voice morphology of verbs in anticausative vs. transitive constructions and subject animacy in the Koine Greek New Testament and the corpus of later Greek biblical translations (and in the LXX): The verb *afxano* 'grow'

Note: Recall that (non-)active (in)animate refers to constructions with (in)animate subjects and (non-)active voice forms. I follow a similar strategy in the way I refer to all terms here.

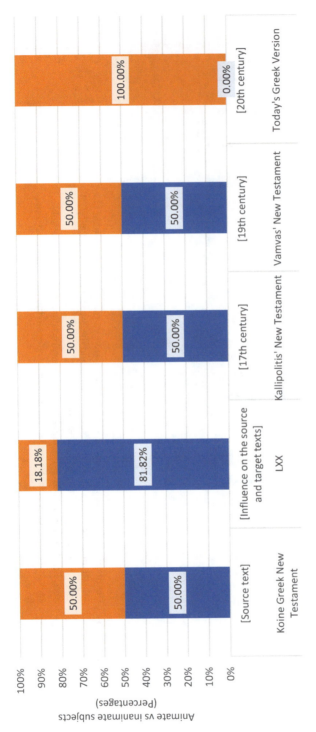

FIGURE 8.16 Subject animacy in the Koine Greek New Testament and the corpus of later Greek biblical translations (and in the LXX): The verb *afxano* 'grow'

GREEK DATA 251

The examples in (56a–e) "stop" in the Koine Greek source text, and the same passage in later Greek translations of the corpus (and an example with the same verb in the LXX).

Acts 19:20

(56) a. Koine Greek New Testament

Οὕτως κατὰ κράτος τοῦ Κυρίου ὁ λόγος
hoútōs katà krátos toû Kyríou ho lógos
so with strength ART.GEN Lord.GEN ART.SG word.SG
ηὔξανεν
ēúxanen
grew.ACT.3SG

b. Kallipolitis

ὁ λόγος τοῦ Κυρίου αὔξανε δυνατὰ
ho lógos toû Kyríou aúxane dynatà
ART.SG word.SG ART.GEN Lord.GEN grew.ACT.3SG mightily

c. Vamvas

Οὕτω κραταιῶς ηὔξανε καὶ ἴσχυεν ο
Oútō krataiós ēúxane kai íschyen o
so mightily grew.ACT.3SG and became-stronger.3SG ART.SG
λόγος του Κυρίου.
lógos tou Kyríou.
word.SG ART.GEN Lord.GEN

d. Today's Greek Version (TGV)

Ἔτσι, το μήνυμα του Κυρίου απλωνόταν
Étsi, to ményma tou Kyríou aplōnótan
etsi, to minima tu Kiriu aplonotan
so ART.NOM message.NOM GEN.SG Lord.GEN spread.MP.3SG
και δυνάμωνε.
kai dynámōne.
ke dinamone.
and grew-stronger.3SG
'So the word of the Lord was growing mightily and prevailing.'

252   CHAPTER 8

LXX

(56) e. 4 Maccabees 13:22

καὶ *αὔξονται*   σφοδρότερον   διὰ   συντροφίας
kaì *aúxontai*   sphodróteron dià   syntrophías
and grow.MP.3PL stronger   from companionship
'and they grow stronger from this daily companionship.'

The second corpus search examines the verb *anignimi/ anigo* 'open' (Figure 8.17). The verb *anignimi/ anigo* 'open' shows a clear preference for the newer (in anticausative constructions) active voice in all texts, even in the Koine Greek New Testament. The tendency becomes an "absolute rule", i.e., with a frequency of 100%, in the Today's Greek Version. Moreover, the Today's Greek Version is different than all other texts of the corpus in that it is the only text that follows the Present-day Greek tendency for *active* anticausatives. Active anticausatives are frequent in Vamvas but with a percentage of 40%, and the relative frequency of active anticausatives is even lower in the other texts. Furthermore, all texts of the corpus, except for Vamvas' translation, show preference for active transitives, rather than for active anticausatives. The later biblical Greek translations appear to be closer to the source text with regard to the voice morphology, rather than to follow the overall diachronic development of Greek non-translated verbs.

The distribution of the voice morphologies with animate subjects appears to be the same in all texts of the corpus. The Today's Greek Version is the only text where the verb under examination ("open") bears active voice morphology only; the data of all other texts evidence similar characteristics with a slight preference for non-active morphology with inanimate subjects. Note that the lexical conceptual structure does not appear to play an essential role in the similarities described above: *anignimi/ anigo* 'open' demonstrates similar characteristics in all texts—with a slightly higher percentage of animate subjects in the Septuagint (Figure 8.18). The similar lexical conceptual structural characteristics of the verb *anignimi/ anigo* did not trigger a similar distribution of voice morphologies in all later Greek biblical texts—and especially in the Today's Greek Version.

The examples in (57a–e) "open" in the Koine Greek source text, and the same passage in later Greek translations of the corpus (and an example with the same verb in the LXX).

GREEK DATA 253

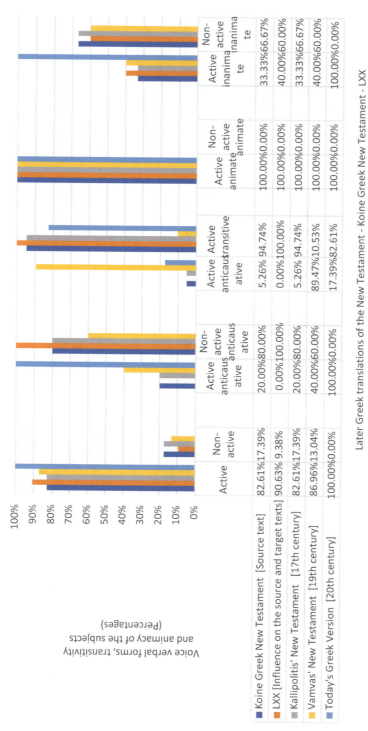

FIGURE 8.17 Later Greek translations of the New Testament - Koine Greek New Testament - LXX
Distribution of voice morphology of verbs in anticausative vs. transitive constructions and subject animacy in the Koine Greek New Testament and the corpus of later Greek biblical translations (and in the LXX): The verb *anigo-anignimi* 'open'

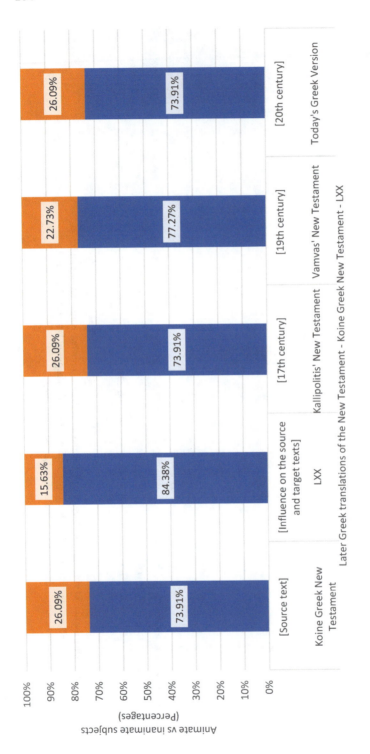

FIGURE 8.18 Subject animacy in the Koine Greek New Testament and the corpus of later Greek biblical translations (and in the LXX): The verb *anigo-anignimi* 'open'

GREEK DATA   255

John 9:14

(57) a. Koine Greek New Testament
  καὶ ἀνέῳξεν   αὐτοῦ τοὺς ὀφθαλμούς
  kaì anéōixen   autoû toùs ophthalmoús
  and opened.ACT.3SG his ART.ACC eyes.ACC

 b. Kallipolitis
  καὶ ἄνοιξε   τὰ   μάτια του
  kaì ánoixe   tà   mátia tou
  and opened.ACT.3SG ART.ACC eyes.ACC his

 c. Vamvas
  καὶ ἤνοιξε   τους οφθαλμούς αυτού
  kai énoixe   tous ophthalmoús autoú
  and opened.ACT.3SG ART.ACC eyes.ACC his

 d. Today's Greek Version (TGV)
  και του άνοιξε   τα μάτια
  kai tou ánoixe   ta mátia
  ke tu anikse   ta matia
  and 3SG.GEN opened.ACT.3SG ART.ACC eyes.ACC
  'and opened his eyes'

LXX

(57) e. Judges 4:19
  καὶ ἤνοιξεν   τὸν ἀσκὸν τοῦ γάλακτος
  kaì énoixen   tòn askòn toû gálaktos
  and opened.ACT.3SG ART.ACC skin.ACC ART.GEN milk.GEN
  'And [she] opened a skin of milk.'

Therapevo 'heal'—both with the same stem as in the source text (*therap-ev-*) or
with a different stem (*iatr-ev-* and *giatr-ev-*)—is attested only with active voice
morphology in all texts of the corpus (Figure 8.19). This fact brings *therapevo* of
biblical Greek texts close to the overall diachronic tendency of Greek attested
in non-tranlated texts, which favors the active voice morphology of the verb
under examination. Furthermore, Vamvas' text includes active anticausatives,
whereas all other texts of the corpus active transitives. The verb *therapevo*
is attested with animate subjects in all texts of the corpus except for the

256 CHAPTER 8

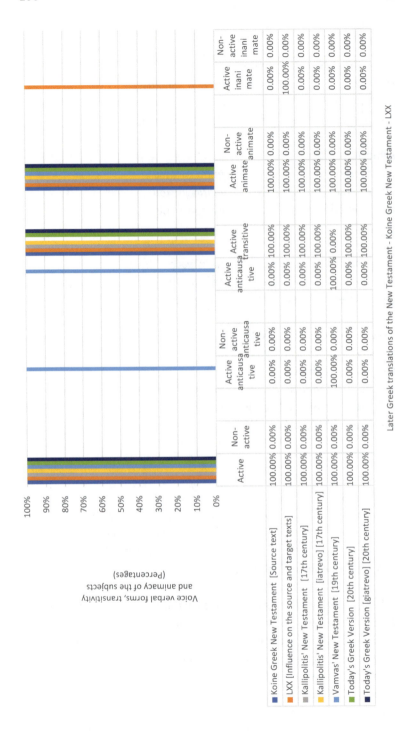

FIGURE 8.19 Distribution of voice morphology of verbs in anticausative vs. transitive constructions and subject animacy in the Koine Greek New Testament and the corpus of later Greek biblical translations (and in the LXX): The verb *therapevo* 'heal'

GREEK DATA

Septuagint, which includes examples with inanimate subjects and active forms of the verb *therapevo*.

The results of the corpus search provide evidence in favor of a similar lexical conceptual structure of *therapevo* in all versions of the biblical texts included in the corpus. The data demonstrate an absolute preference for animate subjects in all texts of the corpus, except for the Septuagint (Figure 8.20). The Septuagint also exhibits a high percentage of animate subjects (85.71%), but it is the only text of the corpus that contains inanimate subjects of the verb *therapevo*.

The examples in (58a–e) "heal" in the Koine Greek source text, and the same passage in later Greek translations of the corpus (and an example with the same verb in the LXX).

Matthew 8:7

(58) a. Koine Greek New Testament

Ἐγὼ ἐλθὼν θεραπεύσω αὐτόν.
Egò *elthòn* **therapeúsō** *autón.*
1SG.NOM come.PRTC.NOM heal.ACT.FUT.1SG this.3SG.ACC.MASC

b. Kallipolitis

Ἐγώ θέλω ἔλθει νὰ τὸν ἰατρεύσω.
Egó *thélō* *élthei nà tòn* **iatreúsō.**
1SG.NOM want.1SG come PRT 3SG.ACC.MASC heal.ACT.FUT.1SG

c. Vamvas

Ἐγώ ἐλθών θέλω θεραπεύσει
Egó *elthón* *thélō* **therapeúsei**
1SG.NOM come.PRTC.NOM want.1SG heal.ACT
αὐτόν.
autón
this.3SG.ACC.MASC

d. Today's Greek Version (TGV)

Εγώ θα έρθω και θα τον θεραπεύσω
Egó *tha érthō* *kai tha ton* **therapeúsō**
egho tha ertho ke tha ton **therapefso**
1SG.NOM FUT come.1SG and FUT 3SG.ACC.MASC heal.ACT.1SG
'I will come and heal him.'

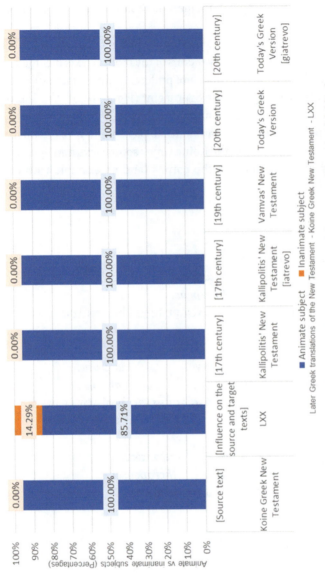

FIGURE 8.20 Subject animacy in the Koine Greek New Testament and the corpus of later Greek biblical translations (and in the LXX): The verb *therapevo* 'heal'

GREEK DATA   259

LXX

(58) e. 1 Esdras 2:14

καὶ	τὰ	τείχη	θεραπεύουσιν
kaì	*tà*	*teíchē*	***therapeúousin***

and ART.ACC walls.ACC heal/restore.ACT.3PL

'They restore [its marketplaces] and walls.'

In the case of *katharizo* 'clean', which was included as one of the two examples of two-place predicates in my data from non-translated texts, all texts present a similar distribution of active and non-active voice morphology and a slight preference for non-active forms, except for the Septuagint which exhibits the opposite preference (Figure 8.21). In addition, all texts of the corpus demonstrate a preference for non-active anticausatives and active transitives. Animate subjects can be found in constructions with active forms of the verb *katharizo* 'clean' more frequently than in constructions with non-active forms in all texts of the corpus, except for the Today's Greek Version. The Today's Greek Version presents no significant difference in the distribution of active and non-active voice morphology in the case of animate subjects. However, inanimate subjects are attested in constructions with non-active voice forms in all texts of the corpus, without exceptions.

Regarding subject animacy, one observes the same distribution of animate and inanimate subjects, with all types of voice morphology, in Kallipolitis' and Vamvas' translations as well as in the source text (Figure 8.22). The data from the Today's Greek Version reflect similar characteristics but a slightly higher frequency of animate subjects, that is, a frequency of 80% vs. 60% in the translations and the source text of the New Testament. The Septuagint exhibits an even higher percentage of animate subjects (87.50%).

The examples in (59a–d) "clean" in the Koine Greek source text, and the same passage in later Greek translations of the corpus (and an example with the same verb in the LXX).

Hebrews 9:14

(59) a. Koine Greek New Testament

τὸ	αἷμα	τοῦ	Χριστοῦ	[...]	καθαριεῖ
tò	*haîma*	*toû*	*Christoû*	[...]	***katharieî***

ART.NOM blood.NOM GEN.SG Christ.GEN   cleanse.ACT.FUT.3SG

τὴν	συνείδησιν	ὑμῶν
tèn	*syneídēsin*	*hymôn*

ART.ACC conscience.ACC your

260   CHAPTER 8

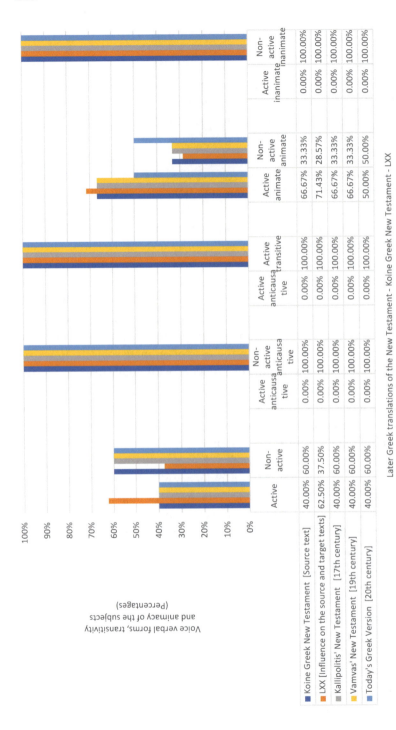

FIGURE 8.21   Distribution of voice morphology of verbs in anticausative vs. transitive constructions and subject animacy in the Koine Greek New Testament and the corpus of later Greek biblical translations (and in the LXX): The verb *katharizo* 'clean'

GREEK DATA

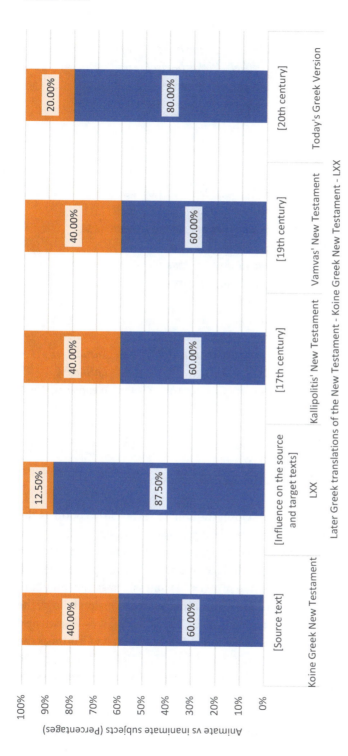

FIGURE 8.22 Subject animacy in the Koine Greek New Testament and the corpus of later Greek biblical translations (and in the LXX): The verb *katharizo* 'clean'

b. Kallipolitis

ὁ	ὁποῖος	[...]	θέλει	**καθαρίσει**	τὴν
ho	*hopoîos*	[...]	*thélei*	***katharísei***	*tèn*
ART.NOM	REL.NOM		want.3SG	cleanse.ACT	ART.ACC

συνείδησίν	σας
syneídēsín	*sas*
conscience.ACC	your

c. Vamvas

το	αίμα	του	Χριστού	[...]	θέλει
to	*aíma*	*tou*	*Christoú*	[...]	*thélei*
ART.NOM	blood.NOM	GEN.SG	Christ.GEN		want.3SG

καθαρίσει	την	συνείδησίν	σας
katharísei	*tēn*	*syneídēsín*	*sas*
cleanse.ACT	ART.ACC	conscience.ACC	your

d. Today's Greek Version (TGV)

το	αίμα	του	Χριστού	[...]	θα	**καθαρίσει**
to	*aíma*	*tou*	*Christoú*	[...]	*tha*	***katharísei***
to	*ema*	*tu*	*Hristu*		*tha*	***katharisi***
ART.NOM	blood.NOM	GEN.SG	Christ.GEN		FUT	cleanse.ACT.3SG

τη	συνείδησή	σας
tē	*syneídēsē*	*sas*
ti	*sinidhisi*	*sas*
ART.ACC	conscience.ACC	your

'The blood of Christ will cleanse your conscience.'

In the case of the verb *klio/ klino* 'close', the source text clearly contrasts the data from the later biblical Greek translations, despite the similarities of the source text to Vamvas' text in various other parameters (Figure 8.23). The source text as well as Vamvas' translation include only non-active examples of the verb 'close'. Moreover, the Koine Greek source text and Vamvas' translation only contain non-active anticausatives, whereas the Today's Greek Version follows the later overall tendency for active anticausatives. The Today's Greek Version also has active verb forms in all examples with inanimate subject and contrasts the Koine Greek source text and Vamvas' translation. The Koine Greek text and Vamvas' text use non-active voice forms in all examples with inanimate subjects.

Even though the texts of the corpus illustrate significant variability with respect to the characteristics of voice morphology and argument structure of *klio/ klino*, the characteristics reflecting its lexical conceptual structure are sim-

GREEK DATA 263

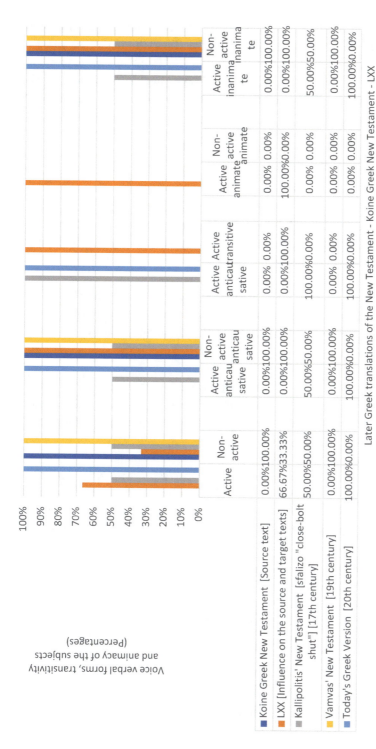

FIGURE 8.23 Distribution of voice morphology of verbs in anticausative vs. transitive constructions and subject animacy in the Koine Greek New Testament and the corpus of later Greek biblical translations (and in the LXX): The verb *kli(n)o* 'close'

264 CHAPTER 8

ilar in all texts (except for the Septuagint). In the source text and all later biblical Greek texts, *klio/ klino* is attested in constructions with inanimate subjects (Figure 8.24).

The examples in (60a–e) "clean" in the Koine Greek source text, and the same passage in later Greek translations of the corpus (and an example with the same verb in the LXX).

Luke 4:25

(60) a. Koine Greek New Testament

ἐκλείσθη	*ὁ*	*οὐρανὸς*	*ἐπὶ*	*ἔτη*	*τρία*	*καὶ*	*μῆνας*	*ἓξ*
ekleísthē	**ho**	**ouranòs**	**epì**	**étē**	**tría**	**kaì**	**mênas**	**héx**
shut.PASS.3SG	ART.NOM	sky.NOM	for	years	three	and	months	six

b. Kallipolitis

ἐσφάλισεν	*ὁ*	*οὐρανὸς*	*τρεισήμισι*	*χρόνους*
esphálisen	**ho**	**ouranòs**	**treisémisi**	**chrónous**
shut.ACT.3SG	ART.NOM	sky.NOM	three-and-a-half	years

c. Vamvas

εκλείσθη	*ο*	*ουρανός*	*επί*	*έτη*	*τρία*	*και*	*μήνας*	*εξ*
ekleísthē	**o**	**ouranós**	**epí**	**étē**	**tría**	**kai**	**ménas**	**ex**
shut.PASS.3SG	ART.NOM	sky.NOM	for	years	three	and	months	six

d. Today's Greek Version (TGV)

Τότε	*ο*	*ουρανός*	*δεν*	*είχε*	*βρέξει*	*για*	*τρία*	*χρόνια*
Tóte	**o**	**ouranós**	**den**	**eíche**	**bréxei**	**gia**	**tría**	**chrónia**
tote	o	uranos	dhen	ihe	**vreksi**	ja	tria	hronia
then	ART.NOM	sky.NOM	NEG	had	rained.ACT	for	three	years

και	*έξι*	*μήνες*[6]
kai	**éxi**	**ménes**
ke	eksi	mines
and	six	months

'The sky was shut./ It did not rain for three and a half years.'

---

6 The Today's Greek Version uses a different verb in the same passage, to express the same meaning.

GREEK DATA 265

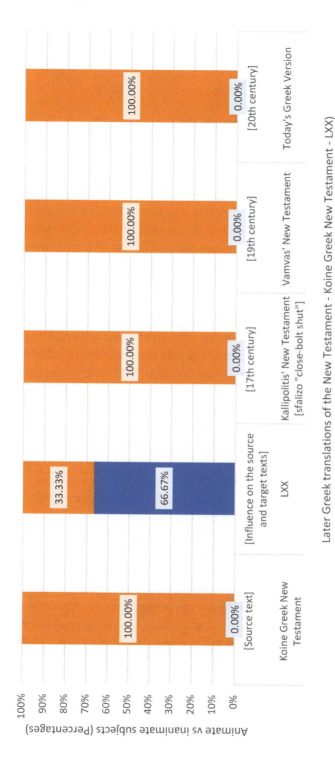

FIGURE 8.24 Subject animacy in the Koine Greek New Testament and the corpus of later Greek biblical translations (and in the LXX): The verb *kli(n)o* 'close'

LXX

(60) e. Joshua 2:7

καὶ ἡ   πύλη   ἐκλείσθη
kaì hē   pýlē   ekleísthē
and ART.NOM gate.NOM shut.PASS.3SG
'and then the gate was shut.'

In this section, I have examined the development of characteristics of voice and argument structure in non-translated texts, focusing on change-of-state verbs. A comparison between data from non-translated texts and data from translated texts reveals that diachronic retranslations do not directly follow changes in grammatical characteristics reflected in non-translated texts. The data on the examined verbal classes (externally vs. internally caused change-of-state verbs) demonstrate a significant change in non-translated texts but not in translated texts prepared in different periods.

On the contrary, diachronic retranslations evidence contact and transfer of grammatical characteristics from the source texts, from earlier texts and from non-translated texts of their period. The Greek data from non-translated texts show a change in contrast to the English data examined in Chapter 7: however, in both cases, translations do not directly follow the diachronic tendencies of change or stability reflected in non-translated texts.

In the following section, I discuss results derived from a corpus-driven survey. The aim is to test the relation between the grammatical characteristics of original texts and of their paraphrases/ intralingual translations prepared in periods of significant grammatical changes. I show that, even in cases of phrase matching where the paraphrased text/ translation follows the original text and repeats the phrase attested in the original text, the differences between translated and non-translated text are not differences that follow a significant grammatical change of the period. On the contrary, these differences reflect a peaceful coexistence of grammatical characteristics in the translated text. This means that, in some examples, the translated text follows earlier grammatical characteristics and differentiates itself from the original text. In other examples, it follows innovative grammatical characteristics and is again different than the original text.

GREEK DATA

8.2 Greek Diachronic Retranslations: Phrase Matching Approach

The corpus survey of the present section confirms my view of parallel grammars and of a contact between them in all periods—even in non-transitional periods. The aim of the present section and of the corpus survey is to test the hypothesis that diachronic (re)translations do not directly follow the grammatical characteristics of the period when the translations are prepared. The data are complex because translations in such cases reflect a contact between new and old grammatical characteristics, transfer from the original text and transfer from contemporary non-translated texts that demonstrate innovative characteristics. The present corpus survey is a corpus-driven case study rather than a corpus-based one—similarly to the second case study on English that was also a corpus-driven study.

8.2.1 *Qualitative and data-driven analysis. Phrase matching approach*

In the present section, I examine intralingual translations of the 14th–16th centuries that aimed at producing texts closer to their contemporary vernacular language. I base my discussion on a methodology applied in Karla & Lavidas' (2004) study of infinitives in source texts and their paraphrases. I use the Thesaurus Linguae Graecae corpus in the present set of corpus searches.

The starting point of the corpus survey—in particular, with respect to the selection of texts—is mainly based on Karla & Lavidas' (2004) diachronic examination of infinitives. Karla & Lavidas' study focuses on texts of the 14th–16th centuries that are available in at least two versions, in an original/ source version and a metaphrase/ paraphrase to a vernacular version (Horrocks 2014, 2017; Hinterberger (ed.) 2014; Churik 2019; Hinterberger 2020; Bentein 2020). Karla & Lavidas have located several factors triggering the presence of infinitive in both versions, its presence only in the vernacular version, and its replacement or absence from the vernacular version. Their conclusion supports a correlation between characteristics of the overall diachronic development of infinitives in Greek in non-translated texts and the coexistence of *parallel grammars* of infinitives in this period.

The criteria of selection of texts in Karla & Lavidas (2004)—which I also follow in the present study—are the following:

(i) The first criterion concerns the aim of investigating texts attested in two versions, such as translations or learned and vernacular paraphrases of the same work. The examination of such texts can contribute to the identification of cases of grammatical change, because any modification in the grammatical characteristics of the newer version may also show what kind of features were not easily understood or accepted by the translator and the audience, and had to change or to be omitted.

(ii) The second criterion is related to an attempt to limit chronologically the data to a significant stage of development of the phenomena under examination. In the beginning of the 14th century, an intense trend appeared for translations or paraphrases of learned texts into a simpler linguistic form, to make them more easily understood by a broad audience.

Such texts include the translation/ paraphrase of Anna Komnene's *Alexiad* (Books XI–XII), the translation/ paraphrase of Nicephorus Vlemmydes' "Imperial Statue" [*Basilikos Andrias*] (written in the beginnings of the 13th century) by Georgios Galesiotes and Georgios Oineotes, the anonymous translations/ paraphrases of the historical texts of *Nicetas Choniates* (12th century) and *Georgios Pachymeres* (13th century). The source texts in the above cases were written in a learned, *atticized* language, with various and complex rhetorical schemas (Horrocks 2014: 264–271). The translations/ paraphrases were prepared in a language that was not the spoken language of the particular period but an intermediate level of the Koine of the period. These texts were addressed to literate people who would like to read the well-known texts without the obstacle of linguistic difficulties, which made them inaccessible to a degree.

The data from the 15th/ 16th century also include the first vernacular, fragmentary, paraphrasis of the novel "Varlaam and Ioasaf" and the vernacular paraphrasis of "Life of Aesop". Moreover, I investigate *Digenis Akritis*, which is different than the other texts because it has a metrical form and belongs to a different period; the source text was probably prepared in the 12th century. It survives in two main versions, the most learned one, Grottaferrata, and the vernacular version of Escorial. Both versions should have been composed before the 16th century.

The data should also be distinguished into two main groups of sources:

(i) the translations of "Alexiad" and of "Imperial Statue" [*Basilikos Andrias*] and the paraphrases of the History of Nicetas Choniates and Georgios Pachymeres represent a middle towards high level of Koine Greek;

(ii) the versions of "Life of Aesop", Varlaam and Ioasaf and the text of Escorial of Digenis Akritis are written in a vernacular variety.

Below I summarize major differences between the two groups of sources, according to Karla & Lavidas' (2004) study on the status of infinitives.

GREEK DATA 269

(*1*) *First group of texts: Anna Komnene's Alexiad, Basilikos Andrias of Nike-phoros Blemmydes, Nicetas Choniates, Georgios Pachymeres.*

In the first group of texts, one does not observe any significant change in the characteristics and function of the infinitive: the infinitive is retained in the paraphrases without significant differences if compared to the Classical Greek infinitive. Most of the changes in the target text concern lexical characteristics and stylistic preferences. I refer to the following indicative examples:

(i) *Retention* of the infinitive in the translation/ paraphrasis: (a) The dependent infinitival form is retained both in case of coreference of the subject and non-coreference (61a). The impersonal matrix verb is either retained, but in a newer form, or changes into a personal verb (61b). (b) The adverbial function of the infinitive is retained, strengthened with a particle (*ὡς hōs / ὥστε hóste*). In most of the examples, other words intervene between the particle and the infinitive.

(ii) *Addition* of infinitives in the translation/ paraphrasis: A dependent infinitive can be added—usually to replace a DP of the source text (61c)—or is used for the formation of a periphrasis.

(iii) *Replacement/ omission* of the infinitive in the translation/ paraphrasis: In this case, the infinitive is replaced with finite forms or is absent from the translated text. One can distinguish the following types of replacement or omission: The verb and the dependent infinitive of the source text are rendered into a simple finite form (62a). However, in other cases, a subordinate clause replaces the infinitive. The subordinate clause is introduced with simple or complex complementizers, such as *ἵνα hína* (62b), *ὡς ἵνα hōs hína, ὡς ἂν hōs àn, ὅπως hópōs* and includes a finite verb in the subjunctive mood, or is introduced with the complementizers *ὅτι hóti* and *ὡς hōs* and includes a finite verb in the indicative mood (Joseph 1983b: 38–44).

(61) a. Anna COMNENA Alexias 11.8.5.11

Χειρώσασθαι	*ταύτην*	*γλιχόμενος*	→
Cheirósasthai	*taútēn*	*glichómenos*	
subdue.INF	this.ACC	strive.PRTC.NOM	

κατακρατῆσαι	*ταύτην*	*ἐπιθυμῶν*
katakratêsai	*taútēn*	*epithymôn*
subdue.INF	this.ACC	wish.PRTC.NOM

'Wishing/ striving to subdue her.'

b. Nicephorus BLEMMYDES Phil. et Theol. Regia statua 45.1

τί δὲ χρὴ λέγειν →
tí dè chrὲ *légein*
what PRT need.3SG say.INF

πῶς δ' ἄν τις δύναιτο λέγειν
pôs d' án tis dýnaito *légein*
how PRT PRT INDF.NOM could.3SG say.INF

'what somebody could say.'

c. Anna COMNENA Alexias 11.8.5.10

ἀνεζήτει ἀπέλευσιν →
anezḗtei *apéleusin*
wanted.3SG leave.ACC

ἐζήτει ἀπελθεῖν
ezḗtei *apeltheîn*
wanted.3SG leave.INF

'He wanted to leave.'

(62) a. Anna COMNENA Alexias 11.10.5.6

ὅσους ἔφθασαν κατασχεῖν →
hósous éphthasan *katascheîn*
as-many.ACC managed.3PL arrest.INF

ὅσους εἰς τὸν πόλεμον ἐπίασαν
hósous eis tòn pólemon *epíasan*
as-many.ACC in ART.ACC war.ACC arrested.3PL

'whoever they [managed to arrest] during a war.'

b. Nicephorus BLEMMYDES Phil. et Theol. Regia statua 16.1

μὴ μόνον αὐτὸν ἀδούλωτον διαπεφυλάχθαι →
mὲ mónon autòn adoúlōton *diapephyláchthai*
NEG only this.ACC free.ACC keep.INF

ἵνα οὐ μόνον αὐτὸς ὑπάρχῃ ἀδούλωτος
hína ou mónon autòs *hypárchēi* adoúlōtos
that NEG only this.NOM exist.3SG free.NOM

'... that not only he will be free.'

(II) *Second group of texts: Digenis Akritis, Life of Aesop, Varlaam and Ioasaf*
In the texts of the second group, one observes more significant changes in the use of infinitives. I distinguish the following three cases:

GREEK DATA 271

(i) *Retention* of the infinitive in the translation/ paraphrasis: (a) Use of a dependent infinitive with coreference or non-coreference of the subject. In several examples, the infinitive can appear in both versions with exactly the same or slightly modified form. Note that retention of an infinitival form can coappear ("coexist") with replacement of an infinitive with a finite verb in the same sentence (63a). (b) There are also instances of infinitives with adverbial function (63b).

(ii) *Addition* of an infinitive in the translation/ paraphrasis: (a) There are only very few instances of a dependent infinitive selected by the lexical verb *θέλω thélō*. (b) Infinitives can also be found with the verb *θέλω thélō* in the vernacular texts under examination, to express a future event. The infinitival form has the suffix [-i] and only rarely retains the early suffix [-in] (Joseph 1983a: 56).

(iii) *Replacement/ omission* of the infinitive in the translation/ paraphrasis: in many cases, the infinitive is replaced by a finite verb. The translation/ paraphrasis includes a main or a subordinate clause, instead of an infinitive.[7]

(63) a. (E) Digenes Acritas (e cod. Escorialense) 1779

οἶδα   φαγεῖν καὶ πιεῖν   ἔχεις   καὶ ⟨νὰ⟩ λουσθῆς
oîda   **phageîn** kaì **pieîn** *écheis*   *kaì* ⟨*nà*⟩ **lousthês**
know.1SG eat.INF and drink.INF have.2SG and PRT   wash.2SG

καὶ ἀλλάξῃς
kaì **alláxēs**
and change.2SG

'I know you should eat and drink and wash your hair and change clothes.'

b. (E) Digenes Acritas (e cod. Escorialense) 1859

πρὸ   τοῦ   γενέσθαι   ταῦτα
prò   *toû*   **genésthai** *taûta*
before ART.GEN happen.INF this.PL

'before all these happened.'

---

7 In the case of *Digenis*, it is evident that the terms *retention, addition, replacement* are conventional because there is no agreement between scholars which of the two versions, Grottaferrata or Escorial, is closer to the source/ original text. On this debate, see also Jeffreys (1998: xxvi–xxx) and the relevant bibliography.

272   CHAPTER 8

The main conclusions of Karla & Lavidas' (2004) study can be summarized as follows: Depending on the syntactic context,[8] the new construction, without infinitive, and the older construction, with infinitive, can be attested in a different ratio, but the new construction does not prevail to an absolute degree in any case. The infinitives, with or without an additional particle or complementizer, alternate with finite forms, and their use is frequent. Following the above remarks, I should refer to a syntactic diglossia of authors—in terms of Kroch (1989, 1994, 2001)—which is the expected situation in periods of grammatical change—but also see my proposal on coexisting multiglossia (Chapter 6). In the texts under examination, this tendency was illustrated, for instance, with the coexistence of cases of addition and replacement of infinitives even in the same sentence.

8.2.2   *Data*

In the present corpus survey, I examine translations/ paraphrases that render the source texts closer to the vernacular language. The data discussed here include examples of possible similarities in the constructions used in both versions, that is cases of intertextual phrase matching: for instance, cases where a ditransitive construction and the same words are used in both texts. This way of examination constitutes a different focus than the one in Karla & Lavidas' (2004) study. I analyze all passages that do not trigger a paraphrasis but contain the main structure and the same words in both versions. In this respect, any kind of slight morphosyntactic difference, e.g. the genitive instead of the dative case, in similar constructions, e.g. ditransitives in both texts, may reflect a significant grammatical change. The data derive from the *Thesaurus Linguae Graecae* (see Appendix 1: 11). The original/ early *vs.* vernacular versions include the following texts:

(a)   An early 14th-century[9] translation of Anna Komnene's *Alexiad* (books XI–XII), which represents middle to high Koine.

---

8   The contexts described in the above-mentioned study are the following: In broad terms, they concern contexts of coreference vs. non-coreference of the subject. More specifically, they include the following sets of constructions: (i) accusativus-cum-infinitivo constructions *vs.* coreference constructions, (ii) control constructions, (iii) with adverbial functions *vs.* in dependent positions, (iv) other words may intervene between the infinitive and the verb that selects it, or other words may intervene between the infinitive and its object (*vs.* adjacency between the verb and the infinitive or the infinitive and its object). For more details, see Karla & Lavidas (2004).

9   According to the Thesaurus Linguae Graecae: "post AD 12".

GREEK DATA 273

(b) A translation of the early 13th-century *Basilikos Andrias* of Nikephoros Blemmydes by Georgios Galesiotes and Georgios Oinaiotes; the variety of this translation represents middle to high Koine.

(c) A paraphrasis of "Life of Aesop" into the vernacular language of the period. I compare Vita W (vita Aesopi Westermanniana) to Vita Pl vel Accursiana (Maximus Planudes). I also compare Vita W (vita Aesopi Westermanniana) to Vita G (e cod. 397 Bibliothecae Pierponti Morgan), again with the aim of analyzing all examples of morphosyntactic variation in intertextual phrase matching.

(d) The last corpus survey concerns *Digenis Akritis*. The source text is a metrical text, written in the vernacular language, prepared circa in the 12th century. The *Grottaferrata Version* offers a more learned version, whereas the *Escorial Version* a more vernacular version. Both of them should have been prepared before the 16th century. I analyze all instances of morphosyntactic variation in cases of intertextual phrase matching in the Grottaferrata and the Escorial Version.

8.2.2.1 Case Study I:
Translation/ paraphrasis of Anna Komnene's *Alexiad* (books XI–XII)

The first corpus study concerns an early 14th-century translation/ paraphrasis of Anna Komnene's *Alexiad* (books XI–XII) (Hunger 1981). The source text is written in middle to high Koine.[10] The data in this part of the study include examples of similar constructions attested in both versions, that is, cases of phrase matching between the source and target text. In this respect, my focus is not the same as the focus of Karla & Lavidas (2004), in that I do not investigate constructions that trigger a paraphrasis in the target/ vernacular text, as in Karla & Lavidas' study. I examine phrases that demonstrate a significant variation with respect to grammatical features, even though they also show phrase matching, i.e., common constructions attested in both versions of the text.

I locate the following cases of variation in constructions that appear in both versions. One observes several cases of addition of a *definite article*, in the genitive case, in the paraphrasis/ intralingual translation: See (64–69). The examples in (70a, b) demonstrate both addition and omission of a definite article in the same phrase of the paraphrased text. In several examples, the paraphrased text omits the dative definite article—or even the accusative definite article,

---

10   On "Alexiad" see, among others, Horrocks (2014: 238–240).

274 CHAPTER 8

with proper nouns—even in cases of overall matching constructions. There are also examples of replacement of the dative form (article and/ or noun) by an accusative type (71a–b).

Moreover, a dative can replace a genitive (72a, b), but also a genitive can replace an accusative in phrases where the target text follows all other characteristics of the source text. A DP in the genitive can be marked overtly with a preposition in the paraphrased text, or it can be replaced by an accusative form, without or with a preposition. A different preposition can also be used instead of the preposition that appears in the source text but is not productive in later texts (73–74).

(64) a. Anna COMNENA Alexias 11.7.4.4
Εὐμάθιον   δοῦκα   Κύπρου
Eumáthion   doûka   Kýprou
Eumathios.ACC duke.ACC Cyprus.GEN

b. Anonyma Metaphrasis 'Alexiadis', lib. XI–XIII 5.2
Εὐμάθιον   δοῦκα   τῆς   Κύπρου
Eumáthion   doûka   tês   Kýprou
Eumathios.ACC duke.ACC ART.GEN Cyprus.GEN
'Eumathios, duke of Cyprus'

(65) a. Anna COMNENA Alexias 11.7.7.6
τὸν   ἀνεψιὸν   αὐτοῦ   Ταγγρὲ
tòn   anepsiòn   autoû   Tangrè
ART.ACC nephew.ACC this.GEN Tancred.ACC

b. Anonyma Metaphrasis 'Alexiadis', lib. XI–XIII 18.3
τὸν   ἀνεψιὸν   αὐτοῦ   τὸν   Ταγγρὲ
tòn   anepsiòn   autoû   tòn   Tangrè
ART.ACC nephew.ACC this.GEN ART.ACC Tancred.ACC
'his nephew Tancred'

(66) a. Anna COMNENA Alexias 11.8.2.16
Ῥωμαῖοι   κατεῖχον
Rhōmaîoi   kateîchon
Romans.NOM occupied.3PL

GREEK DATA

b. Anonyma Metaphrasis 'Alexiadis', lib. XI–XIII 26.2

οἱ   Ῥωμαῖοι   κατεῖχον
hoi   *Rhōmaîoi*   *kateîchon*
ART.NOM Romans.NOM occupied.3PL
'Romans occupied ...'

(67) a. Anna COMNENA Alexias 12.2.1.9

ἀνὴρ   δὲ   οὗτος   εὐγενὴς
anèr   *dè*   *hoûtos*   *eugenès*
man.NOM PRT this.NOM noble.NOM

b. Anonyma Metaphrasis 'Alexiadis', lib. XI–XIII 133.2

οὗτος   ὁ   ἀνὴρ   εὐγενὴς
hoûtos   **ho**   *anèr*   *eugenès*
this.NOM ART.NOM man.NOM noble.NOM
'this noble man'

(68) a. Anna COMNENA Alexias 12.6.3.10

οἶσθα   πάντως, Σολομών
oîstha   *pántōs, Solomón*
know.2SG anyway Solomon.VOC

b. Anonyma Metaphrasis 'Alexiadis', lib. XI–XIII 229.1

γινώσκεις   πάντως, ὦ   Σολομῶν
ginóskeis   *pántōs, ô*   *Solomôn*
know.2SG anyway ART.VOC Solomon.VOC
'You know in any case, Solomon [...]'

(69) a. Anna COMNENA Alexias 12.4.3.8

υἱὸν   Ἰσαακίου   τοῦ   σεβαστοκράτορος   Ἀλέξιον
hyiòn   *Isaakíou*   **toû**   *sebastokrátoros*   *Aléxion*
son.ACC Issac.GEN ART.GEN Sebastokrator.GEN Alexios.ACC

b. Anonyma Metaphrasis 'Alexiadis', lib. XI–XIII 187.2

υἱὸν   Ἰσαακίου   σεβαστοκράτορος   τὸν   Ἀλέξιον
hyiòn   *Isaakíou*   *sebastokrátoros*   **tòn**   *Aléxion*
son.ACC Isaac.GEN Sabastokrator.GEN ART.ACC Alexios.ACC
'Alexios, the son of Sebastokrator Isaac'

(70) a. Anna COMNENA Alexias 11.10.2.14

τὸν ἄπαντα στόλον
tòn hápanta stólon
ART.ACC whole.ACC navy.ACC

b. Anonyma Metaphrasis 'Alexiadis', lib. XI–XIII 61.2

ἄπαντα τὸν στόλον
hápanta **tòn** stólon
whole.ACC ART.ACC navy.ACC
'the whole navy'

(71) a. Anna COMNENA Alexias 12.4.1.8

τεσσαράκοντα νυχθημέροις ὅλοις
tessarákonta nychthēmérois hólois
forty nights-days.DAT whole.DAT

b. Anonyma Metaphrasis 'Alexiadis', lib. XI–XIII 178.2

τεσσαράκοντα γὰρ ὅλα νυχθήμερα
tessarákonta gàr hóla nychthḗmera
forty PRT whole.ACC nights-days.ACC
'[it shined] for whole forty days and nights'

(72) a. Anna COMNENA Alexias 11.11.6.4

καὶ τοῦ Ἰσαγγέλη ἑνωθείς
kaì **toû** Isangélē henōtheís
and ART.GEN Isangeles.GEN join.PRTC.NOM

b. Anonyma Metaphrasis 'Alexiadis', lib. XI–XIII 96.4

καὶ τῷ Ἰσαγγέλη ἑνωθείς
kaì **tôi** Isangélēi henōtheís
and ART.DAT Isangeles.DAT join.PRTC.NOM
'He joined Isangeles.'

(73) a. Anna COMNENA Alexias 11.8.5.7

Ἰσαγγέλης τῆς μεγαλοπόλεως ἐξελθών
Isangélēs tês megalopóleōs exelthṑn
Isangeles.NOM ART.GEN capital.GEN leave.PRTC.NOM

GREEK DATA

277

    b. Anonyma Metaphrasis 'Alexiadis', lib. xi–xiii 39.1

Ἰσαγγέλης	*δὲ*	*ἐκ*	*τῆς*	*μεγαλοπόλεως*	*ἐξελθὼν*
Isangélēs	*dè*	*ek*	*tês*	*megalopóleōs*	*exelthòn*
Isangeles.NOM	PRT	from	ART.GEN	capital.GEN	leave.PRTC.NOM

    'When Isangeles left the capital.'

(74) a. Anna COMNENA Alexias 12.2.2.10

πρὸς	*παρατάξεις*
pròs	*paratáxeis*
towards	lines.ACC

    b. Anonyma Metaphrasis 'Alexiadis', lib. xi–xiii 136.3

εἰς	*παρατάξεις*
eis	*paratáxeis*
in	lines.ACC

    'to lines of battle'

In examples of matching phrases, a verb may appear in a different *tense* in the source text, e.g., in the aorist, than in the paraphrased text, e.g., in the present (75a, b). *Prefixed* forms of the source text appear without a prefix in matching phrases of the translated/ paraphrased version (76–79). A different prefix may also appear in the paraphrased text instead of the verbal prefix attested in the matching phrase of the source text (80a, b). Again, the reverse direction is possible, with addition of a verbal prefix in the paraphrased text (81a, b).

(75) a. Anna COMNENA Alexias 11.7.4.11

βουλὴν	*ἐβουλεύσατο*
boulèn	*ebouleúsato*
decision.ACC	decided.MID.3SG

    b. Anonyma Metaphrasis 'Alexiadis', lib. xi–xiii 7.1

βουλὴν	*βουλεύεται*
boulèn	*bouleúetai*
decision.ACC	decide.MP.3SG

    'He decides/ decided [he conceives/ conceived a plan]'

(76) a. Anna COMNENA Alexias 11.7.6.2

διακειμένου	*βουνοῦ*
diakeiménou	*bounoû*
DIA-situated-opposite.GEN	hill.GEN

b. Anonyma Metaphrasis 'Alexiadis', lib. XI–XIII 14.2

κειμένου   *βουνοῦ*
keiménou   *bounoû*
situated-opposite.GEN hill.GEN
'of the hill opposite [Tripolis]'

(77) a. Anna COMNENA Alexias 11.7.7.6

κατὰ   *τῆς*   *Λαοδικείας*   *ἐκπέμπει*
katà   *tês*   *Laodikeías*   *ekpémpei*
against ART.GEN Laodicea.GEN EK-send.3SG

b. Anonyma Metaphrasis 'Alexiadis', lib. XI–XIII 18.3

κατὰ   *τῆς*   *Λαοδικείας*   *ἔπεμψεν*
katà   *tês*   *Laodikeías*   *épempsen*
against ART.GEN Laodicea.GEN sent.3SG
'... sent them to besiege Laodicea'

(78) a. Anna COMNENA Alexias 11.12.3.12

οὐκ   *ἀπώκνησε*   *ζῆν*
ouk   *apóknēse*   *zên*
NEG APO-shrinked.3SG live.INF

b. Anonyma Metaphrasis 'Alexiadis', lib. XI–XIII 110.3

οὐκ   *ὤκνησε*   *ζῶν*
ouk   *óknēse*   *zôn*
NEG shrinked.3SG live.PRTC
'[For this man, who was not dead except in pretence], did not shrink
from living [with dead bodies].'

(79) a. Anna COMNENA Alexias 12.8.4.6

ἑαυτοὺς   *προσέρριψαν*
heautoùs   *prosérripsan*
themselves.ACC PROS-threw.3PL

b. Anonyma Metaphrasis 'Alexiadis', lib. XI–XIII 266.1

ἔρριψαν   *ἑαυτοὺς*
érripsan   *heautoùs*
threw.3PL themselves.ACC
'... threw themselves [into the sea]'

GREEK DATA

(80) a. Anna COMNENA Alexias 11.11.6.13
πόλεις   ἀναλαμβάνεσθαι
póleis   **analambánesthai**
cities.ACC ANA-take-up.INF

b. Anonyma Metaphrasis 'Alexiadis', lib. XI–XIII 98.3
πόλεις   παραλαμβάνῃς
póleis   **paralambánēis**
cities.ACC PARA-take-up.2SG
'... to take up cities'

(81) a. Anna COMNENA Alexias 12.8.1.1
οὐδὲ τὰ   κατὰ τὸν   Βαϊμοῦντον   ἐλάθετο
oudè tà   *katà tòn*   *Baimoûnton*   **elátheto**
NEG ART.ACC about ART.ACC Bohemund.ACC forgot.MID.3SG

b. Anonyma Metaphrasis 'Alexiadis', lib. XI–XIII 256.4
οὐδὲ τὰ   κατὰ τοῦ   Βαϊμούντου   ἐπελάθετο
oudè tà   *katà toû*   *Baimoúntou*   **epelátheto**
NEG ART.ACC about ART.GEN Bohemund.GEN EPI-forgot.MID.3SG
'He did not [on account of these] forget those related to Bohemund.'

In several cases, *subordination* presents different characteristics in the paraphrased text than in the source text. For example, a relative pronoun can be used to replace the causal complementizer of the source text (82a, b).

Particles and their omission in the paraphrased text also reveal important characteristics of the texts under examination (83–85). For instance, the particle γέ *gé* of the source text is dropped in the paraphrased text in several cases of matching phrases (86–87). In other matching phrases, a particle or an adverbial can be "translated" with particles or adverbials that are more frequent in later texts. See the examples in (88a, b) [πάλαι *pálai* 'long ago' → πώποτε *pópote* 'ever yet'] and (89a, b) [δέ *dé* → γάρ *gár*].

In several examples, the paraphrased text modifies orders related to *hyperbaton* phenomena of Early Greek. The hyperbaton refers to reordering of a part of a phrase, with the result that some elements of the phrase appear as moved outside the phrase; cf., among many others, Devine & Stephens (2000) and Agbayani & Golston (2010). The order in the paraphrased text is similar to the word order attested in post-Koine Greek: the adjective appears before the noun, the object pronoun before the verb, the genitive follows the noun and its other attributes (90–91). In other examples, the paraphrased text adds a pronominal

280   CHAPTER 8

object, which is absent in the matching phrase of the source text. Note that the
overall diachronic tendency reflected in non-translated texts demonstrates a
significant change from Ancient and Koine Greek that allows omission of direct
objects, to post-Koine Greek that does not permit null definite objects: see the
examples in (92a, b).

Infinitives of the source text are replaced in matching phrases of the paraphrased text with finite forms and embedded clauses introduced with *ἵνα/hína*,
or with participles, or with finite verbs in main clauses. See (93–94).

(82) a. Anna COMNENA Alexias 11.8.2.16
          ἐπεὶ   δὲ   τοῦτο   Ῥωμαῖοι   κατεῖχον
          epeì   *dè* *toûto* *Rhōmaîoi*   *kateîchon*
          because PRT this.ACC Romans.NOM occupied.3PL

      b. Anonyma Metaphrasis 'Alexiadis', lib. XI–XIII 26.2
          ὅπερ   οἱ   Ῥωμαῖοι   κατεῖχον.
          hóper   *hoi*   *Rhōmaîoi*   *kateîchon.*
          REL.ACC.SG ART.NOM Romans.NOM occupied.3PL
          'because Romans occupied that ...'

(83) a. Anna COMNENA Alexias 11.11.7.13
          παραλαμβάνει τήν   τε   Λογγινιάδα
          paralambánei tḗn   **te** *Longiniáda*
          seize.3SG   ART.ACC and Longinias.ACC

      b. Anonyma Metaphrasis 'Alexiadis', lib. XI–XIII 103.3
          παρέλαβε   τὴν   Λογγινιάδα
          parélabe *tḕn*   *Longiniáda*
          seized.3SG ART.ACC Longinias.ACC
          '... seizes/ seized Longinias'

(84) a. Anna COMNENA Alexias 12.1.2.3
          Πίσσαν   τὲ   καὶ Γένουαν   καὶ Βενετίαν
          Píssan   *tè* **kaì** *Génouan* *kaì* *Benetían*
          Pisa.ACC and and Genoa.ACC and Venice.ACC

      b. Anonyma Metaphrasis 'Alexiadis', lib. XI–XIII 120.2
          Πίσσαν,   τὴν   Γενούαν,   καὶ τὴν   Βενετίαν
          Píssan, *tḕn*   *Genoúan,* *kaì* *tḕn*   *Benetían*
          Pisa.ACC ART.ACC Genoa.ACC and ART.ACC Venice.ACC
          'Pisa, Genoa and Venice'

GREEK DATA

(85) a. Anna COMNENA Alexias 12.4.5.4
ἐλέγετο δ' οὖν
elégeto *d' oûn*
said.3SG PRT PRT

b. Anonyma Metaphrasis 'Alexiadis', lib. XI–XIII 195.3
ἐλέγετο δὲ
elégeto *dè*
said.3SG PRT
'it was said, then, ...'

(86) a. Anna COMNENA Alexias 11.8.5.1
ὁ δέ γε Ἰσαγγέλης καὶ ὁ Τζίτας
ho *dé ge* Isangélēs *kaì ho* Tzítas
ART.NOM PRT PRT Isangeles.NOM and ART.NOM Tzitas.NOM

b. Anonyma Metaphrasis 'Alexiadis', lib. XI–XIII 36.1
ὁ δὲ Ἰσαγγέλης καὶ ὁ Τζίτας
ho *dè* Isangélēs *kaì ho* Tzítas
ART.NOM PRT Isangeles.NOM and ART.NOM Tzitas.NOM
'Isangeles and Tzitas'

(87) a. Anna COMNENA Alexias 11.9.3.22
ὁ δέ γε Βουτουμίτης
ho *dé ge* Boutoumítēs
ART.NOM PRT PRT Butumites.NOM

b. Anonyma Metaphrasis 'Alexiadis', lib. XI–XIII 56.4
Βουτουμίτης δὲ
Boutoumítēs *dè*
Butumites.NOM PRT
'Butumites meanwhile ...'

(88) a. Anna COMNENA Alexias 12.4.1.5
τῶν πάλαι φανέντων
tôn *pálai* phanéntōn
ART.GEN long-ago appear.PRTC.GEN.PL

282 CHAPTER 8

b. Anonyma Metaphrasis 'Alexiadis', lib. XI–XIII 177.2

τῶν   πώποτε   φανέντων
tôn   **pópote**   phanéntōn
ART.GEN ever-yet appear.PRTC.GEN.PL
'[the largest comet] of all that had ever been seen before'

(89) a. Anna COMNENA Alexias 12.4.1.8

ἐφαίνετο   δὲ
ephaíneto   **dè**
appeared.3SG PRT

b. Anonyma Metaphrasis 'Alexiadis', lib. XI–XIII 178.2

γὰρ ὅλα νυχθήμερα   ἐφαίνετο
gàr hóla nychthémera ephaíneto
PRT all   days-nights   appeared.3SG

'it appeared, then, ...'
'it appeared, then, day and night ...'

(90) a. Anna COMNENA Alexias 12.4.2.15

τὴν   τούτων   αὐτοῦ   που κατάλυσιν   δηλοῖ
tèn   toútōn   autoû   pou katálysin   dēloî
ART.ACC this.GEN.PL this.GEN.SG PRT dissolution.ACC show.3SG

b. Anonyma Metaphrasis 'Alexiadis', lib. XI–XIII 185.2

δηλοῖ   τὴν   τούτων   κατάλυσιν
dēloî   tèn   toútōn   katálysin
show.3SG ART.ACC this.GEN.PL dissolution.ACC
'it shows their dissolution'

(91) a. Anna COMNENA Alexias 11.12.3.12

τέχνη   μὲν οὖν τοῦ   βαρβάρου   αὕτη   πρώτη
téchnē   mèn oûn toû   barbárou   haútē   prótē
device.NOM PRT PRT GEN.SG barbarian.GEN this.NOM first.NOM
καὶ μόνη
kaì mónē
and unique.NOM

GREEK DATA   283

b. Anonyma Metaphrasis 'Alexiadis', lib. XI–XIII 110.3

αὕτη	τέχνη	πρώτη	καὶ μόνη	τοῦ
haútē	*téchnē*	*prótē*	*kaì mónē*	*toû*
this.NOM	device.NOM	first.NOM	and unique.NOM	GEN.SG

βαρβάρου
barbárou
barbarian.GEN

'The device of the barbarian was unique and the first ...'

(92) a. Anna COMNENA Alexias 12.6.3.1

κατὰ	τοῦ	μηδὲν	ἠδικηκότος
katà	*toû*	*mēdèn*	*ēdikēkótos*
against	ART.GEN	nothing	harm.PRF.PRTC.GEN.SG

b. Anonyma Metaphrasis 'Alexiadis', lib. XI–XIII 227.1

κατὰ	τοῦ	μηδὲν	ἀδικήσαντος	**αὐτοὺς**
katà	*toû*	*mēdèn*	*adikḗsantos*	***autoùs***
against	ART.GEN	nothing	harm.AOR.PRTC.GEN.SG.	3PL.ACC

'[...] who had done them no wrong'

(93) a. Anna COMNENA Alexias 11.11.6.13

πόλεις	ἀναλαμβάνεσθαι
póleis	***analambánesthai***
cities.ACC	ANA-take-up.INF

b. Anonyma Metaphrasis 'Alexiadis', lib. XI–XIII 98.3

πόλεις	παραλαμβάνῃς
póleis	***paralambánēis***
cities.ACC	PARA-take-up.2SG

'... to take up cities'

(94) a. Anna COMNENA Alexias 11.12.3.12

οὐκ	ἀπώκνησε	ζῆν
ouk	*apóknēse*	***zên***
NEG	APO-shrinked.3SG	live.INF

284 CHAPTER 8

b. Anonyma Metaphrasis 'Alexiadis', lib. XI–XIII 110.3

οὐκ ὤκνησε   ζῶν
ouk óknēse   *zôn*
NEG shrinked.3SG live.PRTC
'[For this man, who was not dead except in pretence,] did not shrink
from living [with dead bodies].'

The results of the first case study of phrase matching evidence the existence of more than one grammar even in the same text: one clearly observes several cases of change and modification even in phrase matching examples. In other words, intralingual translations/ paraphrases in later periods present examples of coexistence of earlier and late grammatical characteristics even in the same phrase and even in phrases that follow the original text and include the same words and structure.

8.2.2.2   Case study II:
An early 13th-century translation of Nikephoros Blemmydes'
Basilikos Andrias

The data described in the second case study derive from an early 13th-century translation of Nikephoros Blemmydes' *Basilikos Andrias*,[11] which was prepared by Georgios Galesiotes and Georgios Oinaiotes. The source text was written in middle to high Koine. I locate the following cases of variation in constructions that appear in both versions. The paraphrased text does not include word orders showing characteristics of *hyperbaton* in several cases where the source text has examples of hyperbaton.

In several instances, the genitive follows the head of the phrase in the paraphrased text; in (95), however, the pronoun remains in its initial position and the verb breaks the unity between the pronoun and the noun. In other examples of matching phrases, the adjective precedes the noun in the paraphrased text, whereas the source text displays the order noun-adjective (96a, b). In general, there are several examples of the following contrast: the complements follow their head in the matching phrase of the paraphrased text but precede their head in the source text (97a, b).

In addition, the source text exhibits more positions where a *particle* can appear than the corresponding matching phrases of the translated/ paraphrased text do (98–99). However, there are also examples of syntactic contexts where a particle is included in the matching phrase of the paraphrased/ translated text even though it is absent from the source text (100a, b).

---

11   On *Basilikos Andrias* of Nikephoros Blemmydes, see, among others, Ševčenko (1981: 311–312).

GREEK DATA   285

(95) a. Nicephorus BLEMMYDES Phil. et Theol. *Regia statua* 27.1
καὶ   πᾶσαν   Περσῶν   κατέλυσε   τὴν   ἀρχήν
kaì   pâsan   Persôn   katélyse   tèn   archḗn
and whole.ACC Persians.GEN dissolved.3SG ART.ACC power.ACC

   b. Georgius GALESIOTES Rhet. *Metaphrasis "Regiae statuae"* 27.1
καὶ   πᾶσαν   κατέλυσε   τὴν   ἀρχὴν   τῶν
kaì   pâsan   katélyse   tèn   archèn   tôn
and whole.ACC dissolved.3SG ART.ACC power.ACC ART.GEN
Περσῶν
Persôn
Persians.GEN
'He dissolved the whole power of Persians.'

(96) a. Nicephorus BLEMMYDES Phil. et Theol. *Regia statua* 101.6
μεγαληγορία   προφητικὴ
megalēgoría   prophētikè
loftiness.NOM prophetic.NOM

   b. Georgius GALESIOTES Rhet. *Metaphrasis "Regiae statuae"* 101.5
προφητικὴν   μεγαληγορίαν
prophētikèn   *megalēgorían*
prophetic.ACC loftiness.ACC
'the loftiness of the oracular'

(97) a. Nicephorus BLEMMYDES Phil. et Theol. *Regia statua* 159.2
εἰς Ἀθήνας   πολιτογραφηθείς,   Ἀριστείδης
eis Athénas *politographētheís,*   *Aristeídēs*
in Athens   enrolled-as-citizen.NOM Aristides.NOM

   b. Georgius GALESIOTES Rhet. *Metaphrasis "Regiae statuae"* 159.3
πολιτογραφηθείς   εἰς Ἀθήνας,   Ἀριστείδης
politographētheís   **eis Athénas,** *Aristeídēs*
enrolled-as-citizen.PRTC.NOM in Athens   Aristides.NOM
'Aristides, enrolled as a citizen of Athens'

(98) a. Nicephorus BLEMMYDES Phil. et Theol. *Regia statua* 59.4
τῶν   πάλαι   βασιλέων   ἔργοις   τε   καὶ λόγοις
tôn   pálai   basiléōn   érgois   **te**   *kaì lógois*
ART.GEN long-ago kings.GEN works.DAT and and words.DAT

b. Georgius GALESIOTES Rhet. *Metaphrasis "Regiae statuae"* 59.5

τῶν   πάλαι   βασιλέων   ἔργοις   καὶ λόγοις
tôn   pálai   basiléōn   érgois   kaì lógois
ART.GEN long-ago kings.GEN works.DAT and words.DAT
'through the work and words of old kings'

(99) a. Nicephorus BLEMMYDES Phil. et Theol. *Regia statua* 83.5

τοὺς   δέ   γε   φίλους
toùs   dé   ge   phílous
ART.ACC PRT PRT friends.ACC

b. Georgius GALESIOTES Rhet. *Metaphrasis "Regiae statuae"* 83.5

οἱ   φίλοι   δὲ
hoi   phíloi   dè
ART.NOM friends.NOM PRT
'friends, however ...'

(100) a. Nicephorus BLEMMYDES Phil. et Theol. *Regia statua* 138.6

ἐν Φρυγίᾳ   τὸν   Σκάμανδρον
en Phrygíai   tòn   Skámandron
in Phrygia.DAT ART.ACC Scamandros.ACC

b. Georgius GALESIOTES Rhet. *Metaphrasis "Regiae statuae"* 138.7

ἐν Φρυγίᾳ   μὲν τὸν   Σκάμανδρον
en Phrygíai   mèn tòn   Skámandron
in Phrygia.DAT PRT ART.ACC Scamandros.ACC
'Scamandros in Phrygia'

The paraphrased/ translated text adds a *definite article* in examples of syntactic contexts where the matching phrase of the source text does not include an article (101–105). In a restricted number of examples, the reverse direction of modification can be found, in that the matching phrase of the translated text omits the definite article that the source text contains. In these instances, characteristics related to the hyperbaton and other phenomena of early Greek are evidenced in the translated text—which demonstrates overgeneralization of early characteristics (106a, b).

Accordingly, it appears that grammatical differences in such cases cannot mean a simple transfer into the paraphrased texts of grammatical characteristics from non-translated texts of their period. One should recognize a complex situation of parallel grammars, of contact between the grammars and of

GREEK DATA

differences between grammatical characteristics of retranslations that do not depend on grammatical change. Besides the addition of a definite article,[12] the examples in (107a, b) also demonstrate a different order of the noun and the particles in the matching phrase of the translated text.

(101)   a. Nicephorus BLEMMYDES Phil. et Theol. *Regia statua* 27.1

πᾶσαν   Περσῶν   κατέλυσε   τὴν   ἀρχήν
pâsan   *Persôn*   *katélyse*   *tền*   *archến*
whole.ACC Persians.GEN dissolved.3SG ART.ACC power.ACC

b. Georgius GALESIOTES Rhet. *Metaphrasis "Regiae statuae"* 27.1

τὴν   ἀρχὴν   τῶν   Περσῶν
tền   ***archền***   ***tôn***   *Persôn*
ART.ACC power.ACC ART.GEN Persians.GEN
'He dissolved the (whole) power of Persians.'

(102)   a. Nicephorus BLEMMYDES Phil. et Theol. *Regia statua* 37.3

ἀφωμοιωμένος   Θεῷ
aphōmoiōménos   *Theôi*
assimilate.PRTC.NOM God.DAT

b. Georgius GALESIOTES Rhet. *Metaphrasis "Regiae statuae"* 37.5

ἐξομοιούμενος   τῷ   Θεῷ
exomoioúmenos   ***tôi***   *Theôi*
assimilate.PRTC.NOM ART.DAT God.DAT
'assimilating God'

(103)   a. Nicephorus BLEMMYDES Phil. et Theol. *Regia statua* 53.1

Σέσωστρις   Αἰγυπτίων
Sésōstris   *Aigyptíōn*
Sesostris.NOM Egyptians.GEN

b. Georgius GALESIOTES Rhet. *Metaphrasis "Regiae statuae"* 53.1

ὁ   Σέσωστρις   ὁ   τῶν   Αἰγυπτίων
ho   *Sésōstris*   ***ho***   ***tôn***   *Aigyptíōn*
ART.NOM Sesostris.NOM ART.NOM ART.GEN Egyptians.GEN
'Sesostris, king of Egypt'

---

12   Note that the aim of the present section is a qualitative and corpus-driven examination— and not a quantitative analysis. For this reason, I discuss characteristics that appear in the translated text and not their frequency.

(104) a. Nicephorus BLEMMYDES Phil. et Theol. *Regia statua* 147.3

ὑπὸ Σκηπίωνος στρατηγοῦ Ῥωμαίων
hypò Skēpíōnos stratēgoû Rhōmaíōn
by Scipio.GEN general.GEN Romans.GEN

b. Georgius GALESIOTES Rhet. *Metaphrasis "Regiae statuae"* 147.4

ὑπὸ Σκηπίωνος τοῦ στρατηγοῦ Ῥωμαίων
*hypò Skēpíōnos **toû** stratēgoû Rhōmaíōn*
by Scipio.GEN ART.GEN general.GEN Romans.GEN
'by Scipio, the Roman general'

(105) a. Nicephorus BLEMMYDES Phil. et Theol. *Regia statua* 157.7

ὡς Νηρεύς τις
hōs Nēreús tis
as Nereus.NOM INDF.NOM

b. Georgius GALESIOTES Rhet. *Metaphrasis "Regiae statuae"* 157.11

ὡς ὁ Νηρεὺς ἐκεῖνος
*hōs **ho** Nēreùs ekeînos*
as ART.NOM Nereus.NOM that.NOM
'as that Nereus/ a Nereus ...'

(106) a. Nicephorus BLEMMYDES Phil. et Theol. *Regia statua* 159.1

τοὺς διαιτητὰς καὶ τοὺς ἐφόρους
toùs diaitētàs kaì toùs ephórous
ART.ACC umpires.ACC and ART.ACC rulers.ACC

b. Georgius GALESIOTES Rhet. *Metaphrasis "Regiae statuae"* 159.2

καὶ τοῦ λαοῦ διαιτητὰς καὶ ἐφόρους
kaì toû laoû diaitētàs kaì ephórous
and ART.GEN people.GEN umpires.ACC and rulers.ACC
'umpires and rulers (of the people)'

(107) a. Nicephorus BLEMMYDES Phil. et Theol. *Regia statua* 160.1

Γουνεὺς μὲν γὰρ
***Gouneùs** mèn gàr*
Guneus.NOM PRT PRT

GREEK DATA

b. Georgius GALESIOTES Rhet. *Metaphrasis "Regiae statuae"* 160.1

ὁ	μὲν	γὰρ	Γουνεὺς
ho	mèn	gàr	**Gouneùs**
ART.NOM	PRT	PRT	Guneus.NOM

'because Guneus ...'

A different verbal *prefix* in the translated/ paraphrased text can replace the verbal prefix attested in the source text in the matching phrase (108a, b). In other cases, a different *particle* in the matching phrase of the translated/ paraphrased text can be used, for instance, to introduce conditionals; the replaced particle is not frequent in other texts of the period of the translated/ paraphrased text (109a, b).

Infinitives attested in the source text do not appear in all cases of matching phrases in the translated/ paraphrased text: an embedded clause introduced with ὡς *hōs* can be attested in the translation/ paraphrasis instead of the infinitive (110a, b). In other examples, the infinitive is retained, even with more archaic characteristics than in the source text. In the source text, for instance, an article may nominalize the infinitive, whereas the infinitive is not accompanied with an article in the target text (111a, b). Such examples are of significance because they demonstrate characteristics of parallel grammars: translations may show *different characteristics than both the original texts and the texts of their period*. This means that translations may develop their grammatical characteristics, as a result of a contact, through transfer from the innovative grammar of their contemporary non-translated texts and through transfer from the grammar of earlier periods.

Regarding another grammatical characteristic, the source text exhibits a preference for *participial* constructions similarly to early Greek. In several instances, the matching phrase of the translation/ paraphrasis modifies the participial construction or replaces it with a finite verb (112a, b).

(108) a. Nicephorus BLEMMYDES Phil. et Theol. *Regia statua* 37.3
αφωμοιωμένος
aphōmoiōménos
APO-assimilate.PRTC.NOM.SG

b. Georgius GALESIOTES Rhet. *Metaphrasis "Regiae statuae"* 37.5
ἐξομοιούμενος
exomoioúmenos
EK-assimilate.PRTC.NOM.SG
'assimilating'

(109) a. Nicephorus BLEMMYDES Phil. et Theol. *Regia statua* 92.1
   Εἰ δὲ καὶ κόλακες
   Ei dè kaì kólakes
   if PRT and fawners.NOM

b. Georgius GALESIOTES Rhet. *Metaphrasis "Regiae statuae"* 92.1
   ἂν δὲ καὶ κόλακες
   àn dè kaì kólakes
   if PRT and fawners.NOM
   'even though, [they were] fawners ...'

(110) a. Nicephorus BLEMMYDES Phil. et Theol. *Regia statua* 83.5
   τοὺς δούλους εἰπὼν εἶναι τῶν
   toùs doúlous eipòn eînai tôn
   ART.ACC slaves.ACC say.PRTC.NOM be.INF ART.GEN
   ὠνητῶν
   ōnētôn
   bought.GEN.PL

b. Georgius GALESIOTES Rhet. *Metaphrasis "Regiae statuae"* 83.5
   ὡς οἱ δοῦλοι μέν εἰσιν ὠνητοί
   hōs hoi doûloi mén eisin ōnētoí
   that ART.NOM slaves.NOM PRT be.3PL bought.NOM.PL
   '[saying] that slaves may be bought'

(111) a. Nicephorus BLEMMYDES Phil. et Theol. *Regia statua* 132.3
   προμεμελέτητο γὰρ αὐτοῖς καὶ τὸ ἀκοντίζειν καὶ
   promemelétēto gàr autoîs kaì tò akontízein kaì
   trained.3SG PRT 3PL.DAT and ART.NOM hurl-javelin.INF and
   τὸ μεθ' ὅπλων ἱππάζεσθαι καὶ ταχυδρομεῖν
   tò meth' hóplōn hippázesthai kaì tachydromeîn
   ART.NOM with weapons horse-ride.INF and run-fast.INF

b. Georgius GALESIOTES Rhet. *Metaphrasis "Regiae statuae"* 132.3
   ἦσαν γὰρ ἀκριβῶς πρότερον παιδευθέντες
   êsan gàr akribôs próteron paideuthéntes
   were.3PL PRT accurately earlier trained.PRTC.NOM
   ἀκοντίζειν καὶ μεθ' ὅπλων ἱππάζεσθαι καὶ
   akontízein kaì meth' hóplōn hippázesthai kaì
   hurl-javelin.INF and with weapons horse-ride.INF and

GREEK DATA

291

> τᾰχυδρομεῖν
> **tachydromeîn**
> run-fast.INF
> 'They were trained in the past, to hit with a javelin, to ride a horse and carry weapons and to run fast.'

(112) a. Nicephorus BLEMMYDES Phil. et Theol. *Regia statua* 147.3

τὴν	Βιθυνίαν	κατειληφώς
tèn	*Bithynían*	*kateilēphós*
ART.ACC	Bithynia.ACC	seize.PRF.PRTC.NOM

      b. Georgius GALESIOTES Rhet. *Metaphrasis "Regiae statuae"* 147.4

τὴν	Βιθυνίαν	κατέλαβε
tèn	*Bithynían*	*katélabe*
ART.ACC	Bithynia.ACC	seized.3SG

'he seized Bithynia'

The second case study of phrase matching also provided several examples of *coexistence* of *innovative* grammatical characteristics of the period of the translation/ paraphrasis, on the one hand, and of grammatical characteristics of the *original text*. Phrase matching examples are cases where the intralingual translation includes the same words and the same *main* structure as the original text except for one (or even two, in some cases) grammatical characteristic(s) which is (are) different in the original and the translated text. For instance, both the original text and the translation use the same words and a ditransitive construction, but the indirect object bears a dative case in the original text but an accusative in the translation.

The phrase matching data show that translations do not directly follow the grammatical characteristics of their period either in cases of phrase matching but may include earlier or late grammatical characteristics. Besides the fact that they follow the main structure of the original text, and for this reason I characterize the examples as phrase matching, the translations may also follow a grammatical rule of an earlier period and not only the grammatical rules of their period.

292 CHAPTER 8

8.2.2.3   Case study III:
          Two versions of "Life of Aesop"; Accursiana vs. Version W
The third set of corpus surveys examines two versions of "Life of Aesop".[13] I
discuss the main characteristics of the *Accursiana* in comparison to *Version
W*[*estermanniana*].[14] According to the data, I distinguish the following cases of
variation in the constructions that appear in both versions. In several examples
of matching phrases, the dative pronoun expressing an agent in a construction
with a *passive participle* appears after the participle in the Accursiana in contrast to Version W (113a, b). Moreover, in other matching phrases a participle
in the dative is attested in the Accursiana whereas Version W includes a finite
construction in the matching phrase (114a, b). In other examples of matching
phrases, Version W uses a *dative* personal pronoun as complement of a verb,
in contrast to the Accursiana that replaces it with an accusative form. In the
examples in (115a, b), an *adverb* is also attested before the verb in the Accursiana but not in Version W in the matching phrase.

The Accursiana may add an *article* in the vocative case, whereas the article in the vocative is absent from Version W in the matching phrase (116a, b).
The Accursiana adds a *definite article* in a different case than the vocative in
other instances of matching phrases (117–118). In a few examples, Version W
does not include a definite article in constructions in matching phrases where
the Accursiana has a definite article (119–120).

(113)   a. VITAE AESOPI Narr. Fict. *Vita Pl vel Accursiana (sub auctore Max-
           imo Planude)* 230.1
           τὰ   ἑτοιμασθέντα   μοι
           tà   *hetoimasthénta*   *moi*
           ART.NOM prepare.PASS.PRTC.NOM 1SG.DAT

        b. VITAE AESOPI Narr. Fict. *Vita W (vita Aesopi Westermanniana)* 3.4
           τὰ   ἐμοὶ   ἠτοιμασμένα
           tà   *emoì*   *hētoimasména*
           ART.NOM 1SG.DAT   prepare.MP.PRTC.NOM
           '[...] that were prepared by me'

---

13   On "Life of Aesop" see, among others, Karla (2016: 313–315).
14   For Karla (2016), "the Accursiana probably derives from the Westermanniana".

GREEK DATA 293

(114) a. VITAE AESOPI Narr. Fict. *Vita Pl vel Accursiana* (*sub auctore Maximo Planude*) 233.11
τοῦτο   νομίζοντι
toûto   **nomízonti**
this.ACC believe.PRS.PRTC.DAT

b. VITAE AESOPI Narr. Fict. *Vita W* (*vita Aesopi Westermanniana*) 10.6
τοῦτο   νομίζεις
toûto   **nomízeis**
this.ACC believe.2SG
'[...] as you believe this'

(115) a. VITAE AESOPI Narr. Fict. *Vita Pl vel Accursiana* (*sub auctore Maximo Planude*) 246.9
μὴ   οὕτω   σκῶπτέ
mề   **hoútō** skôpté
NEG   SO   mock.IMP.2SG

b. VITAE AESOPI Narr. Fict. *Vita W* (*vita Aesopi Westermanniana*) 31.3
μὴ   σκῶπτέ
mề   skôpté
NEG   mock.IMP.2SG
'do not mock [me] [this way]'

(116) a. VITAE AESOPI Narr. Fict. *Vita Pl vel Accursiana* (*sub auctore Maximo Planude*) 230.1
λέγε   μοι,   ὦ   κατάρατε
lége   moi,   ô   katárate
tell.IMP.2SG 1SG.DAT ART.VOC   accursed.VOC

b. VITAE AESOPI Narr. Fict. *Vita W* (*vita Aesopi Westermanniana*) 3.4
λέγε   μοι,   κατάρατε
lége   moi,   katárate
tell.IMP.2SG 1SG.DAT accursed.VOC
'tell me, accursed person'

(117) a. VITAE AESOPI Narr. Fict. *Vita Pl vel Accursiana (sub auctore Maximo Planude)* 233.9

ἢ   τῶν   κτηνῶν
è̄   *tôn*   *ktēnôn*
or ART.GEN animals.GEN

b. VITAE AESOPI Narr. Fict. *Vita W (vita Aesopi Westermanniana)* 10.4

ἢ   κτῆνος
è̄   *ktênos*
or animal.NOM
'[…] or animal(s)'

(118) a. VITAE AESOPI Narr. Fict. *Vita Pl vel Accursiana (sub auctore Maximo Planude)* 238.18

ὁ   δὲ   Αἴσωπος
ho   *dè*   *Aísōpos*
ART.NOM PRT Aesop.NOM

b. VITAE AESOPI Narr. Fict. *Vita W (vita Aesopi Westermanniana)* 21.8

Αἴσωπος   δὲ
Aísōpos   *dè*
Aesop.NOM PRT
'Aesop, however, […]'

(119) a. VITAE AESOPI Narr. Fict. *Vita Pl vel Accursiana (sub auctore Maximo Planude)* 240.9

ὁ   δὲ   Ξάνθος
ho   *dè*   *Xánthos*
ART.NOM PRT Xanthos.NOM

b. VITAE AESOPI Narr. Fict. *Vita W (vita Aesopi Westermanniana)* 24.14

Ξάνθος
Xánthos
Xanthos.NOM
'Xanthos, however, […]'

GREEK DATA

295

(120) a. VITAE AESOPI Narr. Fict. *Vita Pl vel Accursiana* (*sub auctore Maximo Planude*) 240.1

ὁ	Ξάνθος	τῷ	ἐμπόρῳ	φησί
ho	**Xánthos**	**tôi**	**empórōi**	**phēsí**
ART.NOM	Xanthos.NOM	ART.DAT	seller.DAT	say.3SG

b. VITAE AESOPI Narr. Fict. *Vita W* (*vita Aesopi Westermanniana*) 24.15

Ξάνθος	τῷ	ἐμπόρῳ	ἔφη
Xánthos	*tôi*	*empórōi*	*éphē*
Xanthos.NOM	ART.DAT	seller.DAT	said.3SG

'Xanthos says/ said to the seller [...]'

The Accursiana includes *infinitival* constructions and, in several instances, the infinitives are introduced with ὡς *hōs*. In the matching phrase, Vita W may contain a participle that replaces the infinitive (121a, b). However, there are many examples of participial constructions in the Accursiana that are missing from Version W (122a, b).

A *prefixed* verb of the Accursiana can be attested without a verbal prefix in a matching phrase in Version W (123–124). Verbs attested with two prefixes in Version W are used with one prefix in the Accursiana, in the same construction in a matching phrase (125a, b). In other examples, a different verbal prefix is attested in the Accursiana and Version W in a matching phrase (126–127).

The comparison of the two versions also reveals important differences in the presence of *particles* (128–131). For instance, the Accursiana differs from Version W in adding the particle καίπερ *kaíper* (132a, b). In addition, Version W includes the particle δέ *dé* whereas the Accursiana uses a conjunction (*kaí*) in several matching phrases (133a, b). Version W contains the particle γάρ *gár*, which is omitted in the Accursiana in matching phrases (134a, b). The use of a different—early/ archaic—*preposition* with a similar interpretation in the Accursiana is also one of the main differences between the two versions (135a, b).

(121) a. VITAE AESOPI Narr. Fict. *Vita Pl vel Accursiana* (*sub auctore Maximo Planude*) 230.1

[...]	ὡς	εἰς	τὸ	ταμιεῖον	εἰσελθεῖν
[...]	*hōs*	*eis*	*tò*	*tamieîon*	*eiltheîn*
	that	into	ART.ACC	storehouse.ACC	enter.INF

b. VITAE AESOPI Narr. Fict. *Vita W* (*vita Aesopi Westermanniana*) 3.4

[...] ὅτι	εἰς	τὸ	ταμεῖον	**εἰσελθὼν**
[...] *hóti*	*eis*	*tò*	*tameîon*	**eiselthòn**
that	into	ART.ACC	storehouse.ACC	enter.PRTC

'[...] that he entered the storehouse.'

(122) a. VITAE AESOPI Narr. Fict. *Vita Pl vel Accursiana* (*sub auctore Maximo Planude*) 246.6

ἀπέστρεψε	πρὸς	τὸν	ἄνδρα,	φαμένη	[...]
apéstrepse	*pròs*	*tòn*	*ándra,*	**phaménē**	[...]
turned.3SG	towards	ART.ACC	man.ACC	say.PRTC.NOM.SG	

b. VITAE AESOPI Narr. Fict. *Vita W* (*vita Aesopi Westermanniana*) 31.1

ἀπεστράφη	καί	φησι	πρὸς τὸν	ἄνδρα	[...]
apestráphē	*kaí*	**phēsi**	*pròs tòn*	*ándra*	[...]
turned.3SG	and	say.3SG	to ART.ACC	man.ACC	

'she turned to the man and said [...]'

(123) a. VITAE AESOPI Narr. Fict. *Vita Pl vel Accursiana* (*sub auctore Maximo Planude*) 237.7

ἀπεθαύμασε
apethaúmase
APO-marveled.3SG

b. VITAE AESOPI Narr. Fict. *Vita W* (*vita Aesopi Westermanniana*) 18.6

ἐθαύμασε
ethaúmase
marveled.3SG

'marveled much'

(124) a. VITAE AESOPI Narr. Fict. *Vita Pl vel Accursiana* (*sub auctore Maximo Planude*) 239.10

ἐξεγέλασε
exegélase
EK-laughed.3SG

GREEK DATA

b. VITAE AESOPI Narr. Fict. *Vita W* (*vita Aesopi Westermanniana*)
24.13
ἐγέλασεν
egélasen
laughed.3SG
'laughed out'

(125) a. VITAE AESOPI Narr. Fict. *Vita Pl vel Accursiana* (*sub auctore Max-imo Planude*) 241.9
ἀπόληται
***ap**ólētai*
APO-destroy.AOR.MP.SUBJ.3SG

b. VITAE AESOPI Narr. Fict. *Vita W* (*vita Aesopi Westermanniana*) 25.2
προσαπόληται
***prosap**ólētai*
PROS-APO-destroy.AOR.MP.SUBJ.3SG
'[it] is destroyed'

(126) a. VITAE AESOPI Narr. Fict. *Vita Pl vel Accursiana* (*sub auctore Max-imo Planude*) 238.7
ὑπελείφθη
***hyp**eleíphthē*
HYPO-left.PASS.3SG

b. VITAE AESOPI Narr. Fict. *Vita W* (*vita Aesopi Westermanniana*) 20.2
κατελείφθησαν
***kat**eleíphthēsan*
KATA-left.PASS.3PL
'to be left remaining/ behind'

(127) a. VITAE AESOPI Narr. Fict. *Vita Pl vel Accursiana* (*sub auctore Max-imo Planude*) 240.1
ἀναχωρήσαντος
***ana**chōrésantos*
ANA-leave.AOR.PRTC.GEN.SG

b. VITAE AESOPI Narr. Fict. *Vita W* (*vita Aesopi Westermanniana*) 24.9
ὑπεχώρησεν
hypechṓrēsen
HYPO-left.3SG
'he left/ withdrew'

(128) a. VITAE AESOPI Narr. Fict. *Vita Pl vel Accursiana* (*sub auctore Maximo Planude*) 239.14
"*τί   ποτε ἄρα ἰδὼν   ἐγέλασε;*"
"*tí   pote **ára** idṑn   egélase?*"
what PRT PRT see.PRTC.NOM laughed.3SG

b. VITAE AESOPI Narr. Fict. *Vita W* (*vita Aesopi Westermanniana*) 24.5
τί   ἰδὼν   ἐγέλασεν;
tí   idṑn   egélasen?
what see.PRTC.NOM laughed.3SG
'what did he see and laugh?'

(129) a. VITAE AESOPI Narr. Fict. *Vita Pl vel Accursiana* (*sub auctore Maximo Planude*) 241.9
προσελθὼν   γοῦν τῷ   Αἰσώπῳ
*proselthṑn   **goûn** tôi   Aisṓpōi*
come.PRTC.NOM PRT   ART.DAT Aesop.DAT

b. VITAE AESOPI Narr. Fict. *Vita W* (*vita Aesopi Westermanniana*) 25.2
προσελθὼν   οὖν τῷ   Αἰσώπῳ
*proselthṑn   **oûn** tôi   Aisṓpōi*
come.PRTC.NOM PRT ART.DAT Aesop.DAT
'[...] as, then, he came to Aesop.'

(130) a. VITAE AESOPI Narr. Fict. *Vita Pl vel Accursiana* (*sub auctore Maximo Planude*) 243.18
ἐγὼ   ἄρα ἐλεύθερός   εἰμι
*egṑ   **ára** eleútherós eimi*
1SG.NOM PRT free.NOM be.1SG

b. VITAE AESOPI Narr. Fict. *Vita W* (*vita Aesopi Westermanniana*) 27.9
ἐγὼ   ἐλεύθερός   εἰμι
egṑ   eleútherós eimi
1SG.NOM free.NOM be.1SG
'(Then) I am free.'

GREEK DATA 299

(131) a. VITAE AESOPI Narr. Fict. *Vita Pl vel Accursiana* (*sub auctore Max-imo Planude*) 248.1
διαλλαγήσομαι   τοίνυν αὐτῷ
diallagḗsomai   **toínyn** *autôi*
exchange.FUT.1SG PRT   3SG.DAT

b. VITAE AESOPI Narr. Fict. *Vita W* (*vita Aesopi Westermanniana*) 32.12
διαλλαγήσομαι   αὐτῷ
diallagḗsomai   *autôi*
exchange.FUT.1SG 3SG.DAT
'I will make an exchange with him (now)'

(132) a. VITAE AESOPI Narr. Fict. *Vita Pl vel Accursiana* (*sub auctore Max-imo Planude*) 238.18
Αἴσωπος   δὲ **καίπερ** ὑπὸ πολλῶν σκωπτόμενος
Aísōpos   *dè* **kaíper** *hypò* *pollôn* *skōptómenos*
Aesop.NOM PRT PRT   by   many mock.PASS.PRTC.NOM

b. VITAE AESOPI Narr. Fict. *Vita W* (*vita Aesopi Westermanniana*) 21.8
ὁ   δὲ Αἴσωπος   ὑπὸ πολλῶν σκωπτόμενος
ho   *dè* *Aísōpos*   *hypò* *pollôn* *skōptómenos*
ART.NOM PRT Aesop.NOM by   many mock.PASS.PRTC.NOM
'However, many people mocked Aesop [...]'

(133) a. VITAE AESOPI Narr. Fict. *Vita Pl vel Accursiana* (*sub auctore Max-imo Planude*) 239.2
καὶ θεασάμενος   τοὺς   μὲν δύο παῖδας
kaì theasámenos   *toùs*   *mèn dúo paîdas*
and see.PRTC.NOM.SG ART.ACC PRT two children.ACC

b. VITAE AESOPI Narr. Fict. *Vita W* (*vita Aesopi Westermanniana*) 22.2
θεασάμενος   δὲ τοὺς   μὲν δύο παῖδας
theasámenos   **dè** *toùs*   *mèn dúo paîdas*
see.PRTC.NOM.SG PRT ART.ACC PRT two children.ACC
'[...] as he saw the two children.'

CHAPTER 8

(134) a. VITAE AESOPI Narr. Fict. *Vita Pl vel Accursiana (sub auctore Maximo Planude)* 251.11

μὴ	δεῖ	τῇ	ποικιλίᾳ	τῶν	ἐδεσμάτων
mḕ	*deî*	*têi*	*poikilíai*	*tôn*	*edesmátōn*
NEG	need.3SG	ART.DAT	variety.DAT	ART.GEN	foods.GEN

τοὺς	φίλους	κρίνειν
toùs	*phílous*	*krínein*
ART.ACC	friends.ACC	judge.INF

b. VITAE AESOPI Narr. Fict. *Vita W (vita Aesopi Westermanniana)* 39.5

μὴ	δεῖ	γὰρ τῇ	ποικιλίᾳ	τῶν	ἐδεσμάτων
mḕ	*deî*	*gàr têi*	*poikilíai*	*tôn*	*edesmátōn*
NEG	need.3SG	PRT ART.DAT	variety.DAT	ART.GEN	foods.GEN

τοὺς	φίλους	κρίνειν
toùs	*phílous*	*krínein*
ART.ACC	friends.ACC	judge.INF

'[...] because we should not judge our friends depending on the variety of foods.'

(135) a. VITAE AESOPI Narr. Fict. *Vita Pl vel Accursiana (sub auctore Maximo Planude)* 251.8

ἅμα	τοῖς	φίλοις
háma	*toîs*	*phílois*
together	ART.DAT	friends.DAT

b. VITAE AESOPI Narr. Fict. *Vita W (vita Aesopi Westermanniana)* 39.4

σὺν	τοῖς	φίλοις
sùn	*toîs*	*phílois*
with	ART.DAT	friends.DAT

'together with his friends ...'

Several constructions of the Accursiana display similar characteristics to earlier *hyperbaton* orders. Version W avoids such complex constructions and prefers analytic constructions with prepositions to express the intended meaning (see 136–137). Furthermore, the examples in (138a, b) demonstrate a case strongly related to syntactic contexts that facilitated the reanalysis of early possessive constructions into *indirect objects* in the genitive case. The pronoun is attested immediately after the verb in Version W and can be easily reanalyzed as selected by the verb and as an indirect object: καὶ νίψον μου τοὺς πόδας / καὶ *nípson mou toùs pódas* 'and wash (my) feet (for me)'; (see Horrocks 2014: 116).

GREEK DATA

301

The examples in (139a, b) display an instance of a different *word order* in the two versions. The Accursiana demonstrates a VS order, and both the verb and the subject follow the adverbial πάλιν / *pálin* 'again'. On the contrary, Version W demonstrates an SV order, and the subject appears before the adverbial πάλιν / *pálin* 'again', which precedes the verb in this text. Moreover, in the same example, Accursiana does not contain a *definite article* before Αἴσωπος / *Aísōpos* 'Aesop' (the subject) in contrast to Version W. Another example of variation in matching phrases of the two versions concerns the *position of object pronouns* (140a, b).

The examples in (141a, b) present a significant case of overgeneralization of archaic characteristics in Version W: in the matching phrase, Version W shows an *OV order* with a dative object, whereas the Accursiana demonstrates a VO order with an accusative object. Both texts have an infinitive in this phrase. The dative of Version W can be seen as an instance of a focalized noun (see Gianollo & Lavidas (2013) on focalized datives in the diachrony of Greek). Version W also includes examples with object pronouns in matching phrases where the Accursiana has null objects. The examples in (142a, b) demonstrate a similar case; note that the verb is prefixed in Version W but unprefixed in the Accursiana.

(136)   a. VITAE AESOPI Narr. Fict. *Vita Pl vel Accursiana* (*sub auctore Maximo Planude*) 244.3

καὶ	τῶν	ἱματίων	ἐκείνου	δραξάμενος	ὄπισθεν
kaì	tôn	himatíōn	ekeínou	draxámenos	ópisthen
and	ART.GEN	dress.GEN	this.GEN.SG	grasp.PRTC.NOM	back

b. VITAE AESOPI Narr. Fict. *Vita W* (*vita Aesopi Westermanniana*) 28.3

καὶ	ἐκ	τῶν	ὄπισθεν	τὸ	ἱμάτιον
kaì	ek	tôn	ópisthen	tò	himátion
and	from	ART.GEN	back		ART.ACC	dress.ACC

δραξάμενος
draxámenos
grasp.PRTC.NOM
'and he grasped the back of his dress'

(137)   a. VITAE AESOPI Narr. Fict. *Vita Pl vel Accursiana* (*sub auctore Maximo Planude*) 249.18

τέκνα	ἐκ	τοῦ	πρώτου	ἀνδρὸς	ἔχουσα
tékna	ek	toû	prótou	andròs	échousa
children.ACC	from	ART.GEN	first.GEN	man.GEN	have.PRTC.NOM

302 CHAPTER 8

b. VITAE AESOPI Narr. Fict. *Vita W* (*vita Aesopi Westermanniana*) 37.8

τέκνα ἔχουσα ἐκ προτέρου ἀνδρός
tékna *échousa* *ek* *protérou* *andrós*
children.ACC have.PRTC.NOM from former.GEN husband.GEN
'She has children from her first husband.'

(138) a. VITAE AESOPI Narr. Fict. *Vita Pl vel Accursiana* (*sub auctore Maximo Planude*) 252.1

καὶ νίψον τοὺς πόδας μου
kaì *nípson* *toùs* *pódas* **mou**
and wash.IMP.2SG ART.ACC feet.ACC my

b. VITAE AESOPI Narr. Fict. *Vita W* (*vita Aesopi Westermanniana*) 40.7

καὶ νίψον μου τοὺς πόδας
kaì *nípson* **mou** *toùs* *pódas*
and wash.IMP.2SG 1SG.GEN ART.ACC feet.ACC
'and wash my feet/ wash the feet for me (lit.)'

(139) a. VITAE AESOPI Narr. Fict. *Vita Pl vel Accursiana* (*sub auctore Maximo Planude*) 240.7

πάλιν ἐγέλασεν Αἴσωπος
pálin *egélasen* *Aísōpos*
again laughed.3SG Aesop.NOM

b. VITAE AESOPI Narr. Fict. *Vita W* (*vita Aesopi Westermanniana*) 24.13

ὁ Αἴσωπος πάλιν ἐγέλασεν
ho *Aísōpos* *pálin* *egélasen*
ART.NOM Aesop.NOM again laughed.3SG
'Aesop laughed again.'

(140) a. VITAE AESOPI Narr. Fict. *Vita Pl vel Accursiana* (*sub auctore Maximo Planude*) 244.3

με πώλησον
me *pólēson*
1SG.ACC sell.IMP.2SG

GREEK DATA

b. VITAE AESOPI Narr. Fict. *Vita W (vita Aesopi Westermanniana)* 28.3
πώλησόν   με
*pólēsón   **me***
sell.IMP.2SG 1SG.ACC
'Sell me.'

(141) a. VITAE AESOPI Narr. Fict. *Vita Pl vel Accursiana (sub auctore Max-imo Planude)* 251.11
ἀλλὰ δοκιμάζειν τὴν   προθυμίαν
*allà dokimázein **tḕn**   **prothymían***
but   assay.INF ART.ACC willingness.ACC

b. VITAE AESOPI Narr. Fict. *Vita W (vita Aesopi Westermanniana)* 39.5
ἀλλὰ τῇ   προθυμίᾳ   δοκιμάζειν
*allà **têi**   **prothymíai**   dokimázein*
but   ART.DAT willingness.DAT assay.INF
'but we test their willingness'

(142) a. VITAE AESOPI Narr. Fict. *Vita Pl vel Accursiana (sub auctore Max-imo Planude)* 240.9
ἐρώτησον
erótēson
ask.AOR.IMP.ACT.2SG

b. VITAE AESOPI Narr. Fict. *Vita W (vita Aesopi Westermanniana)* 24.14
ἐπερωτήσω   αὐτόν
*eperōtḗsō   **autón***
EPI-ask.AOR.MID.2SG 3SG.ACC
'you shall ask him'

8.2.2.4   Case study IV:
          Two versions of "Life of Aesop"; Version W vs. Version G
In the present section, I compare *Version W* to *Version G* [*Vita G (e cod. 397 Bib-liothecae Pierponti Morgan)*],[15] with the aim to investigate data that can provide additional information on grammatical similarities and differences that I have already located through the comparative study of Version W and the Accur-

---

15   On Version G, see, among others, Shipp (1983: 96).

siana. According to the data, I distinguish the following cases of variation in constructions that appear in both versions. In several matching phrases, Version G does not include a *definite article* before nouns where Version W does so (143a, b). Note that, in the examples in (143a, b), Version W also omits the *direct object*, whereas Version G includes an object pronoun.

The examples in (144a, b) illustrate more cases of *definite article omission* with subjects in Version W, in contrast to non-omission of the definite article in Version G (see also Lavidas & Tsimpli (2019) on the relation between the omission of definite articles and objects). In the examples in (145a, b), the subject is preceded by a definite article in Version G, which also includes a pronominal subject in the previous clause. On the contrary, Version W omits the definite article that accompanies the subject of the second clause and drops the pronominal subject in the first clause. As evident, in many of the examples, the texts reflect characteristics of possible coexistence of more than one grammatical system. Both characteristics of coexistence and transfer from the one system to the other are systematic and do not occur in a random way.

Moreover, in other examples, Version W includes an *overt indirect object*, whereas Version G omits the indirect object in the matching phrase (146–147). Dative complements can be found in Version W in constructions where they are missing from Version G. In the examples in (148a, b), the prefixed verb in Version W selects a dative complement, whereas the verb in Version G an accusative complement. In the examples in (149a, b), a dative argument is present in Version W, but absent from Version G. In addition, in the same matching phrase, Version W omits the definite article that accompanies the proper noun in the position of the subject—in contrast to Version G. In the examples in (150a, b), one observes that a dative definite article is present in Version G, but, in the matching phrase, Version W omits the definite article.

A *genitive* noun can follow the nominal head in Version G, which is a characteristic order of later Greek, but precedes the nominal head in the matching phrase of Version W—the latter order is representative of early Greek (151a, b). The examples in (152a, b) show that the genitive can appear between the definite article and its nominal head in Version G, but after its nominal head in Version W.

In a similar way, a contrast between Version G and Version W concerns the position of the genitive pronoun in the examples in (153a, b). In Version G, the genitive pronoun appears immediately before the governing participle (*ἰδοῦσα idoûsa see.AOR.PRTC.ACT.FEM*), but, in Version W, the genitive pronoun is attested after the complementizer and the negation, in a distance from the

GREEK DATA 305

governing participle. The above-mentioned contrast is related to the reanalysis of genitive and accusative pronouns with possessive and other interpretations into indirect objects (see above, (138a, b), and Horrocks 2014: 116).

(143) a. VITAE AESOPI Narr. Fict. *Vita G (e cod. 397 Bibliothecae Pierponti Morgan)* 2.20

ὅτι Αἴσωπος αὐτὸ πεποίηκεν
hóti Aísōpos **autò** *pepoíēken*
that Aesop.NOM this.ACC make.PRF.3SG

b. VITAE AESOPI Narr. Fict. *Vita W (vita Aesopi Westermanniana)* 2.16

ὅτι ὁ Αἴσωπος ἐποίησε
hóti ho Aísōpos epoíēse
that ART.NOM Aesop.NOM make.AOR.3SG
'[...] that Aesop did this.'

(144) a. VITAE AESOPI Narr. Fict. *Vita G (e cod. 397 Bibliothecae Pierponti Morgan)* 17.10

ὁ δὲ Αἴσωπος λέγει
ho *dè Aísōpos légei*
ART.NOM PRT Aesop.NOM say.3SG

b. VITAE AESOPI Narr. Fict. *Vita W (vita Aesopi Westermanniana)* 17.6

Αἴσωπος λέγει
Aísōpos légei
Aesop.NOM say.3SG
'Aesop says [...]'

(145) a. VITAE AESOPI Narr. Fict. *Vita G (e cod. 397 Bibliothecae Pierponti Morgan)* 24.3

ὁ δέ "ἐγὼ πάντα." ὁ Αἴσωπος
ho dé "egò pánta." **ho** *Aísōpos*
ART.NOM PRT 1SG.NOM always ART.NOM Aesop.NOM

ἑστὼς ἐγέλασεν
hestòs egélasen
stand-up.PRTC.NOM laughed.3SG

b. VITAE AESOPI Narr. Fict. *Vita W* (*vita Aesopi Westermanniana*) 24.2

ὁ	δέ,	"πάντα."	Αἴσωπος	ἑστὼς
ho	dé,	"pánta."	Aísōpos	hestòs
ART.NOM	PRT	always	Aesop.NOM	stand-up.PRTC.NOM

ἐγέλασεν
egélasen
laughed.3SG

'The other one says "I always." Aesop stood up and laughed.'

(146) a. VITAE AESOPI Narr. Fict. *Vita G* (*e cod. 397 Bibliothecae Pierponti Morgan*) 3.3

δὸς	τὰ	σῦκα
dòs	tà	sûka
give.IMP.2SG	ART.ACC	figs.ACC

b. VITAE AESOPI Narr. Fict. *Vita W* (*vita Aesopi Westermanniana*) 3.1

δός	**μοι**	τὰ	σῦκα
dós	**moi**	tà	sûka
give.IMP.2SG	1SG.DAT	ART.ACC	figs.ACC

'Give [me] the figs.'

(147) a. VITAE AESOPI Narr. Fict. *Vita G* (*e cod. 397 Bibliothecae Pierponti Morgan*) 3.7

λέγε,	ἐπικατάρατε
lége,	epikatárate
tell.IMP.2SG	accursed.VOC

b. VITAE AESOPI Narr. Fict. *Vita W* (*vita Aesopi Westermanniana*) 3.3

λέγε	**μοι,**	κατάρατε
lége	**moi,**	katárate
tell.IMP.2SG	1SG.DAT	accursed.VOC

'Tell me, accursed person.'

(148) a. VITAE AESOPI Narr. Fict. *Vita G* (*e cod. 397 Bibliothecae Pierponti Morgan*) 12.5

ἀπαντήσας	οὖν	ὁ	Ζηνᾶς	γνωστὸν
apantḗsas	oûn	ho	Zēnâs	gnōstòn
meet.PRTC.NOM	PRT	ART.NOM	Zenas.NOM	known.ACC

GREEK DATA

317

ὄντα   ἠσπάσατο
ónta   *ēspásato*
be.PRTC.ACC kissed.3SG

b. VITAE AESOPI Narr. Fict. *Vita W (vita Aesopi Westermanniana)* 12.2
συναντήσας   τῷ   **Ζηνᾷ**   γνωστῷ   αὐτῷ
synantḗsas   ***tôi***   ***Zēnâi***   *gnōstôi*   *autôi*
meet.PRTC.NOM ART.DAT Zenas.DAT known.DAT 3SG.DAT
ὄντι,   ἠσπάσατο
ónti,   *ēspásato*
be.PRTC.DAT kissed.3SG
'As he met Zenas, who knew him, he kissed him.'

(149)   a. VITAE AESOPI Narr. Fict. *Vita G (e cod. 397 Bibliothecae Pierponti Morgan)* 12.8
"... ἔχεις κτήνη   μισθώσασθαι ἢ πωλῆσαι;" ὁ   δὲ
"... *écheis ktḗnē*   *misthṓsasthai è pōlêsai?*" ***ho***   *dè*
have.2SG animals.ACC rent.INF   or sell.INF   ART.NOM PRT
Ζηνᾶς ...
Zēnâs ...
Zenas.NOM

b. VITAE AESOPI Narr. Fict. *Vita W (vita Aesopi Westermanniana)* 12.3
"... ἔχεις μοι   κτήνη   μισθώσασθαι ἢ πωλῆσαι;"
"... *écheis **moi***   *ktḗnē*   *misthṓsasthai è pōlêsai?*"
have.2SG 1SG.DAT animals.ACC rent.INF   or sell.INF
Ζηνᾶς   [...]
Zēnâs   [...]
Zenas.NOM
'"Do you have animals to rent or sell [to me]?" Zenas [...]'

(150)   a. VITAE AESOPI Narr. Fict. *Vita G (e cod. 397 Bibliothecae Pierponti Morgan)* 25.10
ἡ   μήτηρ   μου, πότερον [ἢ] ἐν τῷ
hē   *mḗtēr*   *mou, póteron* [*è*] *en **tôi***
ART.NOM mother.NOM my   whether or in ART.DAT
κοιτῶνι   ἢ ἐν τῷ   τρικλίνῳ
koitôni   *è en **tôi***   *triklínōi*
bed-chamber.DAT or in ART.DAT three-bed-room.DAT

b. VITAE AESOPI Narr. Fict. *Vita W* (*vita Aesopi Westermanniana*) 25.6

ἡ	μήτηρ	μου	πότερον	ἐν	κοιτῶνι	ἤ
hē	*métēr*	*mou*	*póteron*	*en*	*koitôni*	*è*
ART.NOM	mother.NOM	my	whether	in	bed-chamber.DAT	or

ἐν	τρικλίνῳ
en	*triklínōi*
in	three-bed-room.DAT

'[Ask] my mother, whether [she will stay] in a bed-chamber or in a three-bed room.'

(151) a. VITAE AESOPI Narr. Fict. *Vita G* (*e cod. 397 Bibliothecae Pierponti Morgan*) 16.4

ἔχεις	μου	ἤδη	ἀπόδειξιν	τῆς	ἐπαγγελίας
écheis	*mou*	*édē*	*apódeixin*	*tês*	*epangelías*
have.2SG	1SG.GEN	already	proof.ACC	ART.GEN	promise.GEN

b. VITAE AESOPI Narr. Fict. *Vita W* (*vita Aesopi Westermanniana*) 16.3

ἔχεις	μου	ἤδη	τῆς	ἐπαγγελίας	ἀπόδειξιν
écheis	*mou*	*édē*	*tês*	*epangelías*	*apódeixin*
have.2SG	1SG.GEN	already	ART.GEN	promise.GEN	proof.ACC

'You already have a proof of my promise.'

(152) a. VITAE AESOPI Narr. Fict. *Vita G* (*e cod. 397 Bibliothecae Pierponti Morgan*) 18.10

καὶ	τὸ	πάντων	βαρύτερον	ἐξελέξατο
kaì	*tò*	*pántōn*	*barýteron*	*exeléxato*
and	ART.ACC	all.GEN	heaviest.ACC	chose.3SG

b. VITAE AESOPI Narr. Fict. *Vita W* (*vita Aesopi Westermanniana*) 18.5

καὶ	τὸ	βαρύτερον	πάντων	ἐξελέξατο
kaì	*tò*	*barýteron*	*pántōn*	*exeléxato*
and	ART.ACC	heaviest.ACC	all.GEN	chose.3SG

'And he chose the heaviest of all.'

(153) a. VITAE AESOPI Narr. Fict. *Vita G* (*e cod. 397 Bibliothecae Pierponti Morgan*) 29.4

ἵνα	μὴ	ἐξαίφνης	τὴν	σαπρίαν	σου	ἰδοῦσα
hína	*mè*	*exaíphnēs*	*tèn*	*saprían*	*sou*	*idoûsa*
that	NEG	suddenly	ART.ACC	decay.ACC	your	see.PRTC.NOM

GREEK DATA

b. VITAE AESOPI Narr. Fict. *Vita W* (*vita Aesopi Westermanniana*) 29.3

ἵνα μή σου ἐξαίφνης τὴν σαπρίαν
hína mḗ sou exaíphnēs tḕn saprían
that NEG 2SG.GEN suddenly ART.ACC decay.ACC

ἰδοῦσα
idoûsa
see.PRTC.NOM

'So that she does not suddenly see your ugly face.'

A different verbal *prefix* is attested in the two versions in several instances of matching phrases (154–155). The examples in (156a, b) present a case of matching phrase where different prefixes are also associated to different word orders. The different word orders trigger a contrast between a preverbal and a postverbal object pronoun. In the examples in (157a, b), Version G contains an unprefixed verb, whereas the verb is prefixed in the matching phrase of Version W. Version W shows a preference for *finite* constructions in matching phrases where Version G includes participial constructions (158a, b).

Moreover, *particles* appear to play a significant role in the differences between the two versions. For instance, in several cases, Version G includes the particle γάρ *gár*, which is omitted from the matching phrase in Version W (159–160). I should stress the relation of the above-mentioned difference between the matching phrases of the two versions, on the one hand, with the different voice forms (in different tense) which also occur in the relevant phrases, on the other hand. Based on the above observation, one can claim that the differences between the texts do not appear in a random way.

Both versions can include *early or later* grammatical characteristics. In some examples, the differences between the versions are related to syntactic factors (for instance, characteristics of focalized datives), or diachronic factors (for instance, a grammatical characteristic may mark the grammar of an earlier period). In the examples in (161a, b), Version W uses a different particle (οὖν *oûn*) than Version G (δέ *dé*). In addition, in the same sentence, Version W omits the subject (of the participle and the verb); in Version G, the subject appears between the participle and the dative object, which separates the subject from the verb (cf. Haug 2017; Lavidas & Haug 2020). The examples in (162a, b) demonstrate the opposite distribution: οὖν *oûn* is attested in Version G and δέ *dé* in Version W, which shows that there is no direct relation between the versions and the particular particles.

(154) a. VITAE AESOPI Narr. Fict. *Vita G* (*e cod. 397 Bibliothecae Pierponti Morgan*) 3.12

παρεκάλει μικρὸν   ἐπισχεῖν
parekálei mikròn **epischeîn**
asked.3SG for-a-while EPI-hold.INF

b. VITAE AESOPI Narr. Fict. *Vita W* (*vita Aesopi Westermanniana*) 3.7

παρεκάλει μικρὸν   ἀνασχεῖν
parekálei mikròn **anascheîn**
asked.3SG for-a-while ANA-hold.INF
'He asked them to hold up for a while.'

(155) a. VITAE AESOPI Narr. Fict. *Vita G* (*e cod. 397 Bibliothecae Pierponti Morgan*) 10.19

πάλιν καταλλαγέντες   ἐχαρίσαντο
pálin **katallagéntes** *echarísanto*
again KATA-discuss.PRTC.NOM enjoyed.3PL

b. VITAE AESOPI Narr. Fict. *Vita W* (*vita Aesopi Westermanniana*) 10.8

πάλιν διαλλαγέντες   ἐχαρίσαντο
pálin **diallagéntes** *echarísanto*
again DIA-discuss.PRTC.NOM enjoyed.3PL
'They discussed again and they were pleased.'

(156) a. VITAE AESOPI Narr. Fict. *Vita G* (*e cod. 397 Bibliothecae Pierponti Morgan*) 15.3

τί   με   μετεκαλέσω
tí me **metekalésō**
what 1SG.ACC META-call.1SG

b. VITAE AESOPI Narr. Fict. *Vita W* (*vita Aesopi Westermanniana*) 15.2

τί   προσεκαλέσω με
tí **prosekalésō** *me*
what PROS-call.1SG 1SG.ACC
'[...] why to call me [...]'

GREEK DATA   311

(157)   a. VITAE AESOPI Narr. Fict. *Vita G (e cod. 397 Bibliothecae Pierponti Morgan)* 27.15
      κέκραγεν
      kékragen
      shout.PRF.3SG

   b. VITAE AESOPI Narr. Fict. *Vita W (vita Aesopi Westermanniana)* 27.7
      ἀνακέκραγεν
      anakékragen
      ANA-shout.PRF.3SG
      'he has screamed/shouted'

(158)   a. VITAE AESOPI Narr. Fict. *Vita G (e cod. 397 Bibliothecae Pierponti Morgan)* 8.3

καὶ	*τὰ*	*βλεπόμενα*	*ὀνομάζων*
kaì	*tà*	*blepómena*	*onomázōn*
and	ART.ACC	see.PRTC.ACC.PL	name.PRTC.NOM

   b. VITAE AESOPI Narr. Fict. *Vita W (vita Aesopi Westermanniana)* 8.2

καὶ	*τὰ*	*βλεπόμενα*	*ὀνομάζω*
kaì	*tà*	*blepómena*	*onomázō*
and	ART.ACC	see.PRTC.ACC.PL	name.1SG

      'naming/ I name the things I could see […]'

(159)   a. VITAE AESOPI Narr. Fict. *Vita G (e cod. 397 Bibliothecae Pierponti Morgan)* 10.21

λαλεῖν	*γὰρ*	*ἀρξάμενος*	*πάντα*
laleîn	*gàr*	*arxámenos*	*pánta*
tell.INF	PRT	start.PRTC.NOM	all.ACC

   b. VITAE AESOPI Narr. Fict. *Vita W (vita Aesopi Westermanniana)* 10.9

λαλεῖν	*ἀρξάμενος*	*πάντα*
laleîn	*arxámenos*	*pánta*
tell.INF	start.PRTC.NOM	all.ACC

      '[…] starting, then, to tell everything'

(160) a. VITAE AESOPI Narr. Fict. *Vita G* (*e cod. 397 Bibliothecae Pierponti Morgan*) 18.17

ἤδη	γὰρ αὐτοῦ τὴν	τιμὴν	σέσωκα
ḗdē	*gàr autoû tền*	*timền*	*sésōka*
already	PRT his	ART.ACC honor.ACC	save.PRF.1SG

b. VITAE AESOPI Narr. Fict. *Vita W* (*vita Aesopi Westermanniana*) 18.6

ἤδη	αὐτοῦ τὴν	τιμὴν	ἔσωσα
ḗdē	*autoû tền*	*timền*	*ésōsa*
already	his	ART.ACC honor.ACC	save.AOR.1SG

'I [have already] saved his honor.'

(161) a. VITAE AESOPI Narr. Fict. *Vita G* (*e cod. 397 Bibliothecae Pierponti Morgan*) 25.2

προσελθὼν	δὲ ὁ	Ξάνθος	τῷ
proselthền	*dè ho*	*Xánthos*	*tôi*
come.PRTC.NOM	PRT ART.NOM	Xanthos.NOM	ART.DAT

Αἰσώπῳ
Aisṓpōi
Aesop.DAT

b. VITAE AESOPI Narr. Fict. *Vita W* (*vita Aesopi Westermanniana*) 25.2

προσελθὼν	οὖν τῷ	Αἰσώπῳ
proselthền	*oûn tôi*	*Aisṓpōi*
come.PRTC.NOM	PRT ART.DAT	Aesop.DAT

'as [Xanthos] came to Aesop'

(162) a. VITAE AESOPI Narr. Fict. *Vita G* (*e cod. 397 Bibliothecae Pierponti Morgan*) 29.7

εἰσελθὼν	οὖν ὁ	Ξάνθος
eiselthền	*oûn ho*	*Xánthos*
enter.PRTC.NOM	PRT ART.NOM	Xanthos.NOM

b. VITAE AESOPI Narr. Fict. *Vita W* (*vita Aesopi Westermanniana*) 29.4

εἰσελθὼν	δὲ ὁ	Ξάνθος
eiselthền	*dè ho*	*Xánthos*
enter.PRTC.NOM	PRT ART.NOM	Xanthos.NOM

'as Xanthos entered [...]'

GREEK DATA 313

Both examples of case studies on versions of "Life of Aesop" have provided evidence in favor of a *peaceful coexistence* of early and later grammatical characteristics in all versions. It is not the case that one version represents earlier grammatical characteristics only or innovative characteristics only. All versions include both earlier and late grammatical characteristics and this type of grammatical coexistence is apparent even in the same clause or in phrase matching cases. In the following section, I examine phrase matching examples in versions of "Digenis Akritis", again testing the same hypothesis through a corpus-driven approach.

8.2.2.5   Case study V:
Two versions of "Digenis Akritis"; Grottaferrata vs. Escorial

The last part of the present corpus study investigates two versions of Digenis Akritis.[16] The version of the Grottaferrata manuscript (G) is a more learned version of the text; the text of the Escorial (E) is a more vernacular version. Both versions should have been prepared before the 16th century. A comparison between the matching phrases of the two versions leads to useful conclusions.

According to the data, I distinguish the following cases of variation in the constructions that appear in both versions. It is worth noticing that *νὰ σύρω νὰ sýrō* 'to draw' of G appears as *ἂν σύρω ἀν sýrō* 'if I draw' in the matching phrase of E (163a, b). E avoids the use of the newer particle *νά ná* in this sentence (in other instances, the particle *νά ná* replaces the infinitive that functions as complement of verbs; see below).[17] In the same matching phrase, G uses the form *ἐμαυτόν μου emautón mou / myself.ACC my* 'myself' without a definite article in a reflexive construction, whereas E prefers the reflexive form *τὸν ἑαυτόν μου τὸν heautón mou / ART.ACC self.ACC my* 'myself'.

In several matching phrases, G prefers a *participial* construction that includes a nominal postverbal object and the negation *μή mḗ*. On the contrary, E includes a finite construction with the negation *οὐ ou*, and a preverbal object is attested before the negation in the same matching phrases (164a, b). A contrast between a participle and a subjunctive finite verb is also evident in the examples in (165a, b). In the same clause, the object of the participle is not preceded by a definite article in G, whereas, in the matching phrase of E, the object of the finite verb is preceded by a definite article. In other matching phrases, E can also contain a finite construction instead of a participle, which is attested

---

16   On Digenis Akritis, see, among many others, Horrocks (2014: 214–215; 333–334).

17   Previous studies on the development of *na* in Greek provide rich information on the relevant changes and the characteristics of *na* in the diachrony of Greek. Among many others, see Joseph (1983b), di Bartolo (2020).

314 CHAPTER 8

in G (see 166a, b). In the examples in (167a, b), the finite verb selects a *preposition* that is productive in later Greek (ἀπὸ πλαγίου / *apò plagíou* 'from one side'), whereas the more archaic preposition ἐκ *ek* 'from' is attested in G. *Infinitives* of G are absent from matching passages of E that uses *vá/ná-clauses* instead of infinitives. In the examples (168a, b), E includes a *vá/ná-clause* and a postverbal object pronoun with the matrix verb ἀξιώσῃ *axiósē* 'deem worthy', in contrast to G which uses an infinitive and omits the object of the matrix verb.

(163) a. (G) Digenes Acritas (*e cod. Grottaferrata*) 2.195

πάντως νὰ σύρω τὸ σπαθὶν καὶ σφάξω
pántōs *nà* *sýrō* *tò* *spathìn* *kai* *spháxō*
in-any-case PRT draw.1SG ART.ACC sword.ACC and slaughter.1SG

ἐμαυτόν μου
emautón *mou*
myself.ACC my

b. (E) Digenes Acritas (*e cod. Escorialense*) 366

Πάντως ἂν σύρω τὸ σπαθὶν καὶ σφάξω
Pántōs *àn* *sýrō* *tò* *spathìn* *kai* *spháxō*
in-any-case if draw.1SG ART.ACC sword.ACC and slaughter.1SG

τὸν ἑαυτόν μου
tòn *heautón* *mou*
ART.ACC self.ACC my

'[...] to draw the sword and kill myself in any case'

(164) a. (G) Digenes Acritas (*e cod. Grottaferrata*) 2.233

μὴ φοβηθέντες θάνατον
mḕ *phobēthéntes* *thánaton*
NEG fear.PRTC.NOM.PL death.ACC

b. (E) Digenes Acritas (*e cod. Escorialense*) 405

Θάνατον οὐ 'φοβήθητε
Thánaton *ou* *'phobéthēte*
death.ACC NEG fear.AOR.SUBJ.2PL

'Do not be afraid of death.'

(165) a. (G) Digenes Acritas (*e cod. Grottaferrata*) 2.234

μὴ φοβηθέντες θάνατον
mḕ *phobēthéntes* *thánaton*
NEG fear.PRTC.NOM.PL death.ACC

GREEK DATA   315

b. (E) Digenes Acritas (*e cod. Escorialense*) 2

μὴ	φοβηθῆς	τὸν	θάνατον
mè	***phobēthês***	*tòn*	*thánaton*
NEG	fear.AOR.SUBJ.2SG	ART.ACC	death.ACC

'Do not be afraid of death.'

(166) a. (G) Digenes Acritas (*e cod. Grottaferrata*) 4.127

καὶ	σφίγξας	τοὺς	βραχίονας
kaì	***sphínxas***	*toùs*	*brachíonas*
and	tighten.PRTC.NOM	ART.ACC	arms.ACC

b. (E) Digenes Acritas (*e cod. Escorialense*) 770

καὶ	ἔσφιξεν	τοὺς	βραχίονας
kaì	***ésphixen***	*toùs*	*brachíonas*
and	tightened.3SG	ART.ACC	arms.ACC

'[...] and tightening his arms [...]'

(167) a. (G) Digenes Acritas (*e cod. Grottaferrata*) 6.509

ὁ	Φιλοπαπποῦς	καὶ ἐλθὼν	ἐκ	πλαγίου
ho	*Philopappoûs*	*kaì elthòn*	***ek***	*plagíou*
ART.NOM	Philopappos.NOM	and come.PRTC.NOM	from	side

b. (E) Digenes Acritas (*e cod. Escorialense*) 1451

ὁ	Φιλοπαππούς	ἀπὸ	πλαγίου μου	ἦλθεν
ho	*Philopappoùs*	***apò***	*plagíou mou*	*êlthen*
ART.NOM	Philopappos.NOM	from	side my	came.3SG

'Philopappos came from one side [and wounded my horse in the thigh].'

(168) a. (G) Digenes Acritas (*e cod. Grottaferrata*) 4.758

ἀξιώσῃ	χαίρεσθαι	τὰ	ἔτη	τῆς
axiósēi	***chaíresthai***	*tà*	*étē*	*tês*
grant.MID.AOR.2SG	enjoy.INF	ART.ACC	years.ACC	ART.GEN

ζωῆς	σου
zōês	*sou*
life.GEN	your

b. (E) Digenes Acritas (*e cod. Escorialense*) 1058

ἀξιώσῃ   σας   νὰ   χαίρεσθε   τὰ
axiósē   **sas**   **nà**   **chaíresthe**   *tà*
grant.ACT.SBJ.AOR.3SG   2PL.ACC   PRT   enjoy.2PL   ART.ACC

ἔτη   τῆς   ζωῆς   σας
étē   *tês*   *zōês*   *sas*
years.ACC   ART.GEN   life.GEN   your
'[...] and may be graced to enjoy your life.'

The data from the versions of "Digenis Akritis" indicate a similar conclusion as the data from the other texts examined in the present section: earlier and late grammatical characteristics *coexist* even in the same phrase, even in the same clause. The above remarks confirm a hypothesis of *peaceful coexistence of grammars* even in non-transitional periods and of *contact between these grammars*. Phrase matching examples provide useful evidence of transfer from the original text (the paraphrased text uses the same words and same main structure). The grammatical differences in phrase matching cases show that *contact and transfer between the coexistent grammars* is possible and can be of any direction. The paraphrased text may include innovative or early characteristics.

8.3   Greek vs. English Data: An Approach to the Diachrony of Written Language Contact

The data confirm the hypothesis that (re)translations provide evidence of *parallel systems of grammar* both in the case of stability, as seen in the particular phenomena from the history of English, and the case of grammatica change, as described with regard to the particular phenomena from the history of Greek. Translations present characteristics that are similar to the characteristics of the source text (that is, translation effects): this is evident, for instance, in several examples of later Greek biblical translations—even though the case of Greek translations of the New Testament is complex because of the role of the LXX and possible influence from Biblical Hebrew, as well. The analysis of the English translations of the New Testament is not simple for another reason. The interference of the Latin source texts—mainly or together with the Greek source text, and in the form of direct and indirect translations—is a significant factor in the case of English.

It appears that the grammatical characteristics of retranslations have a development of their own, not directly connected to the development of the grammar of non-translated texts but in contact with the grammar of non-translated texts. Diachronic retranslations do *not directly* reflect changes that the language underwent between the period of early and later retranslation. They do *not directly* reflect contact-induced changes either. Diachronic retranslations demonstrate *a parallel grammatical system*, with its own diachrony and its own development, which is in contact with the system of native, non-translated texts. The contact between non-translated and translated texts triggers bidirectional influence—from translated texts on non-translated texts, and the reverse.

The above question is related to the hypothesis of N1 vs. N2 diachronies (*diachronies of first and second order natural languages*; see Section 6). Recall the distinction between natural and non-natural languages which is related to language acquisition. A natural language is acquired as a native language without special instruction ("as a normal part of the process of maturation and socialization"; Lyons 1999: 1). Weiß (2001) calls languages that are subject to native language/ L1 acquisition "first order natural/ N1 languages". Grammatical characteristics of translated texts can be seen as being similar to grammatical characteristics of standard languages (N2 languages) in a way: for instance, they contrast grammatical characteristics of dialects in that they are not entirely subject to L1 acquisition. A source language as well as instruction and learning are involved in several aspects of the linguistic knowledge of the adult speakers/ writers in the case of translations.

Accordingly, grammatical change can also be analyzed as belonging to two different types: that is, the type of natural and semi-natural grammatical change (Section 6.4). I propose that *semi-natural grammatical change* can be relevant to grammatical characteristics of the translated texts and to the evidence they provide on parallel grammars, in a similar way that several studies have shown that standardization processes can be accounted for through characteristics of semi-natural grammatical change.

The above remarks can lead to the following assumption in the context of historical linguistics: some texts of earlier periods reflect parallel grammars of their period as well as the results of a *contact between the grammatical characteristics of non-translated texts and the grammatical characteristics of translated texts*. In this respect, one may interpret Kroch's syntactic diglossia (Kroch 2001) not only as opposition but also as coexistence. I also claim that parallel grammars are in *contact* the one with the other.

In this respect, the main contribution of the present monograph can be described as follows: I examined aspects of the role of written contact in grammatical change in English and Greek in a contrastive way. *Multiple translations/ retranslations* of the same text in different periods are of significant value in a study on the parallel grammars manifested in translated and non-translated texts. I proposed that the characteristics of the diachronic retranslations do not illustrate changes that can be located if one compares non-translated texts of their contemporary period to non-translated texts of the previous period. Moreover, they do not represent contact-induced changes directly. Retranslations demonstrate a parallel grammatical system in both types of examples described in the above case studies, that is, in the examples of stability (English) and change (Greek). Hence, diachronic retranslations illustrate a contrast between natural *vs.* semi-natural diachrony and natural/ N_1 *vs.* non-natural/ N_2 varieties, if compared to the characteristics of non-translated texts belonging to different periods.

CHAPTER 9

Conclusion

Nobody can deny that an account of grammatical change that takes written contact into consideration is a significant challenge for any theoretical perspective. Written contact of earlier periods, or from a diachronic perspective, mainly refers to contact through translation. The main contribution of the present book is to add a contrastive diachronic dimension to the study of written contact by examining aspects of the history of translation focusing on grammatical changes in English and Greek. A special emphasis is placed on the analysis of *diachronic retranslations*: the goal of this monograph is to examine translations from earlier periods of English and Greek, in relation to various grammatical characteristics of these languages in different periods, and in comparison to non-translated texts. Moreover, a second parameter of examination has been added as well, namely, translations seen as the *source of evidence of grammatical change*; a new grammar demands a new translation. Accordingly, one of the basic research questions of this study deals with how diachronic retranslations are associated with the development of grammar, as represented in non-translated texts.

The main aims and structure of this book can be described as follows: I first presented a brief history of translations in the context of English and Greek, to test the ways in which translations—and, mainly, retranslations from earlier periods of English and Greek—are related to grammatical change, and, in broad terms, to the history of the language. The major goal was to present *a theoretical background* accounting for a possible connection between grammatical characteristics of diachronic retranslations and the development of the grammatical systems of the relevant languages. My hypothesis is that diachronic retranslations do not follow and do not evidence grammatical change in a direct way but can reflect grammatical change mainly as intertwined with *semi-natural grammatical characteristics and semi-natural change*. Therefore, the main research questions of this study are linked to the role and characteristics of written language contact evidenced in the case of diachronic (re)translations, that is, translations of the same text prepared in different periods of the history of the language.

Thus, I examined the *types* of relation between the history of (re)translations and grammatical change. The data—in particular, in Part 2 of the study—derive from two languages, English and Greek which have been in written contact for many centuries, and particularly through biblical translations. One should not, however, ignore the fact that the situation regarding the involved

© KONINKLIJKE BRILL NV, LEIDEN, 2022 | DOI:10.1163/9789004503564_011

languages is complex: for instance, the earliest English translations of the New Testament were prepared through a Latin translation (the Vulgate) of the Koine Greek source text.

A special focus is placed on *biblical translations* for various reasons: my emphasis is on early translations, and biblical translations occupy a central position in earlier periods. Moreover, in the case of Greek and in the case of translations from Greek into English, there are various examples of biblical translations that became well-known and republished for several decades; previous research has shown significant differences between biblical and non-biblical translations, and an important part of this study focuses on these differences, by comparing diachronic biblical and non-biblical (re)translations.

An additional important parameter is intralingual translation in the case of biblical translations. Greek data are rich in terms of intralingual retranslations of biblical texts from the 16th century onwards, but they also include the early translation of the Old Testament from Biblical Hebrew. A discussion of a possible connection between the history of translations and grammatical change can be fully enriched if one takes data related to intralingual translations into consideration. For this reason, the data on intralingual retranslations in the history of Greek provide a comparative basis for an analysis of similarities and differences between interlingual and intralingual retranslations. The comparative perspective is pervasive throughout the whole book: the comparison between English and Greek data also offers an example of continuity of characteristics of voice-argument structure in English in contrast to changes in voice-argument structure in Greek.

The book consists of two parts: (i) a theoretical section that discusses the history of translations in relation to grammatical change in Greek and English, including a section on the theoretical framework describing a possible connection between translations and diachrony; and (ii) a more research-based part that presents the results of corpus-based studies in the history of translations in English and Greek. Most of the data in the second part concern characteristics of voice and argument structure. Both parts are directly connected to the main research questions of the book: In Part 1, I analyze the main aspects of the development of translations in English and Greek in relation to grammatical change. In Part 2, I investigate examples of grammatical characteristics and their development as reflected in diachronic retranslations.

Part 1 represents a novel attempt to investigate the possible link between the early history of translations in English and Greek and grammatical change in these languages. My hypothesis concentrates on grammatical characteristics and their development. A detailed presentation of the main hypothesis is provided in Part 1: diachronic (re)translations do not reflect directly

CONCLUSION 321

the grammatical change that is attested in non-translated texts of different periods; (re)translations can demonstrate the *peaceful coexistence between various systems of grammar* (on coexistence and competition of grammars, see Kroch 1989, 2001) and a type of contact between them and transfer of grammatical characteristics from the one to the other. This hypothesis, labelled *Hypothesis of Grammatical Multiglossia*, concerns itself not only with the linguistic community as a whole but also with each speaker and each text that may manifest the coexistence and contact between grammars in all periods and not only in the transitional ones.

In this respect, Part 1 expounds upon the history of early translations, with an emphasis on their relation to grammatical change in English and Greek and on diachronic retranslations. In other words, Part 1 presents a historical linguistic perspective on the history of translations. Written language contact appears to have a twofold role in any study of the history of translations and of grammatical change: it can be associated with grammatical change (contact-induced change) because it reflects *a special type of language contact*, and it can be used as *a source of evidence* of grammatical change.

Any attempt of a historical study of translations should also take into consideration their complex character in terms of the source text: early history of translations demonstrates that it is not always the case that the source text is only one text written in another language; in several examples, the source text can be written in another language but characteristics of intralingual translations may also be found because the translated text is also influenced by earlier translations of the source text in the same language. Biblical translations, in particular, present such complex picture: the question of the source text cannot have a simple answer and multiple influence is available. For instance, early English translations of the New Testament were based on a Latin translation of the Koine Greek text but also on previous English translations of the same text. In addition, the investigation of Greek (biblical) translations raises the question of what characterizes "typical" intralingual translations, which is again not a simple one, in consideration of factors such as the influence of the other biblical text, the Hebrew Old Testament and its translation, the Septuagint, on the text of the New Testament and its translations.

Part 1 also includes a detailed discussion of instances related to external factors which may have affected grammatical change. The discussion of these factors reveals the role of semi-natural linguistic characteristics and change in any relevant explanation of grammatical change. Following the main hypothesis of the study, and on the basis of an investigation of a possible link between the early history of translations and grammatical change, I propose that written language contact should be analyzed as a factor which creates grammatical multiglossia, namely a peaceful coexistence of grammars, that is, coexistence of first- and second-order (learned) grammatical characteristics. In this way, diachronic (re)translations again appear to have a twofold role in any historical linguistic study: they may trigger a type of transfer from the source text language to the target text language as a result of written language contact. Diachronic (re)translations also evidence grammatical characteristics of the target text language of the period when the translation was prepared (especially, in cases of retranslations) and the way that these grammatical characteristics can be influenced by the source text language.

Part 2 examines data that derive from four large corpus surveys. Two corpus surveys investigate data from English and two of these data from Greek. Half of these, both in the case of English and Greek, are corpus-based enquiries and half of these corpus-driven enquiries. I have examined corpora of both biblical and non-biblical, English and Greek, diachronic (re)translations and of both translated and non-translated, English and Greek, texts. All corpus surveys are of contrastive nature in order to test grammatical characteristics of various types of translations against the distribution of the same characteristics in other types of translations and non-translated texts. In addition, all types of comparison also exhibit a diachronic basis: all sub-corpora (biblical vs. non-biblical translations; translated vs. non-translated texts) include texts from different periods of the history of English and Greek.

The corpus-based studies investigate grammatical characteristics related to argument structure and voice, employing a word list methodology. The corpus-driven studies (due to their character) have a broader starting point regarding the transfer from the source text to the translated or paraphrased text. In the case of the English corpus study, the focus is on the transfer of derivational suffixes; in the case of the Greek corpus study, a different methodology was used, starting with phrases where the same words and the main structure is used in both the source and the target or paraphrased text: this in turn makes it possible to single out one difference in grammar (for example, a different case marking in the paraphrased text than in the original text).

Even though various types of corpus surveys have been carried out, all of the data derived from the corpora have been used for testing the same hypothesis: diachronic retranslations do not directly follow the changes attested in non-translated texts of the same period; instead their grammatical characteristics reflect peaceful coexistence of grammatical characteristics of their period and of the source text as well as contact and transfer from the one language to the other—or, from earlier periods, in the case of intralingual translations. The *proposed analysis* of the data is in accordance to the theoretical discussion in Part 1: *the data can be accounted for on the basis of a grammatical multiglossia, peace-*

CONCLUSION

ful coexistence of more than one grammar as well as contact and transfer between grammars, even in non-transitional periods, even in the case of one speaker/ writer, and not only for a whole community. The above-mentioned claim can explain how earlier and late grammatical characteristics coexist in the same translated text or even in the same phrase of a paraphrased text or intralingual translation.

Moreover, following my claims made in Part 1 on the relation between the early history of translations and grammatical change, I argue that *contact and transfer of grammatical characteristics are mainly found in two types of cases.* The first involves contact between prestigious translated texts and the relevant native variety in earlier stages, for instance, between characteristics of Latinate English and native characteristics of early English. The second case involves contact between earlier and late characteristics of the same language in later stages of the history of the language, for instance, between Koine Greek—as archaized Greek—and Modern Greek.

An overall diachronic study of interlingual and intralingual translations in English and Greek, together with a contrastive investigation of the development of grammatical characteristics in (biblical vs. non-biblical) translated and non-translated texts, facilitates the analysis of a complex linguistic issue, namely the possible link between the grammatical characteristics of diachronic (re)translations and the changes attested in the diachrony of non-translated texts. A first significant step to the solution of the above puzzle is to *disambiguate the characteristics and position of translations in the study of the diachrony of language*: translations *can trigger grammatical change but only as a part of grammatical multiglossia*, through contact and transfer to the other coexistent system of grammar, through a type of *semi-natural change*; translations *can reveal paths of change and borrowing* but only if seen as representing the result of coexistence, and semi-natural change (because of its written form), and contact between earlier–late, translated–non-translated, borrowed and native grammatical characteristics.

APPENDIX 1

Further Information on the Texts of the Corpus

1: Section 8.1

Further information on the texts of the corpus:

In the Greek section of the corpus survey, I use the texts of the TLG corpus [http://stephanus.tlg.uci.edu]. With regard to the LXX and the Koine Greek New Testament, I follow:

(a) New Testament: Aland, K., M. Black, C.M. Martini, B.M. Metzger & A. Wikgren. 1968. *The Greek New Testament*, 2nd edn. Stuttgart: Württemberg Bible Society.

(b) LXX: Rahlfs, A. 1971 [1935]. *Septuaginta*, vol. 1, 9th edn. Stuttgart: Württemberg Bible Society.

With regard to the biblical retranslations of Kallipolitis, Vamvas and the Today's Greek Version, I examine the text of the following editions:

(a) 1638. i. Maximos Kallipolitis/ of Gallipoli (Kalliergis): *Η Καινή Διαθήκη του Κυρίου ημών Ιησού Χριστού* / *The New Testament of our Lord Jesus Christ*. Editor: Emmanouil Ch. Kasdaglis. Translator: Maximos Kallipolitis. Athens: National Bank of Greece Cultural Foundation, 1994. vol. 1.

ii. *Η Καινή Διαθήκη του Κυρίου ημών Ιησού Χριστού* / *The New Testament of our Lord, Jesus Christ*. Editor: Emmanouil Ch. Kasdaglis. Translator: Maximos Kallipolitis. Athens: National Bank of Greece Cultural Foundation, 1999. vol. 2.

iii. *Η Καινή Διαθήκη του Κυρίου ημών Ιησού Χριστού: Συναγωγή μεταφρασμάτων*/ *The New Testament of our Lord, Jesus Christ: Collection of translations*. Editor: Eufimia Exisou & Agamemnon Tselikas. Translator: Maximos Kallipolitis. Athens: National Bank of Greece Cultural Foundation, 1999. vol. 3.

(b) 1844 (1850). Archimandrite Neophytos Vamvas, with the help of H.D. Leeves & Chr. Nikolaidis. *Η Καινή Διαθήκη του Κυρίου και Σωτήρος ημών Ιησού Χριστού, παραφρασθείσα εις την καθομιλουμένην γλώσσαν* / *The New Testament of our Lord, Jesus Christ, paraphrased into the vernacular language*. Athens: I mnimosini Ch. Nikolaidou Philadelpheos. Printed for the British and Foreign Bible Society.

(c) 1989. by Profs. P. Vassiliadis, I. Galanis, G. Galitis, & J. Karavidopoulos. *Η Καινή Διαθήκη, Το πρωτότυπο κείμενο με μετάφραση στη δημοτική* / *New Tes-*

tament. The original text and its translation into demotic Greek. Athens: Hellenic Bible Society. Revised edition based on NTTGV-85.

On the edition of the source text, see the data and discussion included in Vasileiadis (to-appear). I am aware that some of the later translations of the New Testament use different source texts than the one published by Aland et al., and some of them use more than one edition of the New Testament. However, the main grammatical characteristics and, in particular, the relative frequencies of the examined characteristics do not differ from Aland et al.'s edition to a significant degree. See also Vasileiadis (to-appear):

> "Amalgams of Greek NT texts are used as the basis for translation. Such a schizophrenic situation is eloquently depicted in the NTTGV-85 [The New Testament in Today's Greek Version, 1985]. While the Modern Greek translation is based on the Greek text of Nestle-Aland (ed. 26)/UBS [United Biblical Society] (ed. 3) with divergences where deemed necessary, it includes, side-by-side, an edition of the *Ecclesiastical Text.*"

II: Section 8.2

Further information on the texts of the corpus:

I cite bibliographical information on the editions provided by the *Thesaurus Linguae Graecae* as well as information on the word count.

(i) *Philol. Anonyma Metaphrasis 'Alexiadis', lib. XI–XIII*

p. AD 12

H. Hunger, *Anonyme Metaphrase zu Anna Komnene, Alexias XI–XIII* [*Wiener Byzantinistische Studien* 15. Vienna: Österreichische Akademie der Wissenschaften, 1981]: 31–151.

Word Count: 19,917.

vs.

Alexias

p. AD 1148

A. Kambylis and D.R. Reinsch, *Annae Comnenae Alexias* [*Corpus Fontium Historiae Byzantinae. Series Berolinensis* XL/1. Berlin—New York: De Gruyter, 2001]: 5–505.

Word Count: 145,850.

FURTHER INFORMATION ON THE TEXTS OF THE CORPUS

(ii) *Metaphrasis "Regiae statuae"*
H. Hunger and I. Ševčenko, *Des Nikephoros Blemmydes Βασιλικὸς Ἀνδριάς und dessen Metaphrase von Georgios Galesiotes und Georgios Oinaiotes: Ein weiterer Beitrag zum Verständnis der byzantinischen Schrift-Koine* [Wiener Byzantinistische Studien 18. Vienna: Österreichische Akademie der Wissenschaften, 1986]: 45–117.
Word Count: 8,981

vs.

Regia statua
H. Hunger and I. Ševčenko, *Des Nikephoros Blemmydes Βασιλικὸς Ἀνδριάς und dessen Metaphrase von Georgios Galesiotes und Georgios Oinaiotes: Ein weiterer Beitrag zum Verständnis der byzantinischen Schrift-Koine* [Wiener Byzantinistische Studien 18. Vienna: Österreichische Akademie der Wissenschaften, 1986]: 44–116.
Word Count: 7,569.

(iii) VITAE AESOPI Narr. Fict.
Vita W (vita Aesopi Westermanniana) (recensio 2)
B.E. Perry, *Aesopica*, vol. 1, Urbana: University of Illinois Press, 1952: 81–107.
Word Count: 13,614.

Vita Pl vel Accursiana (sub auctore Maximo Planude) (recensio 1)
A. Eberhard, *Fabulae romanenses Graece conscriptae*, vol. 1, Leipzig: Teubner, 1872: 226–305.
Word Count: 11,236.

Vita G (e cod. 397 Bibliothecae Pierponti Morgan)
F. Ferrari, *Romanzo di Esopo*, Milan: Biblioteca Universale Rizzoli, 1997: 58–258.
Word Count: 16,795.

(iv) 1. *Digenes Acritas (e cod. Grottaferrata)*
E. Jeffreys, *Digenis Akritis. The Grottaferrata and Escorial versions* [Cambridge Medieval Classics. Cambridge: Cambridge University Press, 1998]: 2–234.
Word Count: 25,918.

2. *Digenes Acritas (e cod. Escorialense)*
E. Jeffreys, *Digenis Akritis. The Grottaferrata and Escorial versions* [Cambridge Medieval Classics. Cambridge: Cambridge University Press, 1998]: 238–374.
Word Count: 14,428.

3. *Digenes Acritas* (*versio Z compilata e codd. T et A*)

E. Trapp, *Digenes Akrites. Synoptische Ausgabe der ältesten Versionen* [Wiener Byzantinistische Studien 8. Vienna 1971]: 73–377.

Word Count: 32,063.

APPENDIX 2

(i) The Corpus of Translations of Biblical Texts; (ii) The Corpus of Translations of Boethius' *De Consolatione Philosophiae*

(i) Section 7.3.1; translations of biblical texts

Penn Parsed Corpus of Historical English (https://www.ling.upenn.edu/hist -corpora/index.html)

I	cmntest-M3	The New Testament (Wycliffite)
		Date a1425 (c1395) (Helsinki gives c1388?)
		Sample: John I.1–XI.56
II	cmotest-M3	The Old Testament (Wycliffite)
		Sample: Genesis I.1–III.24, VI.1–IX.29, XII.1–XIV.20, XXII.1– XXII.19, Numbers XIII.1–XIV.45, XVI.1–XVII.13.
III	tyndnew-E1	Tyndale, William
		1534
		Sample: Exhaustive sample of John and of Acts 1–17.
IV	tyndold-E1	Tyndale, William
		1530
		Sample: Exhaustive sample of Genesis 1–22, (except for the last five verses of Genesis 22, verses 20–24), Numbers 13– 20, and Deuteronomy 1–11.
V	authnew-E2	Authorized Version
		1611
		Exhaustive sample of John and Acts 1–17
VI	authold-E2	Authorized Version
		1611
		Exhaustive sample of Genesis 1–22 (except for the last five verses of Genesis 22, verses 20–24), Numbers 13–20, and Deuteronomy 1–11
VII	purver-new-1764	Purver, Anthony
		1764
		Exhaustive sample of John and Acts 1–17

© KONINKLIJKE BRILL NV, LEIDEN, 2022 | DOI:10.1163/9789004503564_013

APPENDIX 2

(i)   Section 7.3.1; translations of biblical texts (*cont.*)

VIII purver-old-1764   Purver, Anthony
1764
Exhaustive sample of Genesis 1–22 (except for the last five verses of Genesis 22, verses 20–24), Numbers 13–20, and Deuteronomy 1–11

IX   newcome-new-1796   Newcome, William
1796
Exhaustive sample of John and Acts 1–17

X   erv-new-1881   Ellicott, Charles John et al.
1881 (published 1885)
Exhaustive sample of John and Acts 1–17.

XI   erv-old-1885   English Old Testament Revisers
1885
Exhaustive sample of Genesis 1–22 (except for the last five verses of Genesis 22, verses 20–24), Numbers 13–20, and Deuteronomy 1–11

(ii)   Section 7.3.1; translations of Boethius' *De Consolatione Philosophiae*

Penn Parsed Corpus of Historical English (https://www.ling.upenn.edu/hist -corpora/index.html)

I   cmboeth-M3   Chaucer
Date   ?a1425 (c1380)
"Sample   Pp. 429.C1.1–431.C1.195, 431.C2.1–434.C1.250, 434.C2.1– 436.C2.230, 446.C2.1–449.C2.300, 450.C2.1–454.C2.376".

II   boethco-E1   Colville, George
1556
Last half of Book 1 and exhaustive sample of Books 2–4

III boethel-E2   Tudor, Elizabeth I
1593
Last half of Book 1 and exhaustive sample of Books 2–4.

IV   boethpr-E3   Richard Graham, 1st viscount Preston
1695
Last half of Book 1 and exhaustive sample of Books 2–4.

THE CORPUS OF TRANSLATIONS

331

(ii) Section 7.3.1; translations of Boethius' *De Consolatione Philosophiae* (*cont.*)

V	boethri-1785	Ridpath, Philip
		1785
		"The sample includes the last half of Book 1 and all of Books 2–4. It corresponds to the samples in the PPCEME and subsumes that in the PPCME2" (Kroch et al. 2016).
VI	boethja-1897	James, Henry Rosher
		1897
		"The sample includes the last half of Book 1 and all of Books 2–4. It corresponds to the samples in the PPCEME and subsumes that in the PPCME2" (Kroch et al. 2016).

References

Adamou, Evangelia. 2016. *A Corpus-Driven Approach to Language Contact. Endangered Languages in a Comparative Perspective.* Berlin, Boston: De Gruyter Mouton.

Adams, James Noel. 2003. *Bilingualism and the Latin Language.* Cambridge: Cambridge University Press.

Adams, James Noel. 2007. *The Regional Diversification of Latin, 200 BC–AD 600.* Cambridge: Cambridge University Press.

Adams, James Noel, Mark Janse and Simon Swain (eds). 2002. *Bilingualism in Ancient Society: Language Contact and the Written Text.* Oxford: Oxford University Press.

Adams, Sean A. 2013. Ancient Greek history and its methodology for speeches: Is there a relation to Luke? In: Porter, Stanley E. and Andrew W. Pitts, (eds), *Christian Origins and Greco-Roman Culture: Social and Literary Contexts for the New Testament*, 389–411. Leiden, Boston: Brill.

Adamson, Sylvia. 1999. Literary language. In: Lass, Roger (ed.), *The Cambridge History of the English Language Volume III, 1476–1776*, 539–653. Cambridge: Cambridge University Press.

Adelung, Johann Christoph. 1806–1817 [1970]. *Mithridates oder Allgemeine Sprachenkunde: Mit dem Vater Unser als Sprachprobe in Bey Nahe, Fünfhundert Sprachen und Mundarten.* Five volumes. Berlin: Voss [Hildesheim: Olms].

Adger, David. 2006. Combinatorial variability. *Journal of Linguistics* 42: 503–530.

Adger, David. 2007. Variability and modularity: A response to Hudson. *Journal of Linguistics* 43 (3): 695–700.

Adger, David. 2016. Language variability in syntactic theory. In: Eguren, Luis, Olga Fernández Soriano and Amaya Mendikoetxea (eds), *Rethinking Parameters*, 49–63. Oxford: Oxford University Press.

Agbayani, Brian and Chris Golston. 2010. Phonological movement in Classical Greek. *Language* 86 (1): 133–167.

Aitchison, Jean. 2001. *Language Change: Progress or Decay?* Cambridge: Cambridge University Press.

Aitken, James K. 2014a. The language of the Septuagint and Jewish-Greek identity. In: Aitken, James K. and James C. Paget (eds), *The Jewish-Greek Tradition in Antiquity and the Byzantine*, 120–134. Cambridge: Cambridge University Press.

Aitken, James K. 2014b. *No Stone Unturned: Greek Inscriptions and Septuagint Vocabulary.* Winona Lake, IN: Eisenbrauns.

Aland Kurt, Matthew Black, Carlo M. Martini, Bruce M. Metzger and Allen Wikgren. 1968. *The Greek New Testament.* 2nd ed. Stuttgart: United Bible Societies. (Thesaurus Linguae Graecae [TLG]).

Alexiadou, Artemis. 2010. On the morpho-syntax of (anti-)causative verbs. In: Rappa-

REFERENCES

port Hovav, Malka, Edit Doron and Ivy Sichel (eds), *Lexical Semantics, Syntax, and Event Structure*, 177–203. Oxford: Oxford University Press.

Alexiadou, Artemis. 2017. Building verbs in language mixing varieties. *Zeitschrift für Sprachwissenschaft* 36 (1): 165–192.

Alexiadou, Artemis and Elena Anagnostopoulou. 2004. Voice morphology in the causative-inchoative alternation: Evidence for a non-unified structural analysis of unaccusatives. In: Alexiadou, Artemis, Elena Anagnostopoulou and Martin Everaert (eds), *The Unaccusativity Puzzle*, 114–136. Oxford: Oxford University Press.

Allen, Cynthia L. 1999. *Case Marking and Reanalysis: Grammatical Relations from Old to Early Modern English*. Oxford: Clarendon Press.

Allen, Cynthia L. 2008. *Genitives in Early English: Typology and Evidence*. Oxford: Oxford University Press.

Amaral, Luiz and Tom Roeper. 2014. Multiple grammars and second language representation. *Second Language Research* 30 (1): 3–36.

Amenta, Luisa. 2003. *Perifrasi Aspettuali in Greco e in Latino. Origini e Grammaticalizzazioni* [Greek and Latin Aspect Periphrases. Origins and Grammaticalizations]. Milano: Franco Angeli.

Appel, René and Pieter Muysken. 2005. *Language Contact and Bilingualism*. Amsterdam: Amsterdam University Press.

Aschenbrenner, Anne. 2014. *Adjectives as Nouns, mainly as attested in Boethius Translations. From Old to Modern English and in Modern German*. Munich: Herbert Utz.

Baker, Mona. 1996. Corpus-based translation studies: The challenges that lie ahead. In: Somers, Harold (ed.), *Terminology, LSP and Translation: Studies in Language Engineering, in Honour of Juan C. Sager*, 175–186. Amsterdam: John Benjamins.

Baker, Mona and Gabriela Saldanha. 2009. *Routledge Encyclopedia of Translation Studies*. London, New York: Routledge.

Ballard, Michel. 2000. In search of the foreign: A study of the three English translations of Camus's *L'Étranger*. In: Salama-Carr, Myriam (ed.), *On Translating French Literature and Film II*, 19–38. Amsterdam, Atlanta: Rodopi.

Banfi, Emanuele. 1990. The infinitive in south-east European languages. In: Bechert, Johannes, Giuliano Bernini and Claude Buridant (eds), *Toward a Typology of European Languages*, 165–184. Berlin: Mouton de Gruyter.

Barðdal, Jóhanna and Thórhallur Eythórsson. 2006. Control infinitives and case in Germanic: 'Performance error' or marginally acceptable constructions. In: Kulikov, Leonid, Andrej Malchukov and Peter de Swart (eds), *Case, Valency and Transitivity*, 147–177. Amsterdam: John Benjamins.

Barðdal, Jóhanna and Thórhallur Eythórsson. 2012. 'Hungering and lusting for women and fleshly delicacies': Reconstructing grammatical relations for Proto-Germanic. *Transactions of the Philological Society* 110: 363–393.

Barðdal, Jóhanna, Kristian Kristoffersen & Andreas Sveen. 2011. West Scandinavian ditransitives as a family of constructions: With a special attention to the Norwegian 'v-REFL-NP'-Construction. *Linguistics* 49: 53–104.

Barðdal, Jóhanna, Leonid Kulikov, Roland Pooth and Peter Kerkhof. 2020. Oblique anticausatives: A morphosyntactic isogloss in Indo-European. *Poznan Studies in Contemporary Linguistics* 56 (3): 413–449.

Bassnett, Susan. 1991. Translating for the theatre: The case against performability. *TTR: Traduction, Terminologie, Rédaction* 4 (1): 99–111.

Baugh, Albert C. and Thomas Cable. 2013. *A History of the English Language*. 6th ed. London: Routledge.

Baumgarten, Nicole. 2008. Writer construction in English and German popularized academic discourse: The uses of *We* and *Wir*. *Multilingua* 27 (4): 409–438.

Baumgarten, Nicole and Demet Özçetin. 2008. Linguistic variation through language contact in translation. In: Siemund, Peter and Noemi Kintana (eds), *Language Contact and Contact Languages*, 293–316. Amsterdam, Philadelphia: John Benjamins.

Baumgarten, Nicole, Juliane House and Julia Probst. 2004. English as lingua franca in covert translation processes. *The Translator* 10 (1): 83–108.

Beaton, Roderick 1994. *An Introduction to Modern Greek Literature*. Oxford: Clarendon Press.

Becher, Viktor. 2010. Abandoning the notion of 'translation-inherent' explicitation: Against a dogma of translation studies. *Across Languages and Cultures* 11 (1): 1–28.

Becher, Viktor, Juliane House and Svenja Kranich. 2009. Convergence and divergence of communicative norms through language contact in translation. In: Braunmüller, Kurt and Juliane House (eds), *Convergence and Divergence in Language Contact Situations*, 125–152. Amsterdam: John Benjamins.

Benkert, Lysbeth. 2001. Translation as image-making: Elizabeth I's translation of Boethius's consolation of philosophy. *Early Modern Literary Studies* 6 (3): 1–20.

Bennett, Jack A.W. and Geoffrey V. Smithers. 1968. *Early Middle English Verse and Prose*. Oxford: Clarendon.

Bensimon, Paul. 1990. Présentation. *Palimpsestes* XIII (4): ix–xiii.

Bentein Klaas 2020. The distinctiveness of syntax for varieties of Post-classical and Byzantine Greek: Linguistic 'upgrading' from the third century BCE to the tenth century CE. In: Bentein, Klass and Mark Janse (eds), *Varieties of Post-classical and Byzantine Greek*, 304–332. Berlin: De Gruyter Mouton.

Berman, Antoine. 1986. L'essence Platonicienne de la traduction. *Revue d'esthétique* 12: 63–73.

Berman, Antoine. 1990. La retraduction comme espace de la traduction. *Palimpsestes. Revue de Traduction* 4: 1–7.

Bhatia, Tej K. and William C. Ritchie. 1996. Bilingual language mixing, universal grammar, and second language acquisition. In: Ritchie, William C. and Tej K. Bhatia (eds), *Handbook of Second Language Acquisition*, 627–682. San Diego: Academic Press.

REFERENCES

Biberauer, Theresa and Ian Roberts. 2005. Changing EPP-parameters in the history of English: Accounting for variation and change. *English Language and Linguistics* 9 (1): 5–46.

Bisang, Walter. 1998. Grammaticalization and language contact, constructions and positions. *Typological Studies in Language* 37: 13–58.

Blake, Norman F. 1991. *William Caxton and English Literary Culture*. London: The Hambledon Press.

Blake, Norman F. 1992. Translation and the history of English. In: Rissanen, Matti, Ossi Ihalainen, Terttu Nevalainen and Irma Taavitsainen (eds), *History of Englishes: New Methods and Interpretations in Historical Linguistics*, 3–24. Berlin: Mouton.

Blass, Friedrich, Albert Debrunner and Robert W. Funk. 1961. *A Greek Grammar of the New Testament and other Early Christian Literature*. Chicago: University of Chicago Press.

Bolgar, Robert R. 1954. The translations of the Greek and Roman classical authors before 1600. In: Bolgar, Robert R. (ed.), *The Classical Heritage and its Beneficiaries*. Cambridge: Cambridge University Press.

Bons, Eberhard and Jan Joosten (eds). 2016. *Handbuch zur Septuaginta/ Handbook of the Septuagint. Volume 3. Die Sprache der Septuaginta/ The Language of the Septuagint*. Gütersloh: Gütersloher Verlagshaus.

Bons, Eberhard, Ralph Brucker and Jan Joosten. 2014. *The Reception of Septuagint Words in Jewish-Hellenistic and Christian Literature*. Tübingen: Mohr Siebeck.

Borer, Hagit. 1984. *Parametric Syntax: Case Studies in Semitic and Romance Languages*. Dordrecht: Foris.

Bornstein, Diane. 1978. Chaucer's *Tale of Melibee* as an example of the style clergial. *The Chaucer Review* 12: 236–254.

Bortone, Pietro. 2010. *Greek Prepositions: From Antiquity to the Present*. Oxford: Oxford University Press.

Böttger, Claudia and Kristin Bührig. 2003. Translating obligation in business communication. In: Gonzalés, Luis Peréz (ed.), *Speaking in Tongues: Language across Contexts and Users*, 161–183. Valencia: University of Valencia.

Boutcher, Warren. 2000. The Renaissance. In: France, Peter (ed.), *The Oxford Guide to Literature in English Translation*, 45–55. Oxford: Oxford University Press.

Božović, Petar. 2014. Translation and language change. *Mediterranean Journal of Social Sciences* 5 (13): 515–521.

Breul, Carsten. 1999. *Reason clauses in Early Modern English translations: Observations on extracts from translations of Boethius's De Consolatione Philosophiae*. Online at http://www.conlin.uni-wuppertal.de/typescripts/Breul-C-ms-1999b.pdf.

Britain, David and Peter Trudgill. 1999. Migration, new-dialect formation and sociolinguistic refunctionalisation: Reallocation as an outcome of dialect contact. *Transactions of the Philological Society* 97 (2): 245–256.

Brixhe, Claude. 2007. Greek translation of Lycian. In: Christidis, Anastassios Ph. (ed.), *A History of Ancient Greek: From the Beginnings to Late Antiquity*, 924–934. Cambridge: Cambridge University Press.

Brock, Sebastian. 1979. Aspects of translation technique in antiquity. *Greek, Roman, and Byzantine Studies* 20 (1): 69–87.

Brock, Sebastian. 2007. Translation in antiquity. In: Christidis, Anastassios Ph. (ed.), *A History of Ancient Greek: From the Beginnings to Late Antiquity*, 873–886. Cambridge: Cambridge University Press.

Bromhead, Helen. 2009. *The Reign of Truth and Faith: Epistemic Expressions in 16th and 17th Century English*. Berlin: Mouton de Gruyter.

Brook, George L. and Roy F. Leslie (eds). 1963–1978. *Laȝamon: Brut, Edited from British Museum MS Cotton Caligula A. ix and British Museum MS Cotton Otho C. xiii*. 2 vols. London: Oxford University Press.

Brownlie, Siobhan. 2006. Narrative theory and retranslation theory. *Across Languages and Cultures* 7 (2): 145–170.

Bruce, Frederick F. 1970. *The English Bible: A History of Translations from the Earliest English Version to the New English Bible*. London: Lutterworth Press.

Bubenik, Vit. 2010. Hellenistic Koine in contact with Latin and Semitic languages during the Roman period. *Studies in Greek Linguistics* 30: 32–54.

Bubenik, Vit. 2016. The status of the 'progressive aspect' in the Hellenistic Greek of the New Testament. *Graeco-Latina Brunensia* 21 (2): 71–79.

Bubenik, Vit and Emilio Crespo. 2013. Attitudes to language. In: Giannakis, Georgios K. (ed.), *Encyclopedia of Ancient Greek Language and Linguistics*. Online at http://dx .doi.org/10.1163/2214-448X_eagll_COM_000049. First published online: 2013 [Last access: 30 September 2020].

Bullough, Sebastian. 1953. The Revised Standard Version. *Life of the Spirit (1946–1964)* 7 (82): 463–466.

Burke, Peter. 2007a. Translations into Latin in early Modern Europe. In: Burke, Peter and Ronnie Po-Chia Hsia (eds), *Cultural Translation in Early Modern Europe*, 65–80. Cambridge: Cambridge University Press.

Burke, Peter. 2007b. Lost (and found) in translation: A cultural history of translators and translating in Early Modern Europe. *European Review* 15 (1): 83–94.

Burnet, James. 1773–1792 [1967]. *Of the Origin and Progress of Language* (6 vols,) Vol. II. Repr. in English Linguistics 1500–1800, no. 48, ed. by R.C. Alston (Menston, 1967).

Burnley, David. 1986. Curial prose in England. *Speculum: A Journal of Medieval Studies* 61 (3), 593–614.

Burnley, David. 1992. Lexis and semantics. In: Blake, Norman F. (ed.), *The Cambridge History of the English Language. Vol. 2: 1066–1476*, 409–499. Cambridge: Cambridge University Press.

Butterworth, Charles C. 1941. *The Literary Lineage of the King James Bible, 1340–1611*. Philadelphia: University of Pennsylvania Press.

REFERENCES

Cameron, Euan. 2016. *The New Cambridge History of the Bible: Volume 3, From 1450 to 1750*. Cambridge: Cambridge University Press.

Canon, Elizabeth Bell. 2016. Buried treasure in the Tyndale corpus: Innovations and archaisms. *ANGLICA-An International Journal of English Studies* 25 (2): 151–165.

Cennamo, Michela, Thórhallur Eythórsson and Jóhanna Barðdal. 2015. Semantic and (morpho-)syntactic constraints on anticausativization: Evidence from Latin and Old Norse-Icelandic. *Linguistics* 53 (4): 677–729.

Chastoupis, Athanasios. 1981. *Introduction to the Old Testament* [In Greek]. Athens.

Chamberlin, William J. 1991. *Catalogue of English Bible Translations: A Classified Bibliography of Versions and Editions including Books, Parts, and Old and New Testament Apocrypha and Apocryphal Books*. New York: Greenwood.

Chesterman, Andrew. 2000. A causal model for translation studies. In: Olohan, Maeve (ed.), *Intercultural Faultlines*, 15–27. Manchester: St. Jerome Publishing.

Chomsky, Noam. 1995. *The Minimalist Program*. Cambridge, MA: MIT press.

Chomsky, Noam. 2005. Three factors in language design. *Linguistic Inquiry* 36 (1): 1–22.

Chomsky, Noam. 1965. *Aspects of the Theory of Syntax*. Cambridge, Massachusetts: MIT Press.

Churik, Nikolas. 2019. Greek explicating Greek: A study of metaphrase language and style. In: Kinloch, Matthew and Alex MacFarlane (eds), *Trends and Turning Points. Constructing the Late Antique and Byzantine World*, 66–82. Leiden: Brill.

Cichocki, Wladyslaw and Daniel Lepetit. 1986. Intonational variability in language contact: F0 declination in Ontario French. In: Sankoff, David (ed.), *Diversity and Diachrony*, 239–247. Amsterdam: Benjamins.

Ciszek, Ewa. 2004. On some French elements in early Middle English word derivation. *Studia Anglica Posnaniensia* 40: 111–119.

Ciszek, Ewa. 2012. The Middle English suffix *-ish*: Reasons for decline in productivity. *Studia Anglica Posnaniensia* 47 (2–3): 27–39.

Coetsem, Frans van. 1995. Outlining a model of the transmission phenomenon in language contact. *Leuvense Bijdragen* 84: 63–85.

Coetsem, Frans van. 2000. *A General and Unified Theory of the Transmission Process in Language Contact*. Heidelberg: Universitätsverlag C. Winter.

Coetsem, Frans van. 2003. Topics in contact linguistics. *Leuvense Bijdragen* 92: 27–99.

Collombat, Isabelle. 2004. Le XXIe siècle: l'âge de la retraduction. *Translation Studies in the New Millennium* 2: 1–15. Online at https://hal-univ-paris3.archives-ouvertes.fr/hal-01452331.

Connolly, David and Aliki Bacopoulou-Halls. 2011. Greek tradition. In: Baker, Mona and Gabriela Saldanha (eds), *Routledge Encyclopedia of Translation Studies*, 418–426. New York: Routledge.

Consani, Carlo. 2013. Code-mixing. In: Giannakis, Georgios K. (ed.), *Encyclopedia of Ancient Greek Language and Linguistics*. Online at http://dx.doi.org/10.1163/2214

-448X_eagll_SIM_00000426. First published online: 2013 [Last access: 30 September 2020].

Crystal, David and Derek Davy. 2016. *Investigating English Style*. London: Routledge.

Culpeper, Jonathan. 2015. *History of English*. London: Routledge.

Cysouw, Michael and Bernhard Wälchli. 2007. Parallel texts: Using translational equivalents in linguistic typology. *STUF-Language Typology and Universals* 60 (2): 95–99.

Cysouw, Michael, Chris Biemann and Matthias Ongyerth. 2007. Using Strong's numbers in the Bible to test an automatic alignment of parallel texts. *STUF-Language Typology and Universals* 60 (2): 158–171.

Díaz Vera, Javier E. 2000. The development of causation in Old English and its interaction with lexical and syntactic diachronic processes. *Cuadernos de Investigación Filológica* 26: 17–38.

Dahl, Östen. 2007. From questionnaires to parallel corpora in typology. *STUF-Language Typology and Universals* 60 (2): 172–181.

Dalton-Puffer, Christiane. 1992. The status of word formation in Middle English: Approaching the question. In: Rissanen, Matti (ed.), *History of Englishes: New Methods and Interpretations in Historical Linguistics*, 465–482. Berlin: Mouton de Gruyter.

Dalton-Puffer, Christiane. 1997. On the histories of de-verbal adjectives in Middle English. *Studia Anglica Posnaniensia* 31: 41–55.

Dalton-Puffer, Christiane. 2011. *The French Influence on Middle English Morphology: A Corpus-Based Study on Derivation*. Berlin: de Gruyter.

Darlow, T.H. and H.F. Moule. 1911. *The Historical Catalogue of the Printed Editions of Holy Scripture in the Library of the British and Foreign Bible Society. Volume 2: Polyglots and Languages other than English*. London: The Bible House.

Deissmann, G. Adolf. 1895. *Bibelstudien. Beiträge, zumeist aus den Papyri und Inschriften, zur Geschichte der Sprache, des Schriftthums und der Religion des hellenistischen Judenthums und des Urchristenthums*. Marburg: N.G. Elwert.

Deissmann, G. Adolf. 1897. *Neue Bibelstudien Sprachgeschichtliche Beiträge zumeist aus den Papyri und Inschriften*. Marburg: N.G. Elwert.

Deissmann, G. Adolf. 1908. *Licht vom Osten. Das Neue Testament und die neuentdeckten Texte der hellenistisch-römischen Welt*. Tübingen: Mohr.

Dekeyser, Xavier. 1991. Romance loans in late Middle English: A case study. In: Granger, Sylviane (ed.), *Perspectives on the English Lexicon: A Tribute to Jacques Van Roey*, 153–162. Louvain-la-Neuve: Institut de linguistiques.

de Lange, Nicholas. 2007. Jewish Greek. In: Christidis, Anastassios Ph. (ed.), *A History of Ancient Greek: From the Beginnings to Late Antiquity*, 638–645. Cambridge: Cambridge University Press.

Delicostopoulos, Athan. 1998. Major Greek translations of the Bible. In: Krašovec, Jože (ed.), *International Symposium on the Interpretation of the Bible on the Occasion of the Publication of the New Slovenian Translation of the Bible*, 297–316. Sheffield: Sheffield Academic Press.

REFERENCES

Delisle, Jean and Judith Woodsworth. 2012. *Translators through History. Revised Edition.* Amsterdam: John Benjamins.

Dellit, Otto. 1905. *Über lateinische Elemente im Mittelenglischen: Beiträge zur Geschichte des Englischen Wortschatzes.* Marburg: R. Friedrich.

Denison, David. 1993. *English Historical Syntax.* London: Routledge.

Denton, John. 2007. '... Waterlogged somewhere in mid-Atlantic.' Why American readers need intralingual translation but don't often get it. *TTR: Traduction, Terminologie, Rédaction* 20 (2): 243–270.

Devine, Andrew M. and Laurence D. Stephens. 2000. *Discontinuous Syntax: Hyperbaton in Greek.* Oxford: Oxford University Press.

de Vries, Lourens. 2007. Some remarks on the use of Bible translations as parallel texts in linguistic research. *STUF-Language Typology and Universals* 60 (2): 148–157.

di Bartolo, Giuseppina. 2020. Purpose and result clauses: ἵνα-*hína* and ὥστε-*hóste* in the Greek Documentary Papyri of the Roman Period. In: Rafiyenko, Dariya and Ilja A. Seržant (eds), *Postclassical Greek. Contemporary Approaches to Philology and Linguistics*, 19–38. Berlin, New York: de Gruyter.

di Leo, Paolo. 2013. Medieval translation of Greek texts. In: Giannakis, Georgios K. (ed.), *Encyclopedia of Ancient Greek Language and Linguistics.* Online at http://dx.doi.org/10.1163/2214-448X_eagll_COM_00000394. First published online: 2013 [Last access: 30 September 2020].

Donner, Morton. 1986. The gerund in Middle English. *English Studies* 67, 394–400.

Donoghue, Daniel. 2008. Early Old English (up to 899). In: Momma, Haruko and Michael Matto (eds), *A Companion to the History of the English Language*, 156–164. Oxford: Blackwell-Wiley.

Dove, Mary. 2007. *The First English Bible: The Text and Context of the Wycliffite Versions.* Cambridge: Cambridge University Press.

Drinka, Bridget. 2011. The sacral stamp of Greek: Periphrastic constructions in New Testament translations of Latin, Gothic, and Old Church Slavonic. In: Welo, Eirik (ed.), *Indo-European Syntax and Pragmatics: Contrastive Approaches. Oslo Studies in Language* 3 (3): 41–73.

Drinka, Bridget. 2013. Phylogenetic and areal models of Indo-European relatedness: The role of contact in reconstruction. *Journal of Language Contact* 6 (2): 379–410.

Drinka, Bridget. 2017. *Language Contact in Europe. The Periphrastic Perfect through History.* Cambridge: Cambridge University Press.

Du-Nour, Miryam. 1995. Retranslation of children's books as evidence of changes of norms. *Target. International Journal of Translation Studies* 7 (2): 327–346.

Durrell, Martin. 1999. Standardsprache in England und Deutschland. *Zeitschrift für germanistische Linguistik* 27 (3): 285–308.

Ellegård, Alvar. 1953. *The Auxiliary do: The Establishment and Regulation of its Use in English.* Stockholm: Almquist & Wiksell.

Ellis, Roger (ed.). 2008. *The Oxford History of Literary Translation in English. Volume 1: To 1550*. Oxford: Oxford University Press.

Ellis, Roger and Liz Oakley-Brown. 2009. British tradition. In: Baker, Mona and Gabriela Saldanha (eds), *The Routledge Encyclopaedia of Translation Studies*, 333–347. London: Routledge.

Emonds, Joseph. 1979. Appositive relatives have no properties. *Linguistic Inquiry* 10 (2): 211–243.

Emonds, Joseph. 1986. Grammatically deviant prestige constructions. In: Brame, Michael, Heles Contreras and Frederick Newmeyer (eds), *A Festschrift for Sol Saporta*, 93–129. Seattle: Noit Amrofer.

Emonds, Joseph and Jan Terje Faarlund. 2014. *English: The Language of the Vikings*. Olomouc: Palacký University.

Esteban-Segura, Laura. 2011. Suffixal doublets in late Middle English: -ness vs. -ship. *Neuphilologische Mitteilungen* 112 (2): 183–194.

Evans, Trevor V. 1999. The comparative optative: A Homeric reminiscence in the Greek Pentateuch? *Vetus Testamentum* 49 (4): 487–504.

Evans, Trevor V. 2005. Approaches to the language of the Septuagint. *Journal of Jewish Studies* 56 (1): 25–33.

Even-Zohar, Itamar. 1990. The position of translated literature within the literary polysystem. *Polysystem Studies [Poetics Today 11 (1)]*: 45–51.

Fehlauer, Friedrich. 1908. *Die englischen Übersetzungen von Boethius' De Consolatione Philosophiae*. PhD Dissertation, Albertus-Universität zu Königsberg.

Ferguson, Charles A. 1959. Diglossia. *Word* 15: 325–340.

Fernández Marcos, N. 2000. *The Septuagint in Context: Introduction to the Greek Versions of the Bible*. Trans. Wilfred G.E. Watson. Leiden, Boston: Brill.

Filppula, Markku, Juhani Klemola and Heli Paulasto. 2008. *Vernacular Universals and Language Contacts: Evidence from Varieties of English and Beyond*. London: Routledge.

Fischer, Andreas. 1989. Lexical change in late Old English: From æ to lagu. In: Fischer, Andreas (ed.), *The History and the Dialects of English. Festschrift for Eduard Kolb*, 103–114. Heidelberg: Winter.

Fischer, Olga. 1979. A comparative study of philosophical terms in the Alfredian and Chaucerian Boethius. *Neophilologus* 63 (4): 622–639.

Fischer, Olga. 1988. The rise of the *for NP to V* construction: An explanation. In: Nixon, Graham and John Honey (eds), *An Historic Tongue: Studies in English Linguistics in Memory of Barbara Strang*, 67–88. London, New York: Routledge.

Fischer, Olga. 1989. The origin and spread of the accusative and infinitive construction in English. *Folia Linguistica Historica* 8 (1–2): 143–218.

Fischer, Olga. 1991. The rise of the passive infinitive in English. In: Kastovsky, Dieter (ed.), *Historical English Syntax* 141–188, Berlin, New York: Mouton de Gruyter.

REFERENCES

Fischer, Olga. 1992. Syntactic change and borrowing: The case of the accusative-and-infinitive construction in English. In: Gerritsen, Marinel and Dieter Stein (eds), *Internal and External Factors in Syntactic Change*, 17–89. Berlin, New York: Mouton de Gruyter.

Fischer, Olga. 1994. The development of quasi-auxiliaries in English and changes in word order. *Neophilologus* 78 (1): 137–164.

Fischer, Olga. 2007. *Morphosyntactic Change: Functional and Formal Perspectives*. Oxford: Oxford University Press.

Fischer, Olga. 2013. The role of contact in English syntactic change in the Old and Middle English periods. In: Hundt, Marianne and Daniel Schreier (eds), *English as a Contact Language*, 18–40. Cambridge: Cambridge University Press.

Fischer, Olga, Hendrik De Smet and Wim van der Wurff. 2017. *A Brief History of English Syntax*. Cambridge: Cambridge University Press.

Fontana, Josep M. 1993. *Phrase Structure and the Syntax of Clitics in the History of Spanish*. Philadelphia: University of Pennsylvania.

Frantzen, Allen J. 1986. *King Alfred*. Boston: Twayne Publishers.

Fung, Pascale and Kenneth Church. 1994. K-vec: a new approach for aligning parallel texts. *Proceedings of the Fifteenth International Conference on Computational Linguistics (COLING '94)*: 1096–102.

Gamagari, Thomi. to-appear. *Translation and Language Variation*. PhD Dissertation, Aristotle University of Thessaloniki. Supervisor: Dr Nikolaos Lavidas.

Gamagari, Thomi and Nikolaos Lavidas. 2022. How does (not) language change affect translations. A corpus-based study on lexical transfer in Renaissance English and Greek literary texts. In: Lavidas, Nikolaos and Kiki Nikiforidou (eds), *Studying Language Change in the 21st Century. Theory and Methodologies*. Leiden, Boston: Brill.

Gambier, Yves. 1994. La retraduction, retour et détour. *Meta* 39 (3): 413–417.

Gardner, Anne-Christine. 2011. Word formation in early Middle English: Abstract nouns in the Linguistic Atlas of Early Middle English. *Varieng. Studies in Variation, Contacts and Change in English, 6: online*. Online at https://doi.org/10.5167/uzh-58668.

Gardner, Anne-Christine. 2014. *Derivation in Middle English: Regional and Text Type Variation*. Helsinki: Société Néophilologique.

Gehman, Henry S. 1951. The Hebraic character of Septuagint Greek. *Vetus Testamentum* 1 (1): 81–90.

Gelderen, Elly van. 2004. *Grammaticalization as Economy*. Amsterdam: John Benjamins.

Gelderen, Elly van. 2014. *A History of the English Language*. Amsterdam: John Benjamins.

George, Coulter H. 2010. Jewish and Christian Greek. In: Bakker, Egbert J. (ed.), *A Companion to the Ancient Greek language*, 267–280. Oxford: Blackwell.

Gianollo, Chiara. 2011. Native syntax and translation effects: Adnominal arguments in the Greek and Latin New Testament. In: Welo, Eirik (ed.), *Indo-European Syntax and Pragmatics: Contrastive Approaches. Oslo Studies in Language* 3 (3): 75–101.

Gianollo, Chiara and Nikolaos Lavidas. 2013. Cognate adverbials and case in the history of Greek. *Studies in Greek Linguistics* 33: 61–75.

González-Vilbazo, Kay and Luis López. 2011. Some properties of light verbs in code-switching. *Lingua* 121 (5): 832–850.

Görlach, Manfred. 1999. Regional and social variation. In: Hogg, Richard M., Norman F. Blake, Roger Lass and R.W. Burchfield (eds), *The Cambridge History of the English Language*, Vol. 3, 459–538. Cambridge: Cambridge University Press.

Gottlieb, Henrik. 1999. The impact of English: Danish TV subtitles as mediators of Anglicisms. *Zeitschrift für Anglistik und Amerikanistik* 47 (2): 133–153.

Gottlieb, Henrik. 2005. Anglicisms and translation. In: Anderman, Gunilla and Margaret Rogers (eds), *In and out of English: For Better, for Worse*, 161–184. Clevedon: Multilingual Matters.

Goutsos, Dionysis (ed.). 2001. *The Language of Translation: A Collection of Texts of Modern Translation Theories* [In Greek]. Athens. Ellinika Grammata.

Grammenidis, Simos and Georgios Floros. 2019. The Greek-speaking tradition. In: Gambier, Yves and Ubaldo Stecconi (eds), *A World Atlas of Translation*, 323–340. Amsterdam, Philadelphia: John Benjamins.

Grant, W. Leonard. 1954. European vernacular works in Latin translation. *Studies in the Renaissance* 1: 120–156.

Grimshaw, Jane. 1990. *Argument Structure*. Cambridge, MA: MIT Press.

Groningen, Bernhard A. van. 1965. General literary tendencies in the second century AD. *Mnemosyne* 18 (1–4): 41–56.

Grünthal, Riho and Johanna Nichols. 2016. Transitivizing-detransitivizing typology and language family history. *Lingua Posnaniensis* 58 (2): 11–31.

Guerssel, Mohamed, Kenneth Hale, Mary Laughren, Beth Levin and Josie White Eagle. 1985. A Cross-linguistic study of transitivity alternations. *Papers of the Chicago Linguistic Society 21. Part 2: Papers from the Parasession on Causatives and Agentivity*, 48–63.

Gürçağlar, Sehnaz Tahir. 2009. Retranslation. In: Baker, Mona and Gabriela Saldanha (eds), *Routledge Encyclopedia of Translation Studies*, 233–236. London: Routledge.

Häcker, Martina. 2011. French-English linguistic and cultural contact in medieval England: The evidence of letters. *AAA: Arbeiten aus Anglistik und Amerikanistik* 36 (2): 133–160.

Hadley, Dawn M. and Julian D. Richards. 2000. *Cultures in Contact: Settlement in England in the Ninth and Tenth Centuries*. Turnhout: Brepols.

Haeberli, Eric. 2018. Syntactic effects of contact in translations: Evidence from object pronoun placement in Middle English. *English Language and Linguistics* 22 (2): 301–321.

REFERENCES

Hale, Kenneth and Samuel Jay Keyser. 1986. *Some Transitivity Alternations in English*. Cambridge, Mass.: MIT.

Hale, Kenneth and Samuel Jay Keyser. 1987. *A View from the Middle*. Cambridge, Mass.: MIT.

Hale, Kenneth and Samuel Jay Keyser. 1988. Explaining and constraining the middle. In: Tenny, Carol (ed.), *Studies in Generative Approaches to Aspect*, 41–58. Cambridge, Mass.: MIT.

Hale, Kenneth and Mary Laughren. 1983. *The Structure of Verbal Entries*. Walpiri Lexicon Project. Cambridge, MA: MIT.

Hammond, Gerald. 1982. *The Making of the English Bible*. Manchester: Carcanet New Press.

Hankamer, Jorge. 1977. Multiple analyses. In: Li, Charles (ed.), *Mechanisms of Syntactic Change*, 583–607. Austin: University of Texas Press.

Hannick, Christian. 1972. *Das Neue Testament in Altkirchenslavischer Sprache*. Berlin, New York: Walter de Gruyter.

Harris, Alice C. and Lyle Campbell. 1995. *Historical Syntax in Cross-Linguistic Perspective*. Cambridge: Cambridge University Press.

Hartsuiker, Robert J. and Casper Westenberg. 2000. Word order priming in written and spoken sentence production. *Cognition* 75 (2): B27–B39.

Haspelmath, Martin. 1993. More on the typology of inchoative/ causative verb alternations. In: Comrie, Bernard and Maria Polinsky (eds), *Causatives and Transitivity*, 87–121. Amsterdam: John Benjamins.

Haspelmath, Martin. 1997. *Indefinite Pronouns*. Oxford: Oxford University Press.

Haspelmath, Martin, Andreea Calude, Michael Spagnol, Heiko Narrog and Elif Bamyaci. 2014. Coding causal—noncausal verb alternations: A form-frequency correspondence explanation. *Journal of Linguistics* 50 (3): 587–625.

Hatim, Basil and Jeremy Munday. 2004. *Translation: An Advanced Resource Book*. London, New York: Routledge.

Haug, Dag Trygve Truslew. 2017. Backward control in Ancient Greek and Latin participial adjuncts. *Natural Language and Linguistic Theory* 35 (1): 99–159.

Haug, Dag Trygve Truslew and Marius Jøhndal. 2008. Creating a parallel treebank of the old Indo-European Bible translations. *Proceedings of the Second Workshop on Language Technology for Cultural Heritage Data (LaTeCH 2008)*, 27–34.

Heidermanns, Frank. 1993. *Etymologisches Wörterbuch der Germanischen Primäradjektive*. Berlin: Walter de Gruyter.

Heine, Bernd and Tania Kuteva. 2003. On contact-induced grammaticalization. *Studies in Language* 27 (3): 529–572.

Heine, Bernd and Tania Kuteva. 2005. *Language Contact and Grammatical Change*. Cambridge: Cambridge University Press.

Hermodsson, Lars. 1952 *Reflexive und intransitive Verba im älteren Westgermanischen*. Uppsala: Almqvist & Wirksells Boktryckeri.

Hickey, Raymond. 2010a. Contact and language shift. In: Hickey, Raymond (ed.), *Handbook of Language Contact*, 151–169. Malden, MA: Blackwell.

Hickey, Raymond. 2010b. Language contact: Reconsideration and reassessment. In: Hickey, Raymond (ed.), *Handbook of Language Contact*, 1–28. Malden, MA: Blackwell.

Hickey, Raymond. 2012. Assessing the role of contact in the history of English. In: Nevalainen, Terttu and Elizabeth Closs Traugott (eds), *The Oxford Handbook of the History of English*, 485–496. Oxford: Oxford University Press.

Hinterberger, Martin (ed.) 2014. *The Language of Byzantine Learned Literature*. Turnhout: Brepols.

Hinterberger Martin. 2020. From highly classicizing to common prose: The metaphrasis of Niketas Choniates' *History*. In: Bentein, Klaas and Mark Janse (eds), *Varieties of Post-classical and Byzantine Greek*, 179–200. Berlin: Walter de Gruyter.

Hock, Hans Henrich. 2019. Anticausative and passive in Vedic. In: Heltoft, Lars, Iván Igartua, Brian D. Joseph, Kirsten Jeppesen Kragh and Lene Schøsler (eds), *Perspectives on Language Structure and Language Change: Studies in Honor of Henning Andersen*, 181–191. Amsterdam: John Benjamins.

Hoecke, Willy van and Michèle Goyens. 1990. Translation as a witness to semantic change. *Belgian Journal of Linguistics* 5 (1): 109–131.

Hoenen, Maarten J.F.M. and Lodi W. Nauta (eds). 1997. *Boethius in the Middle Ages: Latin and Vernacular Traditions of the Consolatio Philosophiae*. Leiden, Boston: Brill.

Hogg, Richard and David Denison (eds). 2006. *A History of the English Language*. Cambridge: Cambridge University Press.

Holton, David, Geoffrey C. Horrocks, Marjolijne Janssen, Tina Lendari, Io Manolessou and Notis Toufexis. 2019. *The Cambridge Grammar of Medieval and Early Modern Greek*. Cambridge: Cambridge University Press.

Hoof, Henri van. 1993. Histoire de la traduction médicale en Occident. *Cahiers de l'institut de linguistique de Louvain* 19 (1–2): 75–125.

Horrocks, Geoffrey. 2014. *Greek: A History of the Language and its Speakers*. Malden, MA: Wiley-Blackwell.

Horrocks, Geoffrey 2016. The phases of the Greek language. In: Bons, Eberhard and Jan Joosten (eds), *Handbuch zur Septuaginta/ Handbook of the Septuagint. Volume 3. Die Sprache der Septuaginta/ The Language of the Septuagint*, 71–88. Gütersloh: Gütersloher Verlagshaus.

Horrocks, Geoffrey. 2017. 'High' and 'low' in Medieval Greek. In: Bentein, Klaas, Mark Janse and Jorie Soltic (eds), *Variation and Change in Ancient Greek. Tense, Aspect and Modality*, 219–241. Leiden: Brill.

Horsley, Greg H.R. 1989. The fiction of Jewish Greek. In: Horsley, Greg H.R. (ed.), *New Documents Illustrating Early Christianity, 5: Linguistic Essays*, 5–40. Sydney.

Hosington, Brenda M. 2006. 'A poore preasant off ytalyan costume': The interplay of travel and translation in William Barker's *Dyssputacion off the Nobylytye off Wymen*. In: Di Biase, Carmine G. (ed.), *Travel and Translation in the Early Modern Period*, 143–156. Amsterdam: Rodopi.

Hosington, Brenda M. 2015. Translation as a currency of cultural exchange in early Modern England. In: Hackett, Helen (ed.), *Early Modern Exchanges: Dialogues Between Nations and Cultures, 1550–1750*, 27–54. Surrey: Farnham.

House, Juliane. 1997. *Translation Quality Assessment. A Model Revisited*. Tübingen: Gunter Narr.

House, Juliane. 2008. Beyond intervention: Universals in translation? *Trans-kom. Journal of Translation and Technical Communication* 1(1): 6–19.

House, Juliane and Jochen Rehbein (eds). 2004. *Multilingual Communication*. Amsterdam: John Benjamins.

Hunger, Herbert. 1981. *Anonyme Metaphrase zu Anna Komnene, Alexias XI–XIII: Ein Beitrag zur Erschliessung der Byzantinischen Umgangssprache*. Vienna: Verlag der Österreichischen Akademie der Wissenschaften.

Iartseva, Viktoriia N. 1981. The role of translations in the history of literary languages. *Soviet Studies in Literature* 18 (1): 80–87.

Irvine, Susan Elizabeth and Malcolm Godden. 2012. *The Old English Boethius*. Cambridge, MA: Harvard University Press.

Iyeiri, Yoko. 2003. 'God forbid!': A historical study of the verb *forbid* in different versions of the English Bible. *Journal of English Linguistics* 31 (2): 149–162.

Iyeiri, Yoko. 2010. *Verbs of Implicit Negation and their Complements in the History of English*. Amsterdam: John Benjamins.

Jackendoff, Ray. 1988. Conceptual semantics. In: Eco, Umberto, Marco Santambrogio and Patrizia Violi (eds). *Meaning and Mental Representations*, 81–97. Bloomington: Indiana University Press.

Jackendoff, Ray. 1993. On the role of conceptual structure in argument selection: A reply to Emonds. *Natural Language and Linguistic Theory* 11 (2): 279–312.

Jakobson, Roman. 1959. On linguistic aspects of translation. In: Brower, Reuben Arther (ed.), *On Translation* 3: 30–39. Cambridge, MA: Harvard University Press.

Janse, Mark. 2002. Aspects of bilingualism in the history of the Greek language. In: Adams, James Noel, Mark Janse and Simon Swain (eds), *Bilingualism in Ancient Society: Language Contact and the Written Text*, 332–390. Oxford: Oxford University Press.

Janse, Mark. 2007. The Greek of the New Testament. In: Christidis, Anastassios Ph. (ed.), *A History of Ancient Greek: From the Beginnings to Late Antiquity*, 646–653. Cambridge: Cambridge University Press.

Jeffreys, Elizabeth (ed.). 1998. *Digenis Akritis: The Grottaferrata and Escorial Versions*. Cambridge: Cambridge University Press.

Jespersen, Otto. 1940. *A Modern English Grammar on Historical Principles. Part IV. Syntax*. London: George Allen & Unwin.

Jespersen, Otto. 1946. *Mankind, Nation and Individual from a Linguistic Point of View*. London: George Allen & Unwin.

Jespersen, Otto. 1962 [1905]. *Growth and Structure of the English Language*. Oxford: Basil Blackwell.

Johanson, Lars. 2008. Remodeling grammar. Copying, conventionalization, grammaticalization. In: Siemund, Peter and Noemi Kintana (eds), *Language Contact and Contact Languages*, 61–79. Amsterdam, Philadelphia: John Benjamins.

Johanson, Lars. 2011. Contact-induced change in a code-copying framework. In: Jones, Mari C. and Edith Esch (eds), *Language Change: The Interplay of Internal, External and Extra-Linguistic Factors*, 61–79. Berlin: Mouton de Gruyter.

Joosten, Jan. 2008. Reflections on the 'interlinear paradigm' in Septuagintal studies. In: Voitila, Anssi and Jutta Jokiranta (eds), *Scripture in Transition: Essays on Septuagint, Hebrew Bible, and Dead Sea Scrolls in Honour of Raija Sollamo*, 163–178. Leiden, Boston: Brill.

Joosten, Jan. 2016. Septuagint Greek and the Jewish sociolect in Egypt. In: Bons, Eberhard and Jan Joosten (eds), *Handbuch zur Septuaginta/ Handbook of the Septuagint. Volume 3. Die Sprache der Septuaginta/ The Language of the Septuagint*, 246–256. Gütersloh: Gütersloher Verlagshaus.

Joseph, Brian D. 1983a. *The Synchrony and Diachrony of the Balkan Infinitive: A Study in Areal, General and Historical Linguistics*. Cambridge: Cambridge University Press.

Joseph, Brian D. 1983b. Relativization in Modern Greek: Another look at the accessibility hierarchy constraints. *Lingua* 60 (1): 1–24.

Joseph, Brian D. 2000. Is there such a thing as 'Grammaticalization?' *Language Sciences* 23 (2–3): 163–186.

Kakoulidi, Eleni D. 1980. *On the Translation of the New Testament. History—Critique—Views—Bibliography* [In Greek]. Thessaloniki.

Kakoulidi, Eleni D. 1986. The first translator of the Holy Scripture into demotic Greek [In Greek]. Ioannikios Kartanos 1536. *The Translation of the Holy Scripture in the Orthodox Church. Proceedings of the Fourth Orthodox Theological Conference*. Thessaloniki.

Kakoulidi-Panou, Eleni and Eleni Karantzola (ed.). 2000. *Ioannikios Kartanos. Palaia te kai Nea Diathiki (Venice 1536)* [In Greek]. Thessaloniki: Centre for Greek Language.

Kakridis, Ioannis Th. 1961 [1936]. *The Translation Problem* [In Greek]. Athens: I Vivliothiki tou Philologou.

Kakridis, Ioannis Th. 1971. *Homer Revisited*. Lund: Publication of the New Society of Letters at Lund.

Kane, George. 1951. *Middle English Literature*. London: Methuen.

Karla, Grammatiki A. 2016. Life of Aesop: Fictional biography as popular literature. In: de Temmerman, Koen and Kristoffel Demoen (eds), *Writing Biography in Greece and Rome: Narrative Technique and Fictionalization*, 45–160. Cambridge: Cambridge University Press.

REFERENCES

Karla, Grammatiki A. and Nikolaos Lavidas. 2004. The infinitive in the diachrony of Greek [In Greek]. *Proceedings of the 6th International Conference on Greek Linguistics, ICGL 6.* CD-Rom edition (also available online). Heraklio: University of Crete.

Kasinis, Konstantinos G. 2005 [1998]. *Cross-references. Studies on the 19th and 20th Century* [In Greek]. Athens: Chatzinikoli.

Kastovsky, Dieter. 1992. Semantics and vocabulary. In: Hogg, Richard (ed.), *The Cambridge History of the English Language. Vol. 1: The Beginnings to 1066*, 290–408. Cambridge: Cambridge University Press.

Kastovsky, Dieter and Arthur Mettinger (eds). 2000. *The History of English in a Social Context: A Contribution to Historical Sociolinguistics.* Berlin: Mouton de Gruyter.

Katz, Dovid. 1987. *Grammar of the Yiddish Language.* London: Duckworth.

Kaylor, Noel. 2015. The English and German translation traditions of Boethius's De Consolatione Philosophiae. *Studia Litteraria Universitatis Iagellonicae Cracoviensis* 9 (2): 121–129.

Kelly Louis G. 1979. *The True Interpreter: A History of Translation Theory and Practice in the West.* Oxford: Blackwell.

Kemenade, Ans van. 2007. Formal syntax and language change: Developments and outlook. *Diachronica* 24 (1): 155–169.

Kerr, Glenn J. 2011. Dynamic equivalence and its daughters: Placing Bible translation theories in their historical context. *Journal of Translation* 7 (1): 13–20.

Kerswill, Paul. 2003. Dialect levelling and geographical diffusion in British English. In: Britain, David and Jenny Cheshire (eds), *Social Dialectology: In Honor of Peter Trudgill*, 223–243. Amsterdam: John Benjamins.

Keynes, Simon and Michael Lapidge (transl.). 1983. *Alfred the Great. Asser's "Life of King Alfred" and other Contemporary Sources.* Harmondsworth: Penguin.

Kilpiö, Matti. 1989. *Passive Constructions in Old English Translations from Latin: With Special Reference to the OE Bede and the Pastoral Care.* Helsinki: Société néophilologique.

Kim, Lawrence. 2010. The literary heritage as language: Atticism and the second Sophistic. In: Bakker, Egbert J. (ed.), *A Companion to the Ancient Greek Language*, 468–482. Oxford: Wiley-Blackwell.

King, John N. 1982. *English Reformation Literature: The Tudor Origins of the Protestant Tradition.* Princeton: Princeton University Press.

Kitagaki, Muneharu. 1981. *Principles and Problems of Translation in Seventeenth-Century England.* Kyoto: Yamaguchi Shoten.

Kitazume, Sachiko. 1996. Middles in English. *Word* 47 (2): 161–183.

Kitromilides, Paschalis M. 2006. Orthodoxy and the West: Reformation to Enlightenment. In: Angold, Michael (ed.), *The Cambridge History of Christianity* 5: 187–209. Cambridge: Cambridge University Press.

Kmetko, Susan E. 2018. *The Function and Significance of Middle Voice Verbs in the Greek*

New Testament. PhD Dissertation, Australian Catholic University. Online at https://doi.org/10.26199/5c91b01997a0e [Last access: 30 September 2020].

Koch, Karsten. 2011. Revisiting a translation effect in an oral language. In: Kranich, Svenja, Viktor Becher, Steffen Höder and Juliane House (eds), *Multilingual Discourse Production: Diachronic and Synchronic Perspectives*, 281–310. Amsterdam: John Benjamins.

Koch, Peter and Wulf Oesterreicher. 1994. Schriftlichkeit und Sprache. In: Günther, Hartmut and Otto Ludwig (eds), *Writing and its Use. An Interdisciplinary Handbook of International Research*. Volume 1, 587–604. Berlin, New York: de Gruyter.

Kohnen, Thomas. 2003. The influence of 'Latinate' constructions in early Modern English: Orality and literacy as complementary forces. In: Mettinger, Arthur and Dieter Kastovsky (eds), *Language Contact in the History of English*, 171–194. Frankfurt am Main: Peter Lang.

Kohnen, Thomas. 2012. Standardization: Bible translations. In: Bergs, Alexander and Laurel Brinton (eds), *English Historical Linguistics. Vol. 1*, 1039–1050. Berlin: Mouton de Gruyter.

Koivisto-Alanko, Päivi. 1997. The vocabulary of cognition in Early English translations of Boethius from Chaucer to Preston. *Neuphilologische Mitteilungen* 98 (4): 397–414.

Koller, Werner. 1998. Übersetzungen ins Deutsche und ihre Bedeutung für die deutsche Sprachgeschichte. In: Besch, Werner, Anne Betten, Oskar Reichmann and Stefan Sonderegger (eds), *Sprachgeschichte. Ein Handbuch zur Geschichte der deutschen Sprache und ihrer Erforschung*, 210–229. Berlin, New York: de Gruyter.

Koltsiou-Nikita, Anna. 2009. *Translation Issues in the Greek and Latin Christian Literature* [In Greek]. Thessaloniki: University Studio Press.

Konstantinou, Miltiadis. 2012. Bible translation and national identity: The Greek case. *International Journal for the Study of the Christian Church* 12 (2): 176–186.

Koopman, Willem F. 1990. *Word Order in Old English, with Special Reference to the Verb Phrase*. PhD Dissertation, University of Amsterdam.

Koptjevskaja-Tamm, Maria. 2006. The circle that won't come full: Two potential isoglosses in the Circum-Baltic area. In: Matras, Yaron, April McMahon and Nigel Vincent (eds), *Linguistic Areas*, 182–226. London: Palgrave Macmillan.

Koskinen, Kaisa and Outi Paloposki. 2003. Retranslations in the age of digital reproduction. *Cadernos de Tradução* 1 (11): 19–38.

Koskinen, Kaisa and Outi Paloposki. 2010. Retranslation. In: Gambier, Yves and Luc van Doorslaer (eds), *Handbook of Translation Studies: Volume 1*, 294–298. Amsterdam: John Benjamins.

Koskinen, Kaisa and Outi Paloposki. 2015. Anxieties of influence: The voice of the first translator in retranslation. *Target* 27 (1): 25–39.

Kossmann, Maarten. 2008. On the nature of borrowing in Cypriot Arabic. *Zeitschrift für Arabische Linguistik* 49: 5–24.

Kossmann, Maarten. 2010. Parallel system borrowing: Parallel morphological systems due to the borrowing of paradigms. *Diachronica* 27 (3): 459–488.

Kossmann, Maarten. 2013. *The Arabic Influence on Northern Berber.* Leiden: Brill.

Koutsivitis, Vasilis. 1994. *Theory of Translation* [In Greek]. Athens: Ellinikes Panepistimiakes Ekdoseis.

Krahe, Hans and Wolfgang Meid. 1969. *Germanische Sprachwissenschaft, Volume 2: Formenlehre.* 6th ed. Berlin: de Gruyter.

Kranich, Svenja, Viktor Becher and Steffen Höder. 2011. A tentative typology of translation-induced language change. In: Kranich, Svenja, Viktor Becher and Steffen Höder (eds), *Multilingual Discourse Production: Diachronic and Synchronic Perspectives*, 9–44. Amsterdam: John Benjamins.

Krebs, Franz. 1884. *Die Präpositionsadverbien in der späteren historischen Gräcität. I. Teil: 1884; II. Teil: 1885.* Munich: Lindauer.

Krickau, Carl. 1877. *Der Accusativ mit dem Infinitiv in der englischen Sprache, besonders im Zeitalter der Elisabeth.* PhD Dissertation, University of Göttingen.

Kristmannsson, Gauti. 2019. Germanic tradition. In: Gambier, Yves and Ubaldo Stecconi (eds), *A World Atlas of Translation*, 355–374. Amsterdam: John Benjamins.

Kroch, Anthony. 1989. Reflexes of grammar in patterns of language change. *Language Variation and Change* 1 (3): 199–244.

Kroch, Anthony. 1994. Morphosyntactic variation. In: Beals, Kathryn (ed.), *Papers from the 30th Regional Meeting, Chicago Linguistic Society*, 180–201. Chicago: Chicago Linguistic Society.

Kroch, Anthony. 2001. Syntactic change. In: Baltin, Mark and Chris Collins (eds), *The Handbook of Contemporary Syntactic Theory*, 699–729. Oxford: Blackwell.

Kroch, Anthony and Ann Taylor. 1997. The syntax of verb movement in Middle English: Dialect variation and language contact. In: Kemenade, Ans van and Nigel Vincent (eds), *Parameters of Morphosyntactic Change*, 297–325. Cambridge: Cambridge University Press.

Kroch, Anthony and Ann Taylor. 2000. *The Penn-Helsinki Parsed Corpus of Middle English (PPCME2).* Department of Linguistics, University of Pennsylvania. CD-ROM, second edition, release 4 (http://www.ling.upenn.edu/ppche-release-2016/PPCME2-RELEASE-4).

Kroch, Anthony, Beatrice Santorini and Lauren Delfs. 2004. *The Penn-Helsinki Parsed Corpus of Early Modern English (PPCEME).* Department of Linguistics, University of Pennsylvania. CD-ROM, first edition, release 3 (http://www.ling.upenn.edu/ppche -release-2016/PPCEME-RELEASE-3).

Kroch, Anthony, Beatrice Santorini and Ariel Diertani. 2016. *The Penn Parsed Corpus of Modern British English (PPCMBE2).* Department of Linguistics, University of Pennsylvania. CD-ROM, second edition, release 1 (http://www.ling.upenn.edu/ppche-release-2016/PPCMBE2-RELEASE-1).

Kroch, Anthony, Ann Taylor and Donald Ringe. 2000. The Middle English verb-second constraint: A case study in language contact and language change. In: Herring, Susan C., Pieter van Reenen and Lene Schøsler, *Textual Parameters in Older Languages*, 353–391. Amsterdam: John Benjamins.

Kujamäki, Pekka. 2001. Finnish comet in German skies: Translation, retranslation and norms. *Target* 13 (1): 45–70.

Kulikov, Leonid. 1998. Passive, anticausative and classification of verbs: The case of Vedic. In: Kulikov, Leonid and Heinz Vater (eds), *Typology of Verbal Categories: Papers Presented to Vladimir Nedjalkov on the Occasion of his 70th Birthday*, 139–154. Tübingen: Max Niemeyer.

Kulikov, Leonid. 2003. The labile syntactic type in a diachronic perspective: The case of Vedic. *SKY Journal of Linguistics* 16: 93–112.

Kulikov, Leonid. 2011a. Passive to anticausative through impersonalization: The case of Vedic. In: Malchukov, Andrej and Anna Siewierska (eds), *Indo-European Impersonal Constructions: A Cross-linguistic Perspective*, 229–254. Amsterdam: John Benjamins.

Kulikov, Leonid. 2011b. *Voice Typology*. In: Song, Jae Jung (ed.), *The Oxford Handbook of Linguistic Typology*, 368–398. Oxford: Oxford University Press.

Kulikov, Leonid and Nikolaos Lavidas. 2013. Reconstructing passive and voice in Proto-Indo-European. *Journal of Historical Linguistics* 3 (1): 98–121.

Kumaniecki, Kazimierz F. (ed.). 1969. *M. Tulli Ciceronis Scripta Quae Manserunt Omnia. Fasc. 3. De Oratore*. Leipzig: Teubner.

Kurz, Ingrid. 1985. The rock tombs of the princes of elephantine: Earliest references to interpretation in Pharaonic Egypt. *Babel* 31 (4): 213–218.

Kytö, Merja. 1991. *Variation and Diachrony, with Early American English in Focus: Studies on can/may and shall/will*. Frankfurt: Peter Lang.

Kytö, Merja and Matti Rissanen. 1993. "By and by enters [this] my artificiall foole ... who, when Jack beheld, sodainely he flew at him": Searching for syntactic constructions in the Helsinki Corpus. In: Rissanen, Matti, Merja Kytö and Minna Palander-Collin (eds), *Early English in the Computer Age. Explorations through the Helsinki Corpus*, 253–266. Berlin, New York: Mouton de Gruyter.

Labov, William. 1994. *Principles of Linguistic Change. Volume I: Internal Factors*. Oxford: Blackwell.

Lakoff, Robin. 1972. Contextual change and historical change: The translator as time machine. In: Saltarelli, Mario and Dieter Wanner (eds), *Diachronic Studies in Romance Linguistics: Papers Presented at the Conference on Diachronic Romance Linguistics*, 119–134. The Hague: Mouton.

Lampe, G.W.H. (ed.). 1969. *The Cambridge History of the Bible. Vol. II: The West from the Fathers to the Reformation*. Cambridge: Cambridge University Press.

Lanstyák, István. 2003. Code switching and translation. Zooming in on the realities of the Hungarian language in Slovakia [in Hungarian]. *Irodalmi Szemle* 46 (7): 77–94.

REFERENCES

351

Lanstyák, István and Pál Heltai. 2012. Universals in language contact and translation. *Across Languages and Cultures* 13 (1): 99–121.

Lasnik, Howard and Nicholas Sobin. 2000. The who/whom puzzle: On the preservation of an archaic feature. *Natural Language and Linguistic Theory* 18 (2): 343–371.

Lass, Roger. 1997. *Historical Linguistics and Language Change*. Cambridge: Cambridge University Press.

Lass, Roger 1999. Phonology and Morphology. In: Lass, Roger (ed.), *The Cambridge History of the English Language*, 56–186. Cambridge: Cambridge University Press.

Lathrop, Henry Burrowes. 1933. *Translations from the Classics into English from Caxton to Chapman, 1477–1620*. Madison: University of Wisconsin.

Lauxtermann, Marc D. 2020. The *Grammatical Introduction* by Nikolaos Sofianos: Manuscripts, date, and linguistic models. *Byzantine and Modern Greek Studies* 44 (1): 124–136.

Lavidas Nikolaos. 2004. Causative alternations: Synchronic and diachronic tendencies [In Greek]. *Studies in Greek Linguistics* 24: 369–381.

Lavidas Nikolaos 2007. Mechanisms for the emergence of new transitivity alternations in the diachrony of Greek [In Greek]. *Studies in Greek Linguistics* 27: 210–223.

Lavidas, Nikolaos. 2009. *Transitivity Alternations in Diachrony. Changes in Argument Structure and Voice Morphology*. Newcastle upon Tyne: Cambridge Scholars Publishing.

Lavidas, Nikolaos. 2012. Null vs. cognate objects and language contact: Evidence from Hellenistic Greek. *Acta Linguistica Hafniensia* 44 (2): 142–168.

Lavidas Nikolaos. 2014. The Greek Septuagint and language change at the syntax-semantics interface: From null to 'pleonastic' object pronouns. In: Jäger, Agnes, Chiara Gianollo and Doris Penka (eds), *Language Change at the Syntax-Semantics Interface*, 153–182. Berlin: de Gruyter Mouton.

Lavidas, Nikolaos. 2018a. Cognate noun constructions in Early Modern English. The case of Tyndale's New Testament. In: Cuyckens, Hubert, Hendrik De Smet, Liesbet Heyvaert and Charlotte Maekelberghe (eds), *Explorations in English Historical Syntax*, 51–76. Amsterdam, Philadelphia: John Benjamins.

Lavidas, Nikolaos. 2018b. Reorganising voice in the history of Greek. Split complexity and prescriptivism. In: Dammel, Antje, Matthias Eitelmann and Mirjam Schmuck (eds), *Reorganising Grammatical Variation: Diachronic Studies in the Retention, Redistribution and Refunctionalisation of Linguistic Variants*, 175–208. Amsterdam, Philadelphia: John Benjamins.

Lavidas Nikolaos. 2019a. Word order and closest-conjunct agreement in the Greek Septuagint: On the position of a biblical translation in the diachrony of a syntactic correlation. *Questions and Answers in Linguistics* 5 (2): 37–90.

Lavidas, Nikolaos. 2019b. Syntactic borrowability in a Sprachbund setting: Object clitics and definite articles in the West Thracian Greek (Evros) dialect. In: Tzitzilis, Christos and Georgios Papanastassiou (eds), *Language Contact in the Balkans and Asia Minor*, Volume 1, 189–208. Thessaloniki: Institute of Modern Greek Studies.

Lavidas, Nikolaos. 2021. History of translation in the West. A diachronic linguistic perspective. In: Sidiropoulou, Maria (ed.), *Aspects of Meaning-Making through Translation*, 252–298. Athens: Patakis.

Lavidas, Nikolaos and Alexander Bergs (eds). 2020a. Special Issue: Historical Language Contact in English. *Linguistics Vanguard* 6 (2).

Lavidas, Nikolaos and Alexander Bergs. 2020b. On historical language contact in English and its types: State of the art and new directions. *Linguistics Vanguard* 6 (2). Online at https://doi.org/10.1515/lingvan-2020-0010.

Lavidas, Nikolaos and Dag Trygve Truslew Haug. 2020. Postclassical Greek and treebanks for a diachronic analysis. In: Rafiyenko, Dariya and Ilja A. Seržant (eds), *Postclassical Greek. Contemporary Approaches to Philology and Linguistics*, 163–202. Berlin: De Gruyter Mouton.

Lavidas, Nikolaos and Ianthi Maria Tsimpli. 2019. Object omission in contact: Object clitics and definite articles in the West Thracian Greek (Evros) dialect. *Journal of Language Contact* 12 (1): 141–190.

Lavidas, Nikolaos, Georgia Fotiadou and Ianthi Maria Tsimpli. 2012. Active vs. nonactive voice in the Greek diachrony: Real or apparent optionality in the use of voice morphology? In: Gavriilidou, Zoe, Angeliki Efthymiou, Evangelia Thomadaki and Penelope Kambakis-Vougiouklis (eds), *Selected Papers of the 10th International Conference of Greek Linguistics* (electronic publication and limited in-print publication), 390–400. Online at http://www.icgl.gr/files/English/31.Lavidas_et_al_10ICGL_pp.390-400.pdf.

Laviosa, Sara. 1998. The corpus-based approach: A new paradigm in translation studies. *Meta* 43 (4): 474–479.

Laviosa, Sara. 2010. Corpus-based translation studies: 15 years on. *SYNAPS* 24: 3–12.

Lawler, Traugott. 1983. On the properties of John Trevisa's major translations. *Viator* 14: 267–288.

Ledgeway, Adam. 2015. *From Latin to Romance. Morphosyntactic Typology and Change*. Revised 2nd edition. Oxford: Oxford University Press.

Lee, John A.L. 2013. The Atticist grammarians. In: Porter, Stanley E. and Andrew W. Pitts (eds), *The Language of the New Testament. Context, History and Development*, 283–308. Leiden: Brill.

Lefevere, André. 2016. *Translation, Rewriting, and the Manipulation of Literary Fame*. London: Routledge.

Lehiste, Ilse. 1979. Translation from Russian as a source of syntactic change in contemporary Estonian. *CLS: The Elements: A Parasession on Linguistic Units and Levels*, 413–419.

Lehiste, Ilse. 1999. Successive translations as source of evidence for linguistic change. *International Journal of the Sociology of Language* 139 (1): 39–48.

Lendinara, Patrizia. 2013. The world of Anglo-Saxon learning. In: Godden, Malcolm (ed.), *The Cambridge Companion to Old English Literature*, 295–312. Cambridge: Cambridge University Press.

Lendinara, Patrizia. 2014. Glossing the Old Frisian *Psalter*: Pragmatics and competence. *Amsterdamer Beiträge zur älteren Germanistik* 73 (1): 301–327.

Letuchiy, Alexander. 2010. Lability and spontaneity. In: García, Marco and Patrick Brandt (eds), *Transitivity: Form, Function, Acquisition, and Processing*, 237–256. Amsterdam, Philadelphia: John Benjamins.

Levin, Beth. 1993. *English Verb Classes and Alternations: A Preliminary Investigation.* Chicago: University of Chicago Press.

Levin, Beth and Malka Rappaport. 1986. The formation of adjectival passives. *Linguistic Inquiry* 17: 623–661.

Levin, Beth and Malka Rappaport Hovav. 1995. *Unaccusativity.* Cambridge, MA: MIT Press.

Levin, Beth and Malka Rappaport Hovav. 2005. *Argument Realization.* Cambridge: Cambridge University Press.

Levin, Beth and Malka Rappaport Hovav. 2019. Lexicalization patterns. In: Truswell, Robert (ed.), *Oxford Handbook of Event Structure*, 395–425. Oxford: Oxford University Press.

Li, Xingzhong. 2008. Metrical evidence: Did Chaucer translate the *Romaunt of the Rose?* In: Fitzmaurice, Susan M. and Donka Minkova (eds), *Studies in the History of the English Language IV*, 155–179. Berlin: Mouton de Gruyter.

Lianeri, Alexandra. 2014. A regime of untranslatables: Temporalities of translation and conceptual history. *History and Theory* 53 (4): 473–497.

Lianeri, Alexandra and Vanda Zajko. 2008. *Translation and the Classic: Identity as Change in the History of Culture.* Oxford: Oxford University Press.

Liceras, Juana M. 2014. The multiple grammars theory and the nature of L2 grammars. *Second Language Research* 30 (1): 47–54.

Lightfoot, David. 1981. Explaining syntactic change. In: Hornstein, Norbert and David Lightfoot (eds), *Explanation in Linguistics*, 209–240. London: Longman.

Lightfoot, David. 1991. *How to Set Parameters: Arguments from Language Change.* Cambridge, MA: MIT Press.

Lightfoot, David. 1999. *The Development of Language: Acquisition, Change, and Evolution.* Oxford: Wiley-Blackwell.

Linn, Andrew. 2013. Vernaculars and the idea of a standard language. In: Allan, Keith (ed.), *The Oxford Handbook of the History of Linguistics*, 359–374. Oxford: Oxford University Press.

Livingston, Michael (ed.). 2011. *The Middle English Metrical Paraphrase of the Old Testament.* Kalamazoo, MI: Medieval Institute Publications.

Longobardi, Giuseppe. 2001. Formal syntax, diachronic minimalism, and etymology: The history of French *chez. Linguistic Inquiry* 32 (2): 275–302.

Lopes, Alexandra. 2006. Landscaping emotion(s): Translating *Harriet Beecher Stowe* in Portugal. In: Wolf, Michaela (ed.), *Übersetzen—Translating—Traduire: Towards a "Social Turn"*, 199–208. Berlin, Vienna: LIT.

Los, Bettelou. 2005. *The Rise of the to-Infinitive*. Oxford: Oxford University Press.

Lowth, Robert. 1979 [1775]. *A Short Introduction to English Grammar*. Reprinted. New York: Delmar (1775, London).

Luraghi, Silvia. 2013. Contact through translation. In: Giannakis, Georgios K. (ed.), *Encyclopedia of Ancient Greek Language and Linguistics*. Online at http://dx.doi.org/ 10.1163/2214-448X_eagll_COM_00000079. First published online: 2013 [Last access: 30 September 2020].

Luraghi, Silvia and Pierluigi Cuzzolin. 2007. Mediating culture through language. In: Ramat, Paolo and Elisa Roma (eds), *Europe and the Mediterranean as Linguistic Areas*, 133–158. Amsterdam, Philadelphia: John Benjamins.

Lyons, John. 1991. *Natural Language and Universal Grammar. Volume 1: Essays in Linguistic Theory*. Cambridge: Cambridge University Press.

Mackridge, Peter. 2009. A language in the image of the nation: Modern Greek and some parallel cases. In: Beaton, Roderick and David Ricks (eds), *The Making of Modern Greece: Nationalism, Romanticism, and the Uses of the Past (1797–1896)*, 177–188. Farnham: Ashgate.

Mackridge, Peter. 2010a. Korais and the Greek language question. In: Kitromilides, Paschalis M. (ed.), *Adamantios Korais and the European Enlightenment*, 127–150. Oxford: Voltaire Foundation.

Mackridge, Peter. 2010b. Modern Greek. In: Bakker, Egbert J. (ed.), *A Companion to the Ancient Greek Language*, 564–587. Oxford: Wiley-Blackwell.

Mair, Christian and Geoffrey Leech. 2006. Current changes in English syntax. In: Aarts, Bas and April McMahon (eds), *The Handbook of English Linguistics*, 318–342. Oxford: Blackwell.

Maloney, Elliott C. 1981. *Semitic Interference in Marcan Syntax*. Chico, California. Scholars Press.

Manousakas, Manousos. 1986. New findings on the first translation of the New Testament in the vernacular language by Maximos Kallioupolitis [In Greek]. *Medieval and Modern Greek* 2: 7–70.

Marle, Jaap Van. 1997. Dialect versus standard language: Nature versus culture. In: Cheshire, Jenny and Dieter Stein (eds), *Taming the Vernacular. From Dialect to Written Standard Language*, 13–34. London, New York: Longman.

Marlowe, Michael D. 2001. *Bible research. Internet resources for students of Scripture*. Online at http://www.bible-researcher.com/newcome.html [Last access: July 20, 2020].

Maronitis, Dimitris N. 1997. Strong and weak languages in the European Union: Aspects of linguistic hegemonism. *Philologos* 88: 163–168.

Maronitis, Dimitris N. 2001. Issues and problems of intralinguistic translation in education [In Greek]. *Philologiki* 74: 3–7.

Maronitis, Dimitris N. 2008. Intralingual translation: Genuine and false dilemmas. In: Lianeri, Alexandra and Vanda Zajko (eds), *Translation and the Classic: Identity as Change in the History of Culture*, 367–387. Oxford: Oxford University Press.

Marsden, Richard (ed.). 2008. *The Old English Heptateuch and Ælfric's Libellus de veteri testamento et novo. Vol. 1: Introduction and Text*. Oxford: Oxford University Press.

Marsden, Richard. 2012. The Bible in English. In: Marsden, Richard and E. Ann Matter (eds), *The New Cambridge History of the Bible. Vol. 2, From 600 to 1450*, 217–238. Cambridge: Cambridge University Press.

Marsden, Richard and E. Ann Matter. 2012. *The New Cambridge History of the Bible: Volume 2, From 600 to 1450*. Cambridge: Cambridge University Press.

Matras, Yaron. 2009. *Language Contact*. Cambridge: Cambridge University Press.

Matras, Yaron. 2010. Contact, convergence, and typology. In: Hickey, Raymond (ed.), *The Handbook of Language Contact*, 66–85. Oxford: Blackwell.

Matthiessen, Francis Otto 1931. *Translation: An Elizabethan Art*. Cambridge, MA: Harvard University Press.

Mayfield, Elijah and Carolyn Penstein Rosé. 2010. Using feature construction to avoid large feature spaces in text classification. *Proceedings of the 12th Annual Conference on Genetic and Evolutionary Computation*, 1299–1306.

Mayfield, Elijah and Carolyn Penstein Rosé. 2013. LightSIDE: Open source machine learning for text accessible to non-experts. In: Shermis, Mark D. and Jill Burstein (eds), *Handbook of Automated Essay Evaluation*, 124–135. London, New York: Routledge.

McArthur, Tom. 1992. *The Oxford Companion to the English Language*. Oxford: Oxford University Press.

McGrath, Alister. 2001. *In the Beginning: The Story of the King James Bible and How it changed a Nation, a Language, and a Culture*. New York: Doubleday.

McIntosh, Angus. 1963. A new approach to Middle English dialectology. *English Studies* 44: 1–11.

McLaughlin, Mairi. 2011. Tradurre/ Tradire: Translation as a cause of linguistic change from manuscripts to the digital age. *UC Berkeley, The University Library New Faculty Lecture Series*, 4–27. Berkeley: The Doe Library. Online at http://escholarship.org/uc/item/4rc5w95r#page-1.

Metzger, Bruce M. 2001. *The Bible in Translation: Ancient and English Versions*. Grand Rapids, Michigan: Baker Academic.

Mikros, George K. 2006. Authorship attribution in Modern Greek newswire corpora. In: Uzuner, Özlem, Shlomo Argamon and Jussi Karlgren (eds), *Proceedings of the SIGIR 2006 International Workshop on Directions in Computational Analysis of Stylistics in Text Retrieval*, 43–47. Seattle, Washington: ACM.

Mikros, George K. 2007. Stylometric experiments in Modern Greek: Investigating authorship in homogeneous newswire texts. In: Grzybek, Peter and Reinhard Köhler (eds), *Exact Methods in the Study of Language and Text*, 445–456. Berlin, New York: Mouton de Gruyter.

Miller, D. Gary. 2002. *Nonfinite Structures in Theory and Change*. Oxford: Oxford University Press.

Miller, D. Gary. 2011. *Language Change and Linguistic Theory*. Oxford: Oxford University Press.

Miller, D. Gary. 2012. *External Influences on English: From its Beginnings to the Renaissance*. Oxford: Oxford University Press.

Minkova, Donka and Robert Stockwell. 2009. *English Words: History and Structure*. 2nd edition. Cambridge: Cambridge University Press.

Missiou, Vassiliki. 2014. Translation of poetry: Creating or copying? An outline of views of Greek poets-translators. *Intercultural Translation Intersemiotic* 3 (1). Online at http://ejournals.lib.auth.gr/iti/article/viewFile/4255/4339

Mitchell, Bruce. 1985. *Old English Syntax: Concord, the Parts of Speech, and the Sentence*. Oxford: Oxford University Press.

Montanari, Franco. 1991. Tradurre dal greco in greco. In: Nicosia, Salvatore (ed.), *La traduzione dei testi classici. Teoria prassi storia*, 221–236. Napoli: D'Auria.

Montrul, Silvina A. 1998. The L2 acquisition of dative experiencer subjects. *Second Language Research* 14 (1): 27–61.

Morey, James H. 2000. *Book and Verse: A Guide to Middle English Biblical Literature*. Urbana, Chicago: University of Illinois Press.

Möhlig, Ruth and Monika Klages. 2002. Detransitivization in the history of English from a semantic perspective. In: Fanego, Teresa, Maria José López-Couso and Javier Perez-Guerra (eds), *English Historical Syntax and Morphology*, 231–254. Amsterdam: John Benjamins.

Mohrmann, Christine. 1959. *Liturgical Latin: Its Origins and Character. Three Lectures*. London: Burns & Oates.

Mohrmann, Christine. 1961–1977. *Études sur le latin des chrétiens, 4 vols*. Roma: Edizioni di Storia e Letteratura.

Mossé, Fernand. 1938. *Histoire de la forme périphrastique être + participe présent en Germanique*. Vol. 1. Paris: Klincksieck.

Mossop, Brian. 2016. 'Intralingual translation': A desirable concept? *Across Languages and Cultures* 17 (1): 1–24.

Mourigh, Khalid. 2016. *A Grammar of Ghomara Berber*. Köln: Rüdiger Köppe.

Muchnik, Malka. 2003. Changes in word order in two Hebrew translations of an Ibsen Play. *Target* 15 (2): 295–316.

Muraoka, Takamitsu. 2016. Limitations of Greek in representing Hebrew. In: Bons, Eberhard and Jan Joosten (eds), *Handbuch zur Septuaginta/ Handbook of the Septuagint*.

Volume 3. Die Sprache der Septuaginta/ The Language of the Septuagint, 109–118. Gütersloh: Gütersloher Verlagshaus.

Musacchio, Maria Teresa. 2018. The influence of English on Italian: The case of translations of economics articles. In: Anderman, Gunilla and Margaret Rogers (eds), *In and Out of English: For Better, For Worse?*, 71–96. Clevedon: Multilingual Matters.

Mustanoja, Tauno F. 1960. *A Middle English Syntax*. Helsinki: Société Néophilologique.

Muysken, Pieter. 2010. Scenarios for language contact. In: Hickey, Raymond (ed.), *The Handbook of Language Contact*, 265–281. New York: Blackwell Publishing.

Muysken, Pieter. 2014. Wake up, it is 2013! Commentary on Luiz Amaral and Tom Roeper's article. *Second Language Research* 30 (1): 55–58.

Nau, Nicole. 1995. *Möglichkeiten und Mechanismen Kontaktbewegten Sprachwandels: unter besonderer Berücksichtigung des Finnischen*. Munich, Newcastle: Lincom Europa.

Naudé, Jacobus A. 2009. The book of Aristeas and modern translations of the Septuagint. *Acta Patristica et Byzantina* 20 (1): 259–274.

Nehls, Dietrich. 1974. *Synchron-diachrone Untersuchungen zur Expanded Form im Englischen: Eine struktural-funktionale Analyse*. Munich: Max Hueber.

Ness, Lynne and Caroline Duncan-Rose. 1982. A syntactic correlate of style switching in the *Canterbury Tales*. In: Maher, J. Peter, Allan R. Bomhard and E.F. Konrad Koerner (eds), *Papers from the 3rd International Conference on Historical Linguistics*, 293–322. Amsterdam: John Benjamins.

Nevalainen, Terttu. 1999. Early Modern English Lexis and Semantics. In: Lass, Peter (ed.), *The Cambridge History of the English Language* 3: 1476–776, 332–458. Cambridge: Cambridge University Press.

Nevalainen, Terttu. 2006. *Introduction to Early Modern English*. Edinburgh: Edinburgh University Press.

Nevalainen, Terttu. 2008. Mapping change in Tudor English. In: Mugglestone, Lynda (ed.), *The Oxford History of English*, 178–211. Oxford: Oxford University Press.

Newman, Francis William. 1853. *The Odes of Horace: Translated into unrhymed Metres, with Introduction and Notes*. London: Walton and Maberly.

Newman, Francis William. 1856. *The Iliad of Homer faithfully Translated into unrhymed English Metre*. London: Walton and Maberly.

Newton, Brian. 1964. An Arabic-Greek dialect. *Word* [*Papers in Memory of George C. Pappageotes*] 20 (3): 43–52.

Ng, Su Fang. 2001. Translation, interpretation, and heresy: The Wycliffite Bible, Tyndale's Bible, and the contested origin. *Studies in Philology* 98 (3): 315–338.

Nichols, Johanna. 2017. Causativization as non-diversity: Linguistic and non-linguistic causes. *Presented at the 50th annual meeting of the Societas Linguistica Europaea*, Zürich, 10–13 September 2017.

Nichols, Johanna. 2018. Non-linguistic conditions for causativization as a linguistic attractor. *Frontiers in Psychology* 8 (2356). Online at https://doi.org/10.3389/fpsyg.2017.02356.

Nichols, Johanna, David A. Peterson and Jonathan Barnes. 2004. Transitivizing and detransitivizing languages. *Linguistic Typology* 8 (2): 149–211.

Nickel, Gerhard. 1966. *Die Expanded Form in Altenglischen: Vorkommen, Funktion und Herkunft der Umschreibung beon/wesan+ Partizip Präsens*. Neumünster: Karl Wachholtz.

Nida, Eugene A. 1964. *Toward a Science of Translating: With Special Reference to Principles and Procedures involved in Bible Translating*. Leiden: Brill.

Niyogi, Partha and Robert C. Berwick. 1997. Evolutionary consequences of language learning. *Linguistics and Philosophy* 20 (6): 697–719.

Norden, Eduard. 1958. *Die Antike Kunstprosa, II*. Stuttgart: Teubner.

Norton, David. 1985. The Bible as a reviver of words: The evidence of Anthony Purver, a mid-eighteenth-century critic of the English of the King James Bible. *Neuphilologische Mitteilungen* 86 (4): 515–533.

Norton, David. 1993. *A History of the Bible as Literature*. Cambridge: Cambridge University Press.

Noss, Philip A. 2007. A history of Bible translation: Introduction and overview. In: Noss, Philip A. (ed.), *A History of Bible Translation*, 1–25. Rome: Edizioni de storia e letteratura.

Nunnally, Thomas E. 1992. Man's Son/ Son of Man: Translation, textual conditioning, and the history of the English genitive. In: Rissanen, Matti (ed.), *History of Englishes: New Methods and Interpretations in Historical Linguistics*, 359–371. Berlin, Boston: de Gruyter.

Oikonomou, Georgios N. and Georgios K. Angelinara. 1979. *Bibliography of Metrical Modern Greek Translations of Ancient Greek Poetry* [In Greek]. Athens: Saripolos.

Oittinen, Ritta. 2002. *Translating for Children*. London: Routledge.

Olofsson, Staffan. 1988. The translation of Jer 2,18 in the Septuagint: Methodical, linguistic and theological aspects. *Scandinavian Journal of the Old Testament* 2 (2): 169–200.

Olohan, Maeve. 2014. History of science and history of translation: Disciplinary commensurability? *The Translator* 20 (1): 9–25.

Operstein, Natalie. 2015. Contact-genetic Linguistics: Toward a contact-based theory of language change. *Language Sciences* 48: 1–15.

Pace, Sharon. 1984. The stratigraphy of the text of Daniel and the question of theological "Tendenz" in the Old Greek. *Bulletin of the International Organization for Septuagint and Cognate Studies* 17: 15–35.

Packer, James I. (ed.). 2001. *The Holy Bible, English Standard Version. Containing the Old and New Testaments*. Wheaton, Illinois: Crossway.

Pade, Marianne. 2013. Renaissance, translation. In: Giannakis, Georgios K. (ed.), *Encyclopedia of Ancient Greek Language and Linguistics*. Online at http://dx.doi.org/

REFERENCES

10.1163/2214-448X_eagll_COM_00000398. First published online: 2013 [Last access: 30 September 2020].

Paget, James Carleton and Joachim Schaper. 2013. *The New Cambridge History of the Bible: From the Beginnings to 600*. Cambridge: Cambridge University Press.

Pahta, Päivi, Janne Skaffari and Laura Wright (eds). 2018. *Multilingual Practices in Language History: English and Beyond*. Berlin: de Gruyter.

Paloposki, Outi and Kaisa Koskinen. 2004. A thousand and one translations: Revisiting retranslation. In: Hansen, Gyde, Kirsten Malmkjær and Daniel Gile (eds), *Claims, Changes and Challenges in Translation Studies*, 27–38. Amsterdam, Philadelphia: John Benjamins.

Paloposki, Outi and Kaisa Koskinen. 2010. Reprocessing texts. The fine line between retranslating and revising. *Across Languages and Cultures* 11 (1): 29–49.

Panagiotidou, Theodora. 2021. *Argument Structures in Diachrony: Contact Effects of Translation*. PhD Dissertation, Aristotle University of Thessaloniki. Supervisor: Dr Nikolaos Lavidas.

Panagopoulos, Ioannis. 1995. *Introduction to the New Testament* [In Greek]. Athens: Akritas.

Pantelia, Maria C. (ed.). Thesaurus Linguae Graecae Digital Library. University of California, Irvine. Online at http://www.tlg.uci.edu. [Last access: 2 November 2019].

Paradis, Michel. 1998. Language and communication in multilinguals. In: Stemmer, Bridgitte and Harry A. Whitaker (eds), *Handbook of Neurolinguistics*, 417–430. San Diego, CA: Academic Press.

Paradis, Michel. 2004. *A Neurolinguistic Theory of Bilingualism*. Amsterdam: John Benjamins.

Parsons, Mikeal C. and D. Thomas Hanks Jr. 2001. When the salt lost its savour: A brief history of Matthew 5.13/ Mark 9.50/ Luke 14.34 in English translation. *The Bible Translator* 52 (3): 320–326.

Partridge, Astley C. 1973. *English Biblical Translation*. London: André Deutsch.

Pearsall, Derek. 1977a. *Old English and Middle English Poetry*. London: Routledge.

Pearsall, Derek. 1977b. The 'Troilus' frontispiece and Chaucer's audience. *The Yearbook of English Studies* 7: 68–74.

Pietersma, Albert. 2002. A new paradigm for addressing old questions: The relevance of the interlinear model for the study of the Septuagint. In: Cook, Johann (ed.), *Bible and Computer: The Stellenbosch AIBI-6 Conference: Proceedings of the Association Internationale Bible et Informatique "From Alpha to Byte"*, 337–364. Leiden, Boston: Brill.

Pintzuk, Susan. 1991. *Phrase Structures in Competition: Variation and Change in Old English Word Order*. PhD Dissertation, University of Pennsylvania.

Pintzuk, Susan. 1995. Variation and change in Old English clause structure. *Language Variation and Change* 7 (2): 229–260.

Pintzuk, Susan. 2002. Morphological case and word order in Old English. *Language Sciences* 24 (3–4): 381–395.

Pintzuk, Susan. 2005. Arguments against a universal base: Evidence from Old English. *English Language and Linguistics* 9 (1): 115–138.

Pintzuk, Susan and Leendert Plug. 2002. *The York-Helsinki Parsed Corpus of Old English Poetry*. Department of Linguistics, University of York. Oxford Text Archive, first edition (http://www-users.york.ac.uk/~lang18/pcorpus.html).

Pintzuk, Susan and Ann Taylor. 2006. The loss of OV order in the history of English. In: Kemenade, Ans van and Bettelou Los (eds), *The Handbook of the History of English*, 249–278. Oxford: Blackwell.

Plater, William E. and Henry J. White. 1926. *A Grammar of the Vulgate: Being an Introduction to the Study of the Latinity of the Vulgate Bible*. Oxford: Clarendon Press.

Politis, Linos. 1973. *A History of Modern Greek Literature*. Oxford: Oxford University Press.

Polkas, Lambros. 2006. Translation in Greek antiquity [In Greek]. Online at http//www .komvos.edu.gr/endoglwssiki/historiko/episkopisi/klassika/episk_1_1.htm [Last access: 30 September 2020].

Poplack, Shana and Stephen Levey. 2010. Contact-induced grammatical change. A cautionary tale. In: Auer, Peter and Jurgen Erich Schmidt (eds), *Language and Space: An International Handbook of Linguistic Variation. Volume 1: Theories and Methods*, 391–418. Berlin, New York: Mouton de Gruyter.

Porter, Stanley E. 1989. *Verbal Aspect in the Greek of the New Testament*. New York: Peter Lang.

Porter, Stanley E. 2000. Dialect and register in the Greek of the New Testament: Theory. In: Carroll R., M. Daniel and Mark Daniel (ed.), *Rethinking Contexts, Rereading Texts: Contributions from the Social Sciences to Biblical Interpretation*, 190–208. Sheffield: Sheffield Academic Press.

Porter, Stanley E. 2013a. New Testament. In: Giannakis, Georgios K. (ed.), *Encyclopedia of Ancient Greek Language and Linguistics*. Online at http://dx.doi.org/10.1163/2214 -448X_eagll_COM_00000248. First published online: 2013 [Last access: 30 September 2020].

Porter, Stanley E. 2013b. Septuagint. In: Giannakis, Georgios K. (ed.), *Encyclopedia of Ancient Greek Language and Linguistics*. Online at http://dx.doi.org/10.1163/2214 -448X_eagll_COM_000029. First published online: 2013 [Last access: 30 September 2020].

Porter, Stanley E. 2013c. *How we got the New Testament: Text, Transmission, Translation*. Grand Rapids, MI: Baker Academic.

Porter, Stanley E. 2016a. Systemic functional linguistics and the Greek language: The need for further modeling. In: Porter, Stanley E., Gregory P. Fewster and Christopher D. Land (eds), *Modeling Biblical Language: Selected Papers from the McMaster Divinity College Linguistics Circle*, 7–74. Leiden: Brill.

REFERENCES

361

Porter, Stanley E. 2016b. History of scholarship on the language of the Septuagint. In: Bons, Eberhard and Jan Joosten (eds), *Handbuch zur Septuaginta/ Handbook of the Septuagint. Volume 3. Die Sprache der Septuaginta/ The Language of the Septuagint*, 15–38. Gütersloh: Gütersloher Verlagshaus.

Porter, Stanley E. and Donald A. Carson (eds). 2015. *Biblical Greek Language and Linguistics: Open Questions in Current Research*. London: Bloomsbury.

Porter, Stanley E. and Andrew W. Pitts. 2008. New Testament Greek language and linguistics in recent research. *Currents in Biblical Research* 6 (2): 214–255.

Porter, Stanley E., Christopher D. Land and Francis G.H. Pang (eds). 2019. *Linguistics and the Bible: Retrospects and Prospects*. Eugene, Oregon: Pickwick.

Price, David and Charles C. Ryrie. 2004. *Let it go among our People: An Illustrated History of the English Bible from John Wyclif to the King James Version*. Cambridge: The Lutterworth Press.

Psaltes, Stamatios B. 1913. *Grammatik der byzantinischen Chroniken*. Göttingen: Vandenhoeck and Ruprecht.

Pulsiano, Phillip. 1995. The twelve-spoked wheel of the Summoner's tale. *The Chaucer Review* 29: 382–389.

Rahlfs, Alfred. 1971 [1935]. *Septuaginta*, Vol. 1. 9th ed. Stuttgart: Württemberg Bible Society.

Rappaport, Malka, Mary Laughren and Beth Levin. 1993. Levels of lexical representation. In: Pustejovsky, James (ed.), *Semantics and the Lexicon*, 37–54. Dodrecht: Springer.

Remediaki, Ioanna. 2013. Intralingual translation into Modern Greek. In: Giannakis, Georgios K. (ed.), *Encyclopedia of Ancient Greek Language and Linguistics*. Online at http://dx.doi.org/10.1163/2214-448X_eagll_COM_00000193. First published online: 2013 [Last access: 30 September 2020].

Riches, John (ed.). 2015. *The New Cambridge History of the Bible: Volume 4, From 1750 to the Present*. Cambridge: Cambridge University Press.

Rigolio, Alberto. 2016. Syriac translations of Plutarch, Lucian and Themistius: A gnomic format for an instructional purpose? In: Gemeinhardt, Peter, Lieve van Hoof and Peter van Nuffelen (eds), *Education and Religion in Late Antique Christianity: Reflections, Social Contexts, and Genres*, 85–97. London: Routledge.

Rissanen, Matti. 1985. Periphrastic *do* in affirmative statements in early American English. *Journal of English Linguistics* 18 (2): 163–183.

Rissanen, Matti. 1997. In search of *happiness: felicitas and beatitudo* in Early English Boethius translations. *Anglica Posnaniensia* 31: 237–248.

Robbeets, Martine and Hubert Cuyckens (eds). 2013. *Shared Grammaticalization: With Special Focus on the Transeurasian Languages*. Amsterdam: John Benjamins.

Roberts, Ian. 2007. *Diachronic Syntax*. Oxford: Oxford University Press.

Robertson, David and Antonella Sorace. 1999. Losing the V2 constraint. In: Klein,

Elaine C. and Gita Martohardjono (eds), *The Development of Second Language Grammars: A Generative Approach*, 317–361. Amsterdam: John Benjamins.

Rochette, Bruno. 2013. Ancient bidialectalism and bilingualism. In: Giannakis, Georgios K. (ed.), *Encyclopedia of Ancient Greek Language and Linguistics*. Online at http://dx.doi.org/10.1163/2214-448X_eagll_COM_00000023. First published online: 2013 [Last access: 30 September 2020].

Rodríguez-Puente, Paula. 2020. Register variation in word-formation processes: The development of *-ity* and *-ness* in Early Modern English. *IJES* 20 (2): 145–167.

Roeper, Thomas W. 1999. Universal bilingualism. *Bilingualism: Language and Cognition* 2 (3): 169–186.

Roeper, Thomas W. 2016. Multiple grammars and the logic of learnability in second language acquisition. *Frontiers in Psychology* 7: 1–14.

Romaine, Suzanne. 1983. On the productivity of word formation rules and the limits of variability in the lexicon. *Australian Journal of Linguistics* 3: 176–200.

Romaine, Suzanne. 1985. Variability in word formation patterns and productivity in the history of English. In: Fisiak, Jacek (ed.), *Papers from the 6th International Conference on Historical Linguistics*, 451–467. Amsterdam: John Benjamins.

Romaine, Suzanne. 1998. Introduction. In: Romaine, Suzanne (ed.), *Cambridge History of the English Language. Vol. 4. 1776 to 1997*, 1–56. Cambridge: Cambridge University Press.

Romaine, Suzanne. 2005. Change in productivity. In: Booij, Geert, Christian Lehmann and Joachim Mugdan (eds), *Morphology. A Handbook on Inflection and Word Formation*, 1636–1644. Berlin: de Gruyter.

Rosenbach, Anette. 2003. Aspects of iconicity and economy in the choice between the *s*-genitive and the *of*-genitive in English. In: Rohdenburg, Günter and Britta Mondorf, (eds), *Determinants of Grammatical Variation in English*, 379–412. Berlin, New York: Mouton de Gruyter.

Rosenbach, Anette. 2004. The English s-genitive. In: Fischer, Olga, Muriel Norde and Harry Perridon (eds), *Up and Down the Cline. The Nature of Grammaticalization* 59–73. Amsterdam, Philadelphia: John Benjamins.

Ross, Kristiina. 2011. Historical aspects of Estonian Bible translation and the formation of Biblical terminology from the Middle Ages up to the 18th century. *Magyar Terminológia* 4 (1): 19–27.

Ross, Malcolm. 2003. Diagnosing prehistoric language contact. In: Hickey, Raymond (ed.), *Motives for Language Change*, 174–198. Cambridge: Cambridge University Press.

Ross, Malcolm. 2013. Diagnosing contact processes from their outcomes: The importance of life stages. *Journal of Language Contact* 6 (1): 5–47.

Rossoglou, Paraskevi. 2012. *Modern Greek Translations of Euripides' Medea* [In Greek]. PhD Dissertation, Aristotle University of Thessaloniki.

REFERENCES

Roussou, Anna. 2009. Voice morphology and ergativity in Modern Greek. *Proceedings of the 8th International Conference on Greek Linguistics (ICGL8)*, 406–418.

Sankoff, David and Shana Poplack. 1981. A formal grammar for code-switching. *Papers in Linguistics* 14 (1): 3–45.

Sankoff, Gillian. 2008. Linguistic outcomes of language contact. In: Chambers, Jack K., Natalie Schilling-Estes and Peter Trudgill (eds), *The Handbook of Language Variation and Change*, 638–668. Oxford: Blackwell.

Santorini, Beatrice. 1993. The rate of phrase structure change in the history of Yiddish. *Language Variation and Change* 5 (3): 257–283.

Scheffer, Johannes. 1975. *The Progressive in English*. Amsterdam: North-Holland.

Scheler, Manfred. 1961. *Altenglische Lehnsyntax: Die syntaktischen Latinismen im Altenglischen*. Berlin: Ernst Reuter Gesellschaft.

Schendl, Herbert and Laura Wright (eds). 2011. *Code-switching in Early English: Historical Background and Methodological and Theoretical Issues*. Berlin: de Gruyter.

Schmid, Wilhelm. 1887–1897. *Der Atticismus in seinen Hauptvertretern von Dionysius von Halikarnass bis auf den zweiten Philostratus*. 5 vols. Stuttgart: Kohlhammer. Repr.: N.D. Hildesheim: Olms (1964).

Schmitz, Thomas. 1997. *Bildung und Macht: Zur sozialen und politischen Funktion der zweiten Sophistik in der griechischen Welt der Kaiserzeit*. Munich: Beck.

Schreier, Daniel and Marianne Hundt (eds). 2013. *English as a Contact Language*. Cambridge: Cambridge University Press.

Schütze, Carson T. 2001. On the nature of default case. *Syntax* 4: 205–238.

Scouteris, Constantine and Constantine Belezos. 2015. The Bible in the Orthodox Church from the seventeenth century to the present day. In: Riches, John (ed.), *The New Cambridge History of the Bible. Volume 4: From 1750 to the Present*, 523–536. Cambridge: Cambridge University Press.

Screnock, John. 2018. Is rewriting translation? Chronicles and Jubilees in Light of Intralingual Translation. *Vetus Testamentum* 68 (3): 475–504.

Seferis, Giorgos 1980. *Metagraphes*. Ed. by Giorgis Giatromanolakis. Athens: Ikaros.

Selinker, Larry. 1972. Interlanguage. *International Review of Applied Linguistics in Language Teaching (IRAL)* 10 (1–4): 209–232.

Ševčenko, Ihor. 1981. Levels of style in Byzantine literature. *Jahrbuch der österreichischen Byzantinistik* 31: 289–312.

Shipp, George P. 1983. Notes on the language of Vita Aesopi G. *Antichthon* 17: 96–106.

Siemund, Peter. 2008. Language contact. Constraints and common paths of contact-induced language change. In: Siemund, Peter and Noemi Kintana (eds), *Language Contact and Contact Languages*, 3–11. Amsterdam, Philadelphia: John Benjamins.

Sitaridou, Ioanna. 2014. The Romeyka infinitive: Continuity, contact and change in the Hellenic varieties of Pontus. *Diachronica* 31 (1): 23–73.

Sitaridou, Ioanna. 2016. Reframing the phylogeny of Asia Minor Greek: The view from

Pontic Greek. *CHS Research Bulletin, Center for Hellenic Studies, Harvard University* 4 (1): 1–17.

Sitaridou, Ioanna. 2022. On the redundancy of a theory for language contact. In: Lavidas, Nikolaos and Kiki Nikiforidou (eds), *Studying Language Change in the 21st Century. Theory and Methodologies.* Leiden, Boston: Brill.

Skeat, Walter W. 1878. *The Gospel according to Saint John in Anglo-Saxon and Northumbrian Versions synoptically arranged: With Collations exhibiting all the Readings of all the Mss.* Cambridge: Cambridge University Press.

Snow, Don. 2013. Revisiting Ferguson's defining cases of diglossia. *Journal of Multilingual and Multicultural Development* 34 (1): 61–76.

Sobin, Nicholas. 1997. Agreement, default rules, and grammatical viruses. *Linguistic Inquiry* 28 (2): 318–343.

Sollamo, Raija. 1979. *Renderings of Hebrew Semiprepositions in the Septuagint.* Annales Academiae Scientiarum Fennicae, Dissertationes Humanarum Litterarum 19. Helsinki: Suomalain Tiedeakatemia.

Soukup, Paul A. and Robert Hodgson. 1999. *Fidelity and Translation: Communicating the Bible in New Media.* New York: American Bible Society.

Stanton, Robert. 2002. *The Culture of Translation in Anglo-Saxon England.* Rochester, NY: Boydell & Brewer.

Stein, Achim and Carola Trips. 2012. Diachronic aspects of borrowing Aspect: The role of Old French in the development of the 'be going to+INF' construction. *Actes du 3e Congrès Mondial de Linguistique Française (CMLF)*, 227–246. Paris: Institut de Linguistique française. Online at http://dx.doi.org/10.1051/shsconf/20120100254.

Steiner, Erich. 2005. Some properties of lexicogrammatical encoding and their implications for situations of language contact and multilinguality. *Zeitschrift für Literaturwissenschaft und Linguistik* 35: 54–75.

Steiner, Erich. 2008. Empirical studies of translations as a mode of language contact. "Explicitness" of lexicogrammatical encoding as a relevant dimension. In: Siemund, Peter and Noemi Kintana (eds), *Language Contact and Contact Languages*, 317–346. Amsterdam, Philadelphia: John Benjamins.

Steiner, George. 1975. *After Babel: Aspects of Language and Translation.* New York, London, Oxford: Oxford University Press.

Steiner, George. 2004. Homer in English translation. In: Fowler, Robert (ed.), *The Cambridge Companion to Homer*, 363–375. Cambridge: Cambridge University Press.

Strang, Barbara M.H. 1970. *A History of English.* London: Methuen.

Strathearn, Gaye. 2011. Modern English Bible translations. In: Jackson, Kent P. (ed.), *The King James Bible and the Restoration*, 235–259. Provo, UT: Religious Studies Center, Brigham Young University.

Sturz, Friedrich Wilhelm. 1808. *De dialecto Macedonica et Alexandrina.* Leipzig: Weigel.

Swain, Simon. 1996. *Hellenism and Empire: Language, Classicism, and Power in the Greek World, AD 50–250.* Oxford: Clarendon Press.

REFERENCES

Swanton, Michael (ed. and trans.). 1993. *Anglo-Saxon Prose*. London: Dent.

Swete, Henry Barclay. 2003 [1902]. *An Introduction to the Old Testament in Greek*. Cambridge: Cambridge University Press.

Taavitsainen, Irma and Gerold Schneider. 2018. Scholastic argumentation in early English medical writing and its afterlife: New corpus evidence. In: Suhr, Carla, Terttu Nevalainen and Irma Taavitsainen (eds), *From Data to Evidence in English Language Research*, 191–221. Leiden: Brill.

Taylor, Ann. 1994. The change from SOV to SVO in Ancient Greek. *Language Variation and Change* 6 (1): 1–37.

Taylor, Ann, Anthony Warner, Susan Pintzuk and Frank Beths. 2003. *The York-Toronto-Helsinki Parsed Corpus of Old English Prose (YCOE)*. Department of Linguistics, University of York. Oxford Text Archive, first edition (http://www-users.york.ac.uk/~lang22/YcoeHome1.htm).

Teich, Elke. 2003. *Cross-Linguistic Variation in System and Text: A Methodology for the Investigation of Translations and Comparable Texts*. Berlin: Mouton de Gruyter.

Terasawa, Jun. 1985. The historical development of the causative use of the verb *make* with an infinitive. *Studia Neophilologica* 57 (2): 133–143.

Theophanopoulou-Kontou, Dimitra. 1983–1984. Patient vs. non-patient orientation of the action and the voice distinction in Modern Greek. *Glossologia* 2–3: 75–90.

Theophanopoulou-Kontou, Dimitra. 2004. The structure of VP and the mediopassive morphology: Passives and anticausatives in Modern Greek. *Parousia* 15–16: 173–206.

Thiersch, Heinrich W.J. 1841. *De Pentateuchi Versione Alexandrina. Libri Tres*. Erlangen.

Thim-Mabrey, Christiane. 2006. Language change in revised translations between 1846 and 1999. *Neuphilologische Mitteilungen* 107 (3): 361–373.

Thomason, Sarah G. 2001. *Language Contact: An Introduction*. Edinburgh: Edinburgh University Press.

Thomason, Sarah G. 2003. Contact as a source of language change. In: Joseph, Brian D. and Richard D. Janda (eds), *The Handbook of Historical Linguistics*, 686–712. Oxford: Blackwell.

Thomason, Sarah G. 2006. Language change and language contact. In: Brown, Keith (ed.), *Encyclopedia of Language and Linguistics*. 2nd ed., 339–346. Oxford: Elsevier.

Thomason, Sarah G. 2008. Social and linguistic factors as predictors of contact-induced change. *Journal of Language Contact* 2 (1): 43–56.

Thomason, Sarah G. and Terrence Kaufman. 1988. *Language Contact, Creolization, and Genetic Linguistics*. Berkeley, Los Angeles: University of California Press.

Thompson, Steven. 1985. *The Apocalypse and Semitic Syntax*. Cambridge: Cambridge University Press.

Timofeeva, Olga. 2008. Translating the texts where *et verborum ordo mysterium est*: Late Old English idiom vs. ablativus absolutus. *The Journal of Medieval Latin* 18: 217–229.

Timofeeva, Olga. 2010. *Non-finite Constructions in Old English, with Special Reference to Syntactic Borrowing from Latin*. Helsinki: Société Néophilologique.

Timofeeva, Olga. 2011a. Battlefield victory. Lexical transfer in medieval Anglo-Latin. In: Kranich, Svenja, Viktor Becher, Steffen Höder and Juliane House (eds), *Multilingual Discourse Production: Diachronic and Synchronic Perspectives*, 109–134. Amsterdam, Philadelphia: John Benjamins.

Timofeeva, Olga. 2011b. Infinitival complements with the verb *(ge)don* in Old English: Latin influence revisited. In: Hall, Alaric (ed.), *Leeds Studies in English. New Series XLII*, 93–108. Leeds: University of Leeds.

Timofeeva, Olga. 2018. *Aelfred mec heht gewyrcan*: Sociolinguistic concepts in the study of Alfredian English. *English Language and Linguistics* 22 (1): 123–148.

Timofeeva, Olga and Richard Ingham. 2018. Introduction. Special issue on mechanisms of French contact influence in Middle English: Diffusion and maintenance. *English Language and Linguistics* 22 (2): 197–205.

Toury, Gideon. 2012. *Descriptive Translation Studies and Beyond*. Revised edition. Amsterdam: John Benjamins.

Trips, Carola. 2009. *Lexical Semantics and Diachronic Morphology: The Development of -hood, -dom and -ship in the History of English*. Tübingen: Niemeyer.

Trips, Carola. 2014. The position proper of the adjective in Middle English. A result of language contact. In: Sleeman, Petra, Freek van de Velde and Harry Perridon (eds), *Adjectives in Germanic and Romance*, 73–94. Amsterdam, Philadelphia: John Benjamins.

Trips, Carola and Achim Stein. 2008. Was Old French *-able* borrowable? In: Dury, Richard, Maurizio Gotti and Marina Dossena (eds), *English Historical Linguistics 2006. Volume II: Lexical and Semantic Change*, 217–239. Amsterdam: John Benjamins.

Trips, Carola and Achim Stein. 2019. Contact-induced changes in the argument structure of Middle English verbs on the model of Old French. *Journal of Language Contact* 12 (1): 232–267.

Troianos, Spyros and Ioulia Velissaropoulou-Karakosta. 1997. *Legal History: From Ancient to Modern Greece* [In Greek]. Athens, Komotini: Ant. N. Sakkoulas.

Tronci, Liana. 2018. Aorist voice patterns in the diachrony of Greek: The New Testament as a sample of Koine. *Journal of Greek Linguistics* 18 (2): 241–280.

Trudgill, Peter. 2001. Contact and simplification: Historical baggage and directionality in linguistic change. *Linguistic Typology* 5: 371–374.

Trudgill, Peter. 2004. On the complexity of simplification. *Linguistic Typology* 8 (3): 384–388.

Trudgill, Peter. 2009. Sociolinguistic typology and complexification. In: Sampson Geoffrey, David Gill and Peter Trudgill (eds), *Language Complexity as an Evolving Variable*, 98–109. Oxford: Oxford University Press.

Trudgill, Peter. 2012. On the sociolinguistic typology of linguistic complexity loss. In: Seifart, Frank, Geoffrey Haig, Nikolaus P. Himmelmann, Dagmar Jung, Anna Margetts and Paul Trilsbeek (eds), *Potentials of Language Documentation: Methods, Analyses, and Utilization*, 90–95. Honolulu: University of Hawai'i Press.

REFERENCES

Tsimpli, Ianthi Maria. 1989. On the properties of the passive affix in Modern Greek. *UCL Working Papers in Linguistics* 1: 235–261.

Tsimpli, Ianthi Maria. 2006. The acquisition of voice and transitivity alternations in Greek as native and second language. In: Unsworth, Sharon, Teresa Parodi, Antonella Sorace and Martha Young-Scholten (eds), *Paths of Development in L1 and L2 Acquisition*, 15–55. Amsterdam: John Benjamins.

Tsiplakou, Stavroula. 2009. Code-switching and code-mixing between related varieties: Establishing the blueprint. *The International Journal of Humanities* 6: 49–66.

Tsiplakou, Stavroula. 2014. How mixed is a 'mixed' system? The case of the Cypriot Greek Koiné. *Linguistic Variation* 14 (1): 161–178.

Turner, Nigel. 1955. The unique character of Biblical Greek. *Vetus Testamentum* 5 (1): 208–213.

Turville-Petre, Thorlac. 2008. Early Middle English (1066–ca. 1350). In: Momma, Haruko and Michael Matto (eds), *A Companion to the History of the English Language*, 184–190. Malden, Mass., Oxford, Chichester: Wiley-Blackwell.

Tymoczko, Maria. 1999. *Translation in a Postcolonial Context. Early Irish Literature in English Translation*. Manchester: St. Jerome.

Tzitzilis, Christos. 1999. Der Einfluß des Griechischen in Südosteuropa. In: Hinrichs, Uwe (ed.), *Handbuch der Südosteuropa-linguistik*, 585–617. Wiesbaden: Harrassowitz.

Vanderschelden, Isabelle. 2000. Why retranslate the French classics? The impact of retranslation on quality. In: Salama-Carr, Myriam (ed.), *On Translating French Literature and Film II*, 1–18. Amsterdam, Atlanta: Rodopi.

Vaporis, Nomikos M. 1975. The translation of the Scriptures and the Ecumenical Patriarchate: The translation efforts of Hilarion of Tirnovo. *Byzantine and Modern Greek Studies* 1 (1): 141–173.

Vaporis, Nomikos M. 1984. The influence of the foreign Bible societies in the development of Balkan literary languages: The Greek experience. *The Journal of Modern Hellenism* 1: 79–89.

Vaporis, Nomikos M. 1994. *Translating the Scriptures into Modern Greek*. Brookline, MA: Holy Cross Orthodox Press.

Varmazis, Nikos D. 2006. *An historical overview of intralingual translation* [In Greek]. Center for the Greek Language. Online at http://www.greek-language.gr (Ed. by Dimitris N. Maronitis).

Vasileiadis, Pavlos. 2013a. Maximos Kallioupolitis or Kallipolitis [In Greek]. *The Great Orthodox Christian Encyclopedia* 11: 249.

Vasileiadis, Pavlos. 2013b. Translations of the New World [In Greek]. *The Great Orthodox Christian Encyclopedia* 11: 350.

Vasileiadis, Pavlos D. to-appear. An overview of the New Testament translations in vernacular Greek during the printing era. In: Biver-Pettinger, Fränz and Eran Shuali (eds), *Translating the Bible: Past and Present*. Online at https://www.academia.edu/38648487/_An_overview_of_the_New_Testament_translations_in_vernacular_Greek_during_the_printing_era [last access: May 7, 2020].

Vázquez-González, Juan Gabriel and Jóhanna Barðdal. 2019. Reconstructing the ditransitive construction for Proto-Germanic: Gothic, Old English and Old Norse-Icelandic. *Folia Linguistica Historica* 40 (2): 555–620.

Venuti, Lawrence. 2008. *The Translator's Invisibility. A History of Translation*. 2nd ed. London, New York: Routledge.

Vermeer, Hans J. 2000. *Das Übersetzen in Renaissance und Humanismus*. 2 volumes. Heidelberg: TEXTconTEXT.

Verrips, Maaike. 1994. Learnability meets development: The case of pro-drop. In: Tracy, Rosemarie and Elsa Lattey (eds), *How tolerant is Universal Grammar? Essays on Language Learnability and Language Variation*, 111–124. Tübingen: Niemeyer.

Vessella, Carlo. 2014. Atticist lexica and the pronunciation of Greek. *CHS Research Bulletin* 3: 1. Online at http://nrs.harvard.edu/urn-3:hlnc.essay:VessellaC.

Vessella, Carlo. 2018. *Sophisticated Speakers: Atticistic Pronunciation in the Atticist Lexica*. Berlin, Boston: de Gruyter.

Visser, Fredericus Theodorus. 1963–1973. *An Historical Syntax of the English Language*. 4 volumes. Leiden: Brill.

Voitila, Anssi. 2016. Septuagint syntax and Hellenistic Greek. In: Bons, Eberhard and Jan Joosten (eds), *Handbuch zur Septuaginta/ Handbook of the Septuagint. Volume 3. Die Sprache der Septuaginta/ The Language of the Septuagint*, 109–118. Gütersloh: Gütersloher Verlagshaus.

Wälchli, Bernhard. 2007. Advantages and disadvantages of using parallel texts in typological investigations. *STUF-Language Typology and Universals* 60 (2): 118–134.

Waldron, Ronald. 1991. Dialect aspects of manuscripts of Trevisa's translation of the Polychronicon. In: Riddy, Felicity (ed.), *Regionalism in Late Medieval Manuscripts and Texts: Essays celebrating the Publication of a Linguistic Atlas of Late Mediaeval English*, 67–87. Cambridge: D.S. Brewer.

Waldron, Ronald. 2001. Doublets in the translation technique of John Trevisa. In: Kay, Christian and Louise Sylvester (eds), *Lexis and Texts in Early English: Studies presented to Jane Roberts*, 269–292. Amsterdam, Atlanta: Rodopi.

Waldron, Ronald (ed.). 2004. *John Trevisa's Translation of the 'Polychronicon' of Ranulph Higden, Book VI: An Edition Based on British Library MS Cotton Tiberius D.vii*. Heidelberg: Winter.

Walser, Georg A. 2016. Statistical differences between translation Greek and non-translation Greek texts. In: Bons, Eberhard and Jan Joosten (eds), *Handbuch zur Septuaginta/ Handbook of the Septuagint. Volume 3. Die Sprache der Septuaginta/ The Language of the Septuagint*, 221–230. Gütersloh: Gütersloher Verlagshaus.

Warner, Anthony. 1982. *Complementation in Middle English and the Methodology of Historical Syntax*. London and Canberra: Croom Helm.

Warner, Anthony. 1993. *English Auxiliaries: Structure and History*. Cambridge: Cambridge University Press.

Warner, Anthony. 1997. Extending the paradigm: An interpretation of the historical development of auxiliary sequences in English. *English Studies* 78 (2): 162–189.

Wasserstein, Abraham and David J. Wasserstein. 2006. *The Legend of the Septuagint: From Classical Antiquity to Today*. Cambridge: Cambridge University Press.

Weerman, Fred. 1993. The diachronic consequences of first and second language acquisition: The change from OV to VO. *Linguistics* 31: 903–931.

Weinreich, Uriel. 1979 [1953]. *Languages in Contact: Findings and Problems*. Berlin, New York: Mouton de Gruyter.

Weinreich, Uriel, William Labov and Marvin Herzog. 1968. Empirical foundations for a theory of language change. In: Lehmann, Winfred P. and Yakov Malkiel (eds), *Directions for Historical Linguistics: A Symposium*, 95–188. Austin: University of Texas Press.

Weiß, Helmut. 1998. *Syntax des Bairischen: Studien zur Grammatik einer natürlichen Sprache*. Tübingen: Niemeyer.

Weiß, Helmut. 2001. On two types of natural languages. Some consequences for Linguistics. *Theoretical Linguistics* 27 (1): 87–103.

Weiß, Helmut. 2004. A question of relevance: Some remarks on standard languages. *Studies in Language* 28: 648–674.

Weiß, Helmut. 2005a. The double competence hypothesis. On diachronic evidence. In: Kepser, Stephan and Marga Reis (eds), *Linguistic Evidence. Empirical, Theoretical, and Computational Perspectives*, 557–575. Berlin, New York: Mouton de Gruyter.

Weiß, Helmut. 2005b. Inflected complementizers in Continental West Germanic dialects. *Zeitschrift für Dialektologie und Linguistik* 72: 148–166.

Weissbrod, Rachel. 1998. Translation research in the framework of the Tel Aviv School of Poetics and Semiotics. *Meta* 43 (1): 35–45.

Weissbrod, Rachel. 2004. From translation to transfer. *Across Languages and Cultures* 5 (1): 23–41.

Wellhausen, Julius. 1903. *Evangelium Marci*. Berlin: Reimer.

Wellhausen, Julius. 1911. *Einleitung in die drei ersten Evangelien*. 2nd ed. Berlin: Reimer.

Wendland, Ernst and Philip Noss. 2012. Bible translation. In: Chapelle, Carol A. (ed.), *The Encyclopedia of Applied Linguistics*, 1–8. Oxford: Wiley-Blackwell.

Whitmarsh, Timothy. 2005. *The Second Sophistic*. Cambridge: Cambridge University Press.

Wierzbicka, Anna. 2006. *English: Meaning and Culture*. Oxford: Oxford University Press.

Wierzbicka, Anna. 2012. The history of English seen as the history of ideas: Cultural change reflected in different translations of the New Testament. In: Nevalainen, Terttu and Elizabeth Closs Traugott (eds), *The Oxford Handbook of the History of English*, 434–445. Oxford: Oxford University Press.

Wifstrand, Albert. 2005. *Epochs and Styles: Selected Writings on the New Testament, Greek Language and Greek Culture in the Post-Classical Era*. Edited by Rydbeck, Lars and Stanley E. Porter. Translated by Searby, Denis. Tübingen: Mohr Siebeck.

Wigtil, David N. 1982. The translator of the Greek *Res Gestae* of Augustus. *The American Journal of Philology* 103 (2): 189–194.

Wilamowitz-Moellendorff, Ulrich von. 1900. Asianismus und atticismus. *Hermes* 35: 1–52.

Wilson, Derek. 1976. *The People and the Book: The Revolutionary Impact of the English Bible, 1380–1611*. London: Barrie and Jenkins.

Winford, Donald. 2003. *An Introduction to Contact Linguistics*. Oxford: Blackwell.

Wittig, Joseph S. 1982. King Alfred's *Boethius* and its Latin sources: A reconsideration. *Anglo-Saxon England* 11: 157–198.

Wollin, Lars. 2002. Translations and interference by translation in Old Nordic II: Old Swedish and Old Danish. In: Bandle, Oscar, Kurt Braunmüller, Ernst Håkon Jahr, Allan Karker, Hans-Peter Naumann, Ulf Teleman (in cooperation with Lennart Elmevik and Gun Widmark) (eds), *The Nordic Languages. Volume 1*, 1005–1014. Berlin, New York: de Gruyter.

Wollin, Lars. 2005. From Old Nordic to Early Modern Nordic: The language of the translations II: Swedish and Danish translations. In: Bandle, Oscar, Kurt Braunmüller, Ernst Håkon Jahr, Allan Karker, Hans-Peter Naumann, Ulf Teleman (in cooperation with Lennart Elmevik and Gun Widmark) (eds), *The Nordic Languages. Volume 2*, 1201–1212. Berlin, New York: de Gruyter.

Wollin, Lars. 2007. "Hoo haffuer honom lärdt then grammaticam?" Die Flexion lateinischer Lehnwörter im älteren Schwedisch. In: Lindqvist, Christer (ed.), *Hochdeutsch in Skandinavien III*, 33–50. Frankfurt am Main, New York: Peter Lang.

Wood, Johanna L. 2007. Demonstratives and possessives: From Old English to Present-Day English. In: Abraham, Werner, Elisabeth Leiss and Elisabeth Stark (eds), *Nominal Determination: Typology, Context Constraints, and Historical Emergence*, 339–361. Amsterdam: Benjamins.

Workman, Samuel K. 1940. *Fifteenth Century Translation as an Influence on English Prose*. Princeton: Princeton University Press.

Wright, Laura. 2018. A multilingual approach to the history of Standard English. In: Pahta, Päivi, Janne Skaffari and Laura Wright (eds), *Multilingual Practices in Language History: English and Beyond*, 339–358. Boston, MA, Berlin: de Gruyter Mouton.

Wurff, Wim van der. 1989. A remarkable gap in the history of English syntax. *Folia Linguistica Historica* 9 (2): 117–159.

Wurff, Wim van der. 1990. The easy-to-please construction in Old and Middle English. In: Adamson, Sylvia M., Vivien A. Law, Nigel Vincent and Susan Wright (eds), *Papers from the 5th International Conference on English Historical Linguistics*, 519–536. Amsterdam: John Benjamins.

REFERENCES

Wülfing, Ernst Peter. 1894/ 1897. *Die Syntax in den Werken Alfreds des Großen*. 2 vols. Bonn: Hanstein.

Yang, Charles D. 2002. *Knowledge and Learning in Natural Language*. Oxford: Oxford University Press.

Yerkes, David. 1982. *Syntax and Style in Old English: A Comparison of the Two Versions of Wærferth's Translation of Gregory's Dialogues*. Binghamton, NY: Center for Medieval and Early Renaissance Studies.

Zaviras, Georgios. 1972. *New Greece, or Greek Theater* [In Greek]. Athens: Etaireia Makedonikon Spoudon.

Zbierska-Sawala, Anna. 1989. On the status of French derivational suffixes in Early Middle English. *Studia Anglica Posnaniensia* 22: 91–99.

Zethsen, Karen. 2009. Intralingual translation: An attempt at description. *Meta* 54 (4): 795–812.

Zobl, Helmut and Juana M. Liceras. 2005. Accounting for optionality in nonnative grammars: Parametric change in diachrony and L2 development as instances of internalized diglossia. In: Dekydtspotter, Laurent, Rex A. Sprouse and Audrey Liljestrand (eds), *Proceedings of the 7th Generative Approaches to Second Language Acquisition Conference*, 283–291. Somerville, MA: Cascadilla.

Index

accuracy numbers 205–206

accusativus-cum-infinitivo (AcI) 48–50, 103–106, 176

active voice morphology 136–137, 139, 141–142, 145, 150, 153–155, 157, 164, 214–216, 223, 229, 240, 244, 248–249, 257, 259

Aeschylus 57–58

Aesop 8, 270, 294, 298, 301, 305–306, 312

life of Aesop 8, 268, 270, 273, 292, 303, 313

Alfred 30, 34–35, 40, 50–52, 114, 192

Ælfric 35, 40

Anglican Church 72

Anglo-Norman 36

Anglo-Saxon Chronicle 103

animacy 145, 154, 164, 240

subject animacy 155, 158, 160, 167, 170, 212, 214, 249–265

anticausative

active anticausative 150, 164, 220, 234, 237, 246–248, 252, 255, 262

anticausative construction 130–136, 139, 141–142, 150, 153–155, 157, 164, 169, 211–216, 218–220, 229, 232–236, 238, 246–248, 252–253

non-active anticausative 139, 211, 214, 220, 229, 247, 259, 262

anticausativizations 130

archaism 33–34, 41, 88, 93, 95

argument structure 5, 7–8, 104, 129–130, 132, 134–136, 173, 177–179, 209–213, 216, 228, 246–247, 320, 322

Aristeas 29–30, 75

Atticism 54, 92–93, 95–96, 102, 107, 119

Atticists 95–98

authorization of translations 37, 42–43, 72–73

Authorized Version 12–13, 43–44, 78–80, 85–88, 139, 142–145, 157, 162–164, 172–173, 180, 184, 187, 191, 204

auxiliary 62, 78–79, 108, 111, 114, 175

Batrachomyomachia 94

Bede 25, 30, 35

biblical

biblical corpus 85

biblical retranslations 36, 145, 189, 228

biblical translations 4–6, 13, 19–21, 31, 35–36, 39–43, 48, 56–57, 60–61, 63–65, 72, 74–79, 81, 83, 85–87, 108, 120, 177–178, 197, 319–321

bilingualism 7, 10–11, 70, 110, 114–115, 117

historical bilingualism 12, 117

Boethius 30, 35, 37–38, 50–51, 100–101, 106, 177, 181, 183, 185, 188, 191–192, 196–198, 206

borrowing 8–12, 23–25, 41, 45, 48, 51, 117–118, 121, 189, 194, 196

borrowing scale 25

British Bible Society 72–73

Byzantine

Byzantine Atticism 97–98

Byzantine paraphrasis 64

early Byzantine period 55

Catholic Church 37, 41

causative 130–133, 173, 215

causativizations 130

change

contact-induced change 9–12, 16–17, 21, 83, 117, 317–318

grammatical change 3–7, 28–29, 31–76, 83, 88, 91, 101, 109–112, 115–117, 122–123, 129, 183, 266–267, 272, 317–321, 323

natural change 76, 122

semi-natural changes 7, 23, 46, 114, 121, 123–124, 317–319, 323

Chartophylax, Manuel 94

Chaucer 24, 27, 36–38, 50–52, 101, 133, 174, 181, 185, 188, 192, 196–198, 200–201

coexistence

coexistence of influence 10

coexistence of parallel grammars 107, 191, 209

coexistence of varieties 117

stable coexistence 118

coexistent grammars 69, 88, 113, 316, 323

cognate noun constructions 13, 87

Colville, George 100 181, 185, 188, 198, 200–201

INDEX 373

comparative analysis 11, 53
competence
    competence of Latin 12
    diglossic competence 113, 115
    literary competence 104
    native competence 123, 125
    partial competence 126
    standard competence 126
Competing Grammars Hypothesis 4, 111–116
complements
    non-finite complements 86
Consolation of Philosophy/ De consolatione philosophiae 8, 35, 37–38, 100, 177, 181, 185, 188, 191, 194, 196–198, 206
Constant Rate Effect 111–112
constructions
    analytic constructions 300
    auto-benefactive constructions 215
    causative constructions 88, 104, 130–132, 215
    ditransitive constructions 133, 272, 291
    matching constructions 47, 274
    nominativus-cum-infinitivo constructions 49
    reflexive constructions 313
    semi-natural constructions 121
contact
    contact effects 17–18, 46, 48, 110
    contact-induced changes 6, 9–12, 16–17, 21, 83, 117, 208, 317–318, 321
    contact varieties 17–18
    cultural contact 9
    early contact 23, 57
    indirect contact 19
    intense contact 21, 22, 25, 105
    long-term contact 11
    modern contact 23
    short-term contact 11
corpus
    corpus of biblical translations 75
    corpus of English translations 137–138, 146–147, 155–156, 158–161, 166–168, 170–171, 181, 185, 188
    corpus of non-translated texts 8, 150, 230–233, 237–239, 242–246
    historical corpus 108
    parallel corpora 77

Penn Parsed Corpora of Historical English 135, 139, 150–153, 177–179, 186, 188, 190, 197
York-Toronto-Helsinki Parsed Corpus of Old English Prose 47, 150
Coverdale, Miles 42–43
cultural filtering 16

demoticism 56, 95
Digenis Akritis 9, 268, 270–273, 313–316
    Escorial 9, 268, 271, 313
    Grottaferrata 268, 271, 273, 313–315
diglossia 15, 57, 70, 88, 107, 114, 116–119, 122
    grammatical diglossia 118
    internalized diglossia 111, 115–117
    modern diglossia 119
    morphosyntactic diglossia 97
    revived diglossia 119
    syntactic diglossia 4–5, 7, 81, 111–115, 122, 125, 272, 317
    traditional diglossia 119
diglossic variants 125
discriminators 193, 198–199, 201–208
ditipias 211, 216
ditransitives 272
document classification analysis 189, 192–197
domestication 33, 98
Dryden, John 15 31, 33, 46

Elizabeth's translations 50–51, 101, 106, 192, 196
Elytis 59
English
    Biblical English 44
    Early Middle English 41, 45, 132–133, 192
    Early Modern English 43, 98, 132, 176, 188, 192, 206
    Late Modern English 139, 150
    Middle English 13, 35–37, 39, 48–49, 101, 110, 132–133, 174–178, 183, 192–193, 200, 205–208
    Modern English 78, 87–88, 91–92, 130, 133, 174–175
    Old English 25–27, 35–36, 39–40, 46–49, 104–109, 111, 131–133, 174–177, 192–196, 199–201, 204–205
    Present-Day English 174–176

English Old Testament Revisers 180, 184, 187
English Revised Version 134, 139, 142–145, 149, 162–163, 172–173, 191
English Standard Version 134, 139, 142–145, 149, 162–164, 169, 172–173, 191
equivalence 16, 20, 45, 105
  formal equivalence 16, 23
  functional equivalence 21
  structural equivalence 105
Evangelika 57, 64, 73, 95
explicitation 16–17, 82

faithfulness 15, 33, 76
feature weight 196–198, 200, 202–204, 206–208
focalized datives 301, 309
foreignization 33–34

Galesiotes, Georgios 8, 268, 273, 284
Generative Grammar 116
Geneva Bible 42–43
genitive case 174
German
  Middle Low German 23
  Old High German 132
  Standard German 123–125
Germanic 39, 51, 176, 193–194, 200
glosses 12, 24–25, 35–36, 39, 47, 61, 105, 109
Gospels 39–40, 49, 57–58, 64, 66, 73, 76, 94
Gothic 19, 50, 76, 83–84
grammars
  diglossic grammars 112
  interlanguage grammars 126
  multiple grammars 67, 113, 115, 183
  natural grammars 121, 123–124
  parallel antagonistic grammars 88
  standard grammars 126
grammaticalization 20–21, 50, 105, 125
grammatical viruses 120, 125
Greek
  Atticizing Greek 54, 67, 95–96
  archaized Greek 323
  Biblical Greek 6, 19, 59–60, 63, 67–68
  Byzantine Greek 177
  Classical Greek 57, 111, 234, 269
  demotic Greek 56, 58
  Early Modern Greek 94, 238, 242–246
  Greek Language Question 56

Greek Orthodox Church 73
Homeric Greek 94, 234
Medieval Greek 21, 63, 234, 238–240, 242–244
post-Koine Greek 279–280
pre-Koine Greek 248
Present-Day Greek 211, 213–214, 216, 220, 234, 237–240, 242–246, 252
purified Greek 88

Hebrew 30, 39–40, 60, 62–65, 67, 70, 75, 78, 84, 259
  Biblical Hebrew 4–5, 83, 316, 320
  Hebrew Old Testament 29, 63, 78, 321
Homer 31–33, 45, 70, 93
humanism
  religious humanism 94–95
Hypothesis of Grammatical Multiglossia 7, 69, 113, 116, 122, 125, 189, 321

Iliad 31–32, 45–46, 58, 93–94
inanimate
  inanimate subject 136, 145–147, 154, 156–157, 159, 161, 168–169, 211, 213–214, 223–226, 240, 247–248, 257, 259, 262
inchoative 131
Inertial Theory 110
influence
  bidirectional 6, 317
  direct 23
  indirect 48
  multiple 321
interference 6, 16–17, 70, 316
intransitives 8, 132–133, 137, 173, 178

Jerome 19, 30, 40, 76–77
Jewish
  Jewish communities 60
  Jewish dialect 67
  Jewish Greek Hypothesis 68

Kallipolitis, Maximos 57, 64, 71, 94, 210, 216, 221–223, 225, 227–228, 234, 248, 251, 255, 257, 259, 262, 264
Kartanos, Ioannikios 57, 94
King James 12, 31, 43–44, 78, 80, 85, 87
Komnene, Anna 8, 268–270, 272–283
Korais, Adamantios 57–59, 95

INDEX

375

lability 137
language acquisition 3, 113, 116, 123, 317
language attrition 30
Latin 12–15, 19, 23, 25, 29–32, 34–38, 40, 45–51, 54–55, 57, 75–77, 84, 103–109, 119, 192–194
    Biblical Latin 46–47
    Latin Vulgate 19, 40, 77, 83, 134
Latinate
    Latinate constructions 38
    Latinate English 49, 323
lexical conceptual structure (LCS) 148, 154, 157, 164, 169, 211–214, 225, 229, 234, 247–248, 252, 257
lexicalization resources 51
LightSide 193
literacy 34, 121
logistic regression 192–193, 208
Lucaris, Cyril I 71–72, 94–95
Luke 19, 62, 84, 97, 148, 162, 221, 264
Luther, Martin 80, 120

machine learning approach 192, 194–195
Masoretic Text 65, 75, 78
matching phrases 210, 272–273, 277, 279–280, 284, 286–287, 289, 291–292, 295, 301, 304, 309, 313
Matthew 49, 142–145, 163, 172, 222, 225, 257
mediopassive 137, 176, 211, 215
middle voice 95, 214
mixing 11, 96, 126
multiglossia 88, 116, 118, 122, 183, 209, 322
    grammatical multiglossia 4, 7, 53, 67, 69, 110, 113, 116–118, 122, 125, 129, 321–323

naturalization 32, 98
Neo-Latin 45
Newcome, William 178, 180, 184, 187, 191
New English Bible 44, 85, 108
New Revised Standard Version 43, 87–88
New Testament
    Koine Greek New Testament 61–64, 134–136, 139, 142–144, 148–149, 162–163, 172, 216, 222–223, 225, 227, 249–265
non-active (marked) voice morphology 137–139, 150–151, 157, 164, 169, 188–189, 214–216, 223, 225, 229, 240, 242–244, 259

non-transitional periods 117–118, 189, 194, 209, 267, 316, 323
normalization 16–17

object
    direct object 174–176, 178, 280, 304
    indirect object 86, 107, 175, 291, 300, 304–305
    object clitics 122
Odyssey 31–32, 93
Old Church Slavonic 19, 83–84
Old Frisian 133
Old Saxon 132
Old Swedish 23
Old Testament 30, 35, 39–40, 43, 63, 65–66, 72, 75, 84, 180, 183–184, 187
one-place predicates 154, 214, 229, 244
optionality 110–111, 115–116, 214
Orestiaka 95
Orthodox Church 57, 72–73, 75

Pallis, Alexandros 57–58, 64, 73, 95
papyri 68, 96–97
parallel grammars 4–5, 88, 91, 107, 114, 116, 118, 122, 125–126, 209, 267, 286, 289, 317
parameters 4, 8, 12–13, 23, 44–45, 76, 82, 100, 112–113, 134, 136
paraphrasis 8, 32, 39, 92–94, 210, 266–269, 271–273, 284, 289, 291
passive 107, 174–176, 215
    direct passives 175
    indirect passives 175
    passive infinitives 49, 175–176
periphrasis 55, 62, 269
phrase matching 8, 267, 291
Planoudes, Maximos 94, 177
Polybius 96, 234
Pope Gregory 35, 108
prefixes 131–132, 277, 289, 295, 309
prescriptive 19, 121, 125
prestige
    high prestige 16, 22–23
    prestige of classical languages 31, 93
    prestige of source language 22
    prestige status 11
Protestant Church 73, 119–120

reanalysis 300, 305
reconstruction 121

registers
  educated registers   63
  standardized registers   77
retranslation
  diachronic retranslations   3–6, 59, 81, 129, 173, 181, 183, 188–189, 193, 208–209, 225, 266, 317–322
  intralingual retranslation   4, 59, 216, 320
  Retranslation Hypothesis   98–99, 102
Revised Standard Version   43, 88
Romance   31, 47, 54, 110, 119, 201–202, 204–208

sacral stamp   83–85
Scandinavian   13, 110
Seferis, Giorgos   59
Semitism   55, 60, 70
Septuagint (LXX)   29–30, 54, 60–70, 75, 83–84, 210, 216, 220–223, 225, 227–228, 248–261, 263–266, 321
Septuagintisms   66
Shakespeare   13, 55, 58
simplification   11, 16–17
Sofianos, Nikolaos   55, 94
Somaki, Ioulia   73
Sprachbund   10–11, 110
standardization   21–23, 39, 50, 75, 119–120, 122, 124–125, 317
standard languages   11, 15, 69, 119–125, 317
  modern standard languages   119, 121, 125
Strong's Numbers   77–78, 81
subordinate   23, 86, 269, 271, 279
substratum   11, 24
suffixes
  derivational suffixes   8, 194, 199, 201–204, 322
Swedish   21, 23

target text   6, 8, 16–17, 19, 58, 78, 81–83, 92, 107, 269, 273–274
Textus Receptus   64, 74, 78
Thesaurus Linguae Graecae   8, 139, 267, 272
Today's Greek Version (TGV)   65, 220–223, 225, 227–229, 237, 240, 242, 248, 251–252, 255, 257, 259, 262, 264
Toledo School of Translators   30
transitional periods   5, 88, 113, 118, 191, 194

transitives   8, 150, 173, 176, 178, 213, 215, 237, 247
  auto-benefactive transitives   215
  non-active transitives   211, 247
transitivity   8, 155, 158, 160, 165, 167, 170, 173, 178, 183, 189, 194, 209
  transitivity alternations   130, 137
translatability   90
translational equivalents   77, 79–80, 106
translation
  direct translation effects   47
  domesticating translation   99
  English biblical translations   5, 12, 14, 78, 80, 85, 87, 164, 173, 177, 180, 184–185, 187
  Greek biblical translations   63, 65, 72, 74, 229, 237, 240, 249–265, 316
  Greek intralingual translations   56, 74, 92, 101
  indirect translation   53, 316
  interlingual translations   55, 58–59, 63, 71, 82, 90–92, 134, 210
  intralingual biblical translations   23, 81
  literal translation   37, 44, 51, 55, 84
  literary translation   22, 90, 99
  Middle English translations   31, 36, 205
  Modern Greek translations   57, 64, 72
  non-biblical translations   6, 8, 39, 47–48, 53, 57, 59, 178, 183, 204–207, 320, 322
  Old English translations   35, 50, 103–104, 107
  overt translation strategy   23
  sense-for-sense translation   30
  translation effects   5–7, 22, 46, 49, 52, 59–60, 69, 76, 134, 316
  translation-induced changes   15
  translation-induced interference   106
  translation norms   99
  translation techniques/strategies   65, 68, 76
  vernacular translation   64
T-score   78–80
two-place predicate   148, 154, 214, 229, 242, 244, 259
Tyndale, William   12–13   30, 41–42, 86, 136, 139, 143–145, 148–149, 162–164, 172–176, 180, 184, 187, 192–193, 196–197, 199
typological closeness   21

INDEX

United Bible Society 74
universal bilingualism 7, 81, 88, 111–125
Universal Grammar 112, 115

Vamvas, Neofytos 56, 64, 72–73, 216, 221–
   223, 227–229, 234, 237, 240, 251–252,
   255, 257, 259, 262, 264
variation 27, 33, 47, 49, 106, 111–112, 115, 273,
   284, 301, 304
   intraspeaker variation 115
   systematic grammatical variation 112
variety
   colloquial variety 63
   conservative variety 111, 114
   low prestige variety 118
verb
   causative-anticausative verb 176
   change-of-state verb 7–8, 130, 266
   deponent verb 109
   labile verb 132

vernacular 15, 23, 36–37, 40, 54, 56, 58, 108,
   111, 119
voice morphology 8, 211–212, 214–218, 224–
   225, 229, 231–233, 243–246, 248–249,
   252–253, 256, 259–260, 262–263
Vulgate 4, 19, 76, 86, 109, 320

West Saxon Gospels 35, 108–109
word formation 42, 50–51, 191, 197
word list 7–8, 134–137, 154, 178–179, 210, 212,
   225, 229–233, 235–236, 243–245, 247–
   248, 322
word order 13, 37, 44, 50, 107, 111, 175, 279,
   284, 301, 309
Wycliffe 12, 36, 40–41, 52, 80, 86, 139, 142–
   144, 148–149, 162–163, 172, 180, 184, 187,
   199

Yiddish 111, 122, 124